Critical Essays on George Orwell

Critical Essays on George Orwell

Bernard Oldsey
and
Joseph Browne

G. K. Hall & Co. • Boston, Massachusetts

Copyright © 1986 by Bernard Oldsey and Joseph Browne
All Rights Reserved

Library of Congress Cataloging in Publication Data

Critical essays on George Orwell.

(Critical essays on modern British literature)
Bibliography: p. 229
Includes index.
1. Orwell, George, 1903-1950 — Criticism and interpretation.
I. Oldsey, Bernard Stanley, 1923-   . II. Browne, Joseph.
III. Series.
PR6029.R8Z6278 1986   828'.91209   86-4816
ISBN 0-8161-8750-9

This publication is printed on permanent/durable acid-free paper
MANUFACTURED IN THE UNITED STATES OF AMERICA

CRITICAL ESSAYS ON MODERN BRITISH LITERATURE

Bernard Oldsey's introduction to the volume is biographical, with special attention paid to the circumstances of composition of Orwell's major works. It serves as an introductory background for those unfamiliar with Orwell's work and as a clear and precise introduction to the critical essays covering the 1984 year of dystopia, a date made famous by Orwell's most influential novel. Oldsey's essay includes brief introductory remarks on Orwell's major fiction and nonfiction.

The volume includes one section of essays on *Animal Farm* and *1984*, a section of essays on individual works of secondary fiction, a section dealing with each of Orwell's nonfiction books, and a concluding comprehensive Orwell bibliography. The first major edition of critical essays on the entire canon of one of Britain's most influential writers, this volume should prove valuable to students and Orwell scholars alike.

ZACK BOWEN, GENERAL EDITOR

University of Delaware

This book is dedicated to a new generation

Matthew and Michael Oldsey
Timothy and Patrick Browne

It is a necessary pleasure to thank James Kain for his help in preparing the manuscript and Ann Re Oldsey for her editorial assistance.

CONTENTS

INTRODUCTION

Bernard Oldsey

Between the man and the public falls the mask: a shock of dark hair that looks as though it were cut with the aid of a bowl, the small sad eyes that penetrate, the long sharp blade of a nose pointing toward a Parisian line of mustache, the square protruding jaw, and the hollow cheeks lined with tubercular sadness.[1] Here is "The Last Man in Europe," as he once thought of calling *Nineteen Eighty-Four*; here is the lank figure of Abe Quixote, all six feet three of him, one of the most honest and quixotic men ever to wield either word or lance; and yet here, too, is the creator of Winston Smith, who crumbles before the terrible onslaught of dictatorial power and learns to love Big Brother.

Before the almost sacrificial mask came the private man, Eric Blair; and before the man, a lonely and imaginative child who at the age of four created a fictive confidant named "Fronky." By the time he reached the age of thirty, and was about to publish his first book, Blair created another alter ego, or familiar, named George Orwell — "George" after the patron saint of England, and "Orwell" after a river in the East Anglia section of the country.

It was *Down and Out in Paris and London* that prompted the split between private man and public figure through the selection of a nom de plume. Blair felt that certain expressions and materials in his account of low-life in the two capitals might prove embarrassing, especially for his family, who were members of what he would later call, with almost parodistic English precision, the "lower-upper-middle class." He suggested a number of pseudonyms, including P. S. Burton, Kenneth Miles, and H. Lewis Allways. Although he himself expressed a preference for Orwell, Blair had publisher Victor Gollancz to thank for the final choice of a name, as he did for the eventual title of the book (Blair had suggested "Lady Poverty," "In Praise of Poverty," and "Confessions of a Dishwasher," and had earlier sent the manuscript out under the working title of "Days in London and Paris").

Orwell né Blair never did relinquish his family name, but continued to use it for private and legal purposes throughout his life. Nor did he ever really relinquish the political position he somewhat jokingly described as

1

that of a "Tory-anarchist." He did, however, undergo a transformation from the "chubby little boy" of genteel upbringing to the enfant terrible of the political-pamphlet world. The central question to be asked, then, is how Eric Blair, graduate of St. Cyprian's and of Eton, dropped out of the lower-upper-middle class into the lower depths of London and Paris, and then rose to fame as George Orwell, author of some of the most meaningful political-literary works of the century, including two novels that promise never to be forgotten, *Animal Farm* and *1984*.

Eric Arthur Blair was born in Motihar in Bengal, India, on 25 June 1903.[2] His father, Richard Walmesley Blair, was an undistinguished civil servant in the Opium Department of the Government of India, the opium trade with China then having been legalized under a state monopoly. His mother, Ida Mabel Limouzin Blair, was descended from a French-English family that had commercial holdings in Burma. It was not unusual for the children of British families in India to be sent or taken back to Britain for their schooling, and Ida Blair returned to England with Eric and his older sister, Marjorie, just a year after the boy was born. They were established at Henley-on-Thames, where they made their home from 1904 to 1917.

Here in this pleasantly Edwardian setting Eric spent his early boyhood and began his education at an Anglican convent school called Sunnylands. Mrs. Blair was something of a whist- and bridge-playing gadabout with mildly feminist friends. Mr. Blair rejoined his family for a three-month sojourn in 1907, during which time Eric's younger sister, Avril, was conceived. In an essay entitled "Why I Write," Orwell would later characterize much of his boyhood in this manner:

> I was the middle child of three, but there was a gap of five years on either side, and I barely saw my father before I was eight. For this and other reasons I was somewhat lonely, and I soon developed disagreeable mannerisms which made me unpopular throughout my schooldays. I had the lonely child's habit of making up stories and holding conversations with imaginary persons, and I think from the very start my literary ambitions were mixed up with the feelings of being isolated and undervalued.

The feeling of being unpopular and undervalued came after Sunnylands. Mr. Blair returned from India for good in 1911, and in September of that year Eric left home for St. Cyprian's, a preparatory boarding school in Eastbourne. He was eight years old, the age when boys of his social class were typically sent away to school. As an intelligent, "clever," boy whose parents could not readily afford to pay the full tuition of a school like St. Cyprian's, Eric was taken in on a half-scholarship. In return he was expected to study very hard, to become a "swot," and thus earn entrance into one of the great public (actually private) schools—of which there were hardly more than a half-dozen in England, including Eton, Harrow, Rugby, Shrewsbury, Winchester, Westminster, and Charterhouse.

Whether St. Cyprian's was the making or near-breaking of Eric Blair is hard to say, but it certainly left scars on one of its most famous old boys. With irony aforethought, taking his title from Blake's "Songs of Innocence," Orwell wrote a vitriolic attack on St. Cyprian's entitled "Such, Such Were the Joys," which was published for the first time in 1953, three years after Orwell's death, and at that time only in the United States. In this somewhat fictionalized account, Orwell heaps unadorned opprobrium on the headmaster of the school and his wife, a Mr. and Mrs. Wilkes, who are referred to as Sambo and Flip, respectively. The essay begins with the outraged cry of a young bed-wetter torn away from the "warm nest" of his home, and it ends with these only seemingly relenting words: "I even conceived a prejudice against Sussex, as the county that contained St. Cyprian's, and as an adult I have only once been in Sussex, on a short visit. Now, however, the place is out of my system for good. Its magic works no longer, and I have not even enough animosity left to make me hope that Flip and Sambo are dead or that the story of the school being burnt down was true."

Blair was at St. Cyprian's during a very formative period of his life, from 1911 to 1916. Cyril Connolly, who would himself become a man of letters, editor of *Horizon*, and lifelong friend of Orwell's, also wrote about St. Cyprian's, where he and Eric were close companions, as they would be later at Eton. Connolly perceived that he and Blair were probably the kind of young rebels who would be bound to criticize any school they attended during their boyish days. He also felt that Eric Blair's character "was already formed by the time he arrived at Eton." But he saw that his friend's experience at St. Cyprian's was not unrelievedly work and humiliation. Blair had gone on hikes, played schoolboy sports, like "fives" and football, and read many of the authors who would stay with him the rest of his life—Kipling, Swift, Dickens, Gissing, and H. G. Wells. According to Connolly, Blair liked walking, natural history, reading, arguing, and debunking: "his eyes were made to glitter with amusement, his schoolboy chubbiness persisted until his face grew cavernous from two pneumonias. And he was emotionally independent with the egotism of all natural writers; his friendships were constant but seldom close."

If nothing else, St. Cyprian's made a worker out of young Blair. During his last two years there he buckled down to hard studying for those competitive examinations that determined the careers and lives of English youths at the tender age of thirteen or fourteen. If a boy were accepted, for example, at Eton or Harrow his future seemed assured; he did not necessarily have to go on to Oxford or Cambridge, but could enter directly into a career with the church, military, or civil service.

Blair did very well in his examinations and qualified as a King's Scholar at Eton. He entered as a "Colleger" in May 1917 (scholarship students lived on the school grounds; others, the so-called "Oppidans," were settled in more comfortable quarters within the town). In a 1948 essay entitled "Forever Eton," which contrasts sharply with "Such, Such Were the Joys," Orwell praises Eton for its "tolerant and civilised" atmosphere, and for providing a Colleger with at least a semblance of privacy. But the youthful Blair neither thrived nor triumphed in this atmosphere. He did manage to read what he wanted, which was a great deal; he wrote some juvenilia and helped edit the perennial literary magazine; and he established himself as a liberalizing, if somewhat cynical, force within his class. But as biographer Bernard Crick declares, Eric Blair mainly "rested on his oars" during his four years at Eton. And in typically blunt and honest fashion, Orwell later summed up his case this way, in a 1942 entry for *Twentieth Century Authors*: "I had been lucky enough to win a scholarship [to Eton], but I did not work and learned very little." As a result, there was really no question of his going on to a university; in the July 1921 examinations at Eton, Eric Blair placed 138th on a list of 167.

The same year Eric left Eton the Blairs moved to the small resort town of Suffolk on the east coast, and it was here the nineteen-year-old Blair attended a "crammers" course for six months of preparation for the India Office's examination. He qualified seventh in the examination, although a compulsory horse-riding test moved him down to twenty-first on a list of twenty-three successful applicants. On 27 October 1922 Blair sailed for Burma, where he landed in Rangoon. Burma was at that time still part of Anglo-Indian governance. It was Blair's primary choice of station partly because his grandmother Limouzin was still in residence there. The service he selected was the British Imperial Police, a paramilitary organization akin to the Spanish Guardia Civil. Why he chose this form of service remains something of a mystery even today. In an introduction to *The Road to Wigan Pier*, Orwell gives this laconic account of this period of his life: "In 1922 I went to Burma where I joined the Indian Imperial Police. It was a job for which I was totally unsuited; so, at the beginning of 1928, while on leave in England, I gave in my resignation. . . ."

Of course, there was much more to the matter than that: Blair underwent training in Mandalay; and as an assistant superintendent of police he served at various Kiplingesque posts—like Syriam, Insein (near Rangoon), Moulmein, and Katha (on the northern road to Mandalay). He later characterized this period of his life as "five boring years within the sound of bugles." Nonetheless, his experience in the East would lead to the production of one of his best essays, "Shooting an Elephant," and of a novel, *Burmese Days*, which takes its place alongside *A Passage to India* and *The Heart of Matter* as an estimable post-Kipling representation of British imperialism.

Burmese Days has often been read as an open attack on imperialism. The protagonist of this semibiographical work, Flory, berates himself and his countrymen in passages like the following:

Your whole life is a life of lies. Year after year you sit in Kipling-haunted little Clubs, whisky to the right of you, *Pink'un* to the left of you. . . . You hear your Oriental friends called "greasy little babus," and you admit, dutifully, that they *are* greasy little babus. You see louts fresh from school kicking greyhaired servants. The time comes when you burn with hatred of your own countrymen, when you long for a native rising to drown their Empire in blood. . . . And in this there is nothing honourable. . . . You are a creature of the despotism, a pukka sahib. . . .

But as a number of critics have discovered, Flory is also a creature of self-doubt, and at times a form of Conradian ambiguity creeps into his attitude toward himself as well as others who shoulder the white man's burden:

you could forgive the Europeans a great deal of their bitterness. Living and working among Orientals would try the temper of a saint. . . . The life of the Anglo-Indian officials is not all jam. In comfortless camps, in sweltering offices, in gloomy dank bungalows smelling of dust and earth-oil, they earn, perhaps, the right to be a little disagreeable.

What becomes apparent in conflicting passages like these is that the burden which Flory carries is not so much a general imperialist concern as it is a personal dilemma. Here in *Burmese Days* Orwell fixed on a thematic question that would dominate his next three novels: how does an individual formed by the English middle-class transcend, or at least escape, the dictates of his or her society? Played with slight variations, Orwell's thematic answer is that alienated people of this sort cannot in good conscience live within the pale, and yet they lack strength to live outside it. This is true of Dorothy Hare in *A Clergyman's Daughter*, Gordon Comstock in *Keep the Aspidistra Flying*, and to a lesser extent of George Bowling in *Coming Up for Air*.

Eric Blair's personal attempt to live outside the pale was both dramatic and productive. It began with his return on leave to England from Burma. With the steaming delta lands and rich jungles of the East still fresh in his mind, he asked for and received a discharge from the Imperial Police. After five years service, which he later claimed had an ill effect on his health as well as his conscience, Blair left the department on 1 January 1928 — near the end of an economic boom, and just in time to explore fully the lives of the poor and exploited during the period of world depression that followed.

Blair dropped precipitously out of the middle class and the pukka sahib category into the lower depths of London and Paris, and then the coal-mining town of Wigan, just north of Liverpool, with a few side excursions as a bum on the road and as an occasional hop-picker. He was determined in the process of his experiment in misery to become a writer; but at the same time, as this confessional passage from *The Road to Wigan Pier* indicates, he also wanted to do penance for his social sins: "I was conscious of an immense weight of guilt that I had got to expiate. . . . I felt that I had got to escape not merely from imperialism but from every form of man's dominion over man. I wanted to submerge myself, to get right down among the oppressed; to be one of them and on their side against their tyrants."

Blair's entry into the East End of London was almost a duplication of another writer's descent into a world of down-and-outers. A generation earlier Stephen Crane had gone into New York's Bowery and emerged with the material for *Maggie: A Girl of the Streets*, which he published under the pseudonym of Johnston Smith. But it was an American contemporary of Crane's whom Blair would actually emulate. In 1902, when he was already famous, Jack London had donned old clothes, just as Blair would, and had entered the very same territory, the East End, for material to be used in the writing of *The People of the Abyss*. This book and London's attack on dictatorial tyranny, *The Iron Heel*, are what Orwell would later characterize as "bad-good books." He was much impressed by these two works, and thought the latter to be a much better prediction of the future than H. G. Wells's *The Shape of Things to Come* or Aldous Huxley's *Brave New World*. Of course, he retained the impression of London's iron heel for the unforgettable emblem in *1984* of a "boot stamping on a human face—forever."

Blair had no visible success during his first year as a suffering writer among the poor of London, and in the spring of 1928 set off for Paris, to learn the language and to live cheaply while working on two novels, which he never published. Here he was hardly more successful than he had been in London. By his own reckoning, his literary efforts that year brought him no more than twenty pounds. His first professional publication, "La Censure en Angleterre," was translated into French for Henri Barbusse's journal, *Le Monde*, where it appeared on 6 October 1928, and was followed by several others similarly translated. His first professional piece in English, "A Farthing Newspaper," came out on 29 December 1928 in *G. K.'s Weekly*, a small journal owned by G. K. Chesterton.

Hampered by a "weak chest" since early childhood, Blair experienced a bout of pneumonia in Paris that put him in the hospital for several weeks. He emerged almost penniless and, too proud to seek money from his parents, took a job as a dishwasher and porter in a luxury hotel-restaurant in Paris. At the end of that year, he headed for England and his parents' home in Southwold. Using some of the material from his fugitive articles, he set to work on "A Scullion's Confessions," an early version of *Down and Out in Paris and London*. During this period he occasionally returned to the poorer sections of London, and in the fall went out into the country hop-picking. But finally, with his manuscript finished, he took a job as a teacher, at The Hawthorns, a small private school in Middlesex. There, in the summer of 1932, he learned that his first book had been accepted for publication.

Earlier that year, Orwell had met Leonard Moore, who was to remain his literary agent for life. After the manuscript for *Down and Out in Paris and London* had been rejected by two leading publishers (Cape, and Faber & Faber), Moore succeeded in placing it with Victor Gollancz, a socialist publisher who believed the world should know what life was like for the poor during a depression. Gollancz settled on a title for the book and advised Blair on the matter of a pen name. And in January 1933, with publication of the book, George Orwell emerged from the chrysalis of E. A. Blair. Like John Steinbeck, an American counterpart, Orwell had had to serve a long and hard apprenticeship to achieve a literary position above that of a hack writer.

Down and Out might very well be called one of the early-day nonfictional novels. It is autobiographical in subject matter and fictional in manner. The unidentified narrator rehearses a tale of two cities — and it should be remembered that Orwell added the London material only later, to help flesh out the book. In short, it is a dual book about a marginal life among the poor, and it is filled with strange inner anecdotes and extraordinary "characters." The book was reviewed widely and well, but it did not suddenly catapult its author into either fame or fortune. Orwell earned only about 200 pounds from combined U.S. and English sales for the first two years. (Not until 1940, when Penguin brought out an edition of 55,000 copies, and listed it under the rubric of "Fiction," did it earn a substantial amount.) What the initial publication did, though, was to establish Orwell as a writer deserving serious attention from editors and publishers.

In the meantime, there was a living to be earned; so Eric Blair returned to teaching — only this time at Brays College in Middlesex, and just for a short period because he was once more beset by pneumonia. After nearly a month of enforced hospitalization, he retreated to his parents' home in Southwold, where he spent the better part of the year. Then in the fall of that year he decamped for Hampstead and a bookshop called Booklovers' Corner, which provided him a living, as well as an opportunity to see new books and to write.

Actually, Orwell had finished writing a draft of *Burmese Days* before he left Brays College, and a draft of *A Clergyman's Daughter* before he left his parents for Hampstead. He had begun to write in that constant, compulsive, manner that would remain with him the rest of his life. Gone forever was the Eton loafer: in his stead slaved the zealous convert to the Protestant work ethic. As Orwell would confess in one of his last notebooks — "there has literally been not one day in which I did not feel that I was idling. . . . Even at periods when I was working ten hours a day on a book, or turning out four or five articles a week, I never have been able to get away from this neurotic feeling that I was wasting time."

Obviously Orwell wasted very little time during the period 1933–39, when he published a book a year for seven years: *Down and Out in Paris and London* (1933), *Burmese Days* (1934), *The Clergyman's Daughter* (1935), *Keep the Aspidistra Flying* (1936), *The Road to Wigan Pier* (1937), *Homage to Catalonia* (1938), and *Coming Up for Air* (1939). Also during this period, he turned out scores of book reviews and articles that would eventually find their way into a remarkable four-volume collection of his fugitive pieces. Like his best books, many of these essays were done in the name of what Orwell considered to be truth and social justice. As he indicates in "Why I Write," his best work would always have a political edge, and his best prose would always aim at being "like a window pane."

Orwell's first seven books fall into two neat categories: four are middle-class novels; three are autobiographical accounts of economic depression and of civil war. As earlier indicated, all four of these novels have different settings and dissimilar protagonists, but they all have to do with breaking away from the establishment. Flory, of *Burmese Days*, is something of a misfit; like Orwell, he is eminently "unclubbable." He does not fit in with the pukka sahibs and he is betrayed by a wily Burmese. A weak, ranting, lonely figure, Flory tries to find some kind of personal escape through a liaison with a priggish young woman of his own caste, Elizabeth Lackersteen. When that fails, he is ripe for suicide; and, according to John Atkins, *Burmese Days* is a fictive extrapolation of Orwell's own life in the Orient, and an indication of how it might have ended.

Dorothy Hare, the titular clergyman's daughter, is a figure out of an Arnold Bennett novel, or one by H. G. Wells. Stifled by life in her provincial home town, she becomes the victim of a fictionally convenient amnesia, which allows her to go off to a bohemian life of sorts, picking hops with itinerants, and lying about one cold night with other vagrants in Trafalgar Square (Orwell indulges himself here in the last part of the novel with a pseudo-Joycean ramble). Dorothy is offered a chance to escape her middle-class background by a sybaritic fellow named Warburton, but she is sexually repressed and full of morbid fears; so she finally retreats to her parental home in Knype Hill.

Gordon Comstock, protagonist of *Keep the Aspidistra Flying*, is another of Orwell's would-be escapees from the middle class. In many ways he prefigures those characters that were to emerge from the novels of a later generation's "Angry Young Men." Gordon is a would-be poet who has grown bitter about a world where money (of which he has little) is all important. He sees everything in British society from a monetary viewpoint: "Social failure, artistic failure, sexual failure—they are all the same. And lack of money is at the bottom of them all." Having dropped out of the middle class, giving up a job in an advertising firm, Gordon has an affair with a young woman named Rosemary, who later informs him they are going to have a baby. Under these circumstances, Comstock emerges as the first indication of Orwell's almost mystical appreciation of the common folk of England, the salt of the earth that might be the hope of the land. Comstock accepts his responsibility, marries Rosemary, and in the process comes to perceive, somewhat ruefully, that the lives of common men and women may be the salvation of us all:

> The lower middle-class people in there, behind their lace curtains, with their children and their scraps of furniture and their aspidistras [a favorite indoor plant which serves as an emblem of the middle-class in this novel] — they lived by the money-code, sure enough, and yet they contrived to keep their decency. . . . They were bound up in the bundle of life. They begot children, which is what the saints and the soul-savers never by any chance do.

Orwell's own life had taken a Comstockian turn. In March of 1935 he had met Eileen Shaughnessy, who was to become his first wife. An Oxford graduate, Eileen was at the time studying for an M.A. in psychology at University College London. Orwell's association with this strong, independent, and loving woman gave a new coloration to his life; and it may also have influenced the rather accommodating conclusion of *Keep the Aspidistra Flying*. In any case, 1936 was a full and significant year for Orwell: he published the novel in question, married Eileen, and went to live with her in "The Stores" in Wallington, where he was able to keep a few goats and do some gardening. In this same year, he accepted a commission from Victor Gollancz to do another book on poverty — this time on the plight of coal miners in Yorkshire and Lancashire.

The resulting work, *The Road to Wigan Pier*, came out in March of 1937, in both a public and a Left Book Club edition. The first half of the book is a documentary equivalent of Emile Zola's *Germinal*, describing the dangerous working conditions of the miners and the squalid living conditions of their families. One of the most telling passages in this section of the book shows the young wife of a miner kneeling on stones outside her house in frigid weather trying to poke a stick into a filthy drain pipe to unclog it. Her arms are coarse and red with the cold; her face is pasty; she looks exhausted. But she is not without the intelligence the middle class might deny her. "For what I saw," Orwell writes, "was not the ignorant suffering of an animal. She knew well enough what was happening to her — understood as well as I did how dreadful a destiny it was to be kneeling there in the bitter cold, on the slimy stones of a slum backyard, poking a stick up a foul drain-pipe."

It was the second half of the book that gave Gollancz and others of the Left Book Club fits. In this section Orwell traces his own development from childhood and Burma through to the book's present, explaining how he had arrived at the choice of socialism as a political philosophy. But here also he makes a series of idiosyncratic attacks on intellectual English Communists who idolized Russia, and certain socialists whom he considered phonies: "One sometimes gets the impression that the mere words 'Socialism' and 'Communism' draw towards them with magnetic force every fruit-juice drinker, nudist, sandal-wearer, sex maniac, Quaker, 'Nature Cure' quack, pacifist and feminist in England." Because of passages like these, Gollancz felt the necessity to append a mollifying foreword to the book, chastising his young colleague for trailing middle-class snobbery into the ranks of socialism. And yet it was this ability never to be simply a partisan in a narrow sense that was Orwell's greatest attribute. Over and over again he would prove that he was owned by no group or movement, that he would speak what he considered to be the truth on all occasions. Nowhere would that trait be more apparent than in his next book, *Homage to Catalonia*, which helped establish him as an international figure in the company of such other political writers as Ignazio Silone and Arthur Koestler.

The Spanish Civil War broke out on 18 July 1936, and just before Christmas of that year Orwell left for Barcelona, bearing the credentials of a journalist. Within two weeks, however, he had joined a militia unit of the POUM (Partido Obrero de Unificacíon Marxista), a Trotskyist organization affiliated with the International Labor Party. All told, Orwell would spend about three months in the combat area of northern Spain, first with the POUM unit near Saragossa, and then later with a British ILP unit near Huesca. It was here that he was wounded by a sniper's bullet that passed clean through his throat, narrowly missing both the larynx and the carotid artery, but nicking one of his vocal chords. According to Orwell, the sensation was that of being "*at the centre* of an explosion." After being treated back in Lerida (where he received an incorrect prognosis that he would never speak again), Orwell was sent to Barcelona to recuperate. While he was still there, trying to obtain his discharge, the POUM was declared illegal by the Republican government, under Communist urging. Orwell and his wife, who had joined him in Barcelona, then spent two weeks on the run from the Communists, until they crossed the French border on 23 June 1937.

The political infighting among other segments of the popular front and the Communists would stay in Orwell's memory for a long time, as would Andrés Nim, the POUM leader who was kidnapped and killed by Communist agents, and who would share with Leon Trotsky a place in Orwell's depiction of Goldstein in *1984*. If serving with common men in the militia and being traumatically wounded inspired Orwell to write *Homage to Catalonia*, so did the perception that totalitarianism was *the* great threat to liberty and the liberal heritage. Like a number of disillusioned left-wing writers, Silone and Koestler among them, he now found communism to be as much a threat as fascism.

Orwell expressed this attitude in letters to his publisher and declared his intention to "spill the beans about Spain" in a book. Still dismayed by Orwell's animadversions upon left-wingers in *The Road to Wigan Pier*, Victor Gollancz was in no mood for more of the same; and so without even seeing a manuscript of the work, he refused to publish *Homage to*

Catalonia. For awhile, Gollancz appeared to have made the right decision. Published by Secker & Warburg in April of 1938, the book immediately became the target of a massive attack by the leftist press. By the time Orwell died in 1950, no more than 900 copies of the book had been sold; and it was not published in the United States until 1952. But in the long run, it was Secker & Warburg that made the right decision. Not only did they earn the opportunity later to publish Orwell's first best-seller (*Animal Farm*); but *Homage to Catalonia*, which began life as a "succes d'estime" among the knowledgeable, continued over the years to grow in critical esteem until now very few students of Orwell would deny it a place among his three best books, along with *Animal Farm* and *1984*.

Before *Homage to Catalonia*, Orwell's autobiographical and documentary writing had a tinge of fiction about it, as with "Shooting an Elephant"; and his fiction had more than a slight autobiographical tinge, as with *Burmese Days*. *Homage to Catalonia*, on the other hand, is about as honest and straightforward a work of personal reportage as one man could manage. Orwell's accounts of the democratic proceedings of the POUM militiamen in combat, his description of the filth and boredom of war, his analyses of the machinations of the government and its supporters, the internecine squabbling and betrayals — all these constitute a form of homage to people like the idealist Andrés Nim and a young militiaman who had impressed Orwell as the very type of the working man fighting for his rightful place in the world. Later in a 1942 essay called "Looking Back on the Spanish War," Orwell would commemorate this emblematic young man in the last stanza of a poem with which the essay concludes:

> But the thing that I saw in your face
> No power can disinherit:
> No bomb that ever burst
> Shatters the crystal spirit.

After his return from Spain, Orwell fell ill, in March 1938, with a tubercular lesion in one lung, and had to be put into a sanitarium for six months. He learned that he had actually been tubercular since about 1928; the damp Burmese climate had obviously been harmful and the winter months in the Aragon region of Spain could not have helped. An anonymous donation (by fellow novelist J. H. Myers) allowed Orwell and his wife to stay for seven months in the sunny climate of Marrakesh, in Morocco. Here he was able to work on a new novel that would bear the psychosomatic-sounding title of *Coming Up for Air*.

Published in June 1939, *Coming Up for Air* is narrated by its protagonist, George Bowling. A middle-aged insurance salesman with no intellectual pretensions, George is filled with dread of the world war he fears will break out. In fact, most of the modern world fills him with discontent, and he is pulled back toward his Edwardian past in search of something to hold onto in life. The novel is a cautionary tale that says the world is going to hell with itself, and that we may have to hark back to the past to find stable and worthwhile ideals; but it also says, through Bowling's disappointing return to his home town, that there can be no real returning to the past. In some respects, then, *Coming Up for Air* reads like a commonsensical reworking of a Proustian theme—in search of things past—although there is no evidence that Orwell ever read Proust.

The war that Bowling feared did, of course, break out in September 1939, and Bowling's creator tried to find some means of actively supporting Britain's war effort. In his state of health, however, all Orwell could manage was to join the Home Guard, act as an air-raid warden, and later become part of the BBC's staff as a "Talks Producer," responsible for education programs being beamed to India. He continued to write reviews and political commentary for such journals as *Tribune* and *Horizon*, and also began a regular series of columns for American left-wing intelligentsia in *Partisan Review*. Here, in 1941, he explained his attitude toward the writing of fiction during the desperate early stages of the war: "Only the mentally dead are capable of sitting down and writing novels while this nightmare is on. . . . There is such a doubt about the continuity of civilization as can hardly have existed for hundreds of years. . . ."

By 1943, however, when the fortunes of war had begun to shift, Orwell resigned from his patriotic tasks and took over as literary editor of *Tribune*. At about the same time, he began working on a book destined to make him world-famous as a political satirist comparable with Voltaire and Jonathan Swift. But the matter of getting the book published in wartime Britain proved very difficult, because of its attack on Soviet Russia, which was still a valued ally. Once again, socialist publisher Victor Gollancz refused the opportunity, but so too did staunch Tory T. S. Eliot on behalf of Faber & Faber. In an admiringly specious note, Eliot said he did not think "this the right point of view from which to criticise the political situation at the present time." So the task of publishing Orwell once again fell to Secker & Warburg—a firm that greatly enhanced its financial and literary reputation by bringing out *Animal Farm* in August 1945.

The book became an immediate success: the first English edition sold out in a month; within a year it was translated into eight languages; and after the Book of the Month Club in America placed it on their list, it sold over a half-million copies. Although certain leftists and die-hard Communists lambasted the book, most reviewers on both sides of the Atlantic saw it as a small masterpiece, deserving of comparison with Koestler's *Darkness at Noon* and Swift's *Gulliver's Travels* (although it is not literarily much like either of these works).

Animal Farm is a slender book, a political-fictional pamphlet just over a hundred pages in length. The fable it presents reads something like a script for one of Walt Disney's more serious animated cartoons. But the strength of the book lies in its clear style and objective narrative tone. A touch more cleverness or elaboration might have spoiled the entire work. Never before or after was Orwell able to fuse political subject and esthetic intent in such a balanced and polished fashion. The simplicity and clarity of the book meant that contemporary readers would need little or no prompting to align real-life counterparts with the roman à clef figures in Orwell's modern beast fable. A double dramatis personae, somewhat like the following, grew out of even the most cursory of readings:

Animal Farm Figure	Real-life Counterpart
Old Major, founder of "Animalism"	Karl Marx
Napoleon, leader of the pigs	Joseph Stalin
Snowball, theoretician of the pigs	Leon Trotsky
Boxer, worker-hero cart horse	Member of proletariat
Clover, Boxer's helpmate	A worker with curiosity
Squealer, maker of mottoes and news	A commissar-propagandist
The Dogs, caretakers	OGPU (state police)
Farmer Jones, former owner of farm	Western World capitalist
Frederick of Pinchfield	Hitler (with mustache)
Mr. Whymper	Communist sympathizer
Pilkington	Churchillian Tory

The central target of the book is the Stalinist ruination of a cause, the betrayal of world socialism. In a special preface prepared for a Ukrainian version of *Animal Farm* (brought out in 1947 for Russian refugees), Orwell explains clearly why he wrote his fable:

> it was of the utmost importance to me that people in Western Europe should see the Soviet regime for what it really was. Since 1930 I had seen little evidence that the USSR was progressing towards anything that one could truly call Socialism. On the contrary, I was struck by clear signs of its transformation into a hierarchical society, in which the rulers have no more reason to give up their power than any other ruling class.

The book itself emphasizes this hierarchical shift through a series of amendments made in Animalism by the pigs, who become the new ruling class of what was once Manor Farm. Gradually and surreptitiously the pigs change the basic beliefs of Animal Farm. One of the prime command-ments, "No animal shall kill any other animal," is eventually provided with an added tag—"*without cause.*" A leading slogan, originated by the clever Snowball, distinguishes the animals from man: "Four legs good, two legs bad." This is chanted constantly by the sheep on the farm until the pigs become ascendant and begin to walk around on their hind legs. Then Squealer, a *Pravda*-derived figure, informs the animals that the slogan has really been, all along, "Four legs good, two legs better." Of course, the most famous of these redactions is one that even people who have never read Orwell can cite. Overnight the democratic creed of Animalism, summed up in one sentence painted on the barn, is changed by the addition of a second clause so that it finally reads:

ALL ANIMALS ARE EQUAL
BUT SOME ARE MORE EQUAL THAN OTHERS.

After *Animal Farm* was completed, Orwell's own life seemed to rush toward its completion. Publication of the book would make him both famous and financially well off; and even before the book came out, he and his wife, Eileen, had adopted a baby, whom they named Richard Horatio Blair. But fame, fortune, and family were not to represent any lasting happiness. Orwell went off to France as a war correspondent for the *Observer* in 1945, and while he was abroad Eileen was admitted to the hospital for an operation variously reported as "minor" and for "cancer." According to J. R. Hammond, she died "while the anaesthetic was being administered." Himself ill, and grief-stricken, Orwell came back to attend to the funeral. A bit later, almost as a form of therapy, he returned to war reporting for a brief time. Then, in the autumn of 1945, he paid his first visit to Jura — an island near the southernmost tip of the Inner Hebrides, which he and Eileen had been considering as a new place of residence. It was here that he made his last real stand against the tuberculosis which was slowly killing him. It was here also — having as company his son, a housekeeper, a caretaker, and occasional visitors — that he wrote his most famous work, an anti-utopian novel destined to make the year 1984 balefully eponymous.

Actually, as a letter to his agent shows, Orwell had made a start on the novel as early as the summer of 1945. But not until 1947, upon his return to Jura from London (with his sister Avril as replacement housekeeper), did he fully develop the manuscript. He finished a first draft before October of that year. Then his lungs became inflamed once again and he had to take to his sick bed. The condition worsened and a few days before Christmas he was ordered into a Glasgow hospital for a lengthy stay. After a brief return to Jura the next summer, he managed to finish the final draft of *1984* in November 1948. (The title of the book, which Orwell spelled out as *Nineteen Eighty-Four*, is simply a reversal of the last two digits in the year of its completion — *48* turned into *84*.)

Orwell's original title for the novel, "The Last Man in Europe," would have stressed the moribund condition of freedom and of his protagonist, Winston Smith. It is not difficult to understand how the equally moribund author must have incorporated himself in the final stages of Smith's torturous dissolution. Under the goading of his inquisitor, Smith is forced to view himself in a full-length mirror:

A bowed, gray-colored skeletonlike thing was coming toward him. Its actual appearance was frightening, and not merely the fact that he knew it to be himself. He moved closer to the glass. The creature's face seemed to be protruded. . . . But the truly frightening thing was the emaciation of his body. . . . The thin shoulders were hunched forward so as to make a cavity of the chest. . . . At a guess he would have said that it was the body of a man of sixty, suffering from some malignant disease.

There can be little doubt that Orwell used himself as a model for this phthisic portrait. But some critics have argued that the author's physical deterioration — as well as psychic wounds left over from St. Cyprian's — determined the thematic defeat and despair of the novel. This is the genetic argument that says the man is his work and vice versa; those who argue in this manner fail to observe that many people who die of tuberculosis, or attend oppressive prep schools, only infrequently write novels with the force and stature of *1984*. Merely completing such a work under the adverse conditions which beset Orwell might well be looked upon as a form of heroism.

Most critics now view the defeat of Winston Smith as a function of the anti-utopian, or dystopian, novel. The dystopian novel always constitutes something of a literary paradox, as does the so-called "nihilistic" novel (a true nihilist would write nothing). The more successful a book like *1984* is as warning, the less successful it can be as prophecy. The more successful it is as prophecy, the less successful it can be as warning. Orwell's book is a dire warning, a knocking-on-wood against the future; and Winston Smith's defeat is of a sacrificial order, for those "last" men and women who may still be capable of achieving true freedom, not simply the substitution of one tyranny for another.

1984 is all about tyranny. Big Brother rules Oceania as the figurehead of absolute tyranny. His government, Ingsoc, enforces mental tyranny by promulgating oxymoronic slogans: "WAR IS PEACE . . . FREEDOM IS SLAVERY . . . IGNORANCE IS STRENGTH." A book within a book — Emanuel Goldstein's "The Theory and Practice of Oligarchical Collectivism" — is a dissertation on the three tyrannies that rule the world of 1984. O'Brien, Winston's torturing mentor, sums up the "why" as well as the "how" of tyranny. Power, he declares, is its own reward, and power is achieved simply by hurting people. "If you want a picture of the future," he concludes, "imagine a boot stamping on a human face — forever."

Oceania perpetuates its tyranny in several ways. All of the members of its upper classes, for example, come under continuous electronic scrutiny. Big Brother's minions check them constantly for signs of "facecrime" and "thoughtcrime." Yet the subtlest means of control is achieved through the corruption of history and language. Winston himself takes part in this process as a worker within the Ministry of Truth ("Minitrue," in officialese). Here he is able to alter records to such an extent that he can make someone who existed into an "unperson," and conversely can create records to prove that someone who never existed did exist. Equally pernicious is Oceania's language reform, by which "Oldspeak," or stand-ard English, is transformed into "Newspeak," the official language of Ingsoc. By systematically reducing and perverting conceptual terms, the government intends to make it impossible for its citizenry to think or speak anything contrary to governmental wishes.

As an appendix to the novel, Orwell provided a short treatise on Newspeak, revealing a language dominated by "doubleplusungood" words that lead to a form of political gibberish called "duckspeak." The appendix stands as a drastic extension of Orwell's 1946 essay on "Politics and the English Language." In similar fashion, the novel as a whole stands as a dramatic extension of a thematic truth Orwell had earlier used in both *Homage to Catalonia* and *Animal Farm*. Winston's harsh mentor, O'Brien, states this powerful truth axiomatically: "Who controls the past controls the future; who controls the present controls the past." Of course, the axiom applies to textbooks publishers and television network owners in a relatively free society as well as to state-controlled agencies like *Pravda* in a dictatorship.

1984 was published in July 1949; within a year it had sold nearly 50,000 copies in England and about 369,000 in the United States. V. S. Pritchett and Lionel Trilling set the standard for excellent reviews of the novel. Far-left and Communist opinion was epitomized by Sam Sillen, who (in the now defunct *Masses and Mainstream*) accused Orwell of being a "maggot of the month" catering to the debauched tastes of the bourgeoi-sie. The book did fulfill a need in the Western mind, and it has continued to be a perennial best-seller in paperback. There was a period of about a decade, in the fifties, when nearly every American college graduate had read the book, often in conjunction with Aldous Huxley's quite dissimilar dystopian novel, *Brave New World*.

Orwell had little time or opportunity to enjoy the increased fame and earnings that *1984* brought him. He had finished typing out copies of the book in December 1948. By 6 January 1949 he was placed in the Cotswold Sanatorium, in Cranham. He was destined never to leave the hospital environment, for when his condition worsened, he was transferred to University College Hospital, London. During the long months of confine-ment, Orwell received many visitors, including old friends like Richard Rees, Malcolm Muggeridge, Anthony Powell, and Cyril Connolly. Among others was an attractive young woman named Sonia Brownell, an editorial assistant of Connolly's at *Horizon*. Having known her for almost five years, Orwell asked her to marry him, in hopes that he would get better. On 13 October 1949 they were married in the hospital; Orwell was forty-six years old, Sonia thirty-one. The last memory photograph of Blair-Orwell might well show him propped up in his hospital bed, dressed in a crimson-to-mauve smoking jacket (purchased for the occasion), marrying the beautiful young Sonia.

After the wedding, Orwell rallied briefly, but on 21 January 1950 he suffered a final tubercular lung hemorrhage and died immediately. Later, in *The Evening Colonnade* (1973), Cyril Connolly was to sum up his friend's hopeless situation in this eloquent passage:

> The tragedy of Orwell's life is that when at last he achieved fame and success he was a dying man and knew it. He had fame and was too ill to leave his room, money and nothing to spend it on, love in which he could not participate; he tasted the bitterness of dying. But in his years of hardship he was sustained by a genial stoicism, by his excitement about what was going to happen next and by his affection for other people.

In death, Orwell returned to the form of his family. As requested in his will, he was buried in a regular Church of England setting—the church-yard of All Saints, Sutton Courtenay, in Berkshire. And the simple headstone shows a final reversion from Orwell to Blair:

Here Lies
Eric Arthur Blair
Born June 25th 1903
Died January 21st 1950.

Notes

1. This biographical sketch is offered as a review for the Orwell expert and as a source of basic information for the reader who knows little of Orwell's life and only a few of his books. It is meant to be used in complementary fashion with the essays that make up this collection. This is especially true of Paul Schlueter's bibliographic essay, which is one of the latest and most comprehensive tracings of Orwellian scholarship and criticism, with particular emphasis on works dating from the key publication of *The Collected Essays, Journalism, and Letters of George Orwell* in 1968.

2. For the basic facts of this biographical account I have relied primarily on Bernard Crick's almost definitive *George Orwell: A Life* (1980), and *The Collected Essays, Journalism, and Letters of George Orwell*, edited by Sonia Orwell and Ian Angus, 4 volumes (1968). I have also consulted John Atkins's *George Orwell* (1954), Richard Rees's *George Orwell: Fugitive from the Camp of Victory* (1962), Peter Stansky and William Abrahams's *The Unknown Orwell* (1972), J. R. Hammond's *A George Orwell Companion* (1982), George Woodcock's *The Crystal Spirit: A Study of George Orwell* (1984), and David Zehr's essay on Orwell in *The Dictionary of Literary Biography*, vol. 15, *British Novelists, 1930–1959*, edited by Bernard Oldsey (1983).

The Man and the Year

If Orwell Were Alive Today

Norman Podhoretz*

"Dickens," George Orwell once remarked, "is one of those writers who are well worth stealing," which was why so many different groups were eager to claim him as one of their own. Did Orwell foresee that someday he too would become just such a writer? Almost certainly he did not. In 1939, when he wrote those words about Dickens, he was still a relatively obscure figure, and among those who knew his work at all, a highly controversial one. Only a year earlier, his book about the Spanish Civil War, *Homage to Catalonia*, had been rejected on political grounds by his own publishers in both Britain and the United States; and far from being claimed by contending factions as one of their own, he was closer to being excommunicated and excoriated by them all. Nevertheless, by the time of his death in 1950 at the age of forty-six, he had become so famous that his very name entered the language and has remained there in the form of the adjective "Orwellian."

At first, this great status rested almost entirely on the tremendous success, both critical and commercial, of his two last novels, *Animal Farm* (1945) and *Nineteen Eighty-Four* (1949). Thanks to them, all his other books, including several early novels that were scarcely noticed at the time of their publication, as well as literary essays, book reviews, and even fugitive pieces of dated journalism, came back into print and are still easily available. As these earlier works became better known, they gradually enhanced Orwell's posthumous reputation. For example, the much maligned *Homage to Catalonia* was pronounced "one of the important documents of our time" by the Great American critic Lionel Trilling when it was finally published in the United States after Orwell's death. And when in 1968 *The Collected Essays, Journalism and Letters of George Orwell* came out in four massive volumes, the occasion was seized upon by another American critic, Irving Howe, to proclaim Orwell not only "the best English essayist since Hazlitt, perhaps since Dr. Johnson"

*Reprinted from *Harper's Magazine*, January 1983, 30–37, by permission of the author.

19

but also "the greatest moral force in English letters during the last several decades." Bernard Crick, one of Orwell's most recent British biographers, goes if possible, even further, placing him with Thomas Hobbes and Jonathan Swift as one of the three greatest political writers in the history of English literature (greater, in other words, than even Edmund Burke and John Stuart Mill).

This enormous reputation by itself would make Orwell "one of those writers who are well worth stealing." It is, after all, no small thing to have the greatest political writer of the age on one's side: it gives confidence, authority, and weight to one's own political views. Accordingly, a dispute has broken out over what Orwell's position actually was in his own lifetime and what it might have been if he had survived to go on participating in the political debates that have raged since the day of his death.

Normally, to speculate on what a dead man might have said about events he never lived to see is a frivolous enterprise. There is no way of knowing whether and to what extent he would have changed his views in response to a changing world; and this is especially the case with a writer like Orwell, who underwent several major political transformations. On the other hand, the main issues that concerned Orwell throughout his career are still alive today, often in different form but often also in almost exactly the same form they took when he wrote about them. This is why so many of his apparently dated journalistic pieces remain relevant. Even though the particular circumstances with which they deal have long since been forgotten, the questions they raise are questions we are still asking today and still trying to answer.

If this is true of much of Orwell's fugitive journalism, it becomes even more strikingly evident when we consider some of his major works: *Animal Farm* and *Nineteen Eighty-Four* among his novels, and among his discursive writings, *Down and Out in Paris and London* (1933), *The Road to Wigan Pier* (1937), and *Homage to Catalonia* (1938), not to mention many of the wonderful essays collected in *Inside the Whale* (1940), *Dickens, Dali and Others* (1946), and *Shooting an Elephant* (1950). So relevant do all these works seem today that to read through them is to be astonished, and a little depressed, at the degree to which we are still haunted by the ghosts of political wars past.

When Orwell wrote his essay on Dickens, the two main groups trying to "steal" Dickens were the Marxists and the Catholics. (That they could automatically be taken as equivalent to Left and Right is one interesting measure of how things have changed in the past forty years.) The two main groups contending over Orwell today are the socialists on the one side and, on the other, the disillusioned former socialists who have come to be known as neoconservatives. The socialists, of whom Crick is a leading representative, declare that Orwell was a "revolutionary" whose values can only be (as Crick puts it) "wilfully misunderstood . . . when he is

claimed for the camp of the Cold War." For their part, the neoconservatives deny that Orwell was a revolutionary; they think of him instead as a
major critic of revolutionism. And they do indeed claim him for "the camp
of the Cold War" in the sense that they see in his work one of the great
prophetic warnings against the threat of Soviet totalitarianism. Thus the
Committee for the Free World, an organization made up mainly of
neoconservative intellectuals (and with which I am associated), publishes
material under the imprint "Orwell Press" and in general regards Orwell
as one of its guiding spirits.

As a writer, Orwell is most admired, and rightly so, for the simplicity
and straightforwardness of his style. "Good prose," he said, "is like a
window pane." He valued such prose for its own sake, on aesthetic
grounds, but he also believed that in political discourse clarity was a
protection against deceit: "In our time, political speech and writing are
largely the defense of the indefensible. . . . Thus political language has to
consist largely of euphemism, question-begging and sheer cloudy vagueness." Since Orwell wrote about politics in a language that not only
avoided those vices but succeeded marvelously in the art of calling things
by their proper names and confronting questions with plainness and
precision, one might think that nothing would be easier than defining his
point of view. The problem is, however, that he wrote so much and
changed his mind so often — mostly on small issues but also on large ones —
that plausible evidence can be found in his work for each of the two
contending interpretations of where he stood.

As a very young man, Orwell was, by his own account, a "Tory
anarchist." But at the age of thirty or thereabouts he converted to socialism
and kept calling himself a socialist until the day he died. Crick therefore
has no trouble in piling up quotations that support the socialist claim to
possession of Orwell. He does, however, have a great deal of trouble in
trying to explain away the side of Orwell that has given so much aid and
comfort to antisocialists of all kinds. For, avowed socialist though he
certainly was, Orwell was also a relentless critic of his fellow socialists
from beginning to end.

Thus no sooner did he declare his allegiance to socialism than he
began taking it upon himself to explain why so many decent people were
put off by his new political faith. "One sometimes gets the impression," he
wrote in *The Road to Wigan Pier*, "that the mere words 'Socialism' and
'Communism' draw towards them with magnetic force every fruit-juice
drinker, nudist, sandal-wearer, sex-maniac, Quaker, 'Nature Cure' quack,
pacifist and feminist in England." Shortly after delivering himself of this
observation, and while he still regarded the Communists as comrades in
the struggle for socialism, he went to fight against Franco in the Spanish
Civil War. There he learned two things: that the Spanish Communists
were more interested in furthering the aims of Soviet foreign policy than in

making a socialist revolution at home, and that the left-wing press in England (and everywhere else) was full of lies about what was actually going on in Spain. For the next few years, much of his writing was devoted to attacks on the Stalinists and their fellow travelers, who, in those days of the "Popular Front," included almost everyone on the Left.

These attacks were written from what can loosely be described as a Trotskyist or revolutionary-socialist perspective based on, among other things the proposition that England was hardly, if at all, better than Nazi Germany. But with the outbreak of World War II, a new Orwell was born—Orwell the English patriot. "My Country, Right or Left," he now declared in one of his most memorable phrases, and went on to excoriate the "anti-British" attitudes that had been so fashionable on the Left throughout the 1930s and to which he himself had temporarily subscribed.

Then, toward the end of the war, and with the defeat of fascist totalitarianism in sight, Orwell began brooding more and more on the possibility that communist totalitarianism might turn out to be the inevitable wave of the future. In *Animal Farm*, written while the Soviet Union was still a wartime ally of the Western democracies, he produced a satire on the Russian Revolution so unsparing that it could be and usually was interpreted as a repudiation of all hopes for a benevolent socialist revolution. Like *Homage to Catalonia* before it, the manuscript was rejected as too anti-Soviet by the first few publishers to whom it was submitted. One of the publishers in this case was no less a personage than T. S. Eliot, whose own aggressive conservatism did not prevent him from doubting that Orwell's was "the right point of view from which to criticize the political situation at the present time."

Finally there was *Nineteen Eighty-Four*, which came out just at the height of the Cold War and very shortly before Orwell's death. In that novel, Orwell portrayed the England of the future as a totalitarian society ruled over by a Communist-like party in the name of "Ingsoc" ("newspeak" for English socialism). He later explicitly denied that in using this term he had intended to cast any aspersions on the British Labour Party, of which he was a (highly critical) supporter, let alone that he was attacking socialism itself. Nevertheless, neither in *Animal Farm* nor in *Nineteen Eighty-Four* was there any trace of the idea that a socialist revolution could be accomplished without a betrayal of the ideas of liberty and equality to whose full realization socialism was in theory committed.

No wonder Crick has so much trouble staking the socialist claim to Orwell. No wonder too that other socialists of varying stripe like Isaac Deutscher and Raymond Williams have said that Orwell was not really one of them.

If Orwell was a great political writer—and I think he was, though I would not place him quite so high as Crick does—it is not because he was always right in his strictly political judgments. The plain truth is that he was more often wrong than right. For example, he predicted that the British Conservatives (the "Blimpocracy") would never go to war against Hitler; then, when they did, he refused to believe, and he doubted "whether many people under fifty believe[d] it either," that England could "win the war without passing through revolution."

In addition to making many mistaken political predictions, he was also capable of serious errors of political valuation, as when he joined briefly in the fashionable cry of the mid-1930s to the effect that there was no difference between fascism and liberalism. And even after correcting errors of this kind, he was capable of backsliding into such similar absurdities as saying that British rule in India was as bad as Hitler's rule in Europe, or that British policy toward Greece in 1945 was no different from "the Russian coercion of Poland."

Wrong though he so often was about particular events, however, Orwell in every stage of his political development was almost always right about one thing: the character and quality of the left-wing literary intellectuals among whom he lived and to whom he addressed himself as a political writer. More than anything else, the ethos of the left-wing literary intelligentsia was his true subject and the one that elicited his most brilliant work. Indeed, whatever ideas were fashionable on the Left at any given moment were precisely the ones he had the greatest compulsion to criticize. And the fact that he criticized them from within only added authority to the things he said — so much so that I wonder whether this was why he insisted on clinging so tenaciously to his identity as a man of the Left.

It is largely because of Orwell's relation to the left-wing intelligentsia that I believe he would have been a neoconservative if he were alive today. I would even suggest that he was a forerunner of neoconservatism in having been one of the first in a long line of originally left-wing intellectuals who have come to discover more saving political and moral wisdom in the instincts and mores of "ordinary" people than in the ideas and attitudes of the intelligentsia. "One has to belong to the intelligentsia to believe things like that," he wrote in 1945 after listing several egregious examples relating to the progress of World War II; "no ordinary man could be such a fool." This remark has become especially well known in recent years, but it is only one of many passages of similar import scattered throughout Orwell's writings.

Nor was it only on political issues that Orwell defended the "ordinary man" against the left-wing intelligentsia. Even in the mid-1930s, during his most radical period, he attacked Cyril Connolly's novel *The Rock Pool* for suggesting that "so-called artists who spend on sodomy what they have gained by sponging" were superior to "the polite and sheep-like Englishman." This, he said, "only amounts to a distaste for normal life and common decency," and he concluded by declaring: "The fact to which we have got to cling, as to a lifebelt, is that it *is* possible to be a normal decent person and yet to be fully alive."

This streak of populism, always strong in Orwell, became even more pronounced with the outbreak of World War II, when it took the form of a celebration of England and the English character. As a corollary to becoming a wholehearted patriot — and in coming to see patriotism as a great and positive force — Orwell lashed out more ferociously than ever at the British intelligentsia:

> . . . the really important fact about so many of the English intelligent-
> sia [is] their severance from the common culture of the country. . . .
> England is perhaps the only great country whose intellectuals are
> ashamed of their own nationality. In left-wing circles it is always felt
> that there is something slightly disgraceful in being an Englishman and
> that it is a duty to snigger at every English institution. . . . All through
> the critical years many left-wingers were chipping away at English
> morale, trying to spread an outlook that was sometimes squashily
> pacifist, sometimes violently pro-Russian, but always anti-British. . . .
> If the English people suffered for several years a real weakening of
> morale, so that the Fascist nations judged that they were "decadent" and
> that it was safe to plunge into war, the intellectual sabotage from the
> Left was partly responsible.

Is it any wonder that the neoconservatives see Orwell as a guiding spirit when everything he says here has been echoed by them in talking about the American intellectuals of today? And when Orwell was charged with "intellectual-hunting" by a leading young pacifist named Alex Comfort (who, as though to confirm Orwell's diagnosis of the phenomenon of which Comfort was a typical specimen, would go on to greater heights of fame in later years as the author of *The Joy of Sex*), he replied in terms that have been echoed in similar arguments by the neoconservatives as well: "It is just because I do take the function of the intelligentsia seriously that I don't like the sneers, libels, parrot phrases and financially profitable back-scratching which flourish in our English literary world. . . ."

Another and related reason for thinking that Orwell would be as neoconservative if he were alive today lies in his attitude toward pacifism. For a very brief period in his youth Orwell flirted with pacifism, but nothing could have been more alien to his temperament and he soon broke off the affair. By 1938 he was writing (and in language that shows how far he was willing to go in speaking plainly even when euphemism might better have served his own political position): "If someone drops a bomb on your mother, go and drop two bombs on his mother. The only apparent alternatives are to smash dwelling houses to powder, blow out human entrails and burn holes in children with lumps of thermite, or be enslaved by people who are more ready to do these things than you are yourself; as yet no one has suggested a practical way out." And again in 1940, when a British defeat seemed likely: "There is nothing for it but to die fighting but one must above all die *fighting* and have the satisfaction of killing somebody else first."

Moved by such feelings, Orwell came to write about pacifism with an even fiercer edge of scorn and outrage than before. Later he would regret using the term "objectively pro-Fascist," but that is what he now accused the pacifists — or "Fascifists," as he called them — of being (for, "If you hamper the war effort of one side you automatically help that of the other"); he also attacked them for "intellectual cowardice" in refusing to admit that this was the inescapable logical implication of their position; and he said that they were hypocritical "for crying 'Peace!' behind a screen of guns." But in trying to imagine where Orwell would have stood if he were alive today, the key sentence in his attack on pacifism is this: "Insofar as it takes effect all all, pacifist propaganda can only be effective *against* those countries where a certain amount of freedom of speech is still permitted; in other words it is helpful to totalitarianism."

Everything I have just quoted was written at a time when Nazi Germany was the main totalitarian enemy. But here is what Orwell said about pacifism at the very moment when the defeat of Hitler was imminent and when the Soviet Union was about to replace Nazi Germany as the most powerful embodiment of totalitarianism in the world:

> Pacifist propaganda usually boils down to saying that one side is as bad as the other, but if one looks closely at the writings of the younger intellectual pacifists, one finds that they do not by any means express impartial disapproval but are directed almost entirely against Britain and the United States. Moreover they do not as a rule condemn violence as such, but only violence used in defense of the Western countries. The Russians, unlike the British, are not blamed for defending themselves by warlike means. . . .

The "real though unadmitted motive" behind such propaganda, Orwell concluded, was "hatred of Western democracy and admiration for totalitarianism."

It is hard to believe that the man who wrote those words in 1945 would have felt any sympathy for the various "objectively" pacifist anti-defense movements of today, about which the very same words could be used without altering a single detail. I can even easily imagine that Orwell would have been still angrier if he had lived to see so many ideas that have been discredited, both by arguments like his own and by historical experience, once again achieving widespread acceptability. It goes without saying that he would have opposed the unilateral disarmament that is now the official policy of the British Labour Party under the leadership of his old journalistic colleague Michael Foot. He understood, after all, that "Despotic governments can stand 'moral force' till the cows come home; what they fear is physical force." But I think he would also have opposed such measures as the nuclear freeze and a unilateral Western pledge of no-first-use of nuclear weapons. Given the conception of totalitarianism he developed in *Animal Farm* and *Nineteen Eighty-Four* as a totally closed system in which lies become truth at the dictate of the party, the notion that a verifiable disarmament agreement could be negotiated with the Soviet Union would surely have struck him as yet another pacifist "illusion due to security, too much money and a simple ignorance of the way in which things actually happen."

As for no-first-use, Orwell surely would have seen this as a form of unilateral disarmament by the West (since it would make Soviet superiority in conventional military power decisive on the European front) as well as a euphemistic screen behind which the United States could withdraw from its commitment to the defense of Western Europe under the hypocritical pretext of reducing the risk of nuclear war.

Nor is it likely that Orwell would have been reconverted to pacifism by the fear of nuclear weapons. As a matter of fact, he thought that "the worst possibility of all" was that "the fear inspired by the atomic bomb and other weapons yet to come will be so great that everyone will refrain from using them." Such an indefinite Soviet-American stalemate, he predicted, would lead to precisely the nightmare he was later to envisage in *Nineteen Eighty-Four* ("the division of the world among two or three vast totalitarian empires unable to conquer one another and unable to be overthrown by any internal rebellion").

This does not mean that Orwell contemplated the possibility of a nuclear war with equanimity, or that he did not on other occasions say that it could mean the destruction of civilization. Nevertheless, in 1947, the very year in which the Cold War officially began, Orwell wrote: "I don't, God knows, want a war to break out, but if one were compelled to choose between Russia and America — and I suppose that is the choice one might have to make — I would always choose America." Later that same year, he made the point again: "It will not do to give the usual quibbling answer, 'I refuse to choose.' . . . We are no longer strong enough to stand alone, and . . . we shall be obliged, in the long run, to subordinate our policy to that of one Great Power or another."

The same essay contains another one of those uncanny passages we so often come upon in Orwell that could be applied to our situation today without altering a single detail:

To be anti-American nowadays is to shout with the mob. Of course it is only a minor mob, but it is a vocal one. . . . I do not believe the mass of the people in this country are anti-American politically, and certainly they are not so culturally. But politico-literary intellectuals are not usually frightened of mass opinion. What they are frightened of is the prevailing opinion within their own group. At any given moment there is always an orthodoxy, a parrot-cry which must be repeated, and in the more active section of the Left the orthodoxy of the moment is anti-Americanism. I believe part of the reason . . . is the idea that if we can cut our links with the United States we might succeed in staying neutral in the case of Russia and America going to war. How anyone can believe this, after looking at the map and remembering what happened to neutrals in the late war, I do not know.

So much for Orwell's attitude toward the neutralism that lies at the basis of what in Western Europe is called the "peace movement" today.

To understand the force and the courage of Orwell's forthright repudiation of the idea that there was no significant moral difference between the United States and the Soviet Union, we have to remind ourselves that neither anti-Americanism nor neutralism was confined exclusively to the pro-Soviet Left. For example, in *The God That Failed* — the famous collection of autobiographical essays in which six prominent writers explained why they had broken with communism — Orwell's friend the poet Stephen Spender insisted that "no criticism of the Communists removes the arguments against capitalism" and that "both sides are forces producing aggression, injustice, destruction of liberties, enormous evils." The Soviet Union was bad, but "America, the greatest capitalist country, seems to offer no alternative to war, exploitation and destruction of the world's resources." This, in 1949 — a time when Stalin was consolidating his imperial hold over Eastern Europe and untold millions were suffering and dying in the Soviet Gulag. This, in 1949 — when the "alternative" America was offering was not "aggression, injustice, and the destruction of liberties" but rather peace, freedom, and prosperity to formerly fascist countries like Germany, Italy, and Japan as well as to the war-torn and wounded democracies of Western Europe. This, in 1949 — when the United States had just expended blood and treasure to save these nations from the totalitarianism of the Right, and was now prepared to spend blood and treasure to defend them from the totalitarianism of the Left.

Orwell recognized it all. "I particularly hate that trick of sucking up to the Left cliques by perpetually attacking America while relying on America to feed and protect us," he wrote in a letter to a friend. Unlike the anti-Americans, the people in the British Labour Party who openly wanted "to appease Russia" at least understood "that the only big political questions in the world today are: for Russia — against Russia, for America — against America, for democracy — against democracy."

Despite Crick's sophistical protestations, then, there can be no doubt that Orwell did belong in "the camp of the Cold War" while he was still alive. Nor can there be much doubt that if he were alive today he would have felt a greater kinship with the neoconservatives who are calling for resistance to Soviet imperialism than with either the socialist supporters of détente or the coalition of neutralists and pacifists who dominate the "peace movement" in Europe and their neoisolationist allies in the United States.

For consider: Orwell's ruling passion was the fear and hatred of totalitarianism. Unlike so many on the Left today, who angrily deny that there is any difference between totalitarianism and authoritarianism, he was among the first to insist on the distinction. Totalitarianism, he said, was a new and higher stage in the history of despotism and tyranny — a system in which every area of life, not merely (as in authoritarian regimes) the political sphere, was subjected to the control of the state. Only in Nazi Germany and the Soviet Union had totalitarianism thus far established itself, and of the two the Soviet variety clearly seemed to Orwell to be the more dangerous.

Indeed, Orwell's loathing for Nazi Germany was mild by comparison with his feeling about the Soviet Union. He was sufficiently serious in his opposition to fascism to risk his life in struggling against it in Spain (where as a soldier he was very nearly killed by a bullet through the neck). Yet he showed surprisingly little awareness of how evil Nazism actually was. Not only did he never write anything like *Animal Farm* about the Nazi regime; there is scarcely a mention in all his writings of the death camps. (Two of his closest friends, Arthur Koestler and T. R. Fyvel, saw a relation between this curious "blind spot" about Nazism and his equally curious hostility to Zionism.)

When Orwell wrote about the dangers of totalitarianism, then, whether in his essays or in *Nineteen Eighty-Four*, it was mainly the communist version he had in mind. To be sure, he followed no party line, not even his own, and he could always be relied on to contradict himself when the impulse seized him. At one moment he would denounce any move to establish good relations with the Russians, and at another moment, he might insist on the necessity of such relations.

But these were transient political judgments of the kind that, as he himself ruefully acknowledged, were never his strongest suit. What he most cared about was resisting the spread of Soviet-style totalitarianism. Consequently he "used a lot of ink" and did himself "a lot of harm by attacking the successive literary cliques" that had denied or tried to play down the brutal truth about the Soviet Union, to appease it, or otherwise to undermine the Western will to resist the spread of its power and influence.

If he were alive today, he would find the very ideas and attitudes against which he so fearlessly argued more influential than ever in left-wing centers of opinion (and not in them alone): that the freedoms of the West are relatively unimportant as compared with other values; that war is the greatest of all evils; that nothing is worth fighting or dying for; and that the Soviet Union is basically defensive and peaceful. It is impossible to imagine that he would have joined in parroting the latest expressions of this orthodoxy if he had lived to see it return to even fuller and more dangerous force.

I have no hesitation, therefore, in claiming Orwell for the neoconservative perspective on the East-West conflict. But I am a good deal more diffident in making the same claim on the issue of socialism. Like Orwell, most neoconservatives began their political lives as socialists; and most of them even followed the same course Orwell himself did from revolutionary to democratic socialism. Moreover, those neoconservatives who were old enough to be politically active in 1950, the year Orwell died, would still at that point have joined with him in calling themselves democratic socialists. About thirty years later, however, most of them had come around to the view expressed by the philosopher William Barrett in explaining why he had finally given up on his long and tenaciously held faith in "democratic socialism" (the telling quotation marks are Barrett's):

> How could we ever have believed that you could deprive human beings of the fundamental right to initiate and engage in their own economic activity without putting every other human right into jeopardy? And to pass from questions of rights to those of fact: everything we observe about the behavior of human beings in groups, everything we know about that behavior from history, should tell us that you cannot unite political and economic power in one center without opening the door to tyranny.

The question is: would Orwell, in the light of what has happened in the three decades since his death, have arrived eventually at a position similar to Barrett's? Crick is certain that he would not — that he would have remained a socialist, and a militant one. I am not so sure.

Orwell was never much of a Marxist and (beyond a generalized faith in "planning") he never showed much interest in the practical arrangements involved in the building of socialism. He was a socialist because he hated the class system and the great discrepancies of wealth that went with it. Yet he also feared that the establishment of socialism would mean the destruction of liberty. In an amazingly sympathetic review of F. A. Hayek's *The Road to Serfdom*, Orwell acknowledged that there was "a great deal of truth" in Hayek's thesis that "socialism inevitably leads to despotism," and that the collectivism entailed by socialism brings with it "concentration camps, leader worship, and war." The trouble is that capitalism, which "leads to dole queues, the scramble for markets, and war," is probably doomed. (It is indeed largely as a result of the failure of capitalism that the totalitarian world of *Nineteen Eighty-Four* comes into being.)

Suppose, however, that Orwell lived to see this prediction about capitalism refuted by the success of the capitalist countries in creating enough wealth to provide the vast majority of their citizens not merely with the decent minimum of food and housing that Orwell believed only socialism could deliver, but with a wide range of what to his rather Spartan tastes would have seemed unnecessary luxuries. Suppose further that he had lived to see all this accomplished — and with the year 1984 already in sight! — while "the freedom of the intellect," for whose future under socialism he increasingly trembled, was if anything being expanded. And suppose, on the other side, he had lived to see the wreckage through planning and centralization of one socialist economy after another, so that not even at the sacrifice of liberty could economic security be assured.

Suppose, in short, that he had lived to see the aims of what *he* meant by socialism realized to a very great extent under capitalism, and without either the concentration camps or the economic miseries that have been the invariable companions of socialism in practice. Would he still have gone on mouthing socialist pieties and shouting with the anticapitalist mob?

Perhaps. Nothing has been more difficult for intellectuals in this century than giving up on socialism, and it is possible that even Orwell, who so prided himself on his "power of facing unpleasant facts," would have been unwilling or unable to face what to most literary intellectuals is the most unpleasant fact of all: that the values both of liberty and equality fare better under capitalism than under socialism.

And yet I find it hard to believe that Orwell would have allowed an orthodoxy to blind him on this question any more than he allowed other "smelly little orthodoxies" to blind him to the truth about the particular issues involved in the struggle between totalitarianism and democracy: Spain, World War II, and communism.

In Orwell's time, it was the left-wing intelligentsia that made it so difficult for these truths to prevail. And so it is too with the particular issues generated by the struggle between totalitarianism and democracy in our own time, which is why I am convinced that if Orwell were alive today, he would be taking his stand with the neoconservatives and against the Left.

Orwell in 1984
John Atkins*

(John Atkins knew George Orwell personally and wrote one of the earliest books on him — *Orwell*, 1954. The following note from Atkins explains the extrapolative nature of his essay: "Now, writing a few months before the 'off,' I feel entitled to do what racing correspondents do habitually:

*Reprinted with permission from *College Literature* 11 (1984):34–43.

consider form. On form, where would Orwell stand in respect to the public issues of 1983, 1984, if he were still alive?")

I doubt if any writer at any time has annexed a year so firmly and convincingly for himself as George Orwell. Except for him, 1984 would be no more significant than 1974 or any other year you can think of. In Orwellian terms, 1984 means menace; it stands for the triumph of Totalitarianism — a useful word with which Orwell familiarized us, preferring it to either Communism or Fascism because it covered both.

Orwell himself stood for Socialism — but immediately we are involved in semantic confusion. For is not Communism a brand of Socialism? Many use the terms interchangeably. One of the most essential ingredients of Socialism for Orwell was democracy. Was he therefore — and more importantly, from my point of view in this paper, would he have been today — a Social Democrat? But what is Social Democracy? The inner meaning of *democracy*, without being too fastidious, is relatively clear. But *social?* Does it mean Socialist? Might not the term Democratic Socialism be more exact? There seems to be little agreement on the point. To add to the confusion, the first Marxist party in Orwell's homeland, Great Britain (although he would probably have used the more limited term England) was Hyndman's Social Democratic Federation. Most of us, including Orwell, roughly identified Marxism with Communism, and in his day this meant the Soviet variety (there are many others and they seem to spawn annually). But Communism, except in its curious Newspeak understanding of the term, is not democratic. Some of the bitterest in-fighting in the history of Socialism and its derivatives has been between the Communists and the Social Democrats. The polemical warfare of Lenin and Kautsky was merely one campaign in a continuing conflict.[1]

We know, from his many biographers and commentators, that until Orwell went to Wigan he had only the haziest idea of Socialist theory. Richard Rees said that he spent more than three years trying, unsuccessfully, to convert his friend to Socialism. When the conversion finally came, it was the result of intense feeling (disgust mingled with outrage), not of doctrinaire theory: it has been compared to Paul's experience on the road to Damascus, but was less mystical. In fact, it was an extremely worldly event, one which might well have been anticipated by anyone knowing Orwell's character: human suffering and injustice moved him on a scale that could not be matched by argument. In fact, he was probably more impressed by the humane Socialism of his brother-in-law, Laurence O'Shaughnessy (who was a doctor, a man whose professional oath obliged him to combat suffering), than by Rees' well-meaning abstractions.

During the period between the Wars it was common practice for British Socialists, even of the democratic variety, to ignore the totalitarian blemishes of the Soviet Union, on the grounds that the system was Socialist, even if imperfect. Few considered the possibility that the imperfections may have more than outweighed the good qualities. By chance Orwell met committed Socialists who had their doubts. In Paris he met and even stayed with his Aunt Nellie's lover, Eugene Adam, an Esperantist who believed passionately in the hope of world peace. According to Bernard Crick, Adam began as a Communist but became a Democratic Socialist after visiting Moscow. It seems likely that he spoke in terms similar to Orwell's. Orwell encountered the same disillusionment on the part of Myfanwy Westrope at the Bookshop, again as a result of a visit to Russia. Mrs. Westrope stressed that her disappointment was with the Soviet Union, and not with Socialism. Orwell was undoubtedly impressed by the reactions of such humane and sincere people.

What, then, are the qualities of traditional Socialism (or English Socialism, as some of us like to call it) that attracted Orwell? Crick lists them in his biography as egalitarian, non-Marxist (which means partly non-systematic and partly non-biblical), moralist, craft-conscious (not class-conscious); and deeply concerned with the balance between "town and country." In other words, English Socialism was not specially designed for the urban proletariat, like Marxism. To be more precise, it was not "specially designed" at all. It grew. It was organic. Later readers of Orwell did not always get the point. *Animal Farm*, for instance, was treated as an attack on Socialism. It was nothing of the kind. It was an attack on Totalitarianism, with the Soviet variety used as a model. Readers of *Tribune* understood this. Others, including many overseas readers, often did not.[2]

Orwell never gave us an analytical account of his Socialist beliefs. This would in fact be a negation of traditional Socialism. Marxism is rejected partly because it is Mosaic in form; English Socialism resembles a New Testament, made of bits and pieces, insights and conclusions, derived from a series of writers ranging from essayists to active politicians, and including names such as Robert Owen and William Morris, R. H. Tawney and E. F. M. Durbin—and now including Orwell himself. There is no comprehensively systematic account we can turn to. Systematic beliefs must be accepted as they stand, but Orwell's essays are starting points, always providing a stimulus for thought. They are the man speaking to us, not commandments engraved on stone. He distrusted "progressives"—who, in any case, are usually self-proclaimed.[3]

Of Orwell's many essays, "Lear, Tolstoy and the Fool" seems particularly relevant today, during the disarmament controversy. Shakespeare's assumption, says Orwell, is that if you make yourself powerless you invite attack. This does not mean that everyone will attack you, but someone will. Tolstoy could not accept this and so adopted a bullying tone. "Creeds like pacifism and anarchism," wrote Orwell, "which seem on the surface to imply a complete renunciation of power, rather encourage this habit of mind. For if you have embraced a creed which appears to be free from the ordinary dirtiness of politics—a creed from which you cannot expect to draw any material advantage—surely that proves that you are in the right?" I select this one example of an Orwellian statement that has a timeless quality about it, for it is as apt today as it was when he wrote it. Are not the unilateralists absolutely right, because their line is absolutely moral? And therefore, are not the rest of us either shockingly stupid or disgustingly immoral?

In 1983 a new political party, the Social Democratic Party, contested a General Election in Britain. Would Orwell have supported it? Its name would have encouraged him but he was too wise a bird to be taken in by such simplicities. He would have wanted to know who these new Social Democrats were. They were for the most part Labour Party members who could no longer accept the activities of the Left. They were naturally dismissed as renegades, even concealed Tories, by the simon-pure Marxists. This brings to mind Orwell's view of Swift: "Politically, Swift was one of those people who are driven into a sort of perverse Toryism by the follies of the progressive party of the moment." (See "Politics vs. Literature: an Examination of Gulliver's Travels.")

Always in discussing Socialism we are bedevilled by the absence of firm definition. That words should have exact meanings (in public discussion, that is—the rules are different for poetry) and should be used meaningfully was central to Orwell's thought. The meaning of Fascism is another example. Most Socialists between the Wars regarded Fascism as "advanced capitalism," even the last resort of capitalism. This view still persists in some quarters, especially among what are now called Left Wingers, who increasingly refer to Mrs. Thatcher's government as Fascist. But if the word is to have meaning, how can it describe at one and the same time Mussolini's single-party, socialist-bashing, castor-oil republic and a system where four main parties send representatives to Parliament, where views of every possible complexion are openly expressed, and Habeas Corpus still applies? Orwell saw Fascism as a grim perversion of Socialism—as was Communism. Fascism for him was a genuine mass movement, with an elitist philosophy and a popular appeal. Orwell was not alone. Borkenau, Silone, and Koestler also recognised the features both of style and method common to Fascism and Stalinism. This is why they preferred the term Totalitarianism to cover all such monsters.

Orwell was greatly impressed by James Burnham's theory of Managerialism. "Second Thoughts on James Burnham," the original title of the essay, with its hint of re-thinking, gives a concentrated account of an emerging political system. It should be read in conjunction with 1984. Burnham illustrated how the Russophile intelligentsia in Western Europe and North America were doing their best to destroy the old egalitarian version of Socialism and replace it by a hierarchical society. Burnham had the honesty to say that Socialism was not coming; the others asserted that Socialism would come inevitably, but meanwhile they had given the word

Socialism a new meaning which made nonsense of the old one. These people thought only of power — people power, they might think it, but in Orwell's view they approached the social problem from a completely wrong angle. The hallmark of Socialism should be freedom from interference. If power was emphasized, then interference became the major pillar of the new structure. Of course, it would be beautifully described: it would be strong; there would be a handsome capital, a firm base, an attractive shaft. It would also prevent free movement. One of Orwell's most explicit accounts (though brief) of what was wrong with the power-complex of the Soviet system was to be found in his Preface to the Ukrainian edition of *Animal Farm*. As usual, he had not only to attack the injustice of the Soviet system but in addition he had to explain that it was not Socialist. So long as the general public believed that the USSR was a Socialist state, an absolutely unjustified view of Socialism would become widespread. Today, in 1984, the situation is even worse than it was in Orwell's lifetime. The media have on the whole constantly referred to the totalitarian regimes of Eastern Europe as Socialist. It is no surprise if the greater part of the general public, largely uninformed and naive about political matters, follow suit.

If we wish to compress Orwell's views into a single proposition (admittedly, a very risky procedure, but probably necessary in a world where slogans rule) it could be this: *Theoretical* Socialism has failed; or, alternatively, Socialism cannot usefully be theoreticized. (Not, please note, theorized, a different matter altogether.) In an article entitled "Our Own Have Nots" (*Time and Tide*, 27 Nov. 1937) Orwell wrote that he wished to overcome "the tragic failure of theoretical Socialism, to make contact with the normal working classes." He saw the "normal working" people as likely to respond to human warmth, sympathy and understanding but to be quite unmoved by such remote notions as *dictatorship of the proletariat* or *economic determinism*. He would not have been surprised by the way in which a Marxist government has been making contact with the normal working classes in Gdansk, Warsaw, and Nova Huta.

Any good novel contains minor touches which help create the tone the author wishes to establish. Flaubert was the past master in this regard, and Graham Greene is the prime modern example. One reason why *Animal Farm* has such a powerful subliminal effect on the reader lies in its use of this method. At the first meeting of the animals, Boxer and Clover enter very slowly and set down "their vast hairy hoofs with great care lest there should be some small animal concealed in the straw." A brood of ducklings, having lost their mother, come in, looking for a place where they will not be trodden on. "Clover made a sort of wall round them with her great foreleg, and the ducklings nestled down inside it and promptly fell asleep." These horses represent great physical power in the animal world, but they use their strength and size for the protection of the small and weak, in great contrast to those who attain power only to abuse it. If

Orwell were with us today he could look around and distinguish, with little difficulty, those who would uncaringly, even deliberately, tread on ducklings to further their aims. They would excuse the act, if they thought any excuse were needed, by the use of incantation: one of the magic key-phrases would be *inner contradiction*. Orwell would look first at the powerful trade unions.

Among his novels, *Coming Up For Air* is the most self-revealing. There is no doubt that the views expressed by George Bowling are basically those of Orwell, but they have been coarsened and simplified to fit the character. It may surprise new readers to find that Orwell, despite his reputation for intense sympathy for, even a desire for identification with, the working class should in fact express his main pity for the struggling lower middle class. (Marxist theory would have forbidden this.) "The prole suffers physically, but he's a free man when he isn't working. But in every one of those little stucco boxes there's some poor bastard who's *never* free except when he's fast asleep and dreaming that he's got the boss down the bottom of a well and is bunging lumps of coal at him." And again:

> We're all respectable householders—that's to say Tories, yes—men and bum-suckers. Daren't kill the goose that lays the gilded eggs! And the fact that actually we aren't householders, that we're all in the middle of paying for our houses and eaten up with the ghastly fear that something might happen before we've made the last payment, merely increases the effect. We're all bought, and what's more we're bought with our own money. Everyone of those poor downtrodden bastards, sweating his guts out to pay twice the proper price for a brick doll's house that's called Belle Vue because there's no view and the bell doesn't ring—everyone of those poor suckers would die on the field of battle to save his country from Bolshevism.

So would Orwell. And it is interesting to note that forty-odd years later this class has increased numerically to become a clear majority. They are still governed by their mortgages, overdrafts, and inflation.

It was the modern way of life Orwell loathed, a way not really challenged by Marxism. Marxism simply wishes to make it more efficient. (As D. H. Lawrence once wrote, Marxism and Capitalism resemble a racing car and an express train each trying to reach the same destination before the other.) Orwell's rebellion grew out of revulsion; it was cultural, not political. He distrusted so many of his apparent "Socialist" colleagues because they promised improvements which bore no relationship to their methods. His picture of the contemporary world ("everything slick and streamlined, everything made out of something else. Celluloid, rubber, chromium-steel everywhere, arc lamps blazing all night, glass roofs over your heads, radios all playing the same tune, no vegetation left, everything cemented over. . . ."). would flourish equally well under Marxism-Leninism as under Toryism.

In *Coming Up For Air*, Bowling's mind is full of traditional images and emotions. The style of the novel harmonizes with the values expressed. Oddity of character and nostalgic description are the main strands; it is closer to the work of Wells' than to that of any other novelist. Despite the hatred expressed for the world around him, it is really written out of love rather than dismay or disapproval or contempt. Love for a lost world is the quality that remains in the reader's mind once the book has been put down. This is a vital point in understanding Orwell: he is a Socialist whose better world is not an unknown Utopia but a reversion to a loved but unsatisfactory world which would be purged of injustice. It was not in his competence to say how this should be done. He only knew it should be done and he believed it could be done. He was convinced that he knew how it should *not* be done. But in 1900 Bowling had been breathing "real air"; and he wonders about it—"Is it gone for ever? I'm not certain. But I tell you it was a good world to live in. I belong to it. So do you." These are the last words of Part I. Part II is largely a celebration of that beautiful bygone, if not quite forsaken, world.

Bowling's parents had no idea of what was to come. (Bowling-Orwell guessed at *1984*.) The old people's condition was by no means admirable yet it seemed to breed contentment. Orwell's point was that bad legs, stewed tea, endlessly buzzing flies and trashy women's magazines were nevertheless preferable to the five a.m. knock on the door and all that it implied. What could be more important than contentment in a life-span of seventy years? Towards the end of their lives his (Bowling's) parents "were a bit shaken, and sometimes a little dispirited. But at least they never lived to know that everything they had believed in was just so much junk. They lived at the end of an epoch, when everything was dissolving into a sort of ghastly flux, and they didn't know it. They thought it was eternity. You couldn't blame them. That was what it felt like." These words are from *Coming Up For Air*, but they sound as if they were written in the year 1984.

The future was being designed by those who had definite opinions and would do anything to realize them. Ordinary people, those who "*don't* want to go around smashing faces with spanners," did not count in practical politics. Porteous, the retired schoolmaster, is an example. Some people no longer think. "They can't defend themselves against what's coming to them because they can't see it, even when it's under their noses." Orwell refused to be carried away by a formula, which included the idea that the bourgeoisie think only of their own interests. In class terms this was true; in individual terms it was nonsense. Bowling encounters Sir Joseph Cheam and is astonished when the powerful capitalist tries to help him. "This important old bloke, who was probably worth at least half a million, was actually taking thought on my behalf, I'd deflected him from his path and wasted at least three minutes of his time. . . ." This is the kind of observation no *apparat*-political type would ever make. Dogmas are layers which coat over decency; the decency is there and if you do not recognize it you cease to understand people. Certainly the abiding weakness of Marxism has been proved to be psychological.

Orwell's writings are permeated by concessions to the "class enemy." The best-known of his essays, "Shooting an Elephant," confesses that "I did not even know that the British Empire is dying, still less did I know that it is a great deal better than the younger empires that are going to supplant it." In "Riding Down From Bangor" he writes of the society that produced *Helen's Babies* and *Little Women*: "It is hard not to feel that it was a better kind of society than that which arose from the sudden industrialization of the later part of the century."

What comes out of all this? If we are to give a name to Orwell's politics it would be the politics of despair. The dominant tone is pessimism. The early Socialists did not despair because they had their Socialism to feed their hope. Orwell's despair was based on the knowledge that much of this "Socialism" had in practice become debased and corrupted. *Happiness of the people* had been replaced by *victory of a system* — a system no longer critically examined by those that support it. There was no way back. "The old life's finished, and to go about looking for it is just waste of time," says Bowling. He doesn't expect others to follow his train of thought. It is a sad conclusion. Among Orwell's friends, Koestler lost his faith altogether. Today, in 1984, a few Orwellians have broken away from the Labour Party in a desperate attempt to refloat the old values. They have invoked the precious word *democratic* and they have qualified it with *social*. The words are right, but is the faith that moves mountains still there?

In one respect I think Orwell was mistaken. (His honesty and concern for people can never be questioned.) *1984* is unrealistically pessimistic. If we look at the world around us we may agree that his vision has already been realized: we are at the mercy of super-powers who play war-games with other people. But Orwell's picture of a dreary though apparently satisfied proletariat is false. He imagined that groups in public houses singing updated versions of *Knees Up Mother Brown* and *Down at the Old Bull and Bush*, all contentedly supping Victory Gin, would be the social norm. The bosses, from Big Brother downwards, would use fear and oppression to maintain their power. But this will not happen and is not happening. The modern British worker wants a "new second-hand" Ford Cortina. Once he gets it, he's happy. Add to this holidays in Benidorm or the Costa Brava, and he feels he is in a Workers' Paradise that makes the Soviet version dull and insipid. This life represents the kind of synthetic texture that Orwell abhorred, but it is winning. Pessimism is justified, but a different kind of pessimism from Orwell's. (There is, of course, another option: atomization.) There is absolutely no point in governing through pain when it is so much easier and less stressful to govern through pleasure: Ultimately, *Brave New World* is a more accurate picture of a predictable future than *1984*. Huxley's mistake was to project his vision six hundred years into the future, thus turning it into a fairy tale.

There is little point in attempting to guess how Orwell would have voted in 1983, or what he would advocate in an actual 1984. But he was a man we admired, whose opinion was welcomed and respected, and it would bring political comfort to be able to say: He would have said or done thus or thus if he were still alive. One thing we do know. He would have resisted mere theory and recipes that remind us of Eastern Europe (e.g., two hundred more nationalized companies, subservient trade unions, a nationalized press). He would have urged policies that give the individual the feeling that he is being considered. He did not know the exact, mathematical answers any more than anyone else but he did know that progress must be piecemeal. If something goes wrong, it can be put right without too much damage. When something goes wrong with a centralized plan, however, the whole world will know about it. Like ripples in a pool, the process cannot be limited. Or to change the metaphor, cut through one beam and the house will fall down.

Notes

1. Karl Kautsky became leader of the Social Democratic Party; and his Erfurt Programme, 1891, committed the party to an *evolutionary* form of Marxism. It was this approach that roused Lenin's antagonism. After the Russian Revolution Kautsky opposed violent measures and minority socialist dictatorships. It is clear from this that Marxism is not considered necessarily undemocratic by its varied disciples. (For a full treatment of this point see *Marxism and Democracy*, by Lucien Laurat.) An attempt to clear up the confusion may be made by calling the two approaches scientific and traditional. Another snare to avoid is use of the word *Utopian*. Marxists have called Social Democratic politics Utopian. Traditional Socialists regard "biblical" Socialism (Marxism) as Utopian. There is no end to all this!

2. There is no end to the confusion one has to contend with in writing about Socialism. In Orwell's *Tribune* days Left meant Socialism. Communism was an extreme expression of the Left. Today the Left *means* Communism, although it is frequently disguised as Bennism, Scargillism, Militant Tendency, Revolutionary Socialism, etc. Both Attlee and Bevan were Left. Today Benn is Left, Hattersley is not.

3. The same with intellectuals. It is only intellectuals who call each other intellectuals.

Major Fiction

The Uses of Form: A Reading of
Animal Farm

Robert A. Lee*

In his retrospective essay "Why I Write" (1947), George Orwell remarked that "*Animal Farm* was the first book in which I tried, with full consciousness of what I was doing, to fuse political purpose and artistic purpose into one whole."[1] Orwell's political impulses had been to that point in his career, though varied, consistently present; however, he was conscious that the difference between propaganda and art could be slight, that art did not automatically rise from intensity or indignation. Instinctively and by profession a polemicist and essayist, concerned with political problems, causes, and effects, he found the forms of art difficult. For Orwell, politics was a *sine qua non*; the common constituents of imaginative writing—character, image, narrative, for example, were for him secondary considerations, if not outright obstructions. He is thinking of his first novel, *Burmese Days*, for example, when he says that it is "invariably where I lacked a *political* purpose that I wrote lifeless books and was betrayed into purple passages, sentences without meaning, decorative adjectives and humbug generally."[2] To Orwell, adjectives are "decorative"; nonpolitical art is humbug. Yet, Orwell's impulses were, as he says, at least equally toward "artistic purpose." Furthermore, his intentions in the last years of his life were purportedly "to make a complete break from his former polemical, propagandist, way of writing and to concentrate on the treatment of human relationships."[3] Despite the notion of a "complete break"—obviously, given *Animal Farm* and *1984*, Orwell had come to see that the overt stance of the polemicist, and attributes of the essayist never left him. But, at the least, Orwell had come to see that the overt stance of the polemicist, never long hidden even in his self-termed "naturalistic" novels, must be abandoned. And no literary form suited the abandonment of this role better than that of the beast fable: not only was the narrator, the potential polemicist, gone, but the demands of the appropriate conventions provided an impersonality and distance that suggested tradition, not immediacy; art, not journalism.

*Reprinted with permission from Robert A. Lee, *Orwell's Fiction* (Notre Dame: Notre Dame University Press, 1969), 105–127. © 1969 by University of Notre Dame Press.

That the beast fable form was a natural choice for Orwell is borne out by John Wain. *Animal Farm* is "so remarkably similar in its tone, and in the balanced fairness of its judgments, to the critical essays as to be, almost, seen as one of them. It is, after all, a fable, and a fable is closer to criticism than to fiction in the full imaginative sense."[4] Yet this is surely not the whole truth. We must give imagination a more important role than Wain is willing to ascribe to it; and the underlying implications of this form seem to me to run contrary to "balanced fairness," which is indeed one of the consistent appearances of Orwell's essays. The essential characteristic of the beast fable is irony: the form provides for the writer "the power to keep his reader conscious simultaneously of the human traits satirized and of the animals as animals."[5] The form demands of the reader a constant awareness of the double vision: animal allegory prescribes two levels of perception that interact to purvey the irony in comparisons and contrasts. Orwell's essays are only ironic when they verge on fiction, as in the near-tales "A Hanging" and "Shooting an Elephant." In the kind of essays that Wain has in mind, Orwell is honest and straightforward; the tone is that of the open, forthright speaker.

The use of the beast fable provided for Orwell an approach to art that he clearly needed, one that differed from the conventional socially oriented novels he had been writing, and in which he had fallen into pitfalls he now was recognizing. The apparently irresistible need Orwell felt to criticize and attack the social evils he was always conscious of in the world could now be subsumed into an artistic mode which by its very nature provided contrast and, hence, criticism. Yet, paradoxically, the gain of impersonality he sought and found in this form brought Orwell a more intense criticism of social injustice and inequity than he had managed in his earlier novels. The difference in degree and implication of the political insights of, say, *Keep the Aspidistra Flying* and of *Animal Farm* is enormous. The beast fable is in many ways the ideal form in which to articulate attack. The presence of animals provides a ready-made vehicle for the tenor of the hatred, in this essentially metaphorical mode. The correlation of a man, or a class of men, as swine or sheep, for example, in the fable, both allows harsh indictment on the sub-narrative level and concurrently provides the coolness of impersonality in the façade of the narrative. As I. A. Richards says of the properly functioning metaphor, the vehicle should not be "a mere embellishment of a tenor which is otherwise unchanged but the vehicle and tenor in co-operation give a meaning of more varied powers than can be ascribed to either."[6]

Yet because the book is so different from anything else that Orwell wrote, it is somewhat unfair to judge it only in relation to his other works. It deserves much praise for the simple fact that it succeeds despite the problems that this form and Orwell's particular use of it contain. I am thinking of the dangers of allegory in general and of the specific political allegory that informs *Animal Farm*. The principal danger of allegory in fiction is artificiality: the secondary level may demand such precise equivalents that it comes to dominate the tale, with the result that the primary narrative loses its pretense of reality and spontaneity. I think it is clear that such does not happen in *Animal Farm*. The allegory of the Russian Revolution and subsequent events is probably only noticeable to the eye that has been made aware of it. Briefly, the narrative of this tale sets up equivalences of the history of political action in Russia from roughly 1917 to the second World War. Major and Snowball are Lenin and Trotsky; Napoleon is Stalin; and the warring farms and farmers around Manor Farm naturally come to stand for Germany (Frederick) and the Allies (Pilkington). Certain events in the course of the story are said to represent events of history: the timber deal, in which Frederick later reneges on the animals, is, of course, the short-lived Russo-German alliance of 1939; the card game at the end of the book apparently represents the Teheran Conference following the war. The correlations are more elaborate than this; and, while there are some inconsistencies in the precise political allegory,[7] it is notable that one need pay little heed to this to understand the full political significance of the book. Instead of being just an allegory of Russian politics throughout the twentieth century, *Animal Farm* is more meaningfully an anatomy of all political revolutions. As A. E. Dyson says, *Animal Farm* "is by no means about Russia alone. Orwell is concerned to show how revolutionary ideals of justice, equality and fraternity always shatter in the event."[8] I would submit that the implications of this little book are wider yet: it is not merely that revolutions are self-destructive — Orwell also is painting a grim picture of the human condition in the political twentieth century, a time that he has come to believe marks the end of the very concepts of human freedom.

Yet the book starts on a relatively light tone. Mr. Jones — the commonplace name serves to diminish the importance of the human being in the story, yet at the same time gives a universal "Everyman" quality — remembers to lock the hen-houses for the night, but he "was too drunk to remember to shut the popholes."[9] The picture of the drunken farmer, drinking his last glass of beer for the night and lurching up to bed while the animals come alive in the barn, reminds us of the cinema cartoons (and Orwell's interest in the popular arts is surely at play here) and is primarily low-keyed; at the same time, however, we note the irresponsibility of the farmer, neglecting — and endangering — those in his care. Nonetheless, the "revolutionary" meeting of the animals while the humans sleep, though latently serious, forms a picture that is primarily whimsical. The description of the animals gathering for the meeting reveals the essential technique of the beast fable: the concurrent awareness of both human and animal qualities and of the several ironies that such perspective creates.

> The two cart-horses, Boxer and Clover, came in together, walking very slowly and setting down their vast hairy hoofs with great care lest there

should be some small animal concealed in the straw. Clover was a stout motherly mare approaching middle life, who had never quite got her figure back after her fourth foal. Boxer was an enormous beast, nearly eighteen hands high, and as strong as any two ordinary horses put together. A white stripe down his nose gave him a somewhat stupid appearance, and in fact he was not of first-rate intelligence, but he was universally respected for his steadiness of character and tremendous powers of work. (p. 5)

The contrast between the strength of the horses and the fragility of the smaller, hidden animals places the scene unmistakably in the beast world; at the same time, the description of Clover's failure to "get back" her figure, a phrase Orwell surely chose for its commonplace cliché quality, is representative of radical human nature. The menagerie, in fact, demonstrates a spectrum of human qualities and types, from the pigs, who take up the front seats in the audience, to Benjamin the donkey, the cynic of the farm, and to Mollie, the white mare, vain and foolish. These introductory descriptions are woven into the structure of the plot: for her vanity, Mollie will ultimately be excluded from the farm; in his cynicism, Benjamin will come to see through but be incapable of changing the reality of the revolution; and the pigs will come to occupy not only the front but the entirety of the farm.

The awareness of simultaneous levels of animal and human existence is nicely maintained by Orwell throughout the story. Major's speech, describing his dream in which man has disappeared from the earth and is replaced by animals, is at once a logical demonstration of wish fulfillment in the dream at a bestial level and at the same time a gospel of economic revolution easily understandable at the human level. ("Man is the only creature that consumes without producing," is, of course, an ironic variation of Marxian anti-capitalism.) Orwell reinforces this irony by casting Major's speech in a mixture of biological and economic language: "The life of an animal is misery and slavery: that is the plain truth. But is this simply part of the order of nature? Is it because this land of ours is so poor that it cannot afford a decent life to those who dwell upon it?" We slide back and forth between reading this as Marxian dogma, excoriating capitalism and calling for a proletarian revolution, and reading it in terms of the mistreated animals—and we are reminded of the irresponsibility of Farmer Jones.

Moreover, there is the possibility of a fourth kind of irony: in his reading of 1984, Irving Howe remarks that Emmanuel Goldstein's book The Theory and Practice of Oligarchical Collectivism imitates Trotsky's style in "his fondness for using scientific references in non-scientific contexts."[10] Although there is a slightly different usage here, the employment of biological language in a political context is obviously related. We begin to be aware of the complexity of this apparently simple little book. It is not simple political allegory, but neither is it merely classical satire built on multiple or "receding planes."[11] The various levels interact thematically: animals are like humans; humans are only pejoratively like animals; humans' politics are really no more profound nor more rational than natural biology.

Animal Farm maintains an insistent dramatic irony, the essence of the beast fable form. Major's speech builds to the rhetorical climax of "All animals are comrades," which apothegm is immediately punctuated by the dogs' pursuit of some rats that they see. A vote is taken and the rats become "comrades," followed by the animals banding together against their common enemy, man, under the aegis of the motto, "All animals are equal" (p. 12). The remainder of the book will be a series of dramatic repudiations of this and other such mottoes and a return to the tyranny and irresponsibility of the beginning. The only change will be in the identity of the masters, and, ironically, even that will be but a partial change.

At the opening of the second chapter, Major dies, the prophet who articulated the revolutionary ideals and in whose name they will be carried out — and perverted. His successors, Snowball and Napoleon, assume the leadership of the rebellion, aided by their public relations man, Squealer. And these three codify the ideals of Major into "Animalism" "a complete system of thought" (p. 18). But Animalism, obviously communism, is significantly not instituted according to plan. The rebellion occurs spontaneously: once again Jones neglects to feed the animals, who break into the barn for food when "they could stand it no longer" (p. 21). Jones and his hired men come in and the animals, "with one accord, though nothing of the kind had been planned beforehand," attack the men and chase them off the farm. "And so almost before they knew what was happening, the Rebellion had been successfully carried through: Jones was expelled, and the Manor Farm was theirs" (pp. 22–23). Orwell stresses the spontaneity of the Rebellion to make clear that no matter how bad things become for the animals later — and they do become bad — the animals "were far better off than they had been in the days of Jones" (p. 97). Though this fact will itself have to be qualified, there is a justness in this statement. Not only does the spontaneity of the revolution diminish the importance of Napoleon and Snowball's plotting — and thus provide a dramatic irony about their supposed accomplishments — but the motive hunger justifies the revolution more basically and irrefutably than the soundest of political theories. The revolution sprung not from theory, but from real, natural need. No matter how corrupt the ideals of the revolution become, Orwell never questions the validity of the uprising: the target of the satire here is not social — and socialistic — revolution, contrary to the many who simply want to see the book as a satire of communism, but rather the inability of humans to live within a community of ideals.

The inevitable corruption of the revolution is presaged immediately. The animals have driven out their former master.

> For the first few minutes the animals could hardly believe in their good
> fortune. Their first act was to gallop in a body right round the
> boundaries of the farm, as though to make quite sure that no human
> being was hiding anywhere upon it; then they raced back to the farm
> buildings to wipe out the last traces of Jones's hated reign. The harness-
> room at the end of the stables was broken open; the bits, the nose-rings,
> the dog-chains, the cruel knives with which Mr. Jones had been used to
> castrate the pigs and lambs, were all flung down the well. The reins, the
> halters, the blinkers, the degrading nosebags, were thrown on to the
> rubbish fire which was burning in the yard. So were the whips. All the
> animals capered with joy when they saw the whips going up in flames.
> (pp. 23–24)

The response is understandable; but the language of the inevitable and
immediate violence that seems to follow all revolutions foreshadows that
this revolution will suffer the common fate of its predecessors: reactionary
cruelty, the search for the scapegoat, the perversion of the ideals of the
revolution, the counter-revolution. Thus, the good intentions of the
animals in this revolution are immediately endangered when it is learned
that the pigs "had taught themselves to read and write from an old spelling
book which had belonged to Mr. Jones's children."[12] The pigs' reading
ability is a valuable skill for the animals, and one that would be necessary
to run a farm. But it is also patently a human attribute, and one that
already violates one of Major's cardinal tenets: "remember also that in
fighting against Man, we must not come to resemble him" (p. 12).

If seeds of destruction are immediately present, the positive aspects of
the rebellion achieve their high peak with the codification of the "unalterable law by which all the animals on Animal Farm must live for ever
after," the Seven Commandments.

1. Whatever goes upon two legs is an enemy.

2. Whatever goes upon four legs, or has wings, is a friend.

3. No animal shall wear clothes.

4. No animal shall sleep in a bed.

5. No animal shall drink alcohol.

6. No animal shall kill any other animal.

7. All animals are equal. (p. 28)

This "unalterable law" provides the major structural basis for the rest of
the fable. The plot, from this point on, reveals a gradual alteration of
these commandments, ending in, of course, the well-known contradiction
that epitomizes the new nature of the farm at the end of the book. But at
this point, Orwell's technique is of immediate irony: the animals are
watching the painting of the commandments on the barn when the cows
begin to low, needing to be milked. They are milked, and the milk is
placed in front of the animals, at which many "looked with considerable
interest." But Napoleon, "placing himself in front of the buckets," will not

even mix it with the hens' mash, as even "Jones used sometimes to," and it disappears, eventually into Napoleon's own mash. Selfishness is the note on which the chapter concludes, following the spontaneous and successful take-over of the farm and the articulation of unselfish ideals by which all the animals are to live.

The next concern on Animal Farm is to get the hay in, and we see a further definition of the spoiling of the revolution's ideals as the pigs supervise rather than work. Obviously, from the beginning, all animals are not equal. But one must be careful. In light of what is to happen, it is easy to see that the pigs' managerial role is further foreshadowing of the seventh commandment. However, this does not mean that the revolution is therefore wrong, or that Orwell thinks that all revolutions are inevitably self-corrupting. Both farms and revolutions need leaders, managers; and, for all their evil, the pigs are the most capable animals on the farm. Orwell may be suggesting—and this is far more profound—that capable people are inevitably evil; or, conversely, that evil people are inevitably the most capable.[13]

The capability of the pigs, and their management, is reflected in the success of the farm: there is no wastage, no stealing. It is the biggest harvest in the history of the farm; in addition, though the animals work hard, there is more leisure. Each animal, in short, works "according to his capacity" (p. 32). The Marxian slogan at the base of the success of the farm seems to me to provide conclusively that Orwell does not—in this book, at least—question socialistic ideology. He does question the failure of ideology to accommodate human variety, implicit in the missing half of the quotation. At this point, Orwell specifically avoids mention of what goes to each animal: the irony of "need" is already evident in what the pigs have taken and will be reinforced by the future miniscule gains of the other animals.

Orwell stresses the human variability that undermines the best—or the worst—of systems in the "character" of Mollie, the vain mare, more interested in ribbons than in harvests, and in the description of the cat, who disappears when there is work to be done. It is important that these animals are portrayed kindly and humorously: the cat, for example, "always made such excellent excuses, and purred so affectionately, that it was impossible not to believe in her good intentions" (p. 33). We learn soon, however, of the real nature of such intentions. The cat is spied one day talking to some sparrows who were "just out of her reach. She was telling them that all animals were now comrades and that any sparrow who chose could come and perch on her paw; but the sparrows kept their distance" (p. 35). If this attempt by the cat is at one level an ironic variant of the pigs' later, horrifying "education" of the puppies into trained killers, it is simultaneously natural—which the pigs' deed is not. Orwell reminds us of natural instinct and its inevitable conflict with political absolutism. It is just to this point that Mollie soon leaves the farm. She is seen one day being stroked by a human on the outskirts of the farm; Clover finds sugar and several ribbons hidden under the straw in her stall. And so Mollie disappears, to be seen by some pigeons pulling a cart, her coat "newly clipped and she wore a scarlet ribbon around her forelock. She appeared to be enjoying herself, so the pigeons said" (p. 53). In political terms, she is, of course, a heretic, and her selfish behavior is inconsistent with selfless social ideals. But there is no indication on Orwell's part of any criticism toward her. He rather suggests that too strict attention to the harsh, social demands of life obscures the love of beauty in the world. Any criticism seems rather to be pointed to a political norm that makes the aesthete the apostate.

For political and social demands dominate life at Manor Farm; and the demands become more complex. Pilkington and Frederick spread stories about horrible conditions on the farm, stories that are contradicted by rumors among *their* animals of the wonderful paradise that exists on Animal Farm. Neither set of rumors is true, of course, but Orwell primarily develops the consequences of such misrepresentation. The farmers' animals begin to revolt in varying degrees—"bulls which had always been tractable suddenly turned savage, sheep broke down hedges and devoured the clover. . . ," while the humans, hearing in the song of the animals of Animal Farm "a prophecy of their future doom," invade the farm (pp. 44–45). It is not the respective social situations or conflicting ideologies that Orwell is concerned with as much as it is the misrepresentations, the falsification and distortion of fact, which he indicates lead ineluctably to disaster and misery. Falsification is at the heart of the main internal struggle on the farm, and the way fact is distorted and misrepresented is graphically pictured in the rivalry between Snowball and Napoleon over the building of the windmill.

Snowball (who is a brilliant orator, compared with Napoleon, who was "better at canvassing support for himself in between times") conceives of a plan for a windmill, which Napoleon graphically disdains (he urinates on the plans). At the meeting in which the animals are to take the final vote for approval, nine enormous dogs, "as ferocious as wolves," suddenly appear and chase Snowball off the farm; the dogs return and sit by Napoleon, wagging their tails, "as the other dogs had been used to do with Mr. Jones" (pp. 60–61). And it is just a short time until Squealer appears to announce blandly that Napoleon, "who had advocated it from the beginning," himself proposes the building of the windmill. More is suggested here than the simple power struggle attendant on all revolutions, or the more specific overthrow of Trotsky, the party theoretician and planner, by calculating, pragmatic Stalin. The symbol of the windmill suggests much about Orwell's complex attitudes toward the political concepts within the story beyond the primary irony of the pigs' manipulation of the concrete representation of the hopes of the animals of Animal Farm. The windmill has Quixotic overtones: Orwell suggests that the way the animals focus all their efforts on building this is a false and deluded if heroic struggle. The windmill becomes the means by which Napoleon controls deviation; he uses it to direct the animals' attention away from the growing shortages and inadequacies on the farm, and the animals ignorantly concentrate all their efforts on building it — but its symbolic nature suggests it is an empty concentration, a meaningless, unheroic effort, for the idea is literally misguided.

The continuing building of the windmill, its subsequent destruction in a storm (during which the hens hear a gun go off in the background; the allusion is probably to World War I), and its rebuilding provide the linear movement of the plot in the rest of the book. Orwell centers the thematic development on the progressive alteration of the Seven Commandments. The animals suffer two monstrous indignities, but even these are thematically secondary to the larger importance of the alteration of the commandments. There is a bitter winter on the farm and rations become scarce; "starvation seemed to stare them in the face."[14] Needing a scapegoat, Napoleon conveniently uses Snowball. He blatantly tells the other animals that not only is Snowball responsible for all the mysterious destruction that suddenly begins to occur on the farm, but that his brave actions in fighting the humans at the Battle of the Cowshed, *which all the animals witnessed*, had never happened. "Four days later," after being warned by Napoleon that Snowball's secret agents were still among them, the animals are ordered to assemble in the yard. Suddenly the dogs attack four of the other pigs and Boxer; but Boxer easily fights off the dogs.

> Presently the tumult died down. The four pigs waited, trembling, with guilt written on every line of their countenances. Napoleon now called upon them to confess their crimes. They were the same four pigs as had protested when Napoleon abolished the Sunday Meetings. Without any further prompting they confessed that they had been secretly in touch with Snowball ever since his expulsion, that they had collaborated with him in destroying the windmill, and that they had entered into an agreement with him to hand over Animal Farm to Mr. Frederick. They added that Snowball had privately admitted to them that he had been Jones's secret agent for years past. When they had finished their confession, the dogs promptly tore their throats out, and in a terrible voice Napoleon demanded whether any other animal had anything to confess. (pp. 93–94)

Three hens come forward and admit to having heard Snowball speak to them "in a dream." They are slaughtered; a goose confesses to pilfering six ears of corn, followed by a sheep who, "urged to do this" by Snowball, had urinated in the drinking pool, in turn followed by two more sheep who had murdered a ram. "And so the tale of confessions and executions went on, until there was a pile of corpses lying before Napoleon's feet and the air was heavy with the smell of blood, which had been unknown there since the expulsion of Jones" (p. 95).

Orwell has managed to dramatize, in two short, terror-laden pages, the very essence of this strange psycho-political phenomenon of our times: the ritualistic, honestly believed but obviously spurious confession. The ramifications of the motif in contemporary literature abound: one is drawn to such a parallel as Rubashov in *Darkness at Noon* and to such a consideration as that, in a political age that denies individual selfhood, the only way of asserting one's self may be through pain or its extension death. Ontologically and eschatologically, it may be preferable to die horribly and perhaps anonymously than to live as a cipher. However, I wish at this point to consider the relative insignificance of the horrors that have passed, as physical terror becomes thematically subsidiary to the falsification of history and the denial of objective reality. Following this scene, the animals, led by Boxer and Clover, leave. Boxer, unable to understand, thinks it "must be due to some fault in ourselves. The solution, as I see it, is to work harder" (p. 96). And so he trots up to the windmill to resume dragging loads of stone to it. The other animals huddle about Clover on the hillside. "It was a clear spring evening. The grass and the bursting hedges were gilded by the level rays of the sun. Never had the farm — and with a kind of surprise they remembered that it was their own farm, every inch of it their own property — appeared to the animals so desirable a place" (pp. 96–97). Clover, looking down on this scene, remembers the promise and the hope of the revolution on the night she heard Major's speech, and Clover's thoughts sum up the earlier images of the strong mare protecting the ducklings and recall the maxim at the base of the society — "each working according to his capacity, the strong protecting the weak." Even here, she has "no thought of rebellion or disobedience," for the fundamental value of the revolution is reasserted: "even as things were, they were far better off than they had been in the days of Jones" (p. 97). But the phrase "even as things were" implies too much, and so Clover, trying to reestablish somehow her continuity with that now quickly changing past, "feeling this to be in some way a substitute for the words she was unable to find," begins to sing the song that epitomized the egalitarian ideals Major expounded, *Beasts of England*. The animals are singing the song when Squealer appears to announce that "by a special decree of Comrade Napoleon, *Beasts of England* had been abolished." Squealer tells the astonished animals that the reason is that "in *Beasts of England* we expressed our longing for a better society in days to come. But that society has now been established. Clearly this song has no longer any purpose" (p. 99).

The obvious irony is of course the final attainment of "the better society," as the animals sit in the shadow of the heap of freshly slaughtered corpses. But the implications are yet more profound. Terror, bestiality, senseless death are all dreadful and shattering experiences; but they are at least comprehensible and do not radically alter the conceptualized values of the survivors. Far more terrifying is the overt alteration of consciousness that follows the slaughter, the blatant misrepresentation of the past, *which goes unchallenged*. The animals can only "sense" that the new song ("Animal Farm, Animal Farm / Never through me shalt thou come to harm") is different from *Beasts of England*. Squealer's pronouncement that the "better society" has now been established is uncontroverted. The commandments, which have begun to be altered recently, are now more rapidly and unquestioningly changed — and change pervades Animal Farm. A proposed timber deal vacillates between Pilkington and Frederick until the animals are forced to admit "a certain bewilderment, but Squealer was soon able to convince them that their memories had been at fault" (p. 107). Ironically, one of Major's prescriptions had been not to indulge in trade with the humans. Here, the animals are not even sure whom the trade is with, much less can they remember past dogma. The animals no longer can recognize reality, but they manage to finish the windmill, concurrent with Napoleon's double-dealing with Pilkington and Frederick. We see the simultaneous strength and weakness, the goodness and corruption, that has evolved from the original rebellion. Despite all, the animals finish the vain windmill — they can accomplish a nearly impossible task — but at the same time, Napoleon, cheating and being cheated in his dealing, precipitates an attack upon the farm by Frederick and his followers (World War II in the allegory). The battle follows, and though the animals win, the windmill is destroyed and many are grievously injured. But Squealer declares that they have a "victory," "we have won back what we had before" (p. 116). And so the animals celebrate — each animal is given an apple, two ounces of corn for each bird, and three biscuits for each dog — while Napoleon gets drunk. The mere inequity, the surface irony is compounded by the inevitable falsification of fact. The next morning the animals discover that the fifth commandment did not read, as they had thought, "No animals shall drink alcohol," but instead "No animal shall drink alcohol *to excess*."[15] It is not the threat of violence, even the radically inexplicable self-violence that the deracinated individual must, ironically, bring upon himself for his own secular salvation in a wholly political world, nor the war, nor the social injustice that man is suffering that is the cancer of our times, but the loss of "objective truth." Choices vanish in a society that has no bases for choice.

The most darkly pessimistic aspect of *Animal Farm* is that the animals are unable even to recognize their new oppression, much less combat it. The difference is the control by the pigs of language; Mr. Jones controlled only action — not thought. Orwell portrays at least three differing animals as being potentially able to stand up to the state (in an admittedly limited yet meaningful way); yet each is inadequate in a vital respect. Boxer has probably enough power and strength to overthrow Napoleon's regime. When Napoleon's vicious dogs attack him, Boxer simply "put out his great hoof, caught a dog in mid-air, and pinned him to the ground. The dog shrieked for mercy and the other two fled with their tails between their legs" (p. 93). But Boxer is stupid; he can not comprehend the present, much less conceptualize the past. He ingenuously looks to Napoleon for judgment as to whether or not he should let the dog go; when the slaughter is over, he retreats to work, thinking the fault must lie within the animals. Thus, his fate is not as pathetic, as some critics read the scene in which he is taken away, kicking in the truck, as it is the inevitable fate of utter stupidity. The most complex thought that Boxer can express is "if Comrade Napoleon says it, it must be right," in the face of blatant lying, gross falsification. Boxer's basic goodness, social self-sacrifice, and impressive strength are simply inadequately used; the stupidity that wastes such qualities suggests interesting qualifications about Orwell's reputed love of the common man.

Clover is more intelligent and perceptive than Boxer, but she has a corresponding lack of strength. Her "character" is primarily a function of her sex: a mare, her instincts are maternal and pacifistic. She works hard, along with the other animals, but there is no picture of any special strength, as there is with Boxer. And even with a greater intelligence, her insights are partial. Things may indeed be better than they "had been in the days of Jones," but, in the context of the slaughter of the animals, "it was not for this that she and all the other animals had hoped and toiled" (p. 98). Both perceptions are right, but both are incomplete. In both cases, Clover senses that there is something further to be understood, but just as Boxer uncomprehendingly moves to toil, so does Clover wistfully retreat to song—only to have this articulation of the ideals of the past suddenly changed, without her dissent. A paradigm appears: Boxer is marked by great strength and great stupidity; Clover has less physical power but has a corresponding increase in awareness; the equation is completed with Benjamin, who sees and knows most—perhaps all—but is physically ineffectual and socially irresponsible.

Benjamin, the donkey, "was the oldest animal on the farm, and the worst tempered. He seldom talked, and when he did, it was usually to make some cynical remark . . ." (pp. 5–6). As archetypal cynic, Benjamin remains aloof and distant, refusing to meddle in the affairs of the farm, but seeing all. He expresses no opinion about the rebellion; he works on Animal Farm "in the same slow, obstinate way" as he did on Manor Farm; he remarks enigmatically that only "Donkeys live a long time" (p. 33). Beneath the surface cynicism, he is, almost inevitably, blessed with a heart of gold: he is devoted to Boxer, and it is he who discovers the plot to deliver Boxer to the glue-maker. But he is essentially selfish, representing a view of human nature that is apolitical, and thus can hardly be, as some readers hold, the spokesman for Orwell within the book. To Benjamin, the social and political situation is irrelevant: human nature suffers and prospers in the same degree, no matter who is the master. He believes "that things never had been, nor ever could be much better or much worse—hunger, hardship, and disappointment being, so he said, the unalterable law of life" (pp. 143–44). We know too much about Orwell's social beliefs from other contexts to assume that Benjamin speaks for Orwell here. Yet, it is only fair to note that Benjamin sees most, knows most, is obviously the most intelligent and perceptive of all the animals on the farm, including the pigs. To a certain extent, he represents intelligence without the effectuating and necessary strength; perhaps more profoundly, he demonstrates the heinous Orwellian sin of irresponsible intelligence. The posture of assuming that only the very worst is inevitable in life, that change for the better is a delusion, and that the only alternative is a retreat into a social self-pity is exactly the posture from which Orwell presumptively jerks Gordon Comstock in *Keep the Aspidistra Flying*.

With the means of opposition to Napoleon's totalitarian rule so portrayed, there is little suspense in the outcome of the situation the novel describes. Years pass. Jones dies in an inebriates' home; all the animals forget Boxer and Snowball, for a new generation of animals has grown up. The situation on the farm is unchanged — for most of the animals. The farm is more prosperous now, but the fruits of prosperity never pass much beyond Napoleon and his comrades. And the attempt to judge whether the present situation is better or worse than it had been under Jones is fruitless. "Sometimes the older ones among them racked their dim memories and tried to determine whether in the early days of the Rebellion, when Jones's expulsion was still recent, things had been better or worse than now. They could not remember. There was nothing with which they could compare their present lives: they had nothing to go upon except Squealer's lists of figures, which invariably demonstrated that everything was getting better and better" (p. 143). The condition is depressing; more significant is the loss of rational criteria. Human judgement has, it seems, become impossible. The denial of the possibility of memory enables control of the present, and hence of the future.

"And yet the animals never gave up hope" (p. 144). For they retain one ineradicable achievement: equality. "If they went hungry, it was not from feeding tyrannical human beings; if they worked hard, at least they worked for themselves. No creature called any other 'Master.' All animals were equal" (p. 145). The social and economic hopes of the revolution may have become lost in the actualities of history, but the fundamental political gain of the revolution remains valid for the animals. Orwell articulates this one, final achievement of the animals. But within a page Squealer and Napoleon appear, walking on their hind legs. Yet even this sight is not the final violation of hope. Clover and Benjamin walk around to the barn to read the seventh commandment:

ALL ANIMALS ARE EQUAL
BUT SOME ANIMALS ARE MORE EQUAL THAN OTHERS
(p. 148)

After this, "it did not seem strange" that the pigs take the the humans' newspapers, that the pigs dress like humans, invite neighboring humans in to feast and drink, that the name of the farm is changed back to Manor Farm, and, in the final image of the book, that the pigs become indistinguishable from the humans. The book has come full circle, and things are back as they were. If this is so, Benjamin's judgment becomes valid: things do remain the same, never much worse, never much better; "hunger, hardship, and disappointment" are indeed the "unalterable law of life."

Power inevitably corrupts the best of intentions, apparently no matter who possesses the power: at the end, all the representatives of the various ideologies are indistinguishable—they are all pigs, all pigs are humans. Communism is no better and no worse than capitalism or fascism; the ideals of socialism were long ago lost in Clover's uncomprehending gaze over the farm. Religion is merely a toy of the corrupter, neither offensive nor helpful to master or slave. But perhaps more distressing is the realization that everyone, the good and the bad, the deserving and the wicked, are not only contributors to the tyranny, are not only powerless before it, but also are unable even to understand it. Boxer thinks that whatever Napoleon says is right; Clover can only vaguely feel, and can not communicate, that things are not exactly right; Benjamin thinks that it is in the nature of the world that things go wrong. The potential hope of the book is finally expressed only in terms of ignorance (Boxer), wistful inarticulateness (Clover), or tired cynicism (Benjamin). The inhabitants of this world seem to deserve their fate.

One must finally ask, however, with all this despair and bleakness, what are the actual bases for the tyranny of Animal Farm. Is the terrorism of the dogs the most crucial aspect? Is it force that rules the animals? Boxer's power is seen as superior to this violence and force. Is the basis of the tonal despair the pessimistic belief in the helplessness of the mass of the animals? Orwell elsewhere states again and again his faith in the common people.[16] It seems to me that the basis of the evil of this society is the inability of its inhabitants to ascertain truth, as demonstrated through the theme of the corruption of language. So long as the animals cannot remember the past, because it is continually altered, they have no control over the present and hence over the future. A society that cannot control its language is doomed, says Orwell, to be oppressed in terms that deny it the very most elemental aspects of humanity: to live in a world that allows the revised form of the seventh commandment of Animal Farm is not merely to renounce the belief in the possibility of human equality—a terrible human fate—but in the perversion of language, the very concept of objective reality is lost.

Notes

1. In *Collected Essays* (London, 1961), p. 426.
2. "Why I Write," in *Collected Essays*, p. 426. Orwell's italics.

3. Tom Hopkinson, *George Orwell*, Writers and Their Work Series, No. 39 (London, 1962), p. 34.

4. "George Orwell (II)," in *Essays on Literature and Ideas* (London, 1963), p. 201.

5. Ellen Douglass Leyburn, "Animal Stories," in *Modern Satire*, Alvin B. Kernan, ed. (New York, 1962), p. 215.

6. *The Philosophy of Rhetoric* (New York, 1936), p. 100.

7. *E.g.*, if Major represents Lenin, there is some difficulty. Lenin died in 1924, well after the revolution had occurred; yet in *Animal Farm*, Major dies prior to the animals' revolt. Moreover, Major seems to represent the prophet of animal equality and class revolution, obviously more in conformance with Marx. But if Major represents Marx, there is an even worse anachronism.

8. "Orwell: Irony as Prophecy," in *The Crazy Fabric: Essays in Irony* (London, 1965), p. 206.

9. *Animal Farm* (New York, 1954), p. 3. Subsequent references are to this edition and are in the text.

10. *Politics and the Novel* (New York, 1957), p. 243.

11. Hopkinson, p. 29.

12. Page 27. It is noteworthy that these children never appear in the book: they obviously would enjoy a natural sympathy that would be contrary to the antipathy the humans receive in the fable.

13. This is certainly one realization of *1984*. The source of this idea in Orwell's writing may be James Burnham's *The Managerial Revolution*, a major source of *1984*.

14. Page 75. Orwell makes an important distinction here. While there is some mismanagement on the farm and a great deal of selfish confiscation and hoarding by the pigs, it is primarily the severe winter that brings the farm into jeopardy. The socialistic system itself is not wrong, though it appears Orwell thinks it cannot survive in isolation.

15. The violation of the commandments develops according to the degree of seriousness of the violation. The first to be altered is the fourth, which merely adds "with sheets" to the pronouncement, "No animal shall sleep in a bed." The final violation is, of course, to the seventh, "All animals are equal."

16. *Cf.* "Looking Back on the Spanish War" (1943). "The struggle of the working class is like the growth of a plant. The plant is blind and stupid, but it knows enough to keep pushing upwards towards the light, and it will do this in the face of endless discouragement." (In *Collected Essays*, p. 200.) The metaphor is suggestive: here Orwell employs the same terms of organic growth that exist in other contexts in *Animal Farm*. However, it seems to me that Orwell comes to see that the implications of the metaphor fail in human, political contexts. The logical extension is the proles of *1984*; but the "hope" that the proles represent is as delusive and feeble as is Boxer.

The Making of *Animal Farm*   Bernard Crick*

In the same month as he joined *Tribune*, November 1943, Orwell began writing *Animal Farm* and he had finished by the end of February 1944. He knew that it would be a short book, for he wrote to Philip Rahv

*Reprinted with permission from *George Orwell: A Life* (Boston: Little, Brown, 1980), 308–19.

in December 1943, "I have got another book under way which I hope to finish in a few months."[1] He was perfectly clear both what it was about (which could not always be said of his pre-war novels) and that it would cause trouble: "I am writing a little squib," he told Gleb Struve in February 1943, "which might amuse you when it comes out, but it is not so OK politically that I don't feel certain in advance that anyone will publish. Perhaps that gives you a hint of its subject." And in the very same letter he reverted to his interest in Zamyatin's *We*: "I am interested in that kind of book, and even keep making notes for one myself that may get written sooner or later."[2] This is the first concrete evidence that he was planning *Nineteen Eighty-Four* even before he began to write *Animal Farm*. Some of these notes have survived.

The relationship between the two books is much closer than many critics have supposed. The form that each took was very different, but there was an intellectual continuity between the story of the revolution betrayed and the story of the betrayers, power-hungry in each case, perpetuating themselves in power for ever. And it was no boast on his part to say: ("*Animal Farm* was the first book in which I tried, with full consciousness of what I was doing, to fuse political purpose and artistic purpose into one whole.") It was to become, its political message quite apart, sometimes indeed forgotten, the very model of good English prose almost everywhere English is learned; and even in the Soviet bloc it circulates in several widely read *samizdat* versions.

He explained the purpose and origins of the book in a preface he wrote in 1947 for a Ukrainian edition:

> . . . for the past ten years I have been convinced that the destruction of the Soviet myth was essential if we wanted a revival of the Socialist movement.
>
> On my return from Spain I thought of exposing the Soviet myth in a story that could be easily understood by almost anyone and which could be easily translated into other languages. However the actual details of the story did not come to me for some time until one day (I was then living in a small village) I saw a little boy, perhaps ten years old, driving a huge cart-horse along a narrow path, whipping it whenever it tried to turn. It struck me that if only such animals became aware of their strength we should have no power over them, and that men exploit animals in much the same way as the rich exploit the proletariat.
>
> I proceeded to analyze Marx's theory from the animal's point of view. . . .[4]

Thus he reminded his readers, just as he was beginning to write *Nineteen Eighty-Four*, that *Animal Farm* had been "in my mind for a period of six years before it was actually written." He took pains to assert the political continuity and coherence of his writing after 1936 when he became both fervently Socialist and fervently anti-Communist. But he also warned his readers that though *Animal Farm* took various episodes from the Russian

Revolution, the demands of the story came before literal history. The final scene of Jones and his men dining with the Pigs, for instance, was not meant to show reconciliation but discord. "I wrote it immediately after the Tehran Conference which everybody thought had established the best possible relations between the USSR and the West. I personally did not believe that such good relations would last long." The division of the world at Tehran and Yalta between superpowers who then fell out also underlies the plot of *Nineteen Eighty-Four*.

There was a peculiarity about the actual composition of *Animal Farm* compared to that of Orwell's earlier books. He discussed it in considerable detail with Eileen. She had been, she told her friends, always a bit disappointed that he did not want her to read through and criticise his manuscripts before typing them out; only rarely, even back in Wallington days, did he even ask her to type for him. After Eileen's death, he told Dorothy Plowman that "she was particularly fond of and even helped in the planning of *Animal Farm*."[5] He read his day's work to her in bed, the warmest place in their desperately cold flat, discussed the next stage and actually welcomed criticisms and suggestions, both of which she gave. Never before had he discussed work in progress with anyone. Then the next morning Lettice Cooper and Eileen's other women friends at the Ministry of Food waited eagerly for a paraphrase of the latest episode.[6] Eileen seemed excited by it. And they shared not just her pleasure in the story, but also a mischievous delight in speculating about the trouble that lay ahead for the reckless author. Intelligent people did not miss the black comedy of Government propaganda, particularly when it was Churchill's government, pumping out plaudits to those "heroic Russian people" who so shortly before had been "the dupes of the Bolsheviks in alliance with Hitler." Had not Churchill himself said, the day after Hitler's invasion of Russia, that if Hitler were to invade Hell he would pay a graceful tribute on the floor of the House of Commons to the Devil? But for most people propaganda seemed to have obliterated all bad memories of the Russian purges and the carving up of Poland and the Baltic States with Hitler. That it was all *pour raison d'état* or "for the emergency" seemed forgotten, even among some British Conservatives, let alone among the Left. Many English Conservatives of the old breed never really took ideology seriously: politics was all a matter of national self-interest, so Russia could be dealt with as Russia. To think of Stalin as "Uncle Joe" might be going too far, but to keep on reminding people that he was a totalitarian was as irrelevant as reminders of his crimes were imprudent. But Orwell was not so much attacking sins of the past, still less the conduct of a wartime ally; rather he was trying to clear men's minds of cant and power worship so as to guard against what he feared would be a future even more threatened by totalitarianism.

When the book was completed Orwell had no doubt of its merits. For the first time he was fully pleased with what he had done. He also had no doubt that he did not want Gollancz to publish it—though quite unfairly he would include Gollancz in his future execrations against those who had seen its worth but had not had the guts to publish it, or who had set themselves up as censors.

> 10a Mortimer Crescent,
> London N.W.6
> 19.3.44

Dear Mr. Gollancz,

I have just finished a book and the typing will be completed in a few days. You have the first refusal of my fiction books, and I think this comes under the heading of fiction. It is a little fairy story, about 30,000 words, with a political meaning. But I must tell you that it is— I think—completely unacceptable politically from your point of view (it is anti-Stalin). I don't know whether in that case you will want to see it. If you do, of course I will send it along, but the point is that I am not anxious, naturally, for the MS to be hanging about too long. If you think that you would like to have a look at it, in spite of its not being politically O.K., could you let either me or my agent (Christy & Moore) know? Moore will have the MS. Otherwise, could you let me know that you *don't* want to see it, so that I can take it elsewhere without wasting time?

> Yours sincerely,
> Eric Blair

Gollancz replied to this provocative letter with understandable huffiness.

> March 23rd 1944

Dear Mr. Blair,

Certainly I should like to see the manuscript.

Frankly, I don't begin to understand you when you say "I must tell you that it is—I think—completely unacceptable politically from your point of view it is anti-Stalin." I haven't the faintest idea what "anti-Stalin" means. The Communists, as I should have thought you were aware, regard me as violently anti-Stalinist, because I was wholly and openly opposed to Soviet foreign policy from the Nazi-Soviet pact until Russia came into the war, because I have been highly critical of illiberal trends in Soviet internal policy, and because the last two issues of the "Left News" have been very largely devoted to uncompromising criticism of the Soviet proposals about East Prussia, Pomerania and Silesia. Personally, I think it both incorrect and unwise to label that anti-Stalinism; I call it the kind of criticism, whether of the Soviet Union or of any other State, that no socialist can renounce. There is, on the other hand, the anti-Stalinism of Hitler, Lord Haw-Haw, and the more reactionary Tories. With the latter, of course, I can have nothing whatever to do—and I should be surprised to learn that you can.

I suppose I ought rather to pat myself on the back that you

apparently regard me as a Stalinist stooge, whereas I have been
banned from the Soviet Embassy for three years as an "anti-Stalinist."

> Yours sincerely,
> Victor Gollancz

Orwell then sent it to him with a covering note asking for a speedy
decision, reiterating that he did not think "that it is the kind of thing you
would print" and saying that, naturally, he was "not criticising the Soviet
regime from the Right, but in my experience the other kind of criticism
gets one into even worse trouble."[7]

Gollancz did give a commendably speedy decision.

> Eric Blair Esq.,
> 10a Mortimer Crescent
> London N.W.6
>
> April 4th 1944
>
> My Dear Blair,
>
> You were right and I was wrong. I am so sorry. I have returned the
> manuscript to Moore.
>
> Yours sincerely,
> Dictated by Mr Gollancz,
> but signed in his absence.

He said a little bit more to Orwell's agent.

> Leonard P. Moore Esq
> The Ride Annexe,
> Duke's Wood Avenue
> Gerrards Cross
>
> April 4th 1944
>
> My Dear Moore,
>
> Here is the manuscript of *Animal Farm*, together with my note to
> Blair. I am highly critical of many aspects of internal and external
> Soviet policy: but I could not possibly publish (as Blair anticipated) a
> general attack of this nature.
>
> Yours sincerely
> [Victor Gollancz]

Years later Gollancz maintained that Orwell was "a much over-rated
writer." This may have been sour-grapes, but it is plain that Gollancz
turned down the book as a matter of policy and principle. Even if he had
had prophetic powers of the book's incredible sales he would probably
have made, though with agony, the same decision. It was his own firm and
he simply did not want to publish such a thing.

So far, so good—from Orwell's point of view. But rage and alarm
began to mount, despite his anticipation of difficulties, at what happened

when he submitted the manuscript to Jonathan Cape. Cape's chief reader and literary adviser, Daniel George (who also reviewed novels regularly for *Tribune*), shrewd and experienced, gave it a fair wind, despite some uncertainty about "its real purpose":

> This is a kind of fable, entertaining in itself, and satirically enjoyable as a satire on the Soviets. The characters of Marx, Lenin, Trotsky and Stalin can clearly be recognised, and incidents in recent Russian politics are cleverly parodied. There is no doubt that it would find many appreciative readers, though these might not be of the class of which the author publicly approves, and its real purpose is not made clear. Publication of it is a matter of policy. I cannot myself see any serious objection to it.[8]

Veronica Wedgwood, although about to leave Cape, also read it and was strongly in favour of publication.

Jonathan Cape must have been eager to publish it for he wrote anxiously to Gollancz about the copyright position. Gollancz had Orwell under contract for his next three novels, and wished to hold him to that; so he told Moore and Cape that *Animal Farm* was both not a "novel" and was below the normal length for a novel (he had no interest in or rights over Orwell's non-fiction). Cape then began to discuss the terms of a contract with Moore, but also seeing it as "a matter of policy" thought it best to talk it over with a friend of his, "a senior official" in the Ministry of Information. The name of this official cannot, alas, be discovered. But to think it incredible that Cape sent the manuscript at all would be hindsight. The chronicler of his firm wrote: "It is not easy to recall now the force of moral rather than governmental pressure which deterred publishers from risking damage to the common war effort. . . ."[9] The friend, in fact, followed up their conversation with a personal letter strongly imploring Cape not to publish a book that would so damage good relations with Russia. Cape was deeply upset and agonised over the decision, but fairly quickly, to the dismay and annoyance of Daniel George and Veronica Wedgwood, wrote to Moore as follows:

19 June 1944

My Dear Moore,

> Since our conversation the other morning about George Orwell, I have considered the matter carefully and I have come to the conclusion that, unless the arrangement that exists whereby our author has to offer two works of fiction to another publisher can be waived, it would be unwise for us to enter into a contract for his future work. However, it does not seem to me unlikely that some compromise could be reached with Gollancz so far as this matter is concerned.
>
> I mentioned the reaction that I had had from an important official in the Ministry of Information with regard to *Animal Farm*. I must confess that this expression of opinion has given me seriously to think. My reading of the manuscript gave me considerable personal enjoy-

ment and satisfaction, but I can see now that it might be regarded as something which it was highly ill-advised to publish at the present time. If the fable were addressed generally to dictators and dictatorships at large then publication would be all right, but the fable does follow, as I see now, so completely the progress and development of the Russian Soviets and their two dictators, that it can apply only to Russia, to the exclusion of other dictatorships. Another thing: it would be less offensive if the predominant caste in the fable were not pigs. I think the choice of pigs as the ruling caste will no doubt give offence to many people, and particularly to anyone who is a bit touchy, as undoubtedly the Russians are. . . . I think it is best to send back to you the typescript of *Animal Farm* and let the matter lie on the table as far as we are concerned. . . .

Yours sincerely,
Jonathan Cape[10]

Orwell was torn between rage and laughter at Cape's procedure. In the margin of a copy of the letter, where it suggested some other animal than pigs, Orwell wrote laconically "balls." (It is debatable whether the word "pig," offensive enough anywhere, is peculiarly offensive to Russians, but that is not the point. Cape had turned it down, not asked for innocent revisions.)

Something nearly came of it. Veronica Wedgwood was leaving to become Literary Editor of *Time and Tide* (a Liberal journal—in a very Right-wing sense). She asked the editor and proprietor, Lady Rhondda, a formidable lady, whether it would be possible to serialise the book. She was taken with the idea, even though it would have meant sacrificing almost all the literary pages for many weeks. But when Veronica Wedgwood took this proposal to Orwell, he expressed gratitude but said that the politics of *Time and Tide* were far too far to the Right for him, he felt it to be the wrong background for the book.

So Orwell then sent the manuscript to T. S. Eliot as a director of Faber & Faber.

10a Mortimer Crescent,
NW6
(Or "Tribune" CEN 2572)
28 June 1944

Dear Eliot,

This MS has been blitzed which accounts for my delay in delivering it and its slightly crumpled condition, but it is not damaged in any way.

I wonder if you could be kind enough to let me have Messrs Fabers' decision fairly soon. If they are interested in seeing more of my work, I could let you have the facts abt my existing contract with Gollancz, which is not an onerous one nor likely to last long.

If you read this MS yourself you will see its meaning which is not an acceptable one at this moment, but I could not agree to make any alterations except a small one at the end which I intended making anyway. Cape or the MOI, I am not certain which from the wording of his letter, made the imbecile suggestion that some other animal than pigs might be made to represent the Bolsheviks. I could not of course make any change of that description.

> Yours sincerely
> Geo. Orwell

P.S. Could you have lunch with me one of the days when you are in town?[11]

Even before Eliot replied, Orwell had made a hidden flick at Cape in a *Tribune* "As I Please" column of 7 July:

> Nowadays this kind of veiled censorship even extends to books. The MOI does not, of course, dictate a party line or issue an *index expurgatorius*. It merely "advises." Publishers take manuscripts to the MOI and the MOI "suggests" that this or that is undesirable or premature, or "would serve no good purpose." And though there is no definite prohibition, no clear statement that this or that must not be printed, official policy is never flouted. Circus dogs jump when the trainer cracks his whip, but the really well-trained dog is the one that turns his somersault when there is no whip. And that is the state we have reached in this country, thanks to three hundred years of living together without a civil war.[12]

Orwell's language was intemperate, but his description of what happened was all too accurate.[13]

T. S. Eliot replied on 13 July.

> I know that you wanted a quick decision about "Animal Farm" but the minimum is two directors' opinions, and that can't be done under a week. But for the importance of speed, I should have asked the Chairman to look at it as well. But the other director is in agreement with me on the main points. We agree that it is a distinguished piece of writing; that the fable is very skilfully handled, and that the narrative keeps one's interest on its own plane—and that is something very few authors have achieved since Gulliver.
>
> On the other hand, we have no conviction (and I am sure none of the other directors would have) that this is the right point of view from which to criticise the political situation at the present time. It is certainly the duty of any publishing firm which pretends to other interests and motives than mere commercial prosperity, to publish books which go against the current of the moment; but in each instance that demands that at least one member of the firm should have the conviction that this is the thing that needs saying at the moment. I can't see any reason of prudence or caution to prevent anybody from publishing this book—if he believed in what it stands for.
>
> Now I think my own dissatisfaction with this apologue is that the effect is simply one of negation. It ought to excite some sympathy with what the author wants, as well as sympathy with his objections to

something: and the positive point of view, which I take to be generally Trotskyite, is not convincing. I think you split your vote, without getting any compensating strong adhesion from either party—i.e. those who criticise Russian tendencies from the point of view of a purer communism, and those who, from a very different point of view, are alarmed about the future of small nations. And after all, your pigs are far more intelligent than the other animals, and therefore the best qualified to run the farm—in fact, there couldn't have been an Animal Farm at all without them: so that what was needed (someone might argue) was not more communism but more public-spirited pigs.

I am very sorry because whoever publishes this will naturally have the opportunity of publishing your future work: and I have a regard for your work, because it is good writing of fundamental integrity. . . .[14]

Orwell bore Eliot no personal ill will for this. They corresponded on routine editorial matters without rancour later in the year. Yet the letter was in some ways a very strange one. Eliot offered such a variety of arguments, not all consistent with each other, to the same conclusion, but at least he took the book very seriously, which must have disarmed Orwell's personal anger. Plainly he says, in his complicated Eliot-like way, that "it is not our kind of book" and that further, whatever its literary merits, a polemical political book needs some positive conviction behind it from the firm. It would have been as odd for Faber & Faber to publish a revolutionary tract as for Victor Gollancz, at that time even, to publish an anti-Russian conservative one. The Trotskyite attribution is neither unfair nor entirely unexpected from Geoffrey Faber and T. S. Eliot's standpoint, and it is a more accurate reading than that it was to receive from some future Cold War warriors across the Atlantic (including his future main American publishers). The insistence on the inevitability of élites, however, that pigs are with us always, so preferably "public-spirited" pigs, is extraordinarily narrowing for any satirist, especially one capable of "good writing of fundamental integrity"; and the point about the integrity of small nations, precisely one of Orwell's own concerns, is either a sad misreading or a bad red-herring. The favourable comparison with Swift's skill and with *Gulliver* itself (how right Eliot was, how specific is the influence of the Yahoos and the Houyhnhnms on Orwell's fable) should surely have settled the matter, if literary merit was the touchstone. Swift too could have been viewed as untimely, imprudent and essentially negative. Eliot was lucky that Orwell never wrote a parody Eliot letter of rejection to Swift.

The touchstone, however, was not purely literary: Orwell had encountered a "political writer" almost as complicated as himself. If, that is, the letter of rejection is necessarily to be taken as Eliot's views in all respects: it could be a composite of several people's views. He was, after all, a partner of Faber & Faber, but Geoffrey Faber was the owner and took the financial risks. Eliot was punctilious and precise in never recommending publication, only commenting on a book's merits. Geoffrey Faber made the hard decisions, but he did not like writing difficult letters of rejection, such disagreeable tasks he often left to the loyal Eliot. What exactly happened in this case is obscure, but it is a simplification to say that "T. S. Eliot" turned down *Animal Farm*. It was rejected by the firm, a different and not wholly consistent animal.[15]

Four days after Eliot's letter arrived, Orwell told Moore that "Warburg again says he wants to see it and would publish it if he can see his way to getting the paper, but that is a big 'if'." If that falls through, he said, he was not "going to tout it round further publishers . . . but shall publish it myself as a pamphlet at 2s. I have already half-arranged to do so and have got the necessary financial backing."[16] Why did he not take it to Warburg in the first place, a publisher who had already handled two of his books? The answer must lie in Orwell's confidence in the merit of the book and his desire to see it published by one of the two best publishing houses in England. Years before, with far less justifiable confidence, he had sent Faber and then Cape the first and the rejected versions of *Down and Out in Paris and London*. He wanted that kind of recognition, at least for this book. Secker & Warburg, before their faith in Thomas Mann, Franz Kafka and Orwell had paid off, looked a very different house—small, lively but precarious and still nicknamed, however unfairly, because of their courage and persistence in bringing out difficult Left-wing books, "the Trotskyite publisher." Political though the fable was, Orwell thought its literary merits should carry it to a wider readership.

It is odd that he lost heart too soon. Perhaps he was shocked that his new reputation did not prevent such a sudden return to the problems of how to get published at all that he had suffered in his youth. To be turned down by two great publishing houses,[17] and to be as yet unwilling even to show the manuscript to Fred Warburg, seemed an inadequate reason for desperate measures like publishing it himself. Perhaps he felt that if the two most distinguished houses had not recognised its merit he would show the lot of them, he would eat worms and do it himself in thoroughly radical fashion. And he may have been affected by American rejections too. At some stage that year it was sent to the Dial Press who returned it, according to Orwell, with the comment that "it was impossible to sell animal stories in the U.S.A."[18] It is possible, of course, that he believed that the hand of the M.O.I., once alerted, would reach everywhere; and also that he believed the rumours, as his excitable *Tribune* friends did, that Victor Gollancz was on the phone warning London publishers that this time that man had gone too far and was damaging the national interest.

Orwell may not have intended literally to publish it himself, although he approached David Astor, with much diffidence, for a loan of £200. Astor was willing but thought the project hare-brained: he counselled him to have patience with real publishers.[19] But Orwell may have wanted the money more as a subsidy, for he next offered it to anarchist friends. George

Woodcock was a member of the board of the Freedom Press, managed by Vernon Richards and Marie Louise Berneri; and he remembers sounding them out. She objected to it strongly, so it is doubtful it was ever formally submitted. Vernon Richards is adamant that it was never submitted, but he was in prison at the relevant time and might not have been told.[20] Probably one or other of them advised Orwell that it would stand a chance if formally submitted, for the board contained many belligerent pacifists who knew his early wartime writings and attacks on them as pacifists only too well. Whatever their common hatred of Stalinism, of all "oligarchic collectivism" and their common ground with Orwell that there had been a revolution but it had been betrayed, they had not liked being called "objectively Fascist" in relation to the war effort. They had neither forgiven nor forgotten. Their feelings are understandable. However, associated with them was Paul Potts who published and sold poems in pubs on broadsheets, mainly his own. (This enterprise grew, for a while, into a pleasant little imprint, the Whitman Press.) In a perceptive, if idiosyncratic, chapter on Orwell called "Don Quixote on a Bicycle" in his *Dante Called You Beatrice* (1960), Potts claims:

> At one point I became the publisher of *Animal Farm* — which only means that we were going to bring it out ourselves. Orwell was going to pay the printer, using the paper quota to which the Whitman Press was entitled. . . . We had actually started to do so. I had been down to Bedford with the manuscript to see the printer twice. The birthplace of John Bunyan seemed a happy omen. Orwell had never spoken about the contents. I had not liked to ask as any questions might appear to have an editorial accent. He had, however, talked about adding a preface to it on the freedom of the Press. . . . That essay on the freedom of the Press was not needed as Secker and Warburg, at the last minute, accepted the book.[21]

The sentimental prose of *Dante Called You Beatrice* raises some of the same problems as Jacintha Buddicom's writing about Orwell's early years: the style has been taken as grounds for doubting the memories and judgments. Mr. Potts' book has its moments when fact and fiction blend rather uneasily and the chronology is a bit wobbly; but he knew Orwell well and he is a valuable and important source. The essential truth of Potts' account is shown by his being the only person who had ever heard of or who could remember "The Freedom of the Press" — a fiery preface to *Animal Farm* which Orwell did in fact write as a blast against self-censorship, but fortunately did not use. It was lost until 1971.[22] People either did not believe Potts or did not notice his claim that there was a lost major essay (reviewers often have to work at such speed).

In the end the much-handled, dog-eared manuscript was sent to Fred Warburg late in July. The dramatic account Warburg gives in *All Authors Are Equal* of it coming to him out of the blue, of Orwell turning up during his lunch one day and dumping the manuscript on him with an urgent explanation of its contents, is contradicted by Orwell's letter to Moore in the previous month (already quoted), in which he says that Warburg knew about it, had not seen it but wanted to publish it. Probably Orwell came to him, rather shamefacedly, as a last resort. But Orwell's letter raises a problem. However enthusiastic Warburg may have been about Orwell, it is unlikely that he would have taken anything sight unseen. He had already, not surprisingly, turned down Orwell's "War-time Diary." Perhaps Orwell was merely making excuses to Moore for not wanting to send it directly to Warburg, as would have seemed to Moore to be less trouble, more sensible and even proper, from the start. Warburg is, however, amusingly frank about his hesitations once he had read it. Its merits were obvious, but so were the dangers of being its publisher in wartime. Warburg in his autobiography does not crow over Cape or Faber. He saw the dilemma very much in their terms but, despite some strong opposition to accepting the book within his firm, decided to run the risk. Under the rationing system, however, he was desperately short of paper, as he had already warned the suspicious Orwell.[23]

The book was over a year in production and it was not published until August 1945, which was a very long time in those days, especially for such a short book. Orwell wrote to a provincial Labour journalist, Frank Barber, on 3 September 1945, "I have been surprised by the friendly reception *Animal Farm* has had, after lying in type for about a year because the publisher dared not bring it out till the war was over."[24] And on 19 August he had written in a letter to Herbert Read that he had stopped writing for *Tribune* while away in France "and didn't start again because Bevan was terrified there might be a row over *Animal Farm* which might have been embarrassing if the book had come out before the election, as it was at first intended to."[25] These two statements must be taken with a large pinch of salt in the absence of other evidence. It had not been "lying in type for about a year," for Orwell wrote in a letter to T. S. Eliot on 5 September 1944: "Warburg is going to do that book you saw but he probably can't get it out until early next year because of paper."[26] Letters between Orwell and his literary agent show that complications about signing the actual contract also dragged on into March 1945. Orwell may well have been laying it on a bit thick about the delay after the difficult experience he had had in getting his masterpiece accepted at all.

For a moment George Orwell seemed to relapse into being Gordon Comstock again and lashed out in all directions. His feeling of being persecuted for plain speaking was heightened by the rejection in March of a review he wrote for *The Manchester Evening News* of Harold Laski's *Faith, Reason and Civilization*. He had agreed with Laski that the Soviet Union, for all its faults, was the "real dynamo of the Socialist movement," but he had criticised him for closing his eyes to "purges, liquidations, the dictatorship of a minority, suppression of criticism and so forth." The editor felt that this was against the national interest. Dwight Macdonald got to hear about it in New York and wrote an editorial in his *Politics* warning "how seriously the feats of the Red army have misled English public opinion about Russia."[27]

So Orwell's harsh and bitter comment in the last paragraph of the unused preface is understandable, given the provocation and the circumstances.

> I know that the English intelligentsia have plenty of reason for their timidity and dishonesty, indeed I know by heart the arguments by which they justify themselves. But at least let us have no more nonsense about defending liberty against Fascism. If liberty means anything at all it means the right to tell people what they do not want to hear. The common people still vaguely subscribe to that doctrine and act on it. In our country . . . it is the liberals who fear liberty and the intellectuals who want to do dirt on the intellect; it is to draw attention to that fact that I have written this preface.[28]

Notes

1. *Collected Essays, Journalism, and Letters of George Orwell* (London: Secker & Warburg, 1968), ed. Sonia Brownell and Ian Angus, III, p. 53.

2. *Ibid.*, pp. 95–96.

3. "Why I Write," *CE* I, p. 7.

4. *CE* III, pp. 405–06.

5. *CE* IV, p. 104.

6. Interview by the author with Lettice Cooper, West Hampstead, 14 Dec. 1977.

7. Extract from a letter of 25 March 1944 in possession of Victor Gollancz Ltd.

8. Quoted by Michael S. Howard in *Jonathan Cape, Publisher* (Jonathan Cape, London, 1971), p. 179.

9. *Ibid.*, p. 180.

10. Letter of Jonathan Cape to Leonard Moore, 19 June 1944, copy in Orwell Archive; and a letter to the author from Dame Veronica Wedgwood of 19 Sep. 1979.

11. *CE* III, p. 176.

12. *Ibid.*, pp. 180–81.

13. Sir Stanley Unwin, for instance, in his self-congratulatory memoirs, relates how the Publishers Association appointed a Mr. W. G. Taylor and himself as their representatives on the Press and Censorship Bureau (of the Ministry of Information) to advise on censorship of books: "Other war measures confronted us almost daily. The one that was handled most successfully was censorship. . . . It was decreed that the only ground for censorship was giving information to the enemy. On that basis the Publishers Association at once promised 100 per cent cooperation. . . . As a matter of fact our services were never required. In doubtful cases publishers voluntarily and gladly submitted typescripts or proofs, and the censors dealt with them expeditiously. The expression of opinions remained free" (Sir Stanley Unwin, *The Truth About a Publisher* [Allen & Unwin, 1960]). They may have muzzled themselves but to say that "opinions remained free" was double-think indeed.

14. A letter in the possession of Mrs Valerie Eliot and communicated by her to *The Times*, 6 Jan. 1969, a copy in Orwell Archive.

15. The suggestion is contained in a letter of Frank Morley (who worked for Faber & Faber in the late 1930s) to the author, 21 Sep. 1972.

16. *CE* III, pp. 186–87.

17. Michael Meyer says in his essay in *The World of George Orwell*, ed. Miriam Gross, p. 131, that he also offered it to Collins; but there is no record of this in the firm nor memory either, nor yet in Orwell's letters to his agent.

18. *CE* IV, p. 110.

19. Interview by the author with David Astor at *The Observer*, 14 Feb. 1973.

20. See George Woodcock, "Recollections of George Orwell," *Northern Review* (Montreal), Aug.–Sep. 1953, p. 18, and a fuller account in a letter to the author, 29 Jan. 1974. And letter from Vernon Richards to this author, 12 May 1972 and subsequent interview.

21. Paul Potts, *Dante Called You Beatrice* (Eyre & Spottiswoode, London, 1960), pp. 76–77.

22. When it was printed as "The Freedom of the Press," *Times Literary Supplement*, 15 Sep. 1972, pp. 1037–39, with a commentary by this author, "How the Essay Came to be Written," pp. 1039–40.

23. Fredric Warburg, *All Authors Are Equal* (Hutchinson, London, 1973), pp. 39–58.

24. *CE* III, p. 402.

25. *Ibid.*, p. 401.

26. Letter to T. S. Eliot of 5 Sep. 1944, in the possession of Mrs. Valerie Eliot.

27. Dwight Macdonald, *Politics*, Nov. 1944.

28. "Freedom of the Press," *op. cit.*, p. 1039.

Of Man's Last Disobedience: Zamiatin's *We* and Orwell's *1984*   Gorman Beauchamp[*]

Utopia can be defined as civilization-only-more-so: that is, as a systematic intensification of the restraints upon which all society rests.[1] All civilization is predicated on order, regulation, some degree of regimentation — limitations that conflict with man's natural or instinctual drives and result in the phenomenon Freud called repression. Because repression is the inevitable cost exacted for civilization, man will, on an instinctual, subconscious level, always remain its enemy. Primitive man, Freud argues, was psychically "better off knowing no restraints on instinct. To counterbalance this, his prospects of enjoying . . . happiness for any length of time were very slender. Civilized man has exchanged a portion of his possibilities for happiness for a portion of security."[2]

In the tradition of rationally planned utopias, from Plato's *Republic* to B. F. Skinner's *Walden Two*, the ideal has been to enlarge that "portion of security" by increasing the degree of civilization — to reorder society into a more harmonious, efficient (but more regimented, repressed) whole, in

*Reprinted from *Comparative Literature Studies* 10 (1973):285–301, by permission of the author and the University of Illinois Press.

which each "unit" plays only his socially determined role. Lewis Mumford has likened the utopian model to the military one: "total control from above, absolute obedience from below," whether the "above" be occupied by philosopher kings or behavioral engineers. The price of utopia, he says, is total submission to a central authority, forced labor, lifetime specialization, and inflexible regimentation.[3] A reader familiar with Freud's psychosocial theory, set out most fully in *Civilization and Its Discontents*, will recognize the utopian ideal as but a more systematic, rigorous application of civilization's existing prohibitions and restraints — will recognize, that is, that the dreamworld of chiliastic social planners can be realized only at further, and extreme, expense of individual, instinctual freedom.[4]

The claims of utopianism are essentially religious ones. In the vacuum created by the breakup of "the medieval synthesis," a *Weltanschauung* that subsumed all social activity in one embracing theocentric enterprise overseen by the Church, there grew up a new secularized religion that dominated men's lives: *étatisme*, or worship of the State. The State, as the Church's successor, became the object of what Paul Tillich has called "ultimate concern" — became, that is, the supreme value in men's lives to which all other values are subordinated. When a people makes the nation its ultimate concern, he wrote, "it demands that all other concerns, economic well-being, health and life, family, aesthetic and cognitive truth, justice and humanity, be sacrificed. . . . Everything is centered in the only god, the nation."[5] Utopianism is the most extreme form of *étatisme*, claiming for the State a godlike efficacy. Like its predecessor in divinity, the State offers salvation, not in the next world, however, but in this; not through eschatology, but through utopianism.[6] The State can effect the millenium, but only, of course, if its creatures obey its dictates. The new god is not less jealous than the old, and, like the old, aspires to omniscience and omnipotence, for only with such divine powers can it know of and punish the deviations of the sinner who would resist its enforced salvation. Thus even the most benevolently intended utopias are, by the very nature of their claims, totalitarian, demanding the ultimate concern of their subjects and asserting ultimate control of their destinies.[7]

The dream of social redemption through the State, dawning with such bright hopes in the decade of the French Revolution and growing ever brighter through the nineteenth century, became for many in the twentieth century a nightmare. The reasons are historical: the rise of messianic totalitarian regimes, whose utopianistic schemas resulted not in man's salvation but his damnation. The more humane among utopian thinkers would claim Nazism and Stalinist Communism to be aberrations, bastards rather than true heirs of Plato and More and Wells; but Mumford has argued — correctly, I believe — that these regimes arose logically from the assumptions of venerable utopian ideals:

> Isolation, stratification, fixation, regimentation, standardization, militarism — one or more of these attributes enter into the conception of the

utopian city, as expounded by the Greeks. And these same features, in open or disguised form, remain even in the supposedly more democratic utopias of the nineteenth century. . . . In the end, utopia merges into the dystopia of the twentieth century; and one suddenly realizes that the distance between the positive ideal and the negative one was never so great as the advocates or admirers of utopia had professed.[8]

Such a realization underlies the emergence of a distinctly twentieth-century literary subgenre, the dystopian novel, a *roman à thèse* whose purpose, clearly ideological, is to assert the ultimate value of man's instinctual freedom over the putatively melioristic repression of utopian civilization.[9]

In two dystopian novels in particular—Eugene Zamiatin's *We* and George Orwell's *1984*—the central conflict of the individual's rebellion against the State reenacts the Christian myth of man's first disobedience, Adam's against God. For in each novel there is a god figure, the embodiment of the State, who demands absolute adoration and obedience. And in each there is an Adam-like protagonist who, for love of an Eve, defies this god by asserting his instinctual freedom and thus "falls" from the utopianistic new Eden. This mythic conflict—Adam rebelling against the *étatist* god figure—is a fictional manifestation of the psychic conflict that Freud posited between the individual and society.

Freud shared, on the one hand, the belief of Dostoevsky's Grand Inquisitor that man needed, and wanted, a dominant figure to rule and protect him. The "coercive characteristic of group formation" Freud traced back to "the fact of their origin from the primal horde. The leader of the group is still the dread primal father; the group still wishes to be governed by unrestricted force; it has an extreme passion for authority, . . . a thirst for obedience."[10] This political führer is "loved" in the same ambivalent way the personal father is "loved"; and, as Philip Rieff points out, "Freud's belief that politics is founded on the group's erotic relation with authority is made concrete by his claim that authority is always *personified.*" Love for this power-as-person, then, constitutes "the most fundamental source of authority."[11] In dystopian fiction, the embodiment of the state is always such a figure: Zamiatin's Well-Doer, Orwell's Big Brother, Huxley's World Controller, even Forster's Machine (in "The Machine Stops"), all of them incarnations of the Grand Inquisitor. And no clearer confirmation of the "displacement" of Eros which Freud saw underlying all authority can be found than in the erotic language Orwell's disobedient Adam uses to express his ultimate submission: "I love Big Brother." In the megacivilization of utopia, man's whole duty is to love the führer and serve him.

On the other hand, however, Freud himself had little faith in the efficacy of utopias. Dostoevsky's implacable dystopian, the Underground Man, accused utopians of wanting to convert society into a human anthill, but man's instincts — his desire to follow "his own foolish will" — would (he asserted) thwart all their efforts to regiment him. Freud, employing a similar insect metaphor, agreed "It does not seem as though any influence could induce a man to change his nature into a termite's. No doubt he will always defend his claim to individual liberty against the will of the group."[12] His "urge to freedom" is forever pitted against the coercive unity of society, so that the conflict between the individual, "I," and the group or State, "We," appears from a Freudian vantage point irreconcilable.

"I do not want to be 'I,' " cried Bakunin a century ago; "I want to be 'We.' " His sentiment informs utopianism, historical as well as fictional, so that in the dream-turned-nightmare world of Koestler's *Darkness at Noon*, the I has become suspect, a "grammatical fiction." "The Party did not recognize its existence. The definition of the individual was: a multitude of one million divided by one million."[13] Whatever encourages individualism, "I-ness," is the enemy, for it separates the one from the many, man from the godlike State. Prime among such estranging emotions is sexuality: in the new Edens, as in the old, the serpent that seduces man into disobedience is sexual, Adam's love for Eve. "Present-day civilization makes it plain," Freud points out in *Civilization and Its Discontents*, "that it does not like sexuality as a source of pleasure in its own right and is only prepared to tolerate it because there is so far no substitute for it as a means of propagating the human race."[14] (In *Brave New World*, of course, a substitute *has* been found: the bottled baby.) Elsewhere, Freud explains the reason for this animus:

> Sexual impulsions are unfavorable to the formation of groups. . . . The more important sexual love became for the ego, and the more it developed the characteristics of being in love, the more urgently it required to be limited to two people. . . . Two people coming together for the purpose of sexual satisfaction, in so far as they seek solitude, are making a demonstration against the herd instinct, the group feeling. . . .
> In the great artificial groups, the church and the army, there is no room for woman as the sexual object. The love relation between man and woman remains outside these organizations. . . . Even in a person who has in other respects become absorbed in a group, the directly sexual impulsions preserve a little of his individual activity. If they become too strong, they disintegrate every group formation.[15]

This conflict, then, that Freud postulated between the individual and civilization adumbrates the central struggle in the dystopian novel: "the dreadful father," a secularized god demanding total allegiance and obedience to the utopian decalogue, challenged by the individual's instinctual will to freedom. And particularly with respect to the sexual nature of that challenge, the conflict recapitulates the myth of Adam's rebellion against God. With this background, let us turn to an examination of the dystopian versions of paradise lost, *We* and *1984*.

"Put me in a System and you negate me," Kierkegaard declared; "I am not just a mathematical symbol—I *am*." This affirmation underlies Zamiatin's *We*, a satirical depiction of a futuristic United State whose members have become, almost literally, mathematical symbols: they have no names and are known only by their numbers, indeed are called Numbers. Sealed off from the natural world in a glass-walled city, they function as interchangeable parts of one vast machine, regulated by a Table of Hours: "Every morning, with six-wheeled precision, at the same hour, at the same minute, we wake up, millions of us at once. At the very same hour, millions like one, we begin our work, and millions like one, we finish it. United in a single body with a million hands, at the very same second, designated by the Tables, we carry the spoons to our mouths; at the very same second we all go out to walk, go to the auditorium, to the halls for Taylor exercises, and then to bed."[16] Zamiatin's imagination has projected the ideal of utopian organization to its logical extreme: "A magnificent celebration of the victory of *all* over *one*, of the *sum* over the *individual*" (p. 44).

In the United States, not surprisingly, freedom is equated with sin. Employing the Eden metaphor, one Number explains:

> That legend referred to us of today, did it not? Yes. Only think of it for a moment. There were two in paradise and the choice was offered to them: happiness without freedom or freedom without happiness. No other choice. . . . They, fools that they were, chose freedom. Naturally, for centuries afterward they longed for fetters, for the fetters of yore. . . . For centuries! And only we found the way to regain happiness. . . . The ancient god and we, side by side at the same table! We helped god defeat the devil definitely and finally. It was he, the devil, who led people to transgression, to taste pernicious freedom—he, the cunning serpent. And we came along, planted a boot on his head, and . . . squash! Down with him! Paradise again! We returned to the simple-mindedness of Adam and Eve. (p. 59)

The god who oversees this paradise regained is the Well-Doer, a remote, ironclad figure who emerges annually to be reelected on the Day of Unanimity: "This was always the most magnificent moment of our celebration: all would remain sitting motionless, joyfully bowing their heads under the salutary yoke of that Number of Numbers" (p. 134) as "He descend[ed] to us from the sky, He—the new Jehovah—in an aero, He, as wise and lovingly cruel as the Jehovah of the ancients" (p. 131).

Since all Eros in this utopian anthill is channeled into worship of the Well-Doer, there are no marriages nor families, and all children become property of the State; so that having precluded all emotional ties and "having identified itself with man's only permissible aspiration," as one writer notes, the State "emerges as the only possible object of man's affection, thus fulfilling his need for emotional relationship."[17] In a State striving for a monopoly on love, sex is suspect, tolerated as a necessary evil, but strictly controlled:

> Naturally, having conquered hunger . . . , the United State directed its attack against the second ruler of the world, against love. At last this element was conquered, that is, organized and put into a mathematical formula. . . . You are carefully examined in the laboratory of the Sexual Department where they find the content of the sexual hormones in your blood, and they accordingly make out for you a Table of sexual days. Then you file an application to enjoy the services of Number so and so, or Number so and so. (p. 22)

On these occasions, one "received a certificate permitting the use of curtains. This right exists in our State only on sexual days. Normally we live surrounded by transparent walls . . . beneath the eyes of everyone" (p. 19). Not content with such restrictions, the State is seeking ways to reduce the number of sexual days, for these moments of privacy are subversive of its group values, impediments to total We-ness.

In his prelapsarian state of the novel's outset, the protagonist, D–503, is perfectly content in this new, de-eroticized Eden: he has his work as a designer of spacecraft, a sweetly simple sex partner, and his love for the State, for the Well-Doer. He prizes his non-freedom: "It is pleasant to feel that somebody's penetrating eye is watching you from behind your shoulder, lovingly guarding you from the most minute mistake, from the most minute incorrect step" (p. 63). Like all good Numbers, D–503 knows that We is of God, I is of the devil, and the reports he hears of a secret organization that "aims at liberation from the beneficient yoke of the State" (p. 34) puzzle and upset him. But just as the United State has not succeeded in eradicating every vestige of desire for freedom for all its Numbers, neither has D–503 succeeded in eradicating all trace of his instinctual, irrational, "animal" nature. His hands are covered with hair, "a stupid atavism," and he hates having anyone look at them; yet this atavism portends deeper, unconscious desires — Freud's instinctual drives — that are soon stirred to life in him. He is tempted to taste the forbidden fruit of love, and he falls.

The Eve who seduces him to experience his own sexuality, and concomitantly his individuality, is a dark, enigmatic Number, I–330. D–503's first encounter with this mysterious woman "had a strange effect on me, like an irrational component of an equation which you cannot eliminate" (p. 10). He becomes fascinated, however, with his temptress, is lured by her to a secret rendezvous, offered a "forbidden fruit," which is liquor ("drink this charming poison with me"), and succumbs: "Suddenly her arms were around my neck . . . her lips grew into mine, even somewhere much deeper, much more terrible" (p. 53). The experience proves a shattering one:

> I became glass-like and saw within myself. There were two selves in me.
> One, the former D-503, Number D-503; and the other. . . . Before,
> that other used to show his hairy paws from time to time, but now that
> whole other self left his shell. The shell was breaking. . . . (p. 54)

The other (unconscious) self emerging from the shell its civilization had
constructed around it begins now to dream, a state symptomatic among
the Numbers of mental disorder. And, indeed, by the utopian standard of
the United State, D-503 has become "sick."[18]

> I *felt* myself. To feel one's self, to be conscious of one's personality, is the
> lot of an eye inflamed by a cinder, or an infected finger, or a bad tooth.
> A healthy eye, or finger, or tooth is not felt; it is non-existent, as it were.
> Is it not clear, then, that consciousness of oneself is sickness? (p. 121)

The question is, of course, ironic, since D-503's "sickness" constitutes for
Zamiatin the essence of being human, that which separates man from the
robot. And sexuality he presents as the force that liberates consciousness,
frees man from civilization's ultrarepression of his instincts, and gives rise
to individuality, to imagination. "I know that I have imagination," the
postlapsarian Adam realizes, "that is what my illness consists of. And more
than that: I know that it is a wonderful illness—one does not want to be
cured, simply does not want to!" (p. 78). Elsewhere Zamiatin wrote that
"there are two priceless fountainheads in man: brains and sex. From the
first proceeds all science, from the second all art. And to cut off all art
from yourself or to force it into your brain would mean to cut
off . . . well, yes."[19] In a society that *has* forced all art into the brain—
whose poetry is all· in praise of mathematics and whose "immortal
tragedy" is entitled *He Who Comes Late to Work!*—the personal, passionate emotions are considered dangerously subversive: thus the attempt to
emasculate the Numbers, to cut off . . . well, yes.

I-330's rebellion against utopia's repression is overtly political: she
belongs to the secret underground movement (MEPHI, derived from
Mephistopheles) dedicated to overthrowing the Well-Doer, to tearing
down the Wall "so that the green wind may blow over the earth, from end
to end" (p. 145). D-503's rebellion, however, is purely instinctual, that of a
man blindly following his heart: "I want to be with I-330. I want her
every minute, every second, to be with me, with no one else. All that I
wrote about Unanimity is of no value. . . . For I know (be it sacrilege, yet
it is the truth) that a Glorious Day is possible only with her and only when
we are side by side" (p. 130). Passion has restored to D-503 his sexuality
and, with it, consciousness, imagination, I-ness; thus disintegrating in
him, in Freud's words, "the herd instinct, the group feeling." Willing now
to do anything to keep her love, Adam follows his Eve into rebellion
against God. He agrees to turn over to the MEPHI the spacecraft he has
built, to be used to destroy the Wall and topple the Well-Doer.

But their plan fails, thwarted by the Gestapo-like Bureau of Guard-

ians, and D–503 is forced to undergo the Great Operation, a fantasiec-
tomy that serves to numericalize completely the wayward sinners against
the State. The proclamation issued by the Well-Doer epitomizes Zamiatin's view of utopia:

> The latest discovery of our State science is that there is a center for
> fancy — a miserable little nervous knot in the lower region of the frontal
> lobe of the brain. A triple treatment of the knot with X-rays will cure
> you of fancy,
>
> *Forever!*
>
> You are perfect; you are mechanized; the road to one-hundred-per-
> cent happiness is open! Hasten then all of you, young and old, hasten to
> undergo the Great Operation! Long Live the Great Operation! Long
> live the United State! Long Live the Well-Doer. (p. 167)

His "fancy" removed, D–503 reverts to perfect Numberhood: docile,
content, unable to feel love for any but the Well-Doer; again a smoothly
functioning part of We. Sitting beside the Well-Doer, D–503 now watches
I–330 tortured to death and knows it to be right, "for reason must prevail"
(p. 218). Rebellion has been rendered impossible in the utopian Eden; his
has been man's last disobedience.

The influence of Zamiatin's work on *1984* is pronounced and pervasive; indeed, one critic has called *We* Orwell's *Holinshed*.[20] Many of the
features of the United State reappear in Orwell's Oceania, not least of
which is the systematic repression of the sexual drives. Thus the rebellion
of the individual against the State, in *1984* as in *We*, is presented as a
sexual one, the struggle for instinctual freedom against the enforced
conformity of an omniscient, omnipotent *étatisme*. Orwell's Winston
Smith, like Zamiatin's D–503, is the last Adam, reenacting the myth of the
Fall, following his Eve into disobedience against God.

The topography of Oceania is well enough known that I need not
dwell on it: the telescreens, Big Brother's electronic eyes that are always
"watching you"; the phenomena of *newspeak* and *doublethink* and
blackwhite; the ubiquitous slogans proclaiming war to be peace and
freedom slavery. Nor need I stress the dystopian nature of Orwell's vision
of utopia at dead end, all its perverted values terroristically enforced by
the Ministry of Love.[21] What should be pointed out, however, is the
remarkably precise way in which Orwell has embodied, in the conditioned
hysteria of love for Big Brother, Freud's theory of eroticism displaced. In
the daily Two-Minute Hate (the Oceanic equivalent of prayer), the
telescreens project the image of Goldstein, the satan of this State, against
whom the increasingly frenzied faithful hurl their hatred. Then (Winston
recounts of one such Hate) "drawing a sigh of relief from everybody, the
hostile figure melted into the face of Big Brother . . . full of power and
mysterious calm, and so vast that it filled the screen. . . . The little sandy-
haired woman had flung herself over the chair in front of her. With a

tremendous murmur that sounded like 'My savior!' she extended her arms to the screen."[22] Julia, Winston's Eve, explains "the inner meaning of the Party's sexual puritanism."

> It was not merely that the sex instinct created a world of its own which was outside the Party's control and which therefore had to be destroyed if possible. What was more important was that sexual privation induced hysteria, which was desirable because it could be transformed into war fever and hero worship. The way she put it was:
> "When you make love you're using up energy; and afterwards you feel happy and don't give a damn for anyone. They can't bear you to feel like that. They want you to be bursting with energy all the time. All this marching up and down and cheering and waving flags is simply sex gone sour. If you're happy inside yourself, why should you get excited about Big Brother?" (pp. 110–11)

In order to ensure that the Oceanians *do* get excited about Big Brother—displace, that is, eroticism from its natural object, another individual, to the State—the Party attempts in every way "to remove all pleasure from the sex act. . . . The only recognized purpose of marriage was to beget children for the service of the Party. Sexual intercourse was to be looked on as a slightly disgusting operation, like having an enema" (p. 57). Thus the Party instigated organizations like the Junior Anti-Sex League, a sort of celibate Scouts, whose chastity, like that of medieval monks and nuns, demonstrated their superior love for and loyalty to their god. For the Party's ultimate aim, as the Inquisitorial figure O'Brien explains to Winston, is the total abolition of the sex instinct: "We shall abolish the orgasm. Our neurologists are at work upon it now. . . . There will be no love, except love for Big Brother" (p. 220). Even more clearly than in Zamiatin's United State, the rulers of Oceania have grasped the threat to utopianism posed by man's sexuality and are moving drastically to destroy or displace it.

As Adam in this perverted paradise, where the only love allowed is the love for Big Brother, Winston differs from D–503 and their biblical archetype in one important respect: even before he is tempted into erotic rebellion, he already hates the führer. In his furtively kept journal, he has written, over and over again, the phrase "DOWN WITH BIG BROTHER." Guilty though he is of *thoughtcrime* (Oceanians like Christians, are culpable not only for what they do but also for what they think), Winston falls into overt rebellion only when he falls in love. In this respect, the biblical myth and the novel's mythos are the same: it is an Eve who lures Adam to sin against God.

This sin—Julia and Winston's—consists essentially of an emotion. They have illicit rendezvous, they attempt to join the Brotherhood (the probably nonexistent underground resistance movement led by the probably nonexistent Goldstein), but their real lese majesty is simply being in love, giving free reign to their instinctual eroticism. Julia, Winston realizes, is thoroughly apolitical, "a rebel only from the waist down"; she falls asleep while he reads her Goldstein's banned exposé of Ingsoc, the philosophy of Oceanic *étatisme*. But because the whole duty of citizens is to love Big Brother, their love for one another is perforce politically subversive. "Their embrace had been a battle, their climax a victory. It was a blow struck against the Party. It was a political act" (p. 105). Thus when they are arrested by the Thought Police, it is not their lives but their love that must be extinguished.

Julia and Winston had all along known that they were doomed, would sooner or later be caught, yet they had held onto the belief that "they can't get inside you" and therefore that their love was inviolable, something beyond the power of even the State to destroy. O'Brien sets about to demonstrate to Winston that it is not. In the long, excruciating torture sessions that make up the last third of the book, O'Brien systematically undercuts and refutes every belief Winston held, beats and brainwashes away every trace of human dignity, until he is left with only one vestige of his humanity, his love for Julia.

> "Can you think of a single degradation that has not happened to you?"
> Winston had stopped weeping, though the tears were still in his eyes. He looked up at O'Brien.
> "I have not betrayed Julia," he said.
> O'Brien looked down at him thoughtfully. "No," he said, "no; that is perfectly true. You have not betrayed Julia." . . . Never did O'Brien fail to understand what was said to him. Anyone else on earth would have answered promptly that he *had* betrayed Julia. For what was there that they had not screwed out of him under torture? He had told them everything he knew about her, her habits, her character, her past life; he had confessed in the most trivial detail everything that had happened at their meetings, all that he had said to her and she to him . . . everything. And yet, in the sense in which he intended the word, he had not betrayed her. He had not stopped loving her; his feelings toward her had remained the same. O'Brien had seen what he meant without the need of explanation. (p. 225)

Winston hopes to be shot quickly, so that he will die still hating Big Brother, still loving Julia. But O'Brien understands this, too. It is not Winston's life he wants, but his soul, what is "inside him." Winston thus must be made to betray Julia, for only then can he be made to love Big Brother—must be emptied of one love to be filled with another. So he is taken to Room 101.

"The thing in Room 101," O'Brien explains, "is the worst thing in the world," each man's innermost fear. "In your case the worst thing in the world happens to be rats" (p. 223). The threat of having his face devoured by the squealing rats sends Winston into sheer panic, a panic that, as

O'Brien had said, was beyond courage or cowardice, beyond all rational choice.

> He suddenly understood that in the whole world there was just *one* person to whom he could transfer his punishment — *one* body that could be thrust between himself and the rats. And he was shouting frantically, over and over:
> "Do it to Julia! Do it to Julia! Not to me! Julia!" (p. 236)

As George Woodcock noted, each dystopian writer stresses "the particular aspects of the trends toward Utopia which seem to him most dangerous." For Zamiatin these were technological, for Orwell they were bureaucratic, "the fear of man's being turned into a mindless robot by predominantly political means."[23] Thus while D–503, technologically lobotomized, sits in contented approval as I–330 is put to death, Winston, psychologically terrorized by a brutally perfected totalitarianism, is reduced to an even more appalling fate: screaming for Julia's death to save his own life. They *have* gotten inside him and destroyed his love.

The State's total victory is made evident when, "rehabilitated" and released from prison, Winston encounters Julia again and feels toward her — as she toward him — only guilt-induced antipathy. This loss of love leaves Winston emptied of personality, malleable, defenseless against the State whose purpose, O'Brien had explained, was to tear the human mind to pieces and put it together in a shape of the State's own choosing. With Winston their success is complete:

> He gazed up at the enormous face. Forty years it had taken him to learn what kind of smile was hidden beneath the dark mustache. O cruel needless misunderstanding! O stubborn, self-willed exile from the loving breast! Two gin-scented tears trickled down the side of his nose. But it was all right, everything was all right, the struggle was finished. He had won the victory over himself. He loved Big Brother (p. 245).

During one of the torture sessions O'Brien had announced, "if you are a man, Winston, you are the last man. Your kind is extinct; we are the inheritors" (p. 222). Winston's, like D–503's, is man's last disobedience; there will be no more Adams and no more Eves in utopia.

Those more humanistically than theologically inclined have tended — perversely, no doubt — to see in Adam's fall something heroic. Despite scriptural intent, they admire in his refusal to forsake Eve, in his following her into disobedience against God, that spark of Promethean grandeur, that unyielding pride of the rebel. From a Freudian perspective, as we have seen, Adam's Fall embodies the eternal struggle of the instinctual against civilization (the "security" of paradise), of the individual against the fatherhood; in more explicitly political terms, the myth serves as symbol of the erotic rebel who puts love, and thus self, above the State. In this sense Aeneas, who deserts Dido at the gods' command to remember his duty to Rome, stands as Adam's antithesis, as the perfect *étatist* hero.

Given the archetypal nature of the myth of the Fall, it is hardly surprising that dystopian novelists should adapt it in terms of the new *étatist* theology, for it contains the essential elements of the conflict between the individual and utopia. Because the dystopian novel is necessarily futuristic (not so much prediction as warning), its redaction of the myth is Janus-like, facing backward and forward: the cast of characters is that of Genesis, the drama follows its accustomed course, yet the outcome is fundamentally different, a denouement possible only in the twentieth century. For only in the twentieth century has the possibility arisen that men could be made *incapable* of falling from some programmed paradise. Through conditioning or drugs, through physiological alteration or subliminal suggestion or technological coercion or sophisticated terrorism, or some combination of all of these, Adam's erotic rebellion could be rendered impossible. Man would be obedient to the State because he could not be otherwise.[24]

The history of our century lends credence to such fears. We have witnessed the rise of messianic regimes that pretend, in Hannah Arendt's words, "to have found a way to establish the rule of justice on earth," that essential promise of utopianism. The very phrasing of Miss Arendt's description of totalitarianism's goal — to impose on men "a band of iron which holds them so tightly together that it is as though their plurality had disappeared into One Man of gigantic proportions" — parallels that of the dystopian writers.[25] History reflects fiction, and vice versa. The critics who censure the dystopians for despairing of the resiliency of the human spirit, its innate will to freedom, have shown less understanding of the potentialities of totalitarian control than have those they criticize. As Miss Arendt has perceived, totalitarianism is an unprecedented phenomenon in human history, more frightening just because more *total* than any previous form of tyranny. Orwell understood the historically unique threat it posed:

> The terrifying thing about modern dictatorships is that they are something entirely unprecedented. Their end cannot be foreseen. In the past every tyranny was sooner or later overthrown, or at least resisted, because of "human nature," which as a matter of course desired liberty. But we cannot be at all certain that "human nature" is constant. It may be just as possible to produce a breed of men who do not wish for liberty as to produce a breed of hornless cows. The Inquisition failed, but then the Inquisition had not the resources of the modern state. The radio, press-censorship, standardized education and the secret police have altered everything. Mass-suggestion is a science of the last twenty years, and we do not know how successful it will be.[26]

The control techniques enumerated in this passage written in 1939 already seem to us primitive as oxcarts: the technology for tyranny is infinitely more sophisticated today. And tomorrow. . . ?

The dystopian novel, to warn against such a totalitarian tomorrow, posits the existence of utopia: a world where Eros is reserved for the State alone, where Adam will have no Eve, where Eden will be inescapable, where the Fall will be as unimaginable as freedom. Utopia's dawning will signal an end to man's disobedience, and paradise, alas, will be regained.

Notes

1. By "utopia" I should be understood to mean not every sort of escapist eudaemonia where a miraculously rewrought mankind lolls about in effortless contentment but only those imagined societies that offer a *systematic program* for reshaping man's nature and restructuring his social relationships. In other words, for an image of man remade to be legitimately utopian, an at least theoretically viable methodology for effecting this remaking must be explicit, whether a political methodology (as in Plato) or a psychological methodology (as in Skinner).

2. Sigmund Freud, *Civilization and Its Discontents*, in *The Standard Edition of the Complete Psychological Works of Sigmund Freud*, trans. James Strachey, XXI (London, 1961), 115. This work is the locus classicus of Freud's views on the individual's conflict with civilization, but also see *The Future of an Illusion*, also in the *Standard Edition*, XXI, 5–20, and the studies of two neo-Freudian social thinkers; Norman O. Brown, *Life Against Death: The Psychoanalytic Meaning of History* (Middleton, Conn., 1959), and Herbert Marcuse, *Eros and Civilization: A Philosophical Inquiry into Freud* (New York, 1962).

3. Lewis Mumford, "Utopia, the City and the Machine," *Daedalus*, 94 (1965), 258.

4. The best known of contemporary utopians, B. F. Skinner, would, of course, dismiss the idea that man has an innate nature. His mouthpiece in *Walden Two* (New York, 1962), says, for instance: "What do you say to the design of personalities? Would that interest you? The control of temperament? Give me the specifications, and I'll give you the man!" (p. 292). The assumption here—one common, implicitly or explicitly, to all utopians—is that the human personality is limitlessly plastic, to be molded to whatever shape society desires. Freud's emphasis on an innate, biological donnée, however, as Lionel Trilling has pointed out, "proposes to us that culture is not all-powerful. It suggests that there is a residue of human quality beyond the reach of culture to control"; *Beyond Culture* (New York, 1968), p. 113. For Skinner's own estimation of his differences with Freud, see his essay "Critique of Psychoanalytic Concepts and Theories," in *Science and Theory of Psychoanalysis*, ed. Irwin G. Sarason (Princeton, N.J., 1965), pp. 137–49.

5. Paul Tillich, *Dynamics of Faith* (New York, 1958), pp. 1–2. See also J. L. Talmon, *The Origins of Totalitarian Democracy* (New York, 1960), pp. 21–24 et passim.

6. See Martin Buber, *Paths in Utopia*, trans. R. F. C. Hull (Boston, 1958), pp. 7–9; and Judith Shklar, "Political Theory in Utopia," *Daedalus*, 94 (1965), 370.

7. No utopian society was more benevolently intended than that of Sir Thomas More, nor more rigorously democratic, yet even there the State directs all major and most minor aspects of its citizens' lives. For example: "Now you see how nowhere is there any license to waste time, nowhere any pretext to evade work—no wine shop, no alehouse, no brothel anywhere, no opportunity for corruption, no lurking hole, no secret meeting place. On the contrary, *being under the eyes of all*, people are bound either to be performing the usual labor or to be enjoying their leisure in a fashion not without decency"; *Utopia*, trans. Edward Surtz, S.J. (New Haven, Conn., 1964), pp. 82–83 (my italics). "Under the eyes of all" foreshadows the Guardians and glass houses of *We* and the telescreens and "Big Brother is watching you" slogan of *1984*.

8. Mumford, "Utopia, the City and the Machine," p. 277.

9. On the factors giving rise to dystopianism, see George Woodcock, "Utopias in Negative," *Sewanee Review*, 64 (1956), 81–97; and Irving Howe, "The Fiction of Anti-Utopia," *The Decline of the New* (New York, 1970), pp. 66–71.

10. Sigmund Freud, *Group Psychology and the Analysis of the Ego*, also in the *Standard Edition*, XVIII (1955), 127.

11. Philip Rieff, *Freud: The Mind of the Moralist* (Garden City, N.Y., 1961), p. 257.

12. Freud, *Civilization and Its Discontents*, p. 96. See also Paul Roazen, *Freud: Political and Social Thought* (New York, 1970), p. 159; "Freud thought deep within man there was an unbreakable nucleus, a central portion of the self ineluctably in opposition to society. Freud once wrote that 'for most people there is a limit beyond which their constitution cannot comply with the demands of civilization.' In that sense, 'every individual is virtually an enemy of civilization.' "

13. Arthur Koestler, *Darkness at Noon*, trans. Daphne Hardy (New York, 1970), p. 208. This point is made *ad nauseam* in Ayn Rand's execrably written but mercifully brief dystopian fiction, *Anthem*.

14. Freud, *Civilization and Its Discontents*, p. 105.

15. Freud, *Group Psychology and the Analysis of the Ego*, pp. 140–41 (see note 10 above). For Plato's parallel view on this matter, see A. E. Taylor, *Plato: The Man and His Works* (New York, 1956), p. 278.

16. Eugene Zamiatan, *We*, trans. Gregory Zilboorg (New York, 1959), p. 17. Page references are hereafter cited in the text.

17. Christopher Collins, "Zamiatin, Wells, and the Utopian Literary Tradition," *Slavonic and East European Review*, 44 (1966), 358.

18. The sentiment, language, and metaphor here and elsewhere clearly echo Dostoevsky's Underground Man. See Robert L. Jackson, *Dostoevsky's Underground Man in Russian Literature* (The Hague, 1958), pp. 150–57.

19. Eugene Zamiatin, quoted by Alex M. Shane, *The Life and Works of Evgenij Zamjatin* (Berkeley and Los Angeles, 1968), p. 142.

20. Christopher Hollis, *A Study of George Orwell* (London, 1956), p. 199. For the most instructive discussions of Orwell's debt to Zamiatin, and their differences, see Woodcock, "Utopias in Negative" (note 9 above); Isaac Deutscher, "*1984* – The Mysticism of Cruelty," *Heretics and Renegades* (London, 1955), pp. 35–50; and Jürgen Rühle, *Literature and Revolution*, trans. Jean Steinberg (New York, 1969), pp. 38–40. Orwell himself wrote an appreciative review of *We* in his column in the *Tribune* (London), 4 January 1946.

21. George Kateb in *Utopia and its Enemies* (New York, 1963), pp. 235–36, argues that Oceania ought not to be considered even a negative utopia, for O'Brien "describes the political system of *1984* as '. . . the exact opposite of the hedonistic utopias that old reformers imagined.' " Kateb has a point, but it is rather strained and overly formalistic. Orwell's vision of the future is clearly intended to show utopian messianism gone sour, reflecting the historical reality of our century. Consider the reflection of Koestler's Rubashov: "Nobody foresaw the new mass movements, the great political landslides, nor the twisted roads, the bewildering stages which the Revolutionary State was to go through; at that time one believed that the gates of Utopia stood open, and that mankind stood on its threshold" (p. 106). For an excellent account of the dashing of these bright hopes, see Sir Isaiah Berlin's essay, "Political Ideas in the Twentieth Century," *Four Essays on Liberty* (New York, 1969), pp. 1–40.

22. George Orwell, *1984* (New York, New American Library, n.d.) p. 17. Page references are hereafter cited in the text.

23. Woodcock, "Utopias in Negative," pp. 91–92.

24. The evidence for this contention may never be deemed conclusive by skeptics, yet that a wide variety of control techniques is being perfected is indisputable: there are, for example, José Delgado's experiments with cerebral electrodes, Georges Unger's isolation and

chemical duplication of a "memory molecule," the behavior-modifying drugs already administered to "problem" children (to 5 to 10 percent of Washington's school population, for instance), and so on. See also Aldous Huxley, *Brave New World Revisited* (New York, 1965); Seymour Farber and Roger Wilson, eds., *Control of the Mind* (New York, 1961); and Perry London, *Behavior Control* (New York, 1971).

25. Hannah Arendt, *The Origins of Totalitarianism* (Cleveland and New York, 1958), pp. 465–66.

26. George Orwell, *The Collected Essays, Journalism, and Letters of George Orwell*, vol. I, *An Age Like This* (New York, 1968), pp. 380–81.

The Death of Big Sister: Orwell's Tragic Message
Joan Weatherly*

Both his defenders and his detractors have noted Orwell's concern in *1984* with the loss of history and humanism in a totalitarian state.[1] Too little attention has been paid, however, to his concern with the attendant loss of art, a concern placing him in the mainstream of English and European letters.[2] The depth of Orwell's feeling for Western tradition and of his understanding of its relationship to tragedy is reflected in his contrast (1941) between the generation of Wells, which lacked awareness beyond "the contemporary English scene," and the generation of Eliot and Joyce, which rediscovered Europe: "They broke the cultural circle in which England had existed for something like a century. They reestablished contact with Europe, and they brought back the sense of history and the possibility of tragedy. On that basis all subsequent English literature that matters twopence has rested, and the development that Eliot and the others started, back in the closing years of the last war, has not yet run its course."[3] The depth of his understanding linguistic and psycholinguistic bases of poetic language is apparent throughout Orwell's work, most obviously perhaps in the 1940 essay "New Words," in which he emphasizes the importance of shared associations for words, the function of imaginative writing, and the difficulty of verbally expressing inner life, especially dreams: "And even if a psychologist interprets your dream in terms of 'symbols,' he is still going largely by guesswork; for the *real* quality of the dream is outside the world of words."[4]

Failure to consider fully Orwell's aesthetic interest — particularly in tragedy and in its descendant modern Jungian psychology — has led to two distracting misconceptions about *1984*: defenders such as Irving Howe and Philip Rahv read it primarily as a political message, only secondarily if at all, a work of art, and more recently Daphne Patai has viewed the final despair of the novel as a reflection of Orwell's own unconscious misogyny.[5] Surely Oceania is dominated by masculinity — precisely Orwell's point,

*Reprinted with permission from *College Literature* 11 (1984):22–33.

else why would he name its tyrant Big Brother and take such pains to dramatize Winston Smith's (and Oceania's) loss of the redeeming feminine archetype associated with tragedy since its Dionysian beginnings; but this is not to say that Orwell himself is a misogynist. Through the relationship in *1984* between history, humanism, and tragic art, Orwell explores the same artistic problems treated by Eliot in "Tradition and the Individual Talent" and by Jung in *Modern Man in Search of a Soul*, but in a post Waste Land where tradition has been annihilated, leaving no fragment of the voice of Tiresias to shore against ruin. This post-Nietzschean world goes so far beyond good and evil (or Yeats' substitute for the classical tragic vision, or existentialism) that the very antinomies needed for becoming, for embracing nothingness, are vanishing with Oldspeak.[6] Hamlet's and Hieronoymo's feigned madness and Crazy Jane's wisdom are impossible for "double-thinkers" and would, in any case, be lost on an audience that laughs at tragedy. Just as Orwell saw that new words must have old, meaningful associations, so Jung saw that meaning depends on memory to connect past and present: "Today" has meaning only if it stands between "yesterday" and "tomorrow." It is "a process of transition" that forms the link "between past and future."[7]

Irving Howe's claim that literature was "the last thing Orwell cared about" as he composed *1984*, was, of course, directed at early critics who failed to see the organic relationship in the novel among political message, flatness of plot and language, and tone of despair.[8] C. E. Jung's theory of archetypes provides one means of approaching this crucial relationship in the novel between the love story and its language and the resulting tone of its tragic message: through Winston's quest for knowledge, Orwell portrays the plight of the artist as "the last man," a tragedian with no opposites to reconcile and with an official language which by forbidding metaphorical union between concrete and abstract images — as it denies joyful sexual union — obliterates all the traditional symbolic meaning by which Jung says man must live.[9] Winston's fragmentary manuscript and Orwell's complex ending, which includes the Newspeak Appendix, both reflect the entropy resulting when the "reconciliation of opposite and discordant qualities," demanded of tragedy by I. A. Richards and by Nietzsche, is absent.[10] Just as Newspeak denies the possibility of creating a new image from the harmonizing comparison of unlikes, the prohibition of art denies the possibility of catharsis or of Dionysian-Apollonian union; and Marx's dialectical materialism, which hoped for proletarian synthesis, is called into question in terms of Jung's law of psychic compensation which, like classical tragedy, demands balancing of discordant elements.[11]

Using INGSOC as a symbol for totalitarianism and Newspeak as a symbol for INGSOC's totally concrete official language, Orwell dramatizes in *1984* the conquest of Winston's self by Big Brother (his animus) over Big Sister (his anima) through the betrayal of O'Brien (his shadow, which on the deeper archetypal level is inseparable from his animus).[12] On the communal surface level of Oceania, INGSOC and Newspeak (rational and animus-dominated) hold supremacy over old Western Europe and Oldspeak, the great sleeping anima-oriented collective unconscious, comprised mainly of the proles. Patai is exactly right in saying that Winston stands "halfway between the powerless personal feminine and the powerful impersonal masculine."[13] Like John Fowles, whose 1964 words *1984* had already dramatized, Orwell understood that poetry is always "more a nation's anima, its particular mystery, its adytum, than any of the [other] arts."[14] Poetry—all literary art—may be mechanically produced in Oceania, but the persistence of anima shines through in the prole songs, in Ampleforth's rhymes, and in Winston's manuscript. Although he at first comes very near murdering Julia, an embodiment of his anima, Winston Smith, "the last man," still possesses enough vague memory of a feminine archetype to achieve temporary reconciliation of his personal opposites. The animus-dominated state wins over individuals, but Big Brother's victory is complete only when Winston at last submerges the healthy anima archetype of his laughing mother, the creative emotional image in whose quest his art had originated. What O'Brien says of Winston as "last" applies not only to Winston, but also to humanism, to Oldspeak, and to art: "Winston you are the last man. Your kind is extinct; we are the inheritors," and "You are outside history, you are non-existent" (p. 222). To be the "last man" is to be at once the last humanist and the last human being with some sense of the anima and the racial unconscious, the last man with enough memory of Oldspeak—not mere language, but *culture* in its broadest sense—to create, albeit in broken Newspeak, consciousness out of his submerged self.

The reader's terrible knowledge of the extinction of the diary, the record of Winston's quest for self-knowledge, is relieved only by the paradox of art (the contradiction doublethink both uses and says is nonexistent): we *have read* the diary and we still know something of Oldspeak and its language. Like Winston we know *"how"* and, in addition, on the eve of 1984, we have still enough Oldspeak to imagine *"why"* (pp. 179, 215). But "why" is figurative and impossible in doublethink's materialistic dialectic which denies the meaning (spirit) represented by the word (logos); it is O'Brien, the embodiment of the negative shadow archetype, who convinces Smith that "two and two makes five" and that his questioning of "the underlying motives" of society had led him to doubt his "own sanity" (pp. 215, 239).

In reality, it had been those questionings which restored his personal health, and as O'Brien knows, Winston is dangerous to the state because he might well become what Jung calls the voice of his age. He might very well call up "the spirits of his ancestors," the anima archetype in which his "age is most lacking," and be ready to transmute "personal destiny into the destiny of mankind." Jung's description of this awakened artist "who seizes" on the image his age needs and raises it from deepest unconsciousness "into relation with conscious values" fits Winston Smith (and Orwell) exactly. According to Jung—

> The normal can follow the general trend without injury to himself; but the man who takes to the back streets and alleys because he cannot endure the broad highway will be the first to discover the psychic elements that are waiting to play their part in the life of the collective. Here the artist's relative lack of adaptation turns out to his advantage; it enables him to follow his own yearnings far from the beaten path, and to discover what it is that would meet the unconscious needs of his age. Thus, just as the one-sidedness of the individual's conscious attitude is corrected by reactions from the unconscious, so art represents a process of self-regulation in the life of nations and epochs.[15]

Through the story of his artist figure, Orwell himself fulfills the function of both the historian and the poet as defined by Aristotle: he tells us "what has happened" and "what may happen" through the tragedy of Winston Smith, who is duped by his negative shadow.[16]

The significance of the loss of memory—Mnemosyne was the mother of the muses and an ancestor of Jung's collective unconscious—as well as history and tragedy is clarified as Winston begins his forbidden diary on "antique" paper purchased "in just what quarter he did not now remember," using an "archaic" pen (p. 9). Writing suddenly "in sheer panic, only imperfectly aware of what he was setting down" for April 4, 1984, he gives a historical account of the war films he had seen the previous evening and a slightly more subjective account of the audience's callous reaction to the tragedies (p. 11). Sensing his isolation and unconsciously evoking the words of Arnold before the Grand Chartreuse, Winston declares that "The past was dead, the future unimaginable" (p. 25). Triggered by the archetypal image of the woman protecting a child in the war movie and by his attempt to imagine an audience for his diary, his anima is aroused and he dreams of his mother, with whom he associates this same protective gesture. Gesture, which both Orwell and Jung found helpful for communicating inner thoughts and dreams, is used here, as Aristotle said it could be, to call forth "recognition" in "a train of memory."[17] Winston is suddenly struck by the feeling that his mother's "death, nearly thirty years ago, had been tragic and sorrowful in a way that was no longer possible":

> Tragedy, he perceived, belonged to the ancient time, to a time when there was still privacy, love, and friendship, and when the members of a family stood by one another without needing to know the reason. His mother's memory tore at his heart because she had died loving him, when he was too young and selfish to love her in return, and because somehow, he did not remember how, she had sacrificed herself to a conception of loyalty that was private and unalterable. (p. 28)

Looking into the eyes of his mother and sister (the sister often accompanies mother in the anima archetype), he saw that "such things . . . could not happen today." "Today there were fear, hatred, pain but no dignity of emotion, or deep or complex sorrows" (pp. 28–29).

As he begins to write "for the unborn," "the magnitude of what he had undertaken came home to him," the "impossibility" of communicating with the future: "Either the future would resemble the present, in which case it would not listen to him, or it would be different from it, and the predicament would be meaningless" (p. 10). Thinking—like an orthodox existentialist—that "nothing was your own except the few cubic centimeters inside your skull" and taking refuge in the very acts of buying paper, pen, and of writing, Winston "wondered again for whom he was writing the diary."

> For the future, for the past—for an age that might be imaginery. And in front of him there lay not death but annihilation. The diary would be reduced to ashes and himself to vapor. Only the Thought Police would read what he had written, before they wiped it out of existence and out of memory. How could you make appeal to the future when not a trace of you, not even an anonymous word scribbled on a piece of paper could physically survive? (p. 26)

"The chiming of the hour" puts "new heart" into Winston as he becomes the voice of his age conjuring up the forms in which the age was most lacking. Sheer urgency forces him to act, to write his "truth" in the face of annihilation in order to maintain his sanity: "He was a lonely ghost uttering a truth that nobody would ever hear. But so long as he uttered it, in some obscure way the continuity was not broken. It was not by making yourself heard but by staying sane that you carried on the human heritage" (p. 26). For Smith, as for Orwell and Jung—and Arnold and Eliot—the individual's artist's main responsibility is to preserve humanism, to maintain the connection with the past by preserving the truth of the moment, however fragmentary, for the future. In the clarity of the moment, Winston, albeit unconsciously, reverts entirely to the heresy of Oldspeak: "To the future or to the past, to a time when thought is free, when men are different from one another and do not live alone—to a time when truth exists and what is done cannot be undone. From the age of uniformity, from the age of solitude, from the age of Big Brother, from the age of doublethink—greetings!" (pp. 26–27).

The "last man" becomes the last "becomer" in the Nietzschean sense, as "only now," through the "decisive step" of his art "he had begun to be able to formulate his thoughts." He embraces the knowledge that "the consequences of every act are included in the act itself" and writes, "Thoughtcrime does not entail death: thoughtcrime IS death" (p. 27). The sanity or psychological health which Winston temporarily gains through his art is paradoxically reflected in his recognition that having become a "dead man," he must now "stay alive as long as possible" (p. 27). As "the last man," the last "human" adrift in a world where "truth" is altered in a split second, where Memory, the mother of the muses is forgotten, and where her daughters are manipulated by godless machines, Winston has no assurance that there is any connection between himself and his contemporaries, much less between himself and the past, and even less between himself and the future. But he looks for balance within as a means of reconciling his inner and outer worlds. At least for the moment, the private vision saves him, and there is enough trace of his Oldspeak — his collective unconscious, culture, tragedy, tradition, and language — for one last restatement of historical significance. But the ultimate aim of humanism is communication and Winston Smith's fatal error is being duped by O'Brien's seeming humanism — the essence of his function as shadow archetype — into sharing with him his most rebellious ideas. Winston's perplexing admission that he had always known O'Brien (p. 197), a crucial point in Patai's reading of the novel as a male-dominated game, might also reflect O'Brien's function as shadow archetype: certainly he is in some ways a mirror character for Winston, whom the latter in his delusion takes as an embodiment of all the good of which he himself is capable. Like the Jungian shadow, O'Brien is the embodiment of a moral problem and lies closer to the surface than the animus Big Brother with whom he is associated. Few of his own examples fit Jung's description of this negative, destructive archetype so well as O'Brien does.

Through his "art," reporting in Newspeak the movie image of the Jewess protecting the child, Winston recovers from his unconscious self the embedded anima image of his mother holding his sister and subsequently that of the dream "girl with dark hair" who emerges at last as Julia. This tripartite image of Jewess, mother-sister, and Julia merges with the prole anima figures, the prostitute who becomes beautiful after lovemaking and the finally beautiful, red-armed washerwoman who is inseparable from her song. The latter's song provides the clearest example in the novel of Winston's belief that the proles — the collective unconscious — still retain some vestige of the ancient meaning of suffering as, moving to and fro in the courtyard, not unlike some figure from Greek tragedy and surely like Jung's anima archetype, the working woman sings:

> They sye that time 'eals all things,
> They sye you can always forget;
> But the smiles an' the tears across the years
> They twist my 'eartstrings yet!
>
> (p. 180)

The ancient feminine principle associated with Dionysus and tragic art is not utterly dead in the animus-oriented world of Big Brother, so long as there is such a song, or the image of Rutherford's two great tears remains extant, or even such lesser human aspects as the smell of real coffee, or the old capitalist's memory of good beer. But memory must, as Jung, Eliot and Orwell knew, be mixed with desire (or in the linguistic realm, the concrete

image with the abstract image to get meaning), and desire for reconciliation has completely failed Winston and Julia — who could have, at least,
made love right in the park had they so desired. Thus Oldspeak goes for
naught.

Winston's mother, the most difficult of the anima images for him to
remember *and* to forget, sits, like Jung's anima figure, or Nietzsche's
spring of joy, or the wells of Greek tragedy, some place "deep beneath
him" and moves ever "downwards" (p. 28). Watching his mother and sister
sinking into the "green waters," Winston strains to know "why" they *know*
that they must die so that "he might remain alive"; all of the self-
knowledge that he gains in attempting to discover "why" stems from his
memory of this gesture of his mother. Then "suddenly," as when Winston
first begins writing, "the girl with dark hair" comes toward him across the
"Golden Country" where his mother's sacrifice had left him (p. 29). The
girl's relationship to the other women, the anima principle associated with
Dionysus himself and with tragedy, is revealed through "the gesture with
which she had thrown her clothes aside." "What overwhelmed him" was
not her beautiful body, which "aroused no desire in him"; instead "what
overwhelmed him in that instant was admiration for the gesture," which
"with its grace and carelessness . . . seemed to annihilate a whole culture,
a whole system of thought." It was "as though Big Brother and the Party
and the Thought Police could all be swept into nothingness by a single
splendid movement of the arm" (p. 29). This, like the movements of the
dying Jewess and of his mother, is a "gesture belonging to the ancient time"
and foreshadows Julia's flinging off her Junior Anti-Sex League sash before
they make love the first time. As if to drive home the point that in tragic
recognition lies liberation, Orwell has Winston awaken from his dream
with the word *Shakespeare* "on his lips," as close as any Oceanian will ever
get to the juice of Dionysus. In worshipful awe, Winston kneels before
Julia (who incidentally is herself quite a "satirical" tragedian and a living
testament to anima power) after she has undressed and "flung" aside her
clothes "with that same magnificent gesture by which a whole civilization
seemed to be annihilated" (p. 104). Julia's unashamed admission that she
has been with many men is perhaps another clue that she is woman-in-
general as well as woman-particular, or an anima image, not unlike Young
Goodman Brown's Faith — the anima is indeed "with" all men. At the
moment of their arrest, Winston through Julia has achieved a perfect
balance: his health is better and he embraces the slumbering collective
unconscious of the age as he finds the washerwoman now beautiful (p.
180). Just now Winston could emerge as a redeeming voice for Oceania,
but he deserts his newly found energizing anima and submits to the
spiritual entropy of the age by loving its animus — his and O'Brien's like —
Big Brother.

The ultimate terror of *1984* is not that Winston Smith is the last
humanist who, after bringing his personal anima to consciousness, will

ponder the question of bringing the proles to consciousness of their power: nor is it the failure of love, nor the fact that the Thought Police can penetrate the very mystery of "the human heart," making arrival at an ironically inverted state of agape through betrayal of eros and philos (or *logos* in Jung's terms) seem "victory" over self (p. 138). Nor is it the tragedy of the death of tragedy which in a sense—it will be remembered that Hitler loved Nietzsche—made the world of *1984* possible. The most terrible revelation for a 1984 audience is the speed with which the Party has perverted the humanistic tradition to its advantage: O'Brien is an "intellectual," a Machiavellian master of irony who skillfully manipulates masks, pitilessly evoking fear to effect an ironic catharsis which leaves fear submerged, and not truth but absolute falsehood in control with hate masquerading as love (pp. 144, 146). As Eric Fromm points out, an "important point in Orwell's discussion is closely related to 'doublethink,' namely that in a successful manipulation of the mind the person is no longer saying the opposite of what he thinks, but he thinks the opposite of what is true" and thus "he feels free because there is no longer any awareness of the discrepancy between truth and falsehood."[18] His mind completely absorbed by matter, Winston is left without even the possibility for Nietzschean salvation through embracing Zoroastrian dualism, for the latter, too, depends on linguistic dialectic—the play between abstract and concrete. *1984* ends as if Iago has been unmasked and put in power, or Erasmus really loves folly, or Swift eats babies, or, perhaps, worst of all, Thebes is left totally uncleansed without ever knowing itself dirty. The literality of Newspeak has absorbed all of the Oldspeak "figures." To betray Julia—and to be betrayed by her—and then to love Big Brother is to deny the anima with all her tragic, saving gestures, poetry (truth and beauty), and the animating life forces embodied in the washerwoman's song and Mrs. Smith's healthy laughter—all the liberating joy of his submerged anima that Winston as the last humanist, the one transitional New-Old Speaker, should and could have shared with humankind.

But it is the catharsis of the audience, not of the character—the error of some of Nietzsche's followers—that most interests Orwell. Still, there is a sense in which 1983 provides the catastasis for *1984* and in which all people living in 1984 will be characters. The only possible relief this spectacle provides for our fear—Aristotle would say Smith arouses our fear because he is like us and our pity because he is a victim—is that pity is still extant and that Oldspeak may not be entirely abolished until the year 2050, or that we will effect in Jungian terms the restoration of a balance between anima and animus, between the discordant elements of the communal collective unconscious, through balance of our individual consciousnesses.[19] We pity Winston precisely because the classical Aristotelian meaning of pity has degenerated into "pity for his own ruined body," but only because we still *know* how Aristotle used the term. Likewise we *know* that the dispelling of hubris is as ironic as his cure (224). But we pity him more because he cannot know the "why" of his archetypal self and his society, matters he (and we) could ponder without Aristotle's help, but not at all without symbolic language and less well without Jung's help. Anyone who doubts that 1984 is a novel should apply Aristotle's distinction between history (which tells what has happened) and poetry (which tells us what may happen, and which is used herein to mean all imaginative literature). Orwell is surely both historian and poet, particularly the latter as 1984 becomes *1984*. What Orwell chronicles dramatically for us is not the failure of tragedy and her modern children, analytical psychology and existentialism, but their brilliant success in the hands of the dictator, the very success which renders them feckless for humanism in a *total* totalitarian state. The human spirit does survive in the most battered of the human species (Winston and to a lesser degree Julia were "hard" cases) and the human archetypes are nearly indestructible (Winston's anima hangs on for a whole month after the brainwashing). But the final discovery here is that it can be perverted by the "mental" training of the overblown animus through "*crimestop, black-white,* and *doublethink,*" which make one "unwilling and unable to think too deeply on any subject whatever" (p. 147). On every count — linguistic or psychological — Jung's law of psychic compensation holds: "No psychic value can disappear without being replaced by another of equivalent intensity."[20]

Unlike his totally defeated character, George Orwell does become the voice of his age, supplying a link between classical humanism and modern Jungian psychology and also between Matthew Arnold's restatement of classical humanism and John Fowles' tragic existentialism. With Yeats, Orwell laments the "death" of tragedy, but unlike Yeats he sees that even the center of a private vision will not hold when Big Brother takes over in Bethlehem. With Eliot he sees perfectly the relationship between tradition and the individual talent, but unlike Eliot he envisions the annihilation of history itself and hence art, in a world where language denies the use of analogy much less an objective correlative. With Fowles he restates the value of classical tragedy for sanity in an absurd world where hazard is our boon companion, and where even the text faces annihilation. Surely 1984 is a literary work of the highest order — a tragedy meeting many of Aristotle's standards, and reflecting Orwell's own sense of tragedy as defined in "Lear, Tolstoy and the Fool." "A tragic situation exists precisely when virtue does *not* triumph but when it is still felt that man is nobler than the forces which destroy him."[21] The desperate intensity so often noted in connection with 1984 reflects the fact that its author was an artist able to find, in Jung's words, a way to express the primordial images of his age: "The moment when this mythological situation reappears is always characterized by a peculiar emotional intensity; it is as though chords in us were struck that had never resounded before, or as though forces whose existence we never suspected were unloosed. . . . At such moments we are no longer individuals, but the race; the voice of all mankind resounds in us."[22]

Notes

1. Irving Howe, *Politics and the Novel* (New York: Horizon Press, 1957), p. 239. See also Erich Fromm, Afterword, *1984* by George Orwell (1949; rpt. New York: New American Library, 1981), pp. 258, 266–267.

2. From the time Eric Blair took the pen name Orwell (which was perhaps suggested to him by the pleasure Chaucer's Merchant took in the trade connection between the continent and the mouth of the Orwell at Orwelle Haven) until the last days of his life when, in preparing notes for a biography of Joseph Conrad, he complimented the Pole on his European perspective, he never lost sight of the crucial relationship between Britain and the continent. See George Orwell, *The Collected Essays, Journalism and Letters of George Orwell*, ed. Sonia Orwell and Ian Angus (New York: Harcourt, Brace and World, 1968), IV, 489.

3. George Orwell, "The Rediscovery of Europe," in *The Collected Essays, Journalism and Letters of George Orwell*, ed. Sonia Orwell and Ian Angus (New York: Harcourt, Brace and World, 1968) II, 206–207.

4. George Orwell, "New Words," in *The Collected Essays, Journalism and Letters of George Orwell*, ed. Sonia Orwell and Ian Angus (New York: Harcourt, Brace and World, 1968), II, 3–4, 5, 9.

5. Howe, p. 237; Philip Rahv, "The Unfuture of Utopia," *Partisan Review*, 16 (1949), 7; and Daphne Patai, "Gamesmanship and Androcentrism in Orwell's *1984*," PMLA, 97 (1982), esp. 866–69. See Richard I. Smyer, *Primal Dream and Primal Crime: Orwell's Development as a Psychological Novelist* (Columbia: University of Missouri Press, 1979), for an interesting Freudian reading of Orwell; see pp. 176–182 for an excellent Bibliography. Richard Rees, *George Orwell: Fugitive from the Camp of Victory* (London: Secker and Warburg, 1961), p. 8, has no recollection of his friend Orwell's mentioning Freud or Jung. There are several references to Freud in Orwell's writings and Bernard Crick, *George Orwell: A Life* (Boston: Little, Brown, 1980), p. 168, reports that Rosalind Obermeyer — the friend and landlady who first introduced George Orwell to his future wife Eileen O'Shaughnessy (who was then completing graduate work in psychology) — was "a psychologist of Jungian persuasion." Aside from these intimate connections with several psychologists, there are striking parallels between Orwell's and Jung's common concerns with the World Community of Modern Man — not to mention such uncanny examples of synchronicity, if nothing else, as their common usage of smelly sinks to depict the plight of Modern Man. Jung's works were available in English translation from 1922 onward and the striking similarities between Orwell and Jung begin appearing years before Orwell met O'Shaughnessy.

6. See Morse Peckham, *Beyond the Tragic Vision* (New York: George Braziller, 1962), esp. 364–372, for excellent discussion of Nietzsche's view of tragedy; and Friedrich Nietzsche, *The Birth of Tragedy and the Case of Wagner*, trans. Walter Kaufman (1886; rpt. New York: Vintage, 1967), esp. pp. 38–81, for Nietzsche's discussion of the reconciliation of Dionysian and Apollonian in tragedy.

7. C. G. Jung. *Modern Man in Search of a Soul*, trans. W. S. Dell and Cary F. Baynes (1934; rpt. New York: Harcourt Brace, 1934), p. 228.

8. Howe, p. 237.

9. C. G. Jung, *The Archetypes and the Collective Unconscious*, trans. R. F. C. Hull (1936; rpt. Princeton, N.J.: Princeton University Press, 1959), esp. pp. 7, 46–49, 64–66; George Orwell, *1984*, (1949; rpt. New York: New American Library, 1981), p. 222. Cited

parenthetically by page number in remainder of text. Orwell had originally planned to call the novel *The Last Man in Europe*.

10. I. A. Richards, *Principles of Literary Criticism* (New York: Harcourt Brace and World, 1925), pp. 245–46.

11. Jung, *Modern Man in Search of a Soul*, p. 241.

12. For an excellent introduction to Jung's concept of archetypes, see Joseph Campbell, Introd., *The Portable Jung*, by C. G. Jung (1971; rpt. New York; Penguin, 1982), pp. xxi–xxxii. See also "Aion: Phenomenology of the Self," pp. 139–162.

13. Patai, p. 866.

14. John Fowles, *The Aristos* (1964; rpt. New York: Plume, 1970), p. 210.

15. C. G. Jung, "On the Relation of Analytical Psychology to Poetry," in *The Portable Jung*, ed. Joseph Campbell, pp. 321–322.

16. Aristotle, *Poetics*, trans. S. H. Butcher (1895; rpt. Great Books Foundation, 1956), Section IX, p. 13.

17. Ibid., Sections XVI and XVII, pp. 24–25. Orwell, "New Words," pp. 5, 11.

18. Fromm, p. 265.

19. Aristotle, Section XIII, pp. 17–18.

20. C. G. Jung, *Modern Man in Search of a Soul*, p. 242.

21. George Orwell, "Lear, Tolstoy and the Fool," *The Collected Essays, Journalism and Letters of George Orwell*, ed Sonia Orwell and Ian Angus (New York: Harcourt, Brace and World, 1968), IV, p. 293.

22. Jung, "On the Relation of Analytical Psychology to Poetry," in *The Portable Jung*, ed. Joseph Campbell, p. 320.

Contradictions

Antinomies of *Nineteen Eighty-Four*

Carl Freedman*

On 31 May 1947, in a letter to his publisher, George Orwell described the book he was working on as "a novel about the future—that is, it is in a sense a fantasy, but in the form of a naturalistic novel." He added: "That is what makes it a difficult job—of course as a book of anticipations it would be comparatively simple to write."[1] On 16 June 1949, only a few days after the publication of *Nineteen Eighty-Four*, he wrote to a representative of the United Auto Workers to explain that the book was intended neither as an attack on socialism nor as a prediction of the future. He also noted, however, that he believed something resembling the society described in *Nineteen Eighty-Four* could arrive—"allowing of course for the fact that the book is a satire" (*CEJL*, IV, 502).

These few comments contain, I think, the clues essential in understanding Orwell's last and most celebrated work. What his remarks point to is the clash and combination of genres within the book. On the one

*Reprinted with permission from *Modern Fiction Studies* 30 (1984):601–20, © Purdue Research Foundation.

hand, there is the loose-jointed, empiricist, Wellsian naturalism. This is the aspect of *Nineteen Eighty-Four* that deals in great particularity of detail with objects and relations of the "real" world and that recalls the author of *A Clergyman's Daughter* and the early work generally. On the other hand, there is the totally controlled, programmatic, Swiftian satire, where complete coherence is achieved through an intricate and thoroughly fantastic two-dimensionality. Here, plainly, is the author of *Animal Farm*. If *Nineteen Eighty-Four* may be said to represent the culmination of Orwell's literary career, this is above all true in a generic sense.[2] Yet this culmination is profoundly fissured. The attempt to combine two such antithetical genres, though handled with real technical skill ("That is what makes it a difficult job . . ."), throws the book into severe contradiction with itself. It is a dialectical contradiction, for the two main generic aspects thoroughly interpenetrate one another, and, indeed, the naturalism ultimately depends on, or by dialectical reversal turns into, the programmatic satire. Furthermore, it is in this contradiction that the primary ideological significance of the book lies. As I will argue, the dialectic of genres formally registers the two main ideological contradictions of *Nineteen Eighty-Four*. Philosophically, the contradiction is between common-sense empiricism — the typical Orwellian stance — and its antithesis, which Isaac Deutscher has usefully named "the mysticism of cruelty," a sort of terrified and terrifying irrationalism. Politically, the contradiction is between the usual Orwellian radicalism and something that may be called quietest despair, a metaphysical resignation from politics and the social field.

That Orwell's attraction toward quietism — growing in strength in his essays written during the later years of the Second World War and almost dominant in *Animal Farm* — should emerge with such unprecedented strength in *Nineteen Eighty-Four* may in a loose way be correlated with the facts of contemporary history that most imposed themselves upon Orwell's consciousness. With Catalonia and the failed Spanish revolution far behind him, his remaining radical and socialist hopes were identified with certain aspects of the rough-and-ready, empiricist reformism of the British Labour Party, then in power. But Britain itself seemed a weak reed in the face of the total demands of the two superpowers, whose growing hegemony filled Orwell with horror (though his horror was greater at the Soviet Union than at the United States). This point about the international situation ought not, however, to be pressed in a deterministic way. The primary point is the intensity of the ideological contradictions within *Nineteen Eighty-Four* as registered generically.[3]

Admittedly, on the surface *Nineteen Eighty-Four* does not *appear* contradictory. On the contrary, it is (with *Animal Farm*, which seems to me minor in comparison) clearly Orwell's most "well-made" production. It possesses the most complex and coherent plot and the most vivid and "life-like" protagonist of all of Orwell's novels. The tour-de-force of the book, however, lies in its completely significant handling of detail. Nearly every particular is meaningful within the framework of the novel as a whole: sometimes atmospherically (as with the "vile wind" and "swirl of gritty dust" in the opening paragraph),[4] sometimes symbolically (as with the beautiful glass paperweight — a symbol of illusory freedom and disinterestedness — which Winston Smith admires), but above all, in the creation of a paranoia-inducing totalitarian world in which every detail demands interpretation. The universally acknowledged power of *Nineteen Eighty-Four* derives largely from Orwell's achievement in conveying a fictional universe where characters and readers alike must worry constantly over the significance of every particular. By this method the peculiar horror of absolute tyranny is communicated. Thus, for instance, the steel engraving that charms Winston in Mr. Charrington's shop is finally meaningful because it hides a telescreen. The intimate glance that O'Brien one day gives Winston in the Ministry of Truth ultimately means something very different from what Winston initially hopes and believes. Winston is an intelligent interpreter, but not an infallible one. Furthermore, the emphatic paranoia induced in the reader is not fully assuaged even after the act of reading is completed, for there are some details of whose significance even the reader can never be certain. There are, for instance, numerous hints in the text that Winston's lover Julia has all along been an agent of the Thought Police; but there is also evidence to the contrary, and, as often in totalitarian life itself, it is not possible to be sure.[5] There is thus a sense in which one never really finishes reading *Nineteen Eighty-Four*, and the unforgettable force of the book has been registered in various ways. Irving Howe, for instance, whose admiration is virtually unqualified, praises the book as a truthful evocation of a contemporary "nightmare."[6] On the other hand, the hostile Stalinist critic James Walsh obliquely (and perhaps unwittingly) acknowledges much the same quality when, attempting to dismiss *Nineteen Eighty-Four*, he describes it as one of "a couple of horror-comics."[7]

There can be no question as to the "success" of *Nineteen Eighty-Four*. But serious questions do remain as to the price at which this success has been won. What follows is a detailed analysis of the generic contradiction between naturalism and satire that is the basic formal determinant of the book. The geography of *Nineteen Eighty-Four* provides a useful introductory example of this contradiction. The London Orwell portrays is for the most part the naturalistically presented city during the Second World War and the years immediately afterward. The dirt, the smells, the buildings in bad repair, the scarcity and poor quality of consumer goods, the cheap oily gin ever available, the hurrying crowds in public places, the occasional dropping of bombs — this is the picture drawn by the writer who, from *Down and Out in Paris and London* on, had always had a special talent for particularizing such environments, especially through the use of olfactory imagery. The first sentence describing Victory Mansions, the block of flats in which Winston Smith lives, is typical: "The hallway smelt of boiled cabbage and old rag mats" (p. 3). Yet rising from and dominating – in more ways than one – this urban landscape are four structures, the four government ministries, which suggest surreal and fantastic satire. Each is "an enormous pyramidal structure of glittering white concrete, soaring up, terrace after terrace, three hundred meters into the air" (p. 5). Winston Smith does his work of endless forgery and historical falsification in the Records Department of the Ministry of Truth, in a small cubicle equipped with such science-fiction devices as "speakwrite" and "memory hole." His cubicle is itself one of about fifty such cubicles in a long windowless hall, which itself is only one subsection in the "huge complexity of the Records Department" (p. 43), which in turn is only one branch of the Ministry of Truth. It's a different fictional universe from that of boiled cabbage and old rag mats. One detail in particular – "a special kind of kaleidoscope known as a versificator" (p. 44), used to produce sentimental songs for the proles – could be from Book III of *Gulliver*. Yet it may be noted (the point is made explicitly in *The Theory and Practice of Oligarchical Collectivism* by "Emmanuel Goldstein") that the general shabbiness of everyday life is the result of policies quite deliberately formulated in the ministries. The locus of surreal satire determines the locus of mundane naturalism. I will return to this point later. For the moment, consider another example of the basic generic contradiction, this one involving characterization. Parsons, with his dimpled knees, pudgy forearms, and "overpowering smell of sweat" (p. 23), is for the most part a naturalistically drawn sketch. His boundless and imbecile enthusiasm seems a natural extension of his foolish appearance. Yet some passages – for example: " 'The Ministry of Plenty's certainly done a good job this year,' he said with a knowing shake of his head. 'By the way, Smith old boy, I suppose you haven't got any razor blades you can let me have?' " (p. 61) – are just a little too extreme, even for Parsons. There has been a subtle slippage into satire. True, the practice of doublethink could explain the coexistence of both quoted sentences; yet doublethink is, as we shall see, a highly satiric notion. It is, however, certain that Parsons must talk in this way if he is to be more than an isolated sketch – if, that is, he is to be truly integrated into the book in his role as a consciously firm Party loyalist.

Common-sense naturalism – the genre in which are presented the geography of London minus the ministries as well as the appearance and character of Parsons minus his most extreme stupidities – was Orwell's native literary genre. The genre may be partly defined as one that combines an acute verisimilitude of vivid particulars with an inability or unwillingness to form those particulars into a coherent whole. This description is, of course, consonant with Georg Lukács' well-known distinction between naturalism and realism.[8] Hence, in *A Clergyman's Daughter* – perhaps the most paradigmatic of Orwell's early novels – the plot falls apart into a series of episodes, and the protagonist Dorothy Hare remains virtually a cipher from beginning to end. The novel's energy is concentrated into such things as the details of the hop-picking life in Kent, the chaos of human sounds in which the Trafalgar Square sleepers exist, and the caricaturing portrayal of minor characters such as Mrs. Creevy. The book provides sharp particulars of a society but, itself fragmented, cannot evoke its society as a whole. Dorothy Hare is as far as possible from what Lukács would call a typical character—that is, a character who, though strongly individuated and, indeed, *because* strongly individuated, so incarnates essential historical forces as to suggest the socioeconomic structure of an entire society. Orwell's naturalism is untotalized or untheoretical realism. It is thus a very English form, for it philosophically depends on a positivistic empiricism, an eagerness to master details as they come, and a distrust of general theories that claim to account for details as a whole. At the same time, of course, it is politically radical—radical with the rejectionism of the petty bourgeois, who may be disgusted with the ugly and stifling details of capitalist life but whose stubborn individualism tends to preclude acceptance of a totalizing theory that would lead to positive collective action. Such was Orwell's primary political position in his earlier years, and, to a large extent, this pre-Catalonia structure of feelings emerges again in the years following the latter part of the Second World War.

There is, however, a further formal property of Orwell's naturalism: its inherent satiric potential. When details—objects, relations, even characters—are presented in relative isolation, not concretely integrated into a literary totality, they become reified to some degree and tend to glow with the weird light of what may be called spontaneous satire. The Dickensian caricaturism so prominent in Orwell's early work is perhaps the clearest example of this satiric aura spontaneously produced by naturalism; one thinks of Mrs. Creevy or even of the "middle-class socialist" in *The Road to Wigan Pier*. Antithetical—not simply opposed—to this sort of spontaneous satire, and indeed to naturalism in general, is what may be designated programmatic or (with the example of *Gulliver* in mind) Swiftian satire. *Animal Farm* is Orwell's first and most nearly pure effort in this genre. Here little attempt at naturalistic factualness or verisimilitude of detail is made. If Lukácsian realism may be said to involve three-dimensionality and naturalism may be said to involve distorted (because fragmented) three-dimensionality, then programmatic satire may be said to involve two-dimensionality. But the details of a programmatic satire, if two-dimensional, are completely integrated into the fabric of the work as a whole. They are firmly held in place by some totally controlling thesis (or theses) that may be substantially immanent in the work but logically prior to it. The world of programmatic satire is a completely coherent Flatland. It is, then, among the most abstract of genres—so abstract that it is extremely difficult to maintain in perfectly pure form. Even in Swift the objects in Gulliver's pockets, for instance, have a certain naturalistic solidity denied to most of the other details of the book. The unusual thing about *Nineteen Eighty-Four* is that it combines these two antithetical genres, naturalism and programmatic satire, in something like equal proportions.[9]

It is not, of course, a matter of simple combination, of an oil-and-water mixture. It is the dialectic of genres that determines the book's overall quality. *Nineteen Eighty-Four* partakes of both the empiricist solidity of *A Clergyman's Daughter* and the total coherence and significance of *Animal Farm* by a constant and, as it were, illicit traffic between naturalism and satire. In portraying London Orwell is able to call upon all the resources of his naturalistic talent. But the rather hyper-real architecture of the four ministries reflects the way in which the smells of boiled cabbage and old rag mats are integrated into the book as a whole: not realistically by being set in a concrete social totality, but satirically, by being programmatically deemed a policy of the fantastic social totality of Oceania. Parsons may be endowed with all the reified energy of a naturalistic sketch, with some aura of spontaneous satire. More than an isolated caricature, he is made an integral part of the whole only through the assumption of doublethink; and doublethink, to which I will return later, is a concept posited in the programmatic satire. The nearly complete significance of detail that gives the text so much of its force is made possible because the most solid and apparently concrete details are not— or not primarily—significant within the same genre in which they "naturally" exist. They are integrated into the book as a whole, but *forcibly* integrated, by means of programmatic satire. Conversely, the programmatic theses of the satire are made truly memorable (and frightening), and the text is made more than "a book of anticipations," as Orwell himself would say, by being able to draw into itself the particularizing "lifelikeness" of naturalism. The steel engraving is in itself a mundane naturalistic detail; the telescreen that it hides and that provides its overall significance is a cog in the fantastic satiric machinery. Even the paperweight, perhaps the most concrete object in the book, can be significant (as fragment of an un-Oceanian past, as prop in the schemes of the Thought Police) only because of the satiric thesis that is itself abstract. Nothing could be more naturalistically presented than the pain that Winston suffers in the Ministry of Love; the significance that O'Brien gives to it is satiric.

The satiric program of *Nineteen Eighty-Four* contains virtually all of the book's large and well-known concepts. It represents a considerable intellectual achievement, and it is fantastic—though not, of course, in the sense of bearing no rational relation to all to the facts of history. What Orwell has done on this level of the book, in the classic manner of the utopian or antiutopian satirist, is to take what he saw as certain features and tendencies of his own world and to caricature them almost but never quite beyond recognition.[10] What he regarded as the perversion of language by political barbarism, which he had discussed in his influential essay "Politics and the English Language," is carried to its fantastic extreme in Newspeak, whose vocabulary grows smaller every year and whose effect is to render an anti-Party thought impossible. Likewise, the general aim of lying propaganda to make the concept of objective truth untenable, which Orwell defined with terror in "Looking Back on the Spanish War," is satirized in the Party's absolute control of documents and its consequent "collective solipsism" (p. 269), in O'Brien's term. Or again, the evils of limitless espionage and official snooping, which had concerned Orwell since *Burmese Days* (and, as he reveals in "Such, Such Were the Joys," even since his days in prep school), reach their diabolical apotheosis in the Thought Police, the telescreens, and the other instruments of the Party's totalitarian rule.

To call these concepts fantastic is neither to denigrate Orwell's intellectual insight nor to deny their relevance to the world today. Indeed, certain developments in contemporary South Africa directly suggest the acuteness of Orwell's thesis—presented, in its details, through the sexual relationship of Winston and Julia—that political regimentation tends to undermine and to be undermined by normal eros. To take another instance, Orwell's vision of the dependence of advanced authoritarian states upon never-ending *limited* war and preparations for war bears an obvious relevance to the international situation in the years since the book was written. The problem with these satiric theses is not so much immediately intellectual as literary. They are strongly posited, but they are for the most part merely posited. They form a comprehensive, abstract, satiric structure that gains illusory solidity through continual commerce with a "lifelike" naturalistic presentation of detail and character. However, being without real concreteness themselves, they cannot be shown as operating within a concrete social totality. In other words—taking the words of Winston Smith—they brilliantly demonstrate a *how* but cannot demonstrate the *why* without which a *how* is necessarily inadequate (p. 79).

This problem, as I shall consider later, becomes crucial, and calls the entire book into question, when Orwell, toward the end of *Nineteen Eighty-Four*, does attempt to supply a *why*. For the moment let us consider the concept of doublethink. It is yet another of the key satiric theses of the text. It completes the Party's collective solipsism, which is primarily enabled by the complete forgery and fabrication of documents. Doublethink at its most complex involves the ability to accept mutually exclusive ideas, or to follow a chain of reasoning while avoiding the conclusion. It also requires the ability to perform this mental operation while avoiding the knowledge that one is performing it: "even to understand the word 'doublethink' involved the use of doublethink" (p. 36). Doublethink enables O'Brien (whose doublethink seems to be of the higher, insane variety, as distinguished from the lower, stupid variety of

Parsons) to drop a compromising photograph down a memory hole and then immediately to say, quite sincerely, that he does not remember it. Doublethink is an intriguing concept and, once posited, seems relevant to actual social-psychological problems — for instance, to the recent popularity of the phrase "Less is More," which sounds as if it were modeled after the official Party slogans in *Nineteen Eighty-Four*. But doublethink, as presented by Orwell, remains satiric and abstract. He gives a fascinating account of *how* the operation works but (torture apart) no indication of *why* the mind should be able to perform it. (That doublethink, like most of the satiric ideas in the book, *could* be given real social and psychological grounding is suggested by the Sartrean concept of *mauvaise foi*. This refers basically to the same process but has been given a real explanation: Sartre, in his later period, maintained that the mind of the bourgeois is driven to self-contradiction through a need to avoid the intolerable remorse that would result from recognizing that the ultimate source of his standard of living is the exploitation of workers. Whether one accepts this contention or not, it is clearly the kind of explanation needed to make a concept such as doublethink historical and concrete.)[11] O'Brien — who, as he emerges as a major character in Part Three of the book, is predominantly satiric, a necessary omniscient mouthpiece for authorial theses — can easily perform doublethink. Winston Smith, until the end a character of considerable naturalistic verisimilitude, cannot — not until the very end.

There is a further point to be made about the book's satiric aspect. Just as Orwell's naturalism has a fissure *within* itself — between the verisimilitude that is its basis and the spontaneous satire it tends to generate — Orwell's programmatic satire contains a (predictably neater and cleaner) split. Most of the main satiric theses, including all of those I have considered thus far, are part of a *generalized* satire of totalitarianism. Orwell constructs a "pure" totalitarian model, and O'Brien is even made to refer to the Roman Catholic Inquisition and the Stalinist purges as comparatively crude and ineffective. Nonetheless, Orwell does also include a considerable amount of specific, allegorical satire.[12] Its primary targets are Roman Catholicism (and, to some extent, Christianity in general) and the Soviet Communism. The anti-Communist elements are reasonably obvious. They include the fact that Ingsoc (English Socialism), the ruling ideology and system of Oceania, renders property nominally collective; the constant use of terms such as "comrade"; references to "the Revolution," which apparently established the rule of the Party; and various details modeled after the Stalin-Trotsky split and the great Soviet purges of the 1930s. Such elements are probably the most widely known aspects of the book. The anti-Communist satire contains some of the most extreme satiric moments in *Nineteen Eighty-Four*, moments when the fantastic, nonnaturalistic level of the book is foregrounded with a vengeance. One example may be cited. The frequent shifts of alliance in the permanent war between Oceania and either of the two other similar superstates are clearly based on the 1939 Nonaggression Pact between Hitler and Stalin, which completely reversed Soviet foreign policy (the Popular Front) until the subsequent reversal two years later when Germany invaded Russia. Likewise, the unceasing campaign against the probably nonexistent Emmanuel Goldstein, held to be the evil genius behind all that goes amiss under the rule of Big Brother, is modeled after the elaborate Stalinist vilification of Trotsky. Even the facial features of Big Brother and Goldstein suggest those of Stalin and Trotsky, respectively, and "Goldstein" is surely a verbal echo of "Bronstein," Trotsky's original surname. Combining the two themes in one of his most extreme satiric masterstrokes, Orwell portrays an Inner Party orator who, haranguing a crowd into hatred of Eurasia on the sixth day of Hate Week, is delivered a note that informs him that alliances have changed, that Eurasia is now the ally and Eastasia the foe. Without pausing, the speaker continues exactly as before, save for the appropriate changes in name, and the crowd immediately grasps that the anti-Eurasian banners and posters around the square must be the work of Goldsteinite sabotage!

The anti-Catholic and anti-Christian elements of Orwell's satire are more subtle and perhaps more interesting. Orwell regarded the Roman Church with much the same sort of horror with which he regarded the Stalinist bureaucracy in Russia: "It's influence is and always must be against freedom of thought and speech, against human equality," he wrote (*CEJL*, IV, 374). Verbal and incidental references to Catholic Christianity abound in *Nineteen Eighty-Four*. The Party's attitude toward sexuality and prostitution seems based upon that of the Church. The Junior Anti-Sex League is in effect a religious order, and *goodsex* is strictly limited to "normal sexual intercourse between man and wife, for the sole purpose of begetting children, and without physical pleasure on the part of the woman" (p. 309). During a Two Minutes Hate, when Big Brother's face is on the screen, a woman murmurs "My Savior!" (p. 17), extends her arms toward his image, and then buries her face in prayer. In the Ministry of Love O'Brien adopts "the air of a doctor, a teacher, even a priest" (p. 249). He says of himself and his Inner Party colleagues, "We are the priests of power" (p. 267), and he tells Winston that Winston has failed "in humility, in self-discipline" (p. 252). "When finally you surrender to us," says O'Brien, "it must be of your own free will" (p. 258). Not for nothing does Orwell give the representative of Party orthodoxy a Catholic name. O'Brien even denounces the Copernican model of the solar system and the Darwinian theory of evolution. And when he says, "It is impossible to see reality except by looking through the eyes of the Party" (p. 252), there is an obvious echo of the claim of the One True Church (though, no doubt, also of the Leninist party). At the end, Winston's full conversion is described in heavily religious terms:

> He was back in the Ministry of Love, with everything forgiven, his soul white as snow. . . . He gazed up at the enormous face [of Big

Brother]. Forty years it had taken him to learn what kind of smile was hidden beneath the dark mustache. O cruel, needless misunderstanding! O stubborn, self-willed exile from the loving breast! Two gin-scented tears trickled down the sides of his nose. But it was all right, everything was all right, the struggle was finished. He had won the victory over himself. He loved Big Brother. (p. 300)

The picture is not of a political dissenter crushed; it is of a heretic reclaimed.[13]

The satire of Christianity cuts far deeper than mere terminology. Just as the notion that economic collectivism could be the basis of tyranny rather than liberty is the primary means whereby the anti-Communist satire can be joined to the more general satiric program, so the anti-Christian satire is joined to this program through the idea that "love," as a social principle, is potentially totalitarian. The aim of Christian love after all is not to demand adherence to a legalistic code in the manner of the Old Testament but to produce a new kind of individual. When O'Brien says that the command of the Party is not "Thou shalt not" or even "Thou shalt" but *"Thou art"* (p. 258), he is as faithful to Christianity as to Ingsoc. When this principle is socially enforced—when law is politically super-seded by love, as in Oceania, where "nothing was illegal, since there were no longer any laws" (p. 8)—then anything can be done to the individual in the name of a *Thou art*. Love can then become practically synonymous with power, whereas law, by its nature, must to some degree restrain power. O'Brien can thus aptly revise the famous Christian formula to "God is power" (p. 267). Christian love without law can, it seems, lead to the same totalitarian result as socialist collectivism without liberty. As Orwell put it in attacking the ideas that motivate Book IV of *Gulliver*: "When human beings are governed by 'thou shalt not,' the individual can practice a certain amount of eccentricity: when they are supposedly governed by 'love' or 'reason,' he is under continuous pressure to make him behave and think in exactly the same way as everyone else." (*CEJL*, IV, 215–216). This is, I think, one of the subtlest insights in the entire programmatic satire of *Nineteen Eighty-Four*. Orwell has, in effect, attempted to refute a whole Christian-influenced literary tradition, with products as diverse as Shakespearian comedy and *Paradise Lost*, in which it is assumed that the supersession of law by love must inevitably be liberating. But how if love turns out to be the love of Big Brother? What is most deeply ironic about the name of the Ministry of Love is that it is finally not ironic at all.[14]

The whole question of power, or love-as-power, is directly relevant to Part Three of the book, where Orwell attempts to add a *why* to his *how*. This is where the generic contradiction between naturalism and program-matic satire becomes most severe. For if *Nineteen Eighty-Four* were *only* programmatic satire—if it were exclusively a book of abstract satiric anticipations of various possible aspects of totalitarian society—then there would be no need to explain the basis of this fantastic society in a rational, historical way. Swift, for example, is under no obligation to explain why it is possible for human beings to be as small as the Lilliputians (it is, in fact, a biological impossibility). But *Nineteen Eighty-Four* is not exclusively satiric. Its satiric side gains the appearance of solidity by constant borrowing from naturalistic elements that range from the smells of London buildings to the character of Winston Smith. Sooner or later this debt must be repaid. Winston has been presented throughout as the representation of a real man. He is a "lifelike" fictional creation who can be obsessed by guilty memories and dreams from childhood, can brace himself with oily Victory Gin, can resolve to rebel against tyranny, can feel acute curiosity and worry, can have tender emotions for Julia, and, not least, can suffer pain, which is presented with amazing vividness. Accordingly, he cannot fall victim merely to a set of satiric notions, however brilliant. The reader must have a concrete *why*, as surely as Winston must himself. Yet we are given none; the debt is not paid. Or rather, it *is* paid, but in the wholly fantastic coin of programmatic satire: "Power is not a means; it is an end. One does not establish a dictatorship in order to safeguard a revolution: one makes the revolution in order to establish the dictatorship. The object of persecution is persecution. The object of torture is torture. The object of power is power. Now do you begin to understand me?" (pp. 266–267). Thus the authoritative O'Brien. As satire, this is as telling as most of the other concepts in the book. As a rational social explanation, it is meaningless, an abstractly posited bogey.

The point is complex. I do not mean that Orwell should necessarily have put forward any *particular* explanation of Oceanian totalitarianism. The basic political issue involved—why does tyranny exist after the capitalistic relations of exploitation have apparently been overthrown?—is surely one of the most difficult and important of this century, and it is one to which rational enquirers have given different answers. Considering the Soviet Union, one could, for instance, agree with Deutscher (in his biography of Stalin and in other writings) that the underdeveloped economy of agricultural Russia made the real overthrow of bourgeois property relations impossible. The oppressiveness of Stalinism resulted (at least in part) from the attempt to build socialism solely in one country where real socialism was economically and culturally unfeasible. Or—an explanation more relevant, potentially, to Orwell's Oceania—one could agree with Djilas (in *The New Class*) that the overthrow of capitalism does not necessarily preclude the ascendance of a new oppressing class of technicians and bureaucrats. There are hints of this explanation in *Nineteen Eighty-Four*. Though membership in the Party and Inner Party is not hereditary, both groups might be considered classes on account of the definite hierarchy in economic standard of living. But Orwell never develops this line of thought. Material perquisities play not the slightest part in O'Brien's supposedly definitive explanation. Indeed, O'Brien explicitly denies any interest in wealth and luxury. Nor does idealistic belief of any sort play a part.[15] The entire structure of Oceanian society rests, apparently, on nothing more solid than the pure lust for cruelty of a relatively few men who yearn for nothing but "progress toward more pain" (p. 270). Neither Winston — who all along grasps how but now why, who breaks off reading the Burnhamite descriptions in *The Theory and Practice of Oligarchical Collectivism* just as the "why" section begins — nor the reader is given anything more rational than that. Orwell, no doubt, would claim that he, like Zamyatin, has grasped "the irrational side of totalitarianism — human sacrifice, cruelty as an end in itself, the worship of a Leader who is credited with divine attributes" (*CEJL*, IV, 75). The claim may be granted.[16] Indeed, the mad but horribly lucid speeches of O'Brien do satirize the basis of this irrational side of totalitarianism with the same skill that marks the satiric program of the book in general. But, by failing to account for a *rational* side as well, Orwell has, in the final and culminating part of *Nineteen Eighty-Four* — in the part that is meant to explain all the rest — made glaringly obvious the generic contradiction that characterizes the book as a whole. Nothing in the book is more vivid and naturalistic than the physical and mental agonies Winston suffers in the Ministry of Love. Nothing is more satiric than the ultimate explanation given for those agonies.

The final dependence of the book upon its programmatic satire to give total significance to its naturalism generically registers the same contradiction that Deutscher describes philosophically as Orwell's "jump from workaday, rationalistic common sense to the mysticism of cruelty."[17] That the Party, the primary concept of *Nineteen Eighty-Four* from which derive all the other major satiric concepts, is ultimately itself purely satiric, that it is, in Deutscher's words, "not a social body actuated by any interest or purpose" but instead "the metaphysical, mad and triumphant, Ghost of Evil,"[18] signals the breakdown of Orwell's reliance upon reason. There is a profound dialectical paradox in this. Orwell was a congenital empiricist. He was willing to trust his senses and the more obvious inferences that can be drawn from sense data, but he remained profoundly suspicious of general, totalizing theory. As he himself put it, he always took "pleasure in solid objects and scraps of useless information" (*CEJL*, I, 6). Generically, he was most at home in loose-jointed, common-sense naturalism. This attitude survives in *Nineteen Eighty-Four* not only formally, in its naturalistic generic aspect, but thematically, in the position of the naturalistic and Orwellian protagonist. Winston Smith takes his stand on what for the Party is the "heresy of heresies" (p. 80): common sense. Common sense consists of "truisms": "The solid world exists, its laws do not change. Stones are hard, water is wet, objects unsupported fall toward the earth's center" (p. 81).[19] Such sense data, along with the simplest mathematical abstractions from them — "Freedom is the freedom to say that two plus two make four" (p. 81) — constitute Winston's basic idea of reason. The final horror of totalitarianism is that it denies such reason. The Party in *Nineteen Eighty-Four* denies "not merely the validity of experience, but the very existence of external reality" (p. 80). Or, as Orwell projected of totalitarianism in "Looking Back on the Spanish War": "The implied objective of this line of thought is a nightmare world in which the Leader, or some ruling clique, controls not only the future but *the past*. If the Leader says of such and such an event, 'It never happened' — well, it never happened. If he says that two and two are five — well, two and two are five. This prospect frightens me much more than bombs . . ." (*CEJL*, II, 259). This is what common sense must fight against.

But how if common sense proves inadequate to the battle? In that case, it turns into the antithesis of itself. And common sense does break down in *Nineteen Eighty-Four*. Orwell cannot explain Oceanian totalitarianism with the only kind of reason that he has ever fully trusted. Totalitarianism is too overwhelming for common sense to grasp, just as O'Brien's elaborate and insane argument for collective solipsism is, it may be noted, more rigorous and intellectually powerful than anything that Winston's (or Orwell's) common sense can set against it. Yet Orwell *will* have an explanation. And his long attachment to empiricist common-sense reason prevents him, even in the act of abandoning it, from considering more complex, more generalizing, more dialectical forms of reason. Hence, just as the naturalism of the book must, for the sake of a total and coherent literary structure, depend on its antithesis, programmatic satire, so common sense, in order to arrive at an explanation of what it cannot explain, calls to its aid what Deutscher has termed "the oldest, the most banal, the most abstract, the most metaphysical, and the most barren of all generalizations": the omnipotence of power-lust and human depravity.[20] Accustomed, in the name of common-sense reason, to distrust generalized theory as "orthodoxy," Orwell has fallen into the most orthodox kind of irrationalism.

The breakdown of common sense — Orwell's as he reaches for the mysticism of cruelty, Winston's as he is eventually transformed into a satirically presented doublethinker who loves Big Brother — parallels the breakdown of the autonomous individual, the bourgeois ego. The historical connection between empiricist rationality and the centered, stable self is illustrated both by Orwell's firm individualism, never fully transcended save during his Spanish experience, and by Winston's. Despite an attempt to join the Brotherhood and some vague hopes about the proles, Winston's rebellion is primarily a series of individual gestures: thought crime, writing a diary, the affair with Julia. Furthermore, the intellectual basis of his rebellion is not only common sense but also individual autonomy. "Nothing," he thinks, "was your own except the few cubic centimeters inside your skull" (p. 28). "They can't get inside you," he says to Julia (p. 167). However, Winston, knowing himself and Julia to be "dead" as the inevitable social result of their actions, cannot accept Julia's more absolute notion of personal autonomy, based on the primacy of immediate sexual pleasure: "Which would you rather sleep with, me or a skeleton?" she demands of him (p. 137). Orwell himself had even more reservations than Winston. He wrote toward the end of the Second World War: "The greatest mistake is to imagine that the human being is an autonomous individual. The secret freedom which you can supposedly enjoy under a despotic government is nonsense, because your thoughts are never entirely your own" (*CEJL*, III, 133). This is, of course, directly relevant to Winston's fate, and it marks the final antinomy of Orwell's individualism. Basing himself on the autonomous, centered subjectivity of bourgeois thought and feeling, he can nonetheless partially grasp the limitations of such a position. He can conceive of the *destruction* of individual autonomy, but he cannot really imagine its *transcendence*. Thus Winston is shown as having his individuality smashed through an elaborate combination of physical torture, mental torture, and indoctrination in the quasi-theological tenets of the Party. But he cannot be placed in a situation where genuine collective thought and action are possible. Once again the contradiction can be expressed in terms of genre: the reversal is from the naturalistically presented individual that Winston is through most of the book to the satirically drawn doublethinker that he has become by the end.

The matter of individualism is crucial to an understanding of the book's final political significance. From the time that he had any clear and articulate political ideas until his death, Orwell considered himself a socialist. He was dismayed to find that his last work was being interpreted as an attack on socialism. That *Nineteen Eighty-Four* should have eventually found its way into John Birch Society book shops — that, in Deutscher's phrase, Orwell's own book should in some circles have become "so prominent an item in the programme of Hate Week"[21] — is surely the greatest irony of his reputation. Nevertheless, the book does contain elements that make an antisocialist interpretation not wholly perverse. What is at issue here is not so much the anti-Stalinist and anti-Communist satire. The book raises no overt question as to whether some version of socialism is *desirable*. Orwell had no conscious doubts about that. Rather, the most profound political contradiction of *Nineteen Eighty-Four* concerns the question of whether it is *possible*. This question, it must be emphasized, does not imply the least overt attachment to capitalism. Orwell, like Marx, believed that capitalism was certainly doomed and that only socialism or barbarism could follow. Increasingly, however, barbarism seemed to him by far the likelier possibility. This was a late development in his thought. Although much of the satiric program of *Nineteen Eighty-Four* (especially as summarized in *The Theory and Practice of Oligarchical Collectivism*) is Burnhamite, Orwell in his lengthy analyses of James Burnham's work had expressed sharp disagreements with the author.[22] He considered the thesis of *The Managerial Revolution* — that totalitarianism is virtually inevitable — too pessimistic and felt that Burnham grossly overemphasized the importance of naked power. As late as 1946 Orwell was protesting that "slavery is no longer a stable basis of human society" (*CEJL*, IV, 180). But in 1947, the year he completed the first draft of his last book, his view had become gloomier. The Cold War between the Soviet Union and the United States was developing, and he now felt that a world of two or three immense slave states was quite likely. The plan for a united socialist Europe, put forward in "Toward European Unity" as the best alternative to world totalitarianism, was offered without much hope, for he knew that such a scheme would incur the bitter hostility of the two increasingly hegemonic superpowers and, he said, of the Roman Church as well.

Yet despite the importance of the immediate international situation during the years Orwell was writing *Nineteen Eighty-Four* (and despite the importance of his physical health, never really good and fast becoming desperate), the book's political gloom has deeper sources in Orwell's individualism. His political individualism was reflected in and partly based on the idea that there were, by and large, socialists of only two kinds. It is relevant here to recall the exposition of this idea in *The Road to Wigan Pier*. There is, on the one hand, the warm, admirable working-class socialist who, though he grasps the essential socialist aims of liberty and justice, tends to be intellectually superficial: "so far as my experience goes, no genuine working man grasps the deeper implications of Socialism."[23] On the other hand, there is the educated middle-class socialist, who is disgusting and unreliable: "Sometimes I look at a Socialist — the intellectual, tract-writing type of Socialist, with his pullover, his fuzzy hair, and his Marxian quotation — and wonder what the devil his motive really *is*."[24] Despising one group, condescendingly admiring the other but unable to be a part of it, and, in addition, distrusting complex theory ("his Marxian quotation"), Orwell was for most of his political life a political loner. Despite Orwell's conscious desire for collective socialist action, the logic of his attitudes must render it extremely problematic. Historically, it requires the active cooperation of the two groups — masses and intellectuals — whom he regarded as such hopelessly different beings, and it requires some theoretical guidance as well. While actively a partisan in the concrete union of socialist practice and theory that was the Spanish revolution, Orwell was able to transcend his individualistic dilemma. But in his last years it recurs in severe form, particularly with regard to his ambiguous attitude toward the working class.

"If there is hope," writes Winston in his diary, "it lies in the proles" (p. 69). Given the general logic of the programmatic satire of *Nineteen Eighty-Four*, the most striking oddity in it is that the proles, quite simply, have little to do with it. The Thought Police occasionally eliminate individual proles who seem potentially dangerous, but, in comparison to

Party members, they are by and large unmolested. Their presence in the book is integrated into its satiric aspect primarily at one point. The Party, we are given to understand, can exploit their labor and then leave them pretty much alone because they pose no threat. The Party also regards them as subhuman yahoos. "The proles are not human beings" (p. 53), says the orthodox Syme. O'Brien says the same: "They are helpless, like the animals. Humanity is the Party. The others are outside—irrelevant" (p. 272). That the proles (who form eighty-five per cent of the population of Oceania) are "outside" the programmatic satire means that the text is free to describe them and their quarters of London with the naturalistic vividness that Orwell had employed for such purposes ever since *Down and Out in Paris and London.* Indeed, the proles of *Nineteen Eighty-Four* have much in common with the submerged classes of that book and other earlier works. Not precisely subhuman, the proles, as both the text and Winston see them, are in some ways the only real human beings left because they alone have been allowed to retain the basic human impulses—for family, for sexuality, for recreation, for simple freedom from constant paranoia—that the Party tries to suppress in its own members. The singing prole housewife beneath the window of Mr. Charrington's shop, with her earthy "vitality which the Party did not share and could not kill" (p. 222), is a typical Orwellian working-class sketch. The sentimental admiration that she inspires in Winston is equally Orwellian: "Out of those mighty loins a race of conscious beings must one day come" (p. 222). Then there will be a *truly* socialist revolution.

This is the one real hope of the book. And it may be significant that O'Brien's brief dismissal of this hope is in marked contrast to the elaborate cogency with which he normally expounds the omnipotence and immortality of the Party and its collective solipsism. (It is also noteworthy that such limited, temporary freedom as does exist for Party members is due to the proles. Surely there would have been no train for Winston to take to his first lovemaking rendezvous with Julia, were trains not necessary for his fellow passengers, the proles.) But the hope is a slender one. The actual portraits of the proles—the saucepan riot that Winston remembers, or the old man in the pub who cannot even understand Winston's request for a general comparison of life before and after the Revolution but thinks only of details from his own experience—give little reason to suppose that they could ever become "conscious" and hence that Oceanian society is not as eternally stable as O'Brien says. For the most part, indeed, *Nineteen Eighty-Four* regards the proles with much more sympathy and affection but, at bottom, with little more respect than that with which *Gulliver* regards the yahoos.[25] Winston himself identifies the defect in the proles as their being "without general ideas" (p. 72), just as Orwell could find no genuine working man who grasped the "deeper" implications of socialism. Yet neither Winston nor Orwell has general ideas sufficiently complex and dialectical to resolve the basic dilemma: "Until they become conscious

[Winston writes in his diary] they will never rebel, and until after they have rebelled they cannot become conscious" (p. 70). This dilemma — an individualist dilemma that precludes collective action — marks the central political contradiction of the book. The working class alone can establish true socialism, but it is unlikely that the working class can. And so — as naturalism in *Nineteen Eighty-Four* must finally yield to programmatic satire, as common-sense reason must yield to the mysticism of cruelty, and as individual autonomy must yield to its destruction — Orwellian socialist hope (inspired, what little of it there is, by the naturalistically presented proles) must yield to its antithesis, quietist despair (inspired by the satirically presented apparatus of the Party's total control). In terms of the geography of the book, the prole quarters of London are finally less significant than the four Party ministries.

It may be added that the past, to which Winston proposes the toast at what he believes to be his and Julia's initiation into the Brotherhood, provides no more basis for hope than does the future. The capitalist past, like the proles who are its most striking remnant, is ambiguously regarded. It includes the lovely glass paperweight, the "Golden Country" so nostalgically remembered by Winston (and by Orwell in *Coming Up for Air*), and the kind of life that Winston and Julia are briefly able to lead in the room above Mr. Charrington's shop. Their life in that room, indeed, bears some resemblance to the sentimental portrait of a modern working-class home in *The Road to Wigan Pier*. The Party's version of the past, as presented, for instance, in the children's history textbook that Winston looks at, is therefore false in what it excludes. Yet — as Winston cannot know, but as the reader can, and as Orwell knew very well indeed — the Party's description of capitalism is largely true in what it includes. The picture has rather a Victorian-moralistic flavor, and a few details are wrong, such as making the law of *jus primae noctis* a capitalist rather than a feudal prerogative. But certainly the dirt, the poverty, the child labor, the luxury and power of the rich — not to mention "the bishops in their lawn sleeves, the judges in their ermine robes, the pillory, the stocks" (p. 73) — are far from fabrications. The few details that Winston hears from the old man in the pub do tend to confirm the Party's official history. That was capitalism — in a sense, the capitalism that Orwell personally witnessed in Wigan and elsewhere. Now it has been succeeded by totalitarian barbarism, a barbarism that may well have no end. The only sort of rebellion possible against it is the purely individual and hopeless rebellion of Winston Smith, "the last man in Europe," in the phrase that was Orwell's working title for *Nineteen Eighty-Four*. What, then, is left but to admit despair? Furthermore, it is the despair not of socialism simply but of positive hope in general. As Winston sadly reflects long before he finds himself in the Ministry of Love: "On the battlefield, in the torture chamber, on a sinking ship, the issues that you are fighting for are always forgotten, because the body swells up until it fills the universe" (p. 102). Heroism of purposeful action is impossible. Not many years before, in "The Art of Donald McGill," Orwell had used some of the same images to make the opposite point: "When it comes to the pinch, human beings are heroic. Women face childbed and the scrubbing brush, revolutionaries keep their mouths shut in the torture chamber, battleships go down with the guns still firing when the decks are awash" (*CEJL*, II, 164). Yet Orwell had increasingly felt the lure of mere hopeless quietism. He had never been able quite to *accept* it, whether in George Bowling of *Coming Up for Air* or in Henry Miller. But it has had rather a sirenlike fascination for him. In *Nineteen Eighty-Four*, much more than in *Animal Farm*, quietism, rather than the socialism he never completely abandoned, is the strongest political attitude.

Finally, then, *Nineteen Eighty-Four* is a remarkable and deeply problematic achievement. By the intellectual force of its satiric theses and by the literary skill with which these theses are made manifest in the totally significant detail of the book, Orwell has unforgettably shown us what to avoid. His premises — empiricist and individualistic — rendered him unable to show us *how* to avoid it, because, in *Nineteen Eighty-Four*, those premises lead to it.

Notes

1. Sonia Orwell and Ian Angus, eds., *The Collected Essays, Journalism and Letters of George Orwell* (London: Secker & Warburg, 1968), IV, 329–330. Henceforth I will refer to this four-volume collection as *CEJL*, and citations will be given by volume and page within the text.

2. Critics, however, have often felt that the book must be placed more unambiguously in one genre or the other. For instance, Jeffrey Meyers, *A Reader's Guide to George Orwell* (London: Thames and Hudson, 1975), p. 144: "The most common cliché of Orwell criticism is that *1984* (1949) is a 'nightmare vision' of the future. I believe, on the contrary, that it is a very concrete and naturalistic portrayal of the present and the past. . . ."

3. These contradictions are also registered linguistically in the dialectic between Newspeak and the Orwellian "plain style." I have discussed this issue in "Writing, Ideology, and Politics: Orwell's 'Politics and the English Language' and English Composition," *College English*, 43 (April 1981), especially pp. 332–335.

4. George Orwell, *Nineteen Eighty-Four* (New York: Harcourt, Brace & World, 1949), p. 3. Further references will be given parenthetically by page number.

5. One of the ways in which Huxley's *Brave New World* differs most sharply from *Nineteen Eighty-Four* is that in the former there is no such intense and constant necessity for both characters and reader to worry over the interpretation of each detail. This is quite proper to a satire the main object of which is *not* totalitarianism but hedonism. Huxley's antiutopia, with its self-consciously "aesthetic" prose, is in almost all respects much less frightening than Orwell's.

6. Irving Howe, *Politics and the Novel* (New York: Horizon Press, 1957), p. 251.

7. James Walsh, "George Orwell," *Marxist Quarterly*, 3 (January 1956), 36.

8. The distinction is central to the theory of realism that Lukács began developing in the 1930s and that remained his primary literary-critical framework for the rest of his career.

Among his most important works on realism are *The Historical Novel*, *Studies in European Realism*, and *Realism in Our Time*.

9. Unless otherwise qualified, all my uses of terms like "satire" or "satiric" in this essay are intended to refer to programmatic, not spontaneous, satire.

10. The basic text of this satiric tradition is, of course, More's *Utopia*. (Plato's *Republic* may be regarded as providing a classical precedent for the utopian satire, and it certainly had a direct influence on More himself.) The twentieth-century development or inversion of the tradition—the antiutopia—is represented not only by *Brave New World* and Zamyatin's *We* but also by Wells's *When the Sleeper Wakes* and, in a way, by Jack London's *The Iron Heel*—all works with which Orwell was thoroughly familiar. *Gulliver*, another favorite of Orwell's, chronologically comes about midway between renaissance utopia and modern antiutopia and has elements in common with both.

11. Sartre's play *The Devil and the Good Lord*, set at the dawn of capitalism, represents the dramatic embodiment of these ideas. Goetz attempts to escape remorse, and the attempt leads him into something very like doublethink: for example, his love for the peasants and his simultaneous desire to see them destroyed. Yet Goetz is always a historically explicable character as an Orwellian doublethinker is not.

12. The use of the term "allegorical" may raise questions here. It can be argued that all satire, and certainly all utopian or antiutopian satire, contains an allegorical moment. I do not disagree. But I think it is justifiable to use the term to refer particularly to local, topical satire because it is in such satire (of which Dryden's *Absalom* is perhaps the classic instance) that the allegorical moment is most strikingly foregrounded. Topical satire *insists* that the reader focus on one-to-one correspondences between text and history.

13. Alan Sandison, *The Last Man in Europe* (London: Macmillan, 1974), makes a relevant point in this connection: "The whole emphasis in the latter part of *Nineteen Eighty Four*, so often misunderstood, is not on punishment but on conversion. That is why it is so prolonged" (p. 182).

14. It is also somewhat ironic that there have been a number of religiously oriented readings of *Nineteen Eighty-Four*, some of them quite interesting and ingenious. See Christopher Hollis, *A Study of George Orwell* (Chicago, IL: Henry Regnery, 1956); Robert A. Lee, *Orwell's Fiction* (Notre Dame, IN: University of Notre Dame Press, 1969); Christopher Small, *The Road to Miniluv* (London: Victor Gollancz, 1975). Lee, for instance, notes the religious qualities of Ingsoc and states: "Orwell's purpose is satirical. He infuses religious metaphors into a completely secular context to suggest the corruption of the system, the perversion of eternal values by the ephemeral demands of politics" (p. 147). The short answer is that, as O'Brien repeatedly makes clear, there is finally nothing secular—or even, in any normal sense, political—about Ingsoc; its values are, precisely, eternal.

15. Ironically, Orwell had always insisted that rulers do need some idealistic ideology as well as an economic base. It was Jack London's awareness of this insight that led, in large part, to Orwell's admiration for *The Iron Heel* (see *CEJL*, IV, 25). London, in a passage discussing the character of his Oligarchs, writes. "The great driving force of the Oligarchs is the belief that they are doing right." Orwell cites this passage to show that "London's understanding of the nature of a ruling class—that is, the characteristics which a ruling class must have if it is to survive—went very deep." Similar statements abound in Orwell's writings.

16. It is, however, noteworthy that cruelty and human sacrifice are stressed much more by Orwell than by Zamyatin. Indeed, Zamyatin, though more interested in totalitarianism than is Huxley, shares with him and does *not* share with Orwell an interest in satirizing hedonism as well.

17. Isaac Deutscher, *Heretics and Renegades* (Indianapolis, IN: Bobbs-Merrill, 1969), p. 48.

18. Deutscher, p. 49.

19. There is perhaps an echo here of one of Shakespeare's common-sense rustics. Corin

in *As You Like It*, III.ii. It may thus be no accident that Winston had earlier waked from a dream "with the word 'Shakespeare' on his lips" (p. 32).

20. Deutscher, p. 48.

21. Deutscher, p. 50.

22. "James Burnham and the Managerial Revolution" (*CEJL*, IV, 160–184) and "Burnham's View of the Contemporary World Struggle" (*CEJL*, IV, 313–326) are Orwell's two major pieces on Burnham. It is interesting that, although insisting that Burnham placed too much emphasis on the role of sheer power in human affairs, Orwell himself concentrates on the part of *The Managerial Revolution* that concerns power and mostly ignores the book's economic argument, which is primary to Burnham's case. Nonetheless, there can be little doubt that, to the extent that *The Theory and Practice of Oligarchical Collectivism* is based on any actual book, that book is *The Managerial Revolution*. Not only are there specific similarities of content — Burnham predicts a world of three immense superstates engaged in never-ending and inconclusive war with one another — but the general style and manner of "Goldstein" is quite Burnhamite. Both deal in sweeping historical generalizations and assume an air of dispassionate calm in relating the most horrible events. The similarities between the "Goldstein" book and another work more frequently suggested as its model, *The Revolution Betrayed*, are much less striking. Trotsky provides detailed analysis of one specific historical event and writes with biting irony and passionate indignation. Such features as "Goldstein" and Trotsky do have in common, such as an authoritative tone, tend also to be found in Burnham (not surprisingly because Burnham was for many years an active Trotskyist and may well have been influenced by the master's style). The relations between Burnham and Orwell are discussed in more detail by William Steinhoff, *George Orwell and the Origins of "1984"* (Ann Arbor: University of Michigan Press, 1975).

23. George Orwell, *The Road to Wigan Pier* (New York: Harcourt Brace Jovanovich, 1958), p. 176.

24. *Wigan Pier*, pp. 178–179.

25. Raymond Williams makes a similar point, but even more strongly: "It needs to be said, however bitterly, that if the tyranny of *1984* ever finally comes, one of the major elements of the ideological preparation will have been just this way of seeing 'the masses,' 'the human beings passing you on the pavement,' the eighty-five per cent who are *proles*. . . . By viewing the struggle as one between only a few people over the heads of an apathetic mass, Orwell created the conditions for defeat and despair." See Williams, *George Orwell* (New York: The Viking Press, 1971), pp. 79–80.

Secondary Fiction

Orwell and the Lower-Middle-Class Novel

Terry Eagleton*

Burmese Days is widely known as an assault upon Anglo-Burma, but what is less often remembered is its half-convinced apology, through the focus of the self-doubting Flory, for some of the regime's worst aspects. "Besides, you could forgive the Europeans a great deal of their bitterness. Living and working among Orientals would try the temper of a saint. . . . The life of the Anglo-Indian officials is not all jam. In comfortless camps, in sweltering offices, in gloomy dank bungalows smelling of dust and earth-oil, they earn, perhaps, the right to be a little disagreeable." "A little disagreeable," in the light of the brutal white-supremacy complex shown in the novel, seems something of an understatement; its real function is not so much to suggest a judicious "balance," but to half-ratify Flory's incapacity to formulate his own confused feelings into an explicit position, to validate his sense of impotent complicity with what he hates. (It is, significantly, the "atmosphere" rather than the political realities of imperialism he detests, a fact which itself implies a less than complete attitude and understanding.)

Flory veers between a frustrated raging at his compatriots (a feeling which the novel suggests is excessive and unfair) and what amounts to a declared cynicism. Neither attitude is really adequate; the first is too suggestive of the sort of committed moral judgement which can be achieved only by detaching oneself from a world of which one is part; the second, if consistently manifested, would make Flory no better than his fellow-countrymen. So the realities of Anglo-Burma can be neither totally accepted nor totally denied. On the one hand, there is this familiarly Orwellian outburst against the Deputy Commissioner:

> Nasty old bladder of lard! he thought, watching Mr. Macgregor up the road. How his bottom did stick out in those tight khaki shorts. Like one of those beastly middle-aged scoutmasters, homosexuals almost to a man, that you see photographs of in the illustrated papers. Dressing

*Reprinted from *Exiles and Emigres: Studies in Modern Literature* (London: Chatto & Windus; New York: Schocken Books, 1970), 78–108, by permission of the author and Chatto & Windus.

111

himself up in those ridiculous clothes and exposing his pudgy, dimpled knees, because it is the pukka sahib thing to take exercise before breakfast — disgusting!

It is the tone of outraged Orwellian decency: the shudder of the "normal" man, with his sober, puritan, self-consciously ordinary values, at "pansy" eccentricity of any kind; the tone of the criticism of the intellectual socialists and "Nancy poets" in *The Road to Wigan Pier*, replete with a tough, swaggering sense of self-righteous masculinity. It is not far removed from the kind of snobbish, physical disgust which characterises the racialist Ellis in *Burmese Days*, and its quality of *physical* repulsion is important: by virtue of it, an emotional rejection can be satisfied which does not press through, in other than a generalized sense, to an evaluation of the system which Macgregor symbolizes. On the other hand, because the feeling is unfocused and uncontrolled, missing the structure for the fragment of physical detail, it can turn, as easily, against Flory himself, in a callous self-deprecation which "realistically" undercuts the possibility of genuine criticism: "Seditious?" Flory said. "*I'm* not seditious. I don't want the Burmans to drive us out of this country. God forbid! I'm here to make money, like everyone else. All I object to is the slimy white man's burden humbug. The pukka sahib pose. It's so boring." This is intended to suggest a toughly attractive honesty — a rejection of colonial pretense, and so, to that degree, a moral superiority to others — at the same time as it binds Flory *to* those others, in his declared corruption of motive. It accepts the burden of guilt in order to avoid the contaminating risks of a moral stance — which would, presumably, be just one more form of "humbug." Flory must resist any suggestion that he is morally more sensitive or altruistic than others (even though, as the novel will show us, he clearly *is*) because this would be to take a stand on principle which his collusion with colonialism denies him, and so to live with the intolerable tension of bad faith. And so "honesty" and "pretense" are substituted, as moral alternatives, for good and bad.

The true corruption of imperialism, in fact, is that it denies the possibility of reliance on one's own "good" feelings:

> You see louts fresh from school kicking grey-haired servants. And the time comes when you burn with hatred of your own countrymen, when you long for a native rising to drown their Empire in blood. And in this there is nothing honourable, hardly even any sincerity. For, *au fond*, what do you care if the Indian Empire is a despotism, if Indians are bullied and exploited? You only care because the right of free speech is denied you. You are a creature of the despotism, a pukka sahib, tied tighter than a monk or a savage by an unbreakable system of tabus.

It is difficult to believe of the Flory we are actually shown that his anti-imperialist feelings are merely selfish; but the point, once more, is to qualify the possibilities of explicit commitment by insisting upon the "unbreakable" bond between moral judge and the situation judged, by seeing man as a puppet of his environment. The pattern of involvement and repulsion becomes a vicious circle: Flory is repelled by his own compromised involvement, and this is as much the source of his anger as any "objective" criticism of the colonialist system; yet the anger is in that sense egoistic — "You care only because the right of free speech is denied you" — and so is not to be trusted, lapsing back into a sullen acceptance of the *status quo*. Flory, one feels, is right to distrust his anger: the blurred, abstractly violent image of "drowning their Empire in blood" revealingly indicates its subjective quality. Yet the implication is then that considered moral judgments, which transcend an immediate condition and the raw response it evokes, are impossible. As in later Orwell novels, it is a choice between some vague, vicariously fulfilling image of apocalyptic destruction (the suppressed yearning for the bombs in *Coming Up for Air*), and the wry sense of "realistic" impotence which continually undermines it. Escape from being a creature of one's environment is possible through Romantic gestures or courageous moral commitments, and these cannot be wholly repudiated because they link one, in the midst of corruption, to one's "better self." Yet they are not only bound to fail, but also detach one from "normal" life into damaging moral isolation: "it is a corrupting thing to live one's real life in secret. One should live with the stream of life, not against it." To strike a radical stance in a conservative society is to risk the loss of identity, since identity is still located among the old, established customs and decencies, and Orwell could not trust to an idea of identity discovered through a *collective* rejection. And so Flory tells Dr. Veraswami that "You've got to be a pukka sahib or die, in this country." He criticizes the system — "if we are a civilizing influence, it's only to grab on a larger scale" — but from the vantage-point of an emotional and unarguable attachment to the old, primitive Burma which qualifies the value of his criticisms.

It is perhaps worth pointing out, at this stage, that there is a striking parallel between *Burmese Days* and Graham Greene's *The Heart of the Matter*. . . . The resemblance lies not only in remarkable congruencies of setting and narrative detail — the seedy colonialist context, the machinations of a corrupt native leader, the arrival of a young English girl, the culminating suicide — but in the instructive parallels between Flory and Henry Scobie. Both Flory and Scobie are morally superior to their environments, yet both are corrupted by a guilty sense of collusion which narrows their awareness of what virtue they have, and so inhibits decisive moral action:

> "Cur, spineless cur," Flory was thinking to himself; without heat, however, for he was too accustomed to the thought. "Sneaking, idling, boozing, fornicating, soul-examining, self-pitying cur. All those fools at the Club, those dull louts to whom you are so pleased to think yourself superior — they are all better than you, every man of them. At least they

are men in their oafish way. Not cowards, not liars. Not half-dead and rotting. But you — "

This self-castigation occurs after Flory has lacked courage to defend his Burmese friend before his compatriots; and it arises because the ethic of "honesty" turns against Flory himself. The racialists at the English club are at least "sincere," whereas Flory himself lives a deception. They may be "oafish," but they have at least a sort of blunt, masculine integrity which Flory, with his ceaseless "soul-examining," does not; they are "dull louts," but their dullness renders them safely impervious to the "Nancy" poet style of self-pitying introspection. It is here that Flory differs decisively from Greene's Scobie. Scobie's self-castigation is intended to convince us, negatively, of his unusual humility and so of his goodness; Flory, who is much more directly a projection of the younger Orwell himself, manifests his author's own guilty self-hatred and uncertainty. The men at the club are dull, but they are also (in a significant Orwellian epithet) "decent"; they may be bigoted and violent but, the novel insists, they are not corrupted, wallowingly self-indulgent, tremulously sensitive, like Flory himself. And part of Orwell wants to affirm this judgement, to approve Flory's self-disgust: a "tough," masculine honesty is once more stressed as superior to objective moral discriminations, to the point where a racialist is excused on the grounds of his sincerity. The choice is between a dull, seedy world of "decent" normality, which can be sworn at, mocked and caricatured but not wholly disapproved of, and a sensitive, isolated self-examination which rides dangerously near to the hated "Nancy" poets, picking over their own fine emotions. As with Wells's Mr. Polly, too much introspection is dangerous: it allows chaos to infiltrate and undermine the ordinary universe.

Burmese Days is hesitant in its choice of these alternatives, and its total attitude is correspondingly uncertain. There is, for instance, the problem of deciding precisely how much validity to allow to Flory's introspections: the problem of steering a safe course between unmanly sensitivity on the one hand and the straight philistinism of Elizabeth Lackersteen or Verrall, the arrogant army officer, on the other. The fluctuations of tone emerge in the following passage:

> Flory leaned over the gate. . . . Some lines from Gilbert came into his mind, a vulgar silly jingle but appropriate — something about "discoursing on your complicated state of mind." Gilbert was a gifted little skunk. Did all his trouble, then, simply boil down to that? Just complicated, unmanly whinings; poor-little-rich-girl stuff? . . . And if so, did that make it any more bearable? It is not the less bitter because it is perhaps one's own fault, to see oneself drifting, rotting in dishonour and horrible futility, and all the while knowing that somewhere within one there is the possibility of a decent human being.
>
> Oh well, God save us from self-pity! Flory went back to the veranda. . . .

The jingle is "vulgar" and Gilbert is a "skunk"; but with these essential, distancing reservations safely made, the voice of English middle-class banality can be seriously attended to as appropriate. Once the significant status of Flory's experience has thus been denied, it is as quickly re-established in the following sentences, until the final gesture intervenes curtly to reconsolidate "common sense." The problem is really intractable: either Flory is to be taken seriously or he is not, and each possibility conflicts with an aspect of Orwell's intentions.

There are other ambiguities in the novel. It is difficult, for instance, to square Flory's sense of the manly integrity of his fellow-colonialists with his previous remarks to Dr. Veraswami about their self-deceptive preten-tiousness; and it is generally difficult to accommodate Flory's forgiving estimations of them, in the light of his own guilt, to what we are shown of their actual brutality. One is forced to conclude that, when Orwell is actually presenting the men at the English club, he indulges his criticism to the full; but when the spotlight moves to Flory and his compatriots recede into the background, they gain a vicarious merit. The continuing conflict within Orwell's own mind, between an impulse to lonely and defiant moral gesture and a sense of the collective decency of drably normative life, goes unresolved. The first can find a vent for real criticism only at the cost of suggesting a corrupting self-indulgence and callow "ideologizing"; the second is admired for its ordinariness, its shrewdly realist refusal of large gestures, but cursed and hated for its petty sterility. In almost all of Orwell's novels, this dialectic hardens into deadlock: "ordinary" living is mocked and caricatured through the dehumanizing eye of a more intelligent observer, who is himself deflated — reduced to normality — by his own or others' scepticism.

When Flory first appears in the novel, our attention is drawn to the disfiguring birthmark which stains his left cheek. The birthmark isolates him socially from others, marking him out as an exile and even a freak; but it is also at the root of that sensitivity which emerges, especially in his doomed relationship with Elizabeth Lackersteen, as his most admirable quality. The birthmark is connected both with his sensitivity and with his habit of passive compromise:

> Meanwhile, Flory had signed a public insult to his friend. He had done it for the same reason as he had done a thousand such things in his life; because he lacked the small spark of courage that was needed to refuse. For, of course, he could have refused if he had chosen; and equally, of course, refusal would have meant a row! The nagging, the jeers! At the very thought of it he flinched; he could feel his birthmark palpable on his cheek, and something happened in his throat that made his voice go flat and guilty.

Flory, who has carried his disfigurement through years of schoolboy taunts, is a victim, not just of Anglo-Burma, but of life; and the upshot of this is to contribute to the ambivalence with which he is characterised. On the one hand, this agonized awareness of his ugliness half-excuses his compromise: the responsibility for his failure to act by moral principle began, not with him, but "in his mother's womb." So in this respect, the birthmark is a telling detail which the novel can mobilize in support of its thesis that moral stances are impracticable. By selecting a hero stamped from birth with the insignia of failure and hypersensitivity, it suggests that Flory's weakness is in the "nature of things" rather than in his response to a particular moral situation. But the birthmark also makes Flory nontypical, estranged at the outset from "normal" human life: Elizabeth comes finally to hate him "as she would have hated a leper or a lunatic." So the scar dignifies Flory, lending him a compassion superior to others, but only at the cost of implying that he — and men like him — are really "half-men" — freaks. And this, again, is detrimental to the validity of his criticisms of others. It is a choice between the "normal," insensitive man — Verrall and his kind — and the lonely eccentric. There is no suggestion that a "normal" man could take up the critical position which Flory assumes: his criticism is a function of his isolation, his desperate need to be understood, which is in turn a function of his bachelorhood, and that of his disfigurement. The novel certainly goes a good way towards endorsing Flory's raging at imperialism; but it suggests, simultaneously, that the anger is privately motivated, the gesture of a man who is out of the ordinary, and to that extent not a reliably "objective" critic of the system. It is finally the birthmark, and not differences of ideology, which seems to Elizabeth her main reason for rejecting Flory: "It was, finally, the birthmark that had damned him." The two elements (the birthmark and ideological conflict) are, of course, closely interrelated in Flory's history; but the fact that the genetic issue finally predominates over the social question seems to throw the burden of Flory's tragedy, not on to his moral and political conflicts with his fellow-countrymen, but on to what he physically and unchangeably is.

In this and in other ways, *Burmese Days* is really less a considered critique of imperialism than an exploration of private guilt, incommunicable loneliness and loss of identity for which Burma becomes at points little more than a setting. The pain which Flory suffers is "the pain of exile"; but because that exile, by virtue of the birthmark, goes "deeper" than social causes, criticism of the imperialist system is again tempered by a sense of overriding futility. Flory's view, common enough in Orwell, that political stances are merely temperamental rationalizations, is more or less endorsed, to the ultimate detriment of the novel's moral judgements. Despite its obvious political context, *Burmese Days*, in comparison with other of Orwell's novels, is perhaps the least directly social; what really occupies its center is the personal relationship of Flory and Elizabeth. (It is worth adding that for this reason the novel succeeds technically more than most of the others, precisely because it avoids that direct confrontation with a social condition which in later works leads to a crude and latently unbalanced generalizing. It also succeeds because Orwell, like Flory, loves Burma as much as he hates it, a fact which reveals itself in the rich precision of physical description (the landscape, the leopard-hunt), and which disappears when Orwell shifts his attention to England, which cannot, as a physical place, be loved at all.

In the case of Flory, then, we have Orwell's earliest working of tensions and contradictions which remained painfully unresolved throughout his career as a writer. Flory can neither accept, nor disengage from, the "normality" of a hated social system; he can refuse complicity with some of its worst aspects, but only at the cost of a compromised cynicism which reveals him as a "half-man," a soulful and self-pitying outcast. His incapacity for decisive action works in his favor, when it is set against the arrogant certainty of a Verrall; yet this ineffectuality is also his major flaw. If he were more determinedly anti-imperialist, he would see Elizabeth Lackersteen for the callous prig she is; his inability to see this is not only exasperating in a man so sensitive to such callousness in others, but reveals the extent to which he himself shares colonialist feelings, leading him to excuse her desertion of him for Verrall. "What right had he to be jealous? He had offered himself to a girl who was too young and pretty for him, and she had turned him down — rightly." Elizabeth's behaviour has, in fact, little "right" about it; but Flory can only be allowed to recognise this at the risk of self-pity. So, once more, the effort to avoid the risks of introspection leads straight into a condonement of arrogantly colonialist behavior. There is no alternative between a full-blooded condemnation of imperialism which would involve the deceptions of self-pity and of a committed moral stance, and a rejection of self-pity, an acknowledgement of one's own complicity, which more than once blunts the edge of the criticism that part of Orwell wants to make.

If what is at stake in *Burmese Days* is an incapacity either to accept or transcend the texture of "normal" social existence, the same can be said of Orwell's next novel, *A Clergyman's Daughter*. The novel's structure is very simple: Dorothy Hare, a rector's daughter devoted to the small duties of his parochial round, loses her memory, undergoes the experience of the Orwellian underworld (hop-picking, destitution, school-teaching), and finally returns to the rectory to continue her old life. She is rescued from the underworld life by Warburton, a middle-aged bohemian roué who wants to marry her; and the novel's crisis (in so far as it has one, given its rambling, social-documentary structure) is Dorothy's rejection of his offer. What Warburton offers her is essentially a kind of hedonist escape from the deadening trivia of the small town parish; but although Dorothy has learnt the emptiness of this world from her London existence, and to this extent transcended its crippling limits by losing her Christian faith, an escape must be refused: "The point is that all the beliefs I had are gone, and I've nothing to put in their place." Warburton, the emancipated aesthete, is willing to accept and live with this lack of meaning; but Dorothy, while rejecting provincial life intellectually, is still emotionally committed to its values of work, duty, usefulness, decency: in a word, to its conformist "normality," despite its newly revealed vacuousness. Experience and belief have proved to be incompatible; but Dorothy, while unable any longer to accept a belief which thrived simply on an ignorance of social experience, is also unable to accept a life of experience as an end in itself.

Because of this inability, the jovial generosity of Warburton comes to seem tainted, fickle, amoral: when he tries to kiss Dorothy she sees him suddenly as a "fat, debauched bachelor." The physical revulsion is again significant: it is really a way of simplifying the argument, in a typically Orwellian device, by linking despised moral positions to physical obscenity:

> She was in the arms of a man—a fattish, oldish man! A wave of disgust and deadly fear went through her, and her entrails seemed to shrink and freeze. His thick male body was pressing her backwards and downwards, his large, pink face, smooth, but to her eyes old, was bearing down upon her own. The harsh odour of maleness forced itself into her nostrils.

Dorothy's sexual frigidity has previously been the target of the novel's satire: it has signified her pious Anglican innocence. But now, in a suddenly shift, it is used in her favor against Warburton: the virginity which the novel has emphasized as a narrowness, in its first chapters, is now enlisted in a campaign against the pressures of worldly, free-thinking emancipation. The life of the rectory is deadly and drab, but the escape which the Dickensian Christmas figure of Warburton offers must be rejected:

> When he put his arm around her it was as though he were protecting her, sheltering her, drawing her away from the brink of grey, deadly poverty and back to the world of friendly and desirable things—to security and ease, to comely houses and good clothes, to books and friends and flowers, to summer days and distant lands.

These alternatives must be denied, because the grey and deadly world, although empty and stifling, is at least *real*: it is where most people have to live, and escape is false and privileged. It is a conflict of the puritan virtues against the hedonist, and although Dorothy has undergone an experience which confirms Warburton's nihilism and casts the puritan virtues into radical question, the alternatives are Romantic and unthinkable. The full consequences of her experience cannot be faced, for there is no middle ground between narrow devotion and emancipated flippancy. Dorothy can no longer accept her world, but neither can she reject it; the movement to freedom and renewal, here as in all of Orwell's novels, ends in failure. Life is hopeless and sterile, but the worst false consciousness is to think you can change it.

Dorothy is acutely aware that what she has lost, in abandoning Christian faith, is a "totalization": a whole structure which can render experience intelligible, linking its smallest parochial details to a general understanding. Once this has broken under the weight of experience, no other totalization is conceivable: "There was, she saw clearly, no possible substitute for faith; no pagan acceptance of life as sufficient to itself, no pantheistic cheer-up stuff, no pseudoreligion of 'progress' with visions of glittering Utopias and antheaps of steel and concrete." She is left, simply, with the amorphous chaos of experience, which is both inferior to such totalizations in that it is meaningless, but superior in that it is "real." Finally, she discovers a sort of refuge in the empirical facts of experience themselves: the solution to her difficulty emerges as the stock Victorian response of "get(ting) on with the job that lies to hand." And so the gently satirized attitude she had when the novel began—the brisk, spinsterish, self-sacrificial attention to minute tasks—is ultimately affirmed, as superior to a radical criticism of contemporary life which could only be, like Warburton's, that of the "Nancy" poets: decadent, self-indulgent, eccentric and in a sense indecent. Dorothy has changed, but only in consciousness: "It is the things that happen in your heart that matter." And although Warburton's view of life is to that extent endorsed, his belief that it can be acted on is by the same token dismissed. Warburton, in fact, is a curious blend of generous wisdom and hard-boiled philandering—partly a Cheeryble, partly a Micawber or Skimpole—and both attitudes are essential: the first is a necessary criticism of Dorothy's way of life; the second heavily qualifies such criticism and so validates the escape back to the rectory. The inescapable implication is that a rejection of ordinary experience is bound to be unprincipled; yet the alternative is not that the common life is to be gladly embraced. On the contrary, the novel's way of seeing that life has from the outset connived at Warburton's distaste for human society: this characteristically Orwellian description of one of the Rector's parishioners, for instance:

> In her ancient, bloodless face her mouth was surprisingly large, loose and wet. The underlip, pendulous with age, slobbered forward, exposing a strip of gum and a row of false teeth as yellow as the keys of an old piano. On the upper lip was a fringe of dark, dewy moustache. . . .

Ordinary experience is physically disgusting, but the disgust must be painfully overcome, as Dorothy conquers her repugnance at rubbing embrocation into an old lady's legs. It is just that any articulate formulation of this repugnance, such as Warburton makes, must be inhibited by the pressure of guilt: the feeling that the "grey, dead" life, however obscene, is where one really belongs.

Dorothy, then, escapes from the limiting perspectives of the rectory into an underground world of broader experience; yet what she gains from that broadening is ambiguous. On the one hand, it must be enough to expose the unreal pieties of the rectory, to allow access to the true emptiness of reality; yet on the other hand it must not be permitted to subvert too deeply a commitment to that life to which she can return. Part of the novel's technique for sustaining this balance is to be found in the process by which Dorothy enters and inhabits the world of hop-picking and vagrancy. Somehow, the novel has to introduce her into this sphere other than by her own conscious decision: for such a decision would not only be mysteriously obscure in the light of her previous, respectably devotional existence, but would also signify the sort of definitive critical rejection of that existence from which extrication back into the rectory would prove difficult. So the novel selects the simple, improbable device of translating Dorothy from the Suffolk rectory to the back-streets of London by a sudden loss of memory, silently eliding the physical process which this dramatic transition involves. Once Dorothy is immersed in this confused amnesiac state, two concomitant problems can be overcome. First, because she moves in a "dazed, witless" trance, a "contented and unreflecting state," the question of adequate motivation for her unlikely behavior in travelling with petty criminals to Kent can be suspended; she can, as it were, undergo the whole "underground" experience of the younger Orwell himself without our questioning the probability of this in terms of her pios and spinsterly temperament. More importantly, by avoiding the *conscious* critical choice which directed Orwell's own callowly Romantic "low-life" explorations, Dorothy is not required to question her previous history in a way which would cause difficulties over her final return to it. The lose-of-memory gambit simply effects a neat transition from rectory to common lodging-house without raising the complicated issues of motive and purpose which, as a *conscious* process, this would inevitably involve.

Secondly, because of the amnesia, the whole episode takes on the quality of a dream. In this state, "You act and plan and suffer, and yet all the while it is as though everything were a little out of focus, a little unreal." Dorothy is a sort of automaton, moving with uncritical and unreflective contentment in a world of grotesquely unfamiliar experience. The consequence of this is to diminish the solid significance of what experience she has, in a way which allows her final return to the rectory to appear as a re-assumption of "normal" life after an interim and unaccountable suspension of it. There is, in other words, a genuine though submerged question in the novel about the status of her underworld adventures: is this the "reality" which the small Suffolk town deceptively concealed, or is it an unreal interpolation, a salutary but eccentric fantasy? It is the question we put to the novelist who stands behind much of Orwell's work and who is detectable in some of the characterizations of this book: is Fagin, or Brownlow, "real" life?

There is a sense in which the novel wants to assert both attitudes at once. It is essential that the underworld should be sufficiently "real" to disclose the lying pretensions of bourgeois normality; yet the alternatives to that normality, whether "above" it, in the cosmopolitanism of Warburton, or "below" it, in the world of tramps and prostitutes, must at the same time be exposed as in some sense "unreal": as unreliably untypical diversions from the ordinary universe. And so Warburton is presented as two-dimensional, and the criminal underworld assumes a quality of fantasy, through the befuddled mind of Dorothy. Because of that befuddlement, she is able to "experience" the broader world, but without reflecting critically upon it; it is noticeable that we are nowhere shown her actual responses to her adventures, but allowed to see her only from the outside. And so the final conclusions she draws are restricted: she has learnt from the underworld the unreality of ordinary life, but only because she has also seen the emptiness of the wider life, which is thus not in any sense an alternative. Like Flory, she is caught between an overwhelming sense of the falsity of contemporary society and a consciousness of the dangers involved in formulating that sense into anything which might resemble a "position."

Orwell's pre-war development, from *Burmese Days* and *A Clergyman's Daughter* to *Keep the Aspidistra Flying* and *Coming Up For Air*, reflects his movement towards an increasingly explicit, more frontal engagement with the tensions which preoccupied him; but it registers, for related reasons, an accelerating artistic decline. As the central dilemmas become less oblique and more urgently intractable, the treatment becomes significantly cruder, the impulse to violent, cursing caricature and uncontrolled loathing progressively less resistible. As the pressures of a disintegrating society, moving quickly to the brink of war, are increasingly taken, the qualities which distinguished *Burmese Days* and even parts of the notably inferior *A Clergyman's Daughter* — the acute sense of physically active life, the shrewd feeling for social detail — become overwhelmed by a generalizing rhetoric. The sense of social reality is still alive in the childhood scenes of *Coming Up For Air*; but it has taken the form of rambling, unstructured social-documentary observation which cannot be significantly related in feeling or quality to contemporary life.

One index of this growing loss of control is the changed relation between author and protagonist: the degree of objectivity possible in the presentation of Flory or Dorothy dwindles damagingly in the later instances of Gordon Comstock and George Bowling. This is not, of course, to suggest that Comstock, in *Keep the Aspidistra Flying*, is uncritically characterized: rather that what is criticized in him is essentially what Orwell criticizes in himself, and that in this respect he does not cease to be a too-direct projection of his author's own confused and unachieved attitudes. Gordon's dogmatic rejection of capitalism for an underworld existence is seen as impossibly histrionic — "The poet starving in a garret — but starving, somehow, not uncomfortably — that was his vision of himself" — yet his modes of feeling are nevertheless strongly endorsed. Comstock's dehumanizing perception is essentially Orwell's: "The pink doll-faces of upper-class women gazed at him through the car window. Bloody nit-witted lapdogs. Pampered bitches dozing on their chains. Better the lone wolf than the cringing dog." In this way, the novel's criticism of its hero is a regulative factor: it allows Orwell to indulge his own less intelligent feelings under the cover of critical detachment from them. The self-pity which was generally avoided in the case of Flory is now either directly unleashed ("It was the feeling of helplessness . . . of being set aside, ignored — a creature not worth worrying about"), or sidestepped only in a way which is really just a more subtle form of the same emotion, coated with a desperate "realism": "He was thirty, moth-eaten, and without charm. Why should any girl ever look at him again?"

By virtue of Gordon's belief that money is the all-determining factor in every human feeling and relationship, the novel is able to maintain the tension between a criticism of the formal, ordinary world and a criticism of attempts to escape it. If the ordinary world is corrupted by money, then a committed stance against it will also be financially undermined. So commitment will fail absurdly, but not in a way which reflects any particular credit on the established society. Moreover, once Gordon's money-doctrine is accepted, we are persuaded to half-excuse his more self-indulgent behavior — his callous treatment of his girl-friend Rosemary, for example — because lack of money becomes a covering formula for all types of weakness: "Social failure, artistic failure, sexual failure — they are all the same. And lack of money is at the bottom of them all." In believing this, Gordon is holding an attitude which merely reflects the views of the bourgeois world: he is, in this respect, thoroughly endorsing bourgeois values, bound to the world he rejects by a simple inversion. Gordon rejects middle-class society from what are essentially middle-class premises: his extraordinary sensitivity to such matters as the social significance of kinds of doorbell indicates the depth of his obsession with the insignia of a social structure he is supposed to reject. The important point is that Gordon, in subscribing to a financial estimation of human qualities ("No woman ever judges a man by anything except his income"), dehumanizes men as thoroughly as does the society he assaults. He would dismiss the view that, even within the corruption of capitalism, men are still men, and their relationships can still partially transcend the crude determinants which limit them, as "unrealistic" humanitarianism; and the novel, at least at points, would seem to confirm his attitude. Like Orwell himself, Gordon oscillates between Romantic gesture and a cynical accommodation to the *status quo*, seeing no other possible standpoint; like Orwell, he is anti-Romantic in the way that only a confirmed Romantic can be.

It is significant, in the light of the choices offered in the novel, that

Gordon's ideological opponent is not an experienced working-class socialist, but Ravelston, the rich, guilty, middle-class left winger. The result is a
typically Orwellian conflict between the amorphous complexities of sordid
"experience" on the one hand and the abstract rigidities of "ideology" on
the other. "Ravelston . . . knew . . . that life under a decaying capitalism
is deathly and meaningless. But this knowledge was only theoretical. You
can't really *feel* that kind of thing when your income is eight hundred a
year." Gordon's "front-line" defense against socialism, then, is an appeal to
the immovable misery of his own life; but his "second-line" defense is a
cynical acknowledgement, in the manner of Flory, that his arguments are
in any case only the arbitrary projections of private feeling. He attacks
Ravelston's socialist argument, but then, in a second move, detaches
himself cynically from his own scepticism:

> "All this about Socialism and Capitalism and the state of the
> modern world and God knows what. I don't give a — — — for the state
> of the modern world. If the whole of England was starving except
> myself and the people I care about, I wouldn't give a damn."
> "Don't you exaggerate just a little?"
> "No. All this talk we make—we're only objectifying our own
> feelings. It's all dictated by what we've got in our pockets. . . ."

Gordon is forced to deny the validity of his own experience, since even this
leads him towards a (purely negative) "position"; in order to express the
full quality of his cynicism he must at the same time negate it by
suggesting that it is, after all, purely subjective and so valueless. He is, of
course, correct—his pessimism *is* a subjective projection—yet at the same
time the novel's own way of looking works to suggest an at least partial
endorsement of the view that "It's all dictated by what we've got in our
pockets." The novel is thus vulnerable to a serious criticism: in order to
affirm the validity of Gordon's dramatic rejection of society, it must show
his evaluation to be objectively true; but in order to protect both itself and
its hero from the dangers of declared moral commitment, it must at the
same time deny the objective validity of the position it takes. The
uncertainty registers itself, once more, in a fluctuation of attitude within
the text:

> He gazed out at the graceless streets. At this moment it seemed to him
> that in a street like this, in a town like this, every life that is lived must
> be meaningless and intolerable. The sense of disintegration, of decay,
> that is endemic in our time, was strong upon him. Somehow it was
> mixed up with the ad-posters opposite. . . . Corner Table grins at you,
> seemingly optimistic, with a flash of false teeth. But what is behind the
> grin? Desolation, emptiness, prophecies of doom. . . . The great death-
> wish of the modern world. Suicide pacts. Heads stuck in gas-ovens in
> lonely maisonettes. French letters and Amen pills. . . . It is all written
> in Corner Table's face.

The vision of meaninglessness begins as Gordon's own: this is how it "seemed to him," and the novel does not rush instantly to confirm his view. His attitude belongs to the decay of the times, which lends it more solid substantiation but still leaves it open to question. Then, as the passage gathers speed, it is no longer clear whether the speaking voice is Comstock's or Orwell's: what began as a character's attitude is generalized to an image of society which seems, in the dogmatism of the final sentence, to have been finally established as "objective."

Similar ambiguities can be found throughout the book. Gordon's stance is revealed as deliberately self-indulgent—"He clung with a sort of painful joy to the notion that because he was poor everyone must *want* to insult him"—yet, equally, the significance of his experience seems confirmed: "He perceived that it is quite impossible to explain to any rich person, even to anyone so decent as Ravelston, the essential bloodiness of poverty." There can, in other words, be no traffic between the raw stuff of experience and the categories of understanding and analysis; like Flory, Gordon insists on the inherent incommunicability of his deprivation, the impossibility of ever being understood, as a way of avoiding an articulate formulation of his experience which might involve him in a "commitment"—to changing the society, for instance. The experience remains jealously private, a mode of defiant self-definition against the world. This attitude is certainly criticized; but because Gordon's poverty is real, a critic of his behavior is placed, for lack of an alternative standpoint, in the shoes of Ravelston. He can risk criticism of Gordon's attitudes only at the cost of a damaging charge of patrician remoteness from the realities of Gordon's existence.

The choice which the novel poses, then, is essentially that defined by Flory in *Burmese Days*: one must either be a pukka sahib or die. "Serve the money-god or go under: there is no other rule." It is a sharper choice than that in *A Clergyman's Daughter*, where the belief still lingered that an external accommodation to society could be made in a way which preserved an interior consciousness from its falsehoods. In *Aspidistra* this posture is much less viable: if attitudes are so mechanically determined by economic environment (and Gordon's belief is that kind of vulgarization of Marxism), then there can be no balanced compromise. Gordon must finally re-enter society, impelled, significantly, by the forces of "decency." That decency is embodied both in Ravelston (who throughout the novel symbolizes one side of Orwell as Gordon symbolizes another: the generous, wryly "realist" compromiser as against the self-indulgent Romantic), and also in Rosemary, who is to bear Gordon's child. The money-god cannot be fought "when he gets at you through your sense of decency"; the struggle between the impulse to determined moral commitment and the undermining claims of a weary "common sense" is decided in favor of the latter.

Yet it is not decided without considerable ambiguity. Gordon's return to society suggests the impracticality of his venture into a social limbo without, however, too radically questioning the validity of that venture. It also indicates the inevitability of a return to routine social life without implying either that this is a sort of betrayal or that it is deeply valuable. Gordon's plan has been to sink low enough in the social structure to free himself from bourgeois claims: "Down in the safe soft womb of earth, where there is no getting of jobs or losing of jobs, no relatives or friends to plague you, no hope, fear, ambition, honour, duty. . . . That was where he wished to be." It is a way of negating the whole range of common drives and feelings without particularly having to act: a passive subsiding into social death, into the fertile darkness at the base of society. This, as Ravelston points out, is a "mistake": one can't live in a corrupt society and escape corruption. Yet it is not particularly suggested that this mode of "social" protest is inherently inadequate: a capitulation rather than a constructive challenge; a selfishly individualist rather than a collective transcendence; a false idealizing of those at the end of the social scale who seem to Gordon most free from oppression but who are in reality most deeply exploited. It is merely suggested that such a gesture might be possible for saints, but not for Gordon.

On the one hand, the return to lower middle-class life is seen as a compromise (Gordon will "sell his soul" to his firm); but it is also seen, suddenly, as a return to "decent, fully human life," in a way which is difficult to square with the descriptions of that life elsewhere in the novel:

> He wondered about the people in houses like this. They would be, for example, small clerks, shop-assistants, commercial travellers, insurance touts, tram conductors. Did *they* know that they were only puppets dancing when money pulled the strings? You bet they didn't. And if they did, what would they care? They were too busy being born, being married, begetting, working, dying. It mightn't be a bad thing, if you could manage it, to feel yourself one of them, one of the ruck of men. Our civilisation is founded on greed and fear, but in the lives of common men the greed and fear are mysteriously transmuted into something nobler. The lower middle-class people in there, behind their lace curtains, with their children and their scraps of furniture and their aspidistras—they lived by the money-code, sure enough, and yet they contrived to keep their decency. The money-code as they interpreted it was not merely cynical and hoggish. They had their standards, their inviolable points of honour. They "kept themselves respectable"—kept the aspidistra flying. Besides, they were *alive*. They were bound up in the bundle of life. They begot children, which is what the saints and the soul-savers never by any chance do.

The transitions of attitude here are interesting. "Ordinary" life is still seen externally, as a kind of curiosity, and the physical setting of the meditation (Gordon is looking at a street of houses) powerfully underlines the sense of a distanced analysis of the inscrutable. People are still "puppets," and the observer thus distinguished from them by his superior insight; yet if one could plunge into the ruck of men, in a movement at once self-conscious and self-abnegating, one might perhaps find value in their lives. The lower middle class are still dehumanizingly described — notice the casual equivalence of status between lace curtains, children and furniture — but they are, at least, "decent," and even in some nebulous sense "alive." We have not previously seen "life" and "respectability" as equivalents, but now we are asked to do so, as a way of ratifying Gordon's return. So the novel finally perceives the humanity which remains at the heart of capitalism, but chiefly, one feels, as a kind of afterthought, a tactic for rendering Gordon's surrender acceptable. Moreover, the sense of nobility in the common life is not allowed to override, even at this point, the more typically negative feelings towards it which have run throughout the novel, the patronizing Orwellian contempt for the "little" men: "He would be a law-abiding little cit like any other law-abiding little cit — a soldier in the strap-hanging army. Probably it was better so." Is it "better so" because Gordon has no other choice (he feels "as though some force outside him were pushing him"), and is thus acquitted of responsibility? Or because a denial of society, although morally admirable, is simply impractical? Or because society is, after all, of value? It is something of all of these: but the shifts of attitude obscure the issue, trying to salvage the value of social rejection while simultaneously affirming the merit of social settlement. (We do not, for instance, know how much Gordon has lost by his abandonment of poetry, and so how truly detrimental his re-integration might be, since neither we nor he can decide whether he is a good poet or a bad one.) Orwell remains ambiguously stranded between two positions: once more, an intensely emotional rejection of the decent aspidistra world clashes head-on with a sense of pragmatic decency which rejects such intense emotions as privileged luxury.

Orwell's next novel, *Coming Up For Air*, represents, not an extension, but a re-working of the problems we have examined so far. It is his most typical "lower middle-class" novel, obsessed with the cheapness of "suburbia," permeated by a tired, cursing, ragged defeatism and underpinned by a semi-hysterical sense of anxiety and estrangement as war approaches. The choice of the first-person narrator, George Bowling, is itself significant. Bowling is fat, seedy and disillusioned, an integral part of the decaying suburban world he criticizes, yet imbued with a quality of ironic insight superior to those who surround him. There is thus, from the outset, no possibility of the experience offered by the novel being "objectively" appraised — not only because no other character is allowed to advance an opposing viewpoint, but because Bowling's disgust with his environment is qualified by a cynically devaluing sense of his own corruption, his inert complicity in the world he despises:

> Don't mistake me. I'm not trying to put myself over as a kind of tender
> flower, the aching heart behind the smiling face and so forth. You

couldn't get on in the insurance business if you were anything like that. I'm vulgar, I'm insensitive, and I fit in with my environment. . . . But also I've got something else inside me, chiefly a hangover from the past. . . . I'm fat, but I'm thin inside. Has it ever struck you that there's a thin man inside every fat man, just as they say there's a statue inside every block of stone?

Bowling, an "ordinary, middling chap," fits in with his environment: but neither so thoroughly that he cannot achieve a reflectively critical standpoint towards it, nor so loosely that he can analyze it as a whole and imagine an alternative. Through the focus of Bowling, then, the novel is able to project a criticism of society which is the more convincing because it emerges, not from the contemptible "abstractions" of the ideologists, but from a man trapped within its limits. Yet by the same token, the criticism cannot be "positive," since Bowling's title to criticize without arrogance or abstraction is gained from the fact that he bears around the seediness he discerns within his own grotesque physique. He is superior in insight to others, but not too much so:

The usual crowd that you can hardly fight your way through was streaming up the pavement, all of them with that insane fixed expression on their faces that people have in London streets. . . . I felt as if I was the only person awake in a city of sleep-walkers. That's an illusion, of course. When you walk through a crowd of strangers it's next to impossible not to imagine that they're all waxworks, but probably they're thinking just the same about you.

The point of this is both to affirm and to qualify his greater perceptiveness: to allow him a partial transcendence of his environment without the deceptions of disengagement. In one sense, Bowling is presented with a greater degree of objectivity than Gordon Comstock: he is a vulgar, philandering philistine, and is seen by the novel to be so. Yet, as with Comstock, the point of this distancing is to permit Orwell to indulge his own cruder feelings—his malicious delight in cruel parody, his own sporadically philistine contempt for intellectuals, his gushingly apocalyptic despair, his desire for destructive violence—while at the same time protecting himself, by virtue of his spokesman's seedy grossness, from any direct commitment to these attitudes.

The qualities which give Bowling a right to be heard, then, are also the qualities which prevent him from achieving any meaningful organization of his experience. The world dramatized through his eyes is fragmented and unreal: the synthetic frankfurter he swallows early in the novel symbolizes an insubstantial world where everything is "slick and streamlined, everything made out of something else." The most interesting point at issue is not the stock quality of this judgement: whatever local force it might have looks less impressive when it is placed in the context of Bowling's pervasively jaundiced world-view, his monotonously one-dimensional perception of his environment. The significant point is that, here as in other novels, this feeling of social unreality conflicts with an opposing sense of the inert solidity of the suburban world. Bowling's perception of his society is colored by the insistent thought of impending war: he is struck by the strangeness of the notion that the routine world of London, its houses and factories, is likely to be brought into destructive collision with an abstract world of political strategy and theory. He imagines "bloomers soaked in blood" on a washing-line, disturbed by this connection of the domestically known and the abstractly feared. And this works both ways: to sharpen a sense of the indestructible *reality* of the experienced social world ("Miles and miles of streets, fried-fish shops, tin chapels, picture houses . . .") in contrast to the intangible forces of international politics; but also to highlight the fragile unreality of the quotidian, its vulnerability to destruction. The question, once again, is which world is more "real." Bowling recoils from suburbia, but satirizes Porteous, his intellectual friend, for his aesthetic escapism. On the other hand, little of the same satire attaches to Bowling's own escapist and ill-fated return to Lower Binfield, his childhood home.

The ambiguity emerges most sharply in the account of the political meeting which Bowling attends in Part Three of the novel. The anti-Fascist speaker is made to seem a purveyor of mindless, ranting hatred; yet the fear of Fascism he articulates is also Bowling's own, and Bowling can therefore equally satirize those in the audience who cannot understand the lecture. Both commitment and apathy are despicable: Bowling's shifts of feeling towards the audience register the contradictions:

> So perhaps after all there *is* a significance in this mingy little crowd that'll turn out on a winter night to listen to a lecture of this kind. Or at any rate in the five or six who can grasp what it's all about. They're simply the outposts of an enormous army. They're the longsighted ones, the first rats to spot that the ship is sinking. Quick, quick! The Fascists are coming! Spanners ready, boys! Smash others or they'll smash you. So terrified of the future that we're jumping straight into it like a rabbit diving down a boa-constrictor's throat.

The audience is "mingy," but is grudgingly allowed a significance — a significance limited in the next breath to the few, like Bowling himself, who can understand, and which thus preserves intact a dismissive attitude towards the rest. The image of the "long-sighted ones" then defines that importance, but the following image — that of the rats leaving the ship — instantly curtails any suggestion of active virtue. Then, with the following, hysterical phrases ("The Fascists are coming . . ."), a fear which is in fact Bowling's most characteristic feeling is detached from himself and projected on to the audience, as a way of distancing himself from their, and his own, involvements. It is only the "we" of the final sentence which acknowledges (lest Bowling be given too much lonely moral distinction) that this is a common condition in which he himself is implicated. Once more, Orwell's novel embodies a paradox: those who escape from the ordinary world by intellectual pursuits or political ideologies are satirized, but so also are those who involve themselves "mindlessly" with it. The only visible stance is one of passive withdrawal *within* the world: the Bowling posture, midway between fool and intellectual, law-abiding "cit" and radical ideologist, stupefied masses and contemptible capitalists, "Progress" and "Culture." It is the classical stance of the lower middle-class hero.

Orwell's A *Clergyman's Daughter*: The Flight from History
Richard I. Smyer*

At one point in George Orwell's novel A *Clergyman's Daughter* (1935) the central figure, Dorothy Hare, having taken a teaching position at a private girls' school in a London suburb, begins to feel that at last she has found a career that will give some meaning and direction to her life. Prior to this she has undergone a series of disturbing experiences—an unhappy home life with an unloving and unlovable father, the Anglican rector Hare, in the village of Knype Hill; exposure to the unwanted advances of Warburton, a local rake; a period of amnesia during which she wanders off to Kent, where she toils as an economically exploited hop picker; and, later, a miserable existence within the sub-world of the London destitute and jobless. And running through her adventures after leaving home are two dark currents that seem constantly to carry her into the deep waters of isolation and despair. One is the growing awareness that modern civilization, having rejected those ancient beliefs and pieties which once served to bind the elements of a Christian society into a state of communal closeness, is now committed to a worship of money which divides and alienates men from their fellows. The other more personal factor working its influence on Dorothy's mind and spirit is the fact that she is popularly believed to have formed an illicit relationship with Warburton and to have run off with him to Europe, where, it is claimed even in the press, she has, at some stage of her adventures abroad, burst out of the drab cocoon of clerical respectability and winged her luridly colorful way from one Continental bordello to another—a story which moves the girl's shocked father to bar her return home.

Despite a number of minor vexations encountered at the school— some springing from the minors themselves, others from the inadequate educational facilities provided by the tightfisted proprietress, Mrs. Creevy—the young woman finds teaching to be an emotionally rewarding way of life. Critical of the distorted, chauvinistic account of the past

*Reprinted with permission from *Modern Fiction Studies* 21 (1975):31–47. © Purdue Research Foundation.

contained in the school's approved textbook, Dorothy triggers an enthusiastic response to history among her pupils by setting them to work on a
historical chart, a roll of wallpaper on which the students paste cutouts
illustrating various significant events of the past. And the children's
eagerness to come to grips with history, the enthusiasm they feel in making
history, as it were, instead of merely learning about it in a superficial,
mindless way, is matched by Dorothy's readiness to embrace teaching as a
life-long career:

> Almost any job that fully occupied her would have been a relief after the
> horrible futility of the time of her destitution. But this was more than a
> mere job; it was — so it seemed to her — a mission, a life-purpose. Trying
> to awaken the dulled minds of these children, trying to undo the swindle
> that had been worked upon them in the name of education — that,
> surely, was something to which she could give herself heart and soul? So
> for the time being, in the interest of her work, she disregarded the
> beastliness of living in Mrs. Creevy's house, and quite forgot her strange,
> anomalous position and the uncertainty of her future.[1]

A typical feature of Orwell's novels is that of the sudden and
unexpected reversal, the unforeseen turn of events which frustrates the
central characters' conscious aspirations and diverts the course of their
lives, sometimes with dire results. Dorothy's reversal of fortune stems from
her responsiveness to the children's curiosity — particularly to their questions regarding the passage in *Macbeth* in which Macduff reveals that he
was "untimely ripp'd" from the womb: "About half the children went
home and asked their parents the meaning of the word 'womb.' There was
a sudden commotion, a flying to and fro of messages, an electric thrill of
horror through fifteen decent Nonconformist homes" (p. 249). The upshot
of this incident is that in addition to being chastised in front of the irate
parents, Dorothy is forced to abandon her innovative teaching methods
and follow the mind-deadening pedagogic rituals favored by proprietress
and parents alike, and finally she is sacked without notice.

Although only one episode in a novel full of rather sensational, even
melodramatic, events, the passages dealing with the heroine's tenure at
Mrs. Creevy's school, and especially those relating to her interest in history
and the puritanical suspiciousness aroused by the word "womb," not only
hint at the complexity lying beneath the apparently simple and straightforward plot of *A Clergyman's Daughter* but also direct our attention
toward themes and ideas which are important to an understanding of
Orwell's vision of reality, particularly as it is expressed in his fiction.

Even a partial list of the outstanding writers of the twentieth
century — Yeats, Eliot, Malraux, Joyce, Faulkner, Musil, Silone, Mann —
serves as an impressive roll call of figures who, in expressing their
imaginative visions of the human condition, have had to recognize the
problematic nature of man's relationship to history, to the often forbidding
realm of political experience, with its social and spiritual dislocations, its

absurdity and dehumanizing violence. And despite the highly individualized stamp borne by their works, each has sought to wrest some meaning from the chaos of man's temporal existence in the belief or hope that among the fragmented bits and pieces of reality which we call history one might discover traces of a design or catch a fleeting glimpse of some non-temporal, ahistoric mode of reality providing justification for the fallen world of historical experience.

Among such writers can be placed Orwell, in whose essays and novels we can note a growing sense of alarm at the course of Western civilization. Underlying Orwell's continuous attacks on specific examples of economic exploitation, journalistic lying, and political bullying is a suspicion, which gradually hardens into certitude, that Western civilization has for some time been moving toward moral and social calamity. For Orwell, the enervation of people living within modern capitalist society is exemplified by the decay and decrepitude he observes among the swarms of tramps aimlessly wandering around England during the early thirties, as described in *Down and Out in Paris and London*, and by the "labyrinthine slums and dark back kitchens with sickly, ageing people creeping round and round them like black beetles," the inevitable byproducts of an industrial civilization.[2]

If the economic imperatives of modern industrial society have reduced human beings to the condition of creeping beetles, the cultural upheavals of the last several centuries have produced even more dire consequences. The understandable rebellion against a socially and philosophically reactionary Christian world view, in which the doctrines of the immortal soul and an after-life served to insure the docility of the lower classes, has resulted in a humanity reduced to the sad state of a wasp which Orwell once cut in two as it was eating off his plate: "Only when [it] tried to fly away did [it] grasp the dreadful thing that had happened. . . . It is the same with modern man. The thing that has been cut away is his soul. . . ."[3]

In Orwell's view, the loss of man's soul has had grave socio-political effects in the twentieth century.

> It is as though in the space of ten years we had slid back into the Stone Age. Human types supposedly extinct for centuries . . . have suddenly reappeared, not as inmates of lunatic asylums, but as the masters of the world. Mechanisation and a collective economy seemingly aren't enough. By themselves they lead merely to the nightmare we are now enduring: endless war and endless underfeeding for the sake of war, slave populations toiling behind barbed wire, women dragged shrieking to the block, cork-lined cellars where the executioner blows your brains out from behind. So it appears that amputation of the soul *isn't* just a simple surgical job. . . . The wound has a tendency to go septic.[4]

Although Orwell grants that material progress does occur, he believes that history, even when it seems to move forward, leaves dead civilizations in its wake.[5] More ominous, in Orwell's opinion, is the circumstance that, in reality, history has tended to follow a downward spiral. Thus, the Puritan Revolution brought neither real liberty nor equality, and there is reason to believe that the age of capitalism, with the horrors of the Industrial Revolution and the imperialistic assault on other cultures, is in fact worse even than the feudal period.[6]

This downward-and-upward spiral movement of modern history contradicts the forward-and-backward progressivist view held by nineteenth-century and Edwardian liberals. Noting the sudden appearance during the thirties and forties of vast slave empires, Orwell points out that the face of Europe has undergone changes incredible to thoughtful men living only a few generations earlier. The widespread infatuation with communist Russia in the late thirties gave new life to what once were thought to be moribund superstitions—patriotism, military greatness, and imperialism; and even in post–World War II France the notion of a humanitarianism unconcerned with national boundaries is, Orwell claims at the time, far less influential than the old idols of Army, Fatherland, and Glory.[7]

Subverting the liberal-humanist belief in progress is the paradox that the same technological sophistication once thought necessary for the development of a humane, enlightened society is, during the second quarter of the century, geared for the destruction of such a society: "Modern Germany is far more scientific than England, and far more barbarous. Much of what [H. G.] Wells has imagined and worked for is physically there in Nazi Germany. The order, the planning, the State encouragement of science, the steel, the concrete, the aeroplane, are all there, but all in the service of ideas appropriate to the Stone Age."[8] It is just this oppressive awareness that the increasingly efficient technology of Western civilization is being used for ever more savage purposes which, in the essay "Shooting an Elephant" (1936), prompts Orwell's half-lament regarding the replacement of British imperialism, bad enough in its own way, by newer, less benign imperial powers (I, 236).

According to Orwell, the retrograde direction of modern history is tied in with recent attempts to alter the course of events by means of revolution. "We are living in a nightmare," Orwell claims in 1940, "precisely *because* we have tried to set up an earthly paradise."[9] Orwell has little doubt that the success of revolutionary activity is the very circumstance that dooms it. Even without a Stalin the Russian Revolution was bound to transform itself into a tyranny because the ideals motivating revolutionaries are "fatally mixed up" with a selfish hankering after power for its own sake.[10]

The anti-Utopian attitude expressed in a number of Orwell's essays and articles appears, to one degree or another, in his novels. Caught between nostalgia for the old pre-colonial Burma (including its backwardness and brutality) and a personal need to avoid the disapprobation of the white colonial ruling class, John Flory (*Burmese Days*, 1934) takes advantage of the few opportunities that present themselves to air his secret misgivings about the future in store for a Europeanized Burma: "Where's it going to lead, this uprush of modern progress. . . ? Just to our . . . swinery of gramophones and billycock hats. Sometimes I think that in two hundred years . . . all this will be gone — forests, villages, monasteries, pagodas all vanished. And instead, pink villas fifty yards apart; all over these hills, as far as you can see, villa after villa, with all the gramophones playing the same tune. And all the forests shaved flat — chewed into pulp for the *News of the World*, or sawn up into gramophone cases."[11] Let him drink himself into degeneracy, Flory comments about a particularly backward native; "it . . . postpones Utopia" (p. 44). In *Animal Farm* and *Nineteen Eighty-Four* Orwell deals at greater length with those inner contradictions which deflect the forward thrust of Utopian aims and direct them down along a spiral into the Tartarean blackness of the modern dystopia.

In order to grasp the imaginative function of Orwell's reaction to history in these later novels, it may be helpful to glance once more at the passage from *A Clergyman's Daughter* described above. Worth noting is the fact that Dorothy's new-found enthusiasm for history, the conviction that her students' collective reconstruction of the past has, along with the teaching of other subjects, given to her own godless existence some meaning and significance, is blighted by a misadventure associated with what appears to be some form of sexual indecency (the utterance of the word "womb"). Moreover, insofar as the project upon which the students are working is a re-created history which is supposedly enhancing the lives of the pupils and their teacher, Dorothy and her girls are, in effect, producing a mini-Utopia within the school. This being the case, an interesting question arises: What connects the term "womb" to the swift collapse of this pocket Utopia and the reassertion of Mrs. Creevy's authoritarian and reactionary control over Dorothy's classroom? What is the link between the outrage over Dorothy's reference to Macduff's parturition and the uneasy relationship between individuals and the historical process.

Although far less popular than *Animal Farm* and *Nineteen Eighty-Four*, *A Clergyman's Daughter* is, for several reasons, worth examining. In addition to expressing psychological and socio-political themes relevant to Orwell's fiction in general, *A Clergyman's Daughter* exhibits the earliest instance of Orwell's attempt to break free from the plot conventions of the realistic novel and to exploit his material for more or less non-naturalistic ends. To be more precise, there is evidence that to a significant degree this novel is characterized by the employment of naturalistically presented details to produce a surrealistic effect and that the traditional linear plot development — by means of which a reader is shown the fictional characters' interactions with various aspects of their social and physical environment — becomes a series of interior adventures, a kind of psychodrama played out within a mental landscape, the inner-space of the mind. And as I shall indicate, in this novel Orwell, by directing our attention toward the subterranean depths of Dorothy's mind, endeavors to throw light on those obscure discontents, anxieties, and longings which in one way or another condition her attitude toward civilization, past and present.

As the novel opens, we see that England's spiritual dryness is not simply an urban phenomenon, for even within pastoral England, as represented by the rural community of Knype Hill, Reverend Hare's congregation is dwindling, and the bulk of the local population is indifferent to religion. The inner decay of traditional religious institutions, and particularly the moral disintegration of the Established Church, is embodied in Dorothy Hare's father, whose concern for his own investments and material comforts blinds him to his parishioners' spiritual needs. Dorothy's wanderings through England sharpen her own awareness of the gap between genuine Christianity and a money-worshipping society: agricultural laborers receive niggardly wages for long, grueling hours spent in the hop fields, while in the city only one commandment is respected: "Thou shalt not lose thy job."

Even before the conscious loss of religious faith that takes place sometime during her experiences in the England beyond the confines of Knype Hill, Dorothy finds herself in a dilemma common in Orwell's novels — the feeling that one is trapped beneath the painful weight of time. The opening paragraph of the novel suggests that for Dorothy time past provides no comfort, nor does time present offer liberation from the burden of the past: "As the alarm clock on the chest of drawers exploded like a horrid little bomb of bell metal, Dorothy, wrenched from the depths of some complex, troubling dream, awoke with a start and lay on her back looking into the darkness in extreme exhaustion" (p. 5). If the nightworld of the unconscious mind generates disturbing dreams, the daylight world of consciousness, of historical and clock time, holds out little more than a life of constant rushing to meet deadlines, of continual commands to be punctual, of onerous parish duties to be fulfilled and expectations to be met.

More upsetting are the reminders of time as destroyer, which — in the form of the decaying church building and the aged, sickly bodies of the parishioners to whom the girl must minister — confront Dorothy at every turn and fill her with foreboding and disgust. Moreover, Dorothy's obsession with the destructive effects of time seems to go hand in hand with a guilty fear regarding the flesh, for her sense of sin remains firm even while her formal religious faith is being eroded. The local butcher's dunning notices become terrifying warnings to her that the flesh must be paid for (p. 19).

Later, fully aware of her loss of faith in immortality, Dorothy finds earthly existence intolerable: "Life, if the grave really ends it, is monstrous and dreadful" (p. 315). Unable to find any source of joy in a world bereft of religious significance, she sinks into a life of drudgery. At the end of the novel, the girl, once again at the rectory and apparently bent on escaping from an awareness that human existence is spiritually meaningless, throws herself back into a mind-numbing life of trivial parish activities.

Although Dorothy's anguish at both her inability to believe and the breakdown of Christian unity in society as a whole is conveyed in a straightforward manner, critics have been disturbed by areas of vagueness in the novel. For one thing, the cause of Dorothy's disbelief seems unclear. Although half the narrative has to do with Dorothy's encounters with a society fragmented by rapacious exploitation, suspicion, and selfishness, apparently Orwell expects the reader to accept without question the validity of Dorothy's claim that these experiences are irrelevant to her apostasy: "Those things don't really matter. I mean, things like having no money and not having enough to eat. Even when you're practically starving—it doesn't *change* anything inside you" (p. 294).

Other questions are raised about Orwell's treatment of the central character's sexual problem, particularly as it relates to the marriage proposal from Warburton, who, tired of playing the rake, offers an alternative to a life of drudgery and spinsterhood. A confirmed atheist, Warburton can enjoy earthly pleasures without demanding immortality or any transcendent justification for human life; and there are signs that despite his godlessness and hedonism, Dorothy is fond of him. Side by side with the life-affirming Warburton, Dorothy can calmly meet the menacing gaze of the local butcher (p. 46); and at the end of the novel, Dorothy seems to be on the verge of accepting Warburton's offer of marriage, only to recoil in disgust at his attempt to kiss her—a revulsion that turns her toward the emotional impoverishment of a lonely spinsterhood.

The nature of Dorothy's sexual anxiety is, I think, meant to be connected to the larger matter of Orwell's vision of history. An examination of this relationship may open new perspectives in regard to the criticisms directed at Orwell's failure to indicate the link joining Dorothy's wanderings to her loss of faith and sexual distress.[12]

Dorothy associates childhood memories of her parents with certain "dreadful scenes," and to these recollections are added others of steel engravings depicting nymphs pursued by satyrs with "furry thighs." Now, for the adult Dorothy, the thought of physical intimacy with a male is unbearable: "They were dreadful when they kissed you—dreadful and . . . disgusting, like some large, furry beast that rubs itself against you . . ." (pp. 91–94 *passim*). Furthermore, the narrative suggests that behind Dorothy's rejection of Warburton lies a fear-provoking, seemingly unrecognized incest fantasy. Dorothy's upsetting vision of an assault by a "furry beast" takes on added meaning when we remember that her father's surname is Hare.

The broader implications of the heroine's troubled sexual life may become clearer if we direct our attention away from the documentary realism of Orwell's style and pay heed to the symbolic import of the narrative, keeping alert to the possibility that the apparently naturalistic treatment possesses a surrealistic dimension through which is objectified Dorothy's inner condition. *A Clergyman's Daughter* can be divided into three more or less distinct sections. Chapter I describes Dorothy's unhappy life at Knype Hill — an existence marked by dunning notices, a tiresome round of parish activities, and an unrewarded devotion to the needs of an emotionally frigid father. The next section (Chapters II through IV), which begins sometime after Dorothy's lapse into amnesia, records the girl's experiences in the Kentish hop fields and in London, first as a tramp and later as a schoolteacher. In the third section (Chapter V) Dorothy returns home and, after rejecting Warburton, throws herself back into the narcotizing existence of parish drudgery. However, another way of looking at these various stages of the narrative is to regard the opening section as primarily dealing with the heroine's conscious feelings of discontent; the second (and longest) section as being, for the most part, an interior drama, a descent into a subconscious *mise en scène* where takes place an obscure struggle between guilt and a longing for innocence and peace; and the third, a return to the daylight world of emotional isolation and a life spent trying to muffle an anxiety-burden consciousness.

What drives Dorothy from Knype Hill is the circumstance that despite the girl's attempt to erect around herself a fortress of unassailable righteousness through obsessive acts of filial self denial and religious piety within the parish, her protective redoubt gradually transforms itself into a hall of mirrors reflecting back the shadowy dimensions of her incest fantasy — which takes on an alarming solidity in the figure of Warburton. Warburton is the complement to the girl's emotionally unresponsive father. The two men are doubles, halves of a single paternal entity. Deaf to the outcries of his creditors, Hare shamelessly allows his debts — such as the butcher's — to go unpaid; Warburton, deaf to the townspeople's censure, has lived in shameless concubinage (pp. 31, 45). To the symbolic equation of behavioral similarities can be added the revealing coincidence that a Van Dyck portrait looks down from a wall in the rectory, while next door to the libertine lives the ever-watchful town scandalmonger, Mrs. Semprill, whose face has the "appearance of a Van Dyck portrait" (pp. 19, 50). The same panic which, triggered at the end of the novel when the suitor hugs Dorothy "pseudo-paternally" (p. 288) and precipitates the severance of their relationship, operates earlier as Warburton, alone with Dorothy in his house, prefaces a seduction attempt with the curious remark that he is "old enough to be [her] father . . ." (p. 88). In this instance, the severance, the girl's subsequent attack of amnesia, is mental — a separation of her past history from her present existence.

Doubling is not, however, limited to Hare and Warburton, for Mrs. Semprill is like a fragmented part of Dorothy, an omniscient conscience relentlessly poisoning the girl's mind with reminders of evil: "No indiscretion, however small, escaped [Semprill's] vigilance." Given the nature of Dorothy's sexual anxiety, it is grimly appropriate that the scandalmonger's stories usually bear "some monstrous tinge of perversion"; and within a fictive world marked by the breakdown of social unity, it is not surprising to find that Semprill's rumormongering has disrupted relationships between men and women: her tales, we learn, have brought about the dissolution of engagements and quarrels between spouses (pp. 51–54).

Dorothy's conscious attempts to mortify the flesh for the purpose of warding off "sacrilegious thoughts" and punishing herself for some "sin of yesterday" prove ineffectual in subduing her terror. At the end of the first section, Dorothy, having fled from the would-be seducer's home to the refuge of the rectory, where she tries to quell her panic by working on costumes for a church pageant, lapses into a fugue condition.

When next we see Dorothy, she is on a London street. With her past a total blank, she is a new-born person, and, in fact, she behaves like a child — haltingly associating sounds with objects and only gradually becoming conscious of her own distinct existence. As though in effect recreating her personal history, Dorothy sets out on a journey to Kent, which, not consciously known by the amnesiac, is her birthplace (pp. 96–105 *passim*).

Dorothy's return to Kent, to the place of her origin, is, however, a return to a special form of the past, for hers is an interior journey, a trek into the mind where traces of the past may still exist. Thus, on the road south, Dorothy enters into a kind of dreamworld: she "seemed almost to be sleeping as she walked," and she arrives at her destination "in a dreamlike state" (pp. 110, 119).

Worth noting is the parallelism between life in the Kentish hop fields and Dorothy's situation at home. Being with Nobby, the laborer whom she accompanies to Kent, is curiously similar to living with Reverend Hare. In both cases Dorothy is nearly destitute, and the domestic services she provides for Nobby are much the same as those she has performed for her father (pp. 6, 118–119, 122). (Indicative of the parallel is the fact that the kitchen table against which Dorothy habitually bumps at the rectory has its counterpart in the sack of potatoes which rubs her hip raw on the road to Kent [pp. 6, 110].)

What lends importance to these similarities is the circumstance that Nobby is a combination of Warburton and Hare (the two facets of the fragmented father), who seems not to call forth the girl's incest anxiety. Nobby is a grubby version of Warburton in that both men resort to a falsehood to lure Dorothy into accompanying them — one to his house, the other to Kent — and neither man loses his composure when his sexual advances are rebuffed (pp. 89, 112). And like Hare, who refuses to pay his creditors, Nobby is a "bold thief" (p. 108). But beneath these similarities lies what would seem to be a crucial difference: Nobby is the good father.

Unlike the improvident Hare, who cannot manage his own household finances, Nobby is an "expert in small economies"; in contrast to the insistently lecherous Warburton, the laborer prefers pilfering orchards to making love (p. 129).

As suggested earlier, the work of Dorothy and her pupils on the historical chart, that re-creation of history which transforms the class period into a meaningful experience for both teacher and students, is a small-scale Utopian gesture. Analogously, Dorothy's activities in the Kentish hop fields become, insofar as this rural setting represents a longed-for condition of purity, an interior pageant, personal instead of public, which, at least for a while, heralds the discovery of a pastorally innocent Utopia within the depths of her own being. For one thing, Kent is a fantasy world, seemingly free of the sense of shame which Dorothy has earlier felt when begging credit from impatient merchants: "All of [the hop pickers] begged, Dorothy with the others; she had no remembered past, no standards of comparison to make her ashamed of it" (p. 108). Her own newspaper photograph conveying "absolutely nothing to her mind," it is small wonder that the sensational press accounts of Warburton's supposed nocturnal flight abroad with a flimsily clad Dorothy have no effect on her (p. 137). Moreover, even the sense of historicity, of the movement from time past toward time future, seems to be abolished in this rural Utopia: "More and more [Dorothy] had come to take her curious situation for granted, to abandon all thoughts of either yesterday or tomorrow." And being an exploited, over-worked laborer is not all bad: her range of consciousness narrowed by the long, stupifying hours of work in the fields, Dorothy, too tired to "struggle with nebulous mental problems," is "profoundly, unquestionably happy" (p. 135).

If at the surface level of narrative A Clergyman's Daughter presents us with a fragmented society, a civilization fractured by mistrust and alienation, fragmentation exists at the psychological level, too, as is indicated by the instances of doubling. Moreover, we may conclude that the reason Dorothy can gain the sanctuary of this apparently guilt-free, joyful Utopia is that Orwell has reduced her to a dream-figure whose sexual identity is sheared off. In fact, Dorothy's habit of addressing herself in the second person (p. 5) suggests the process of fragmentation that allows her to enjoy a blissful existence in the innocent childhood world of Kent. Her other, disreputable libidinous self assumes a separate existence as a tabloid wanton sinning her way through Europe.

But Dorothy's idyll cannot last; the Utopian dream of innocence cannot — for reasons I shall discuss later — remain inviolable to the intrusive nightmare of her incest fear. Nobby's arrest for raiding orchards (at once a symbolic sexual violation and a reminder of mankind's primal transgression) is linked to the other pickers' expressed opinion that he and Dorothy are lovers (pp. 140, 145). Now Dorothy realizes that the sensational newspaper stories — the headlines of which unintentionally suggest incest (PASSION DRAMA IN . . . RECTORY — PARSON'S DAUGHTER AND ELDERLY SEDUCER — WHITE-HAIRED FATHER PROSTRATE WITH GRIEF) — refer to her. And even though Dorothy consciously refuses to believe these accounts, the girl's behavior on the eve of her departure from Kent, her acceptance of a young man's kiss and subsequent dancing around the campfire while holding hands with a "butcher-boy" (p. 155), indicates the re-emergence of sexual guilt and an oppressive awareness of time.

Dorothy's move from Kent to London after her unanswered appeal to return home represents one more stage in the transformation of Utopian illusion into dystopian suffering. Among the London vagabonds, as among the Kentish laborers, "the world, inner and outer, grows dimmer till it reaches almost the vagueness of a dream" (p. 202). It is a dream of cold and hunger and dirt, a place in which the circumstantially described "external" world around Dorothy again becomes a large-scale reflection of her tormented inner life.

The nature of Dorothy's sexual malaise is almost explicitly conveyed in the hallucinatory Trafalgar Square passage (in Chapter III), where Tallboys, a rector defrocked for his sexual relationship with a local spinster, gleefully recalls pinching, "in loco parentis," the behinds of parish Girl Guides and later suggests that Dorothy assist him in a Black Mass (pp. 175–191 passim). In this surrealistic episode, we see more clearly exhibited than elsewhere the splitting technique associated with psychological fragmentation. To protect themselves from the freezing night air, the tramps, including an exhausted Dorothy, wrap themselves in newspapers. "There is," we learn, "some furtive fondling of the women under cover of the paper. Dorothy is too far gone to care" (p. 195). Symbolically, Dorothy's alienated sexual self operates "under cover of the paper" in Europe, while the Dorothy who remains apart in England, literally insulated, enjoys a short-lived illusion of guiltlessness because, in terms of the novel's dreamworld geography, she is "too far gone to care."

However, reminders of sexual evil cannot be escaped. In addition to being repeatedly taken for a fallen woman while in London (pp. 100, 159, 163), Dorothy finds that her first lodging in the city is in a refuge for prostitutes (p. 164). The ineradicable obscenity carved into a wall of this establishment is one more sign of her failure to shake off the incubus of guilt (p. 158). Indeed, there are hints dropped here and there that a sense of sexual evil is too deeply rooted in Dorothy's mind to allow even the return to Kent, to a condition of childhood innocence, to be anything but chimerical; for from the very start of the novel she has been imprisoned within her own private London. Dorothy's longing for innocence, for certainty regarding her righteousness, is bound to be frustrated because, her adult emotional life crippled by the voice of Mrs. Semprill, which she harbors within herself, she carries a load of guilt with her into Kent. Early in the novel Dorothy, busy with her morning chores, hears the "antiphonal snoring of her father and Ellen [Millborough], the maid of all work" (p.

6). In the ambiguous realm of fantasy, this remark calls up a sexually suggestive, albeit amusing, image. Later, as the amnesiac travels to Kent, she calls herself Ellen (p. 102); and as though inadvertently underscoring the symbolic relationship between herself and the maid, Dorothy assumes the girl's surname from the time when the Kentish idyll begins to crumble until her apparent exculpation and return home. Finally, it should be noted that the phrase by which Orwell designates his heroine, "a clergyman's daughter," is a tongue-in-cheek British term for a woman of easy virtue.

Before examining the connection between Dorothy's incest anxiety and the novel's treatment of history, we should grasp the fact that the "sin of yesterday," which leaves the girl emotionally disabled, is not to be understood as an actual incestuous experience, nor is the past, the "yesterday" which she hopes to find, made spotless, simply the girl's literal past. The past with which Dorothy tries to cope is a subjective reality within her adult, guilt-burdened mind.[13] Moreover, even the final reconciliation with her father, who seems a shade less cold than usual, fails to suggest that now she is able to embrace life enthusiastically. Although Mrs. Semprill, the externalized projection of Dorothy's oppressive conscience, has left town, her influence is still at work within the girl. Dorothy's touching of her own breasts before setting out for Kent, the discovery of her womanhood (p. 98), implies that state of adult awareness which makes impossible any return to what might be dimly perceived as the guiltless, spontaneous joy of childhood. Consequently, at the end of the novel, Dorothy signifies her acceptance of an emotionally ossified existence by constructing a "breastplate" for the school pageant (p. 320).

To understand the pertinence of Dorothy's religious and sexual problems to the novel's vision of history, we should bear in mind several important points. As has been indicated, repeatedly in A Clergyman's Daughter the central character's personal history, the series of events and experiences defining her movement through time and space, is initiated by some form of reprehensible sexuality. Furthermore, historical experience, both personal and social, manifests itself through various kinds of disunity—shame, suspicion, distrust, isolation, exploitation, and emotional alienation. Warburton's attempted seduction leads to Dorothy's amnesia (a mental fragmentation) and separation from home and father; her expulsion from an Edenic Kent is traceable to Nobby's violation of the orchard, the theft of forbidden fruit; and the collapse of the heroine's snug classroom Utopia and her eventual dismissal from Mrs. Creevy's school stem from the parents' priggish outrage at the word "womb."

But if Dorothy's historical identity exposes her to a riddled, splintered existence, there are intimations of another, more unified mode of reality which holds out the promise of stasis and wholeness and innocence. The last we see of Dorothy, she is once more hard at work in the rectory, feverishly preparing costumes for the church pageant. "We *must* make that pageant a success! she thought. . . . The problem of faith and no faith had vanished utterly from her mind. It was beginning to get dark, but, too busy to stop and light the lamp, she worked on, pasting strip after strip of paper into place, with absorbed, with pious concentration, in the penetrating smell of the gluepot" (p. 320). What appears to be an obsessive desire to redeem history, to invest the welter of humanity's struggles in time with a ceremonial orderliness and meaning, is, in fact, an escape from history. Pasted together in an obscure rectory, sponsored by a backwater church, directed by a provincial schoolmaster, this pageant bears only the faintest resemblance to the real world outside, to a civilization discarding its ancient beliefs and following a secular code of values based on distrust and ruthless competition. Safely insulated within her father's country church, sealed off by the impenetrable armor of thought-constricting toil, Dorothy can blot from consciousness all knowledge of the chaotic great world. What holds her rapt attention is not the historical pageant but the pot of glue, the fascinating emblem of an intrauterine condition of unchanging peace and wholeness.

Secularized history is open ended, always on the move, a restless and protean reality in which innocence turns into evil, security into uncertainty—a fallen, post-Edenic world of time, decay, and dissolution. It is not surprising, therefore, that Dorothy finds comfort from states of enclosure, from those womb-like places—the rectory, Kentish haystacks, the classroom, the cell of a London jail under the command of a "fatherly sergeant" (p. 203), newspaper swathings—which provide refuge from the divisive gale winds of historical reality, whether public or personal. Indeed, the reaction of one of the pupils to Dorothy's proposal of the historical chart—the child locks herself in the bathroom (p. 243)—serves as an implicit commentary not only on the teacher's rashly optimistic belief that innocents may safely be exposed to historical experience but also on the assumption that an involvement with history is compatible with the actualization of Utopia.

If the ur-longing to return to a condition of stasis and containment stands opposed to the disharmony of historical reality, then we can see how Dorothy's quest to return home, to regain the place of her origin, may be threatened by the historical imperative to move forward in time. As this imperative becomes more insistent, producing more alarming signs of social and personal fragmentation, the need to regain an intimate union with the past becomes more and more urgent, so pressing, in fact, as to assume the extreme form of an incest fantasy. In the fallen, disunified realm of historical time, the alienation of men from women—Dorothy's fear of males, the divisive effects of Mrs. Semprill's rumors, Reverend Hare's coldness toward his daughter, the ill-natured rivalry between Mrs. Creevy's establishment and a neighboring boys' school (p. 215), and even Macduff's violent and "untimely" separation from his mother—is the basic metaphor indicating the unhappy condition of modern society. Consequently, that state of being farthest removed from historical reality takes a form symbolically expressive of an intimate and all-embracing male-female union—that of incest, the ultimate reactionary gesture.

But, obviously, the very nature of such a fantasy stands athwart the road back to an Edenic condition of stasis and contentment, for the awareness of sexual guilt is in itself an ineradicable sign that one belongs to the world of historical experience. And perhaps because of this circumstance, Dorothy finds herself no longer able to believe, to tolerate the idea of an immanent, patriarchal God, close both to her personally and to mankind's historical development. There can be no rebirth into some ahistorical condition of purity because Dorothy's sin-burdened, time-bound sensibility is too splintered ever to be made whole. In fact, the flight from her historical, as well as sensual, identity is itself a symptom of this fragmentation, since her escape involves an obliteration of self-awareness and a rejection of consciousness, the result being that at the end of the novel Dorothy's final state, her mindless fixation on a common gluepot, is little more than a pathetically simulated return to the womb-like wholeness of the past.

An examination of Orwell's later works reveals the presence of this tension—the longing to return to a state of innocence, permanence, and wholeness versus the oppressiveness of one's conscious participation in historical experience. Moreover, in *A Clergyman's Daughter*, we encounter an artistic difficulty which, as the study of Orwell's other novels suggests, is not easily solved—the problem of relating the central characters' inner, sometimes surrealistically expressed anxieties to disorders afflicting the realistically described socio-political milieu. At times it seems as though the familiar, observable "real" world of external reality disintegrates, loses its substantiality, and becomes little more than the epiphenomenal projection of the protagonists' inner conflicts—conflicts, it is important to note, which are frequently too idiosyncratic to shed light on problems affecting society as a whole. In the case of *A Clergyman's Daughter* it is not enough for the narrator to remark glibly that his heroine's sexual neurosis is "too common, nowadays, to occasion any kind of surprise" (p. 94), for the extreme interiorization of the narrative, the claustrophobically psychodramatic quality which marks the rendering of Dorothy's experiences, raises a legitimate doubt regarding the relevance of her personal dilemma to the state of society in general.

The basic incompatibility between Utopian goals and the historical process finds expression almost totally in terms of the central character's personal dilemma: the Utopian quest takes on a private and, therefore, restricted meaning, and the history with which Dorothy has such an uneasy relationship is merely that of her own neurotic existence. In *A Clergyman's Daughter* the downward-and-backward movement of civilization toward the atavistic leader-worship and savagery of twentieth-century totalitarianism, as depicted in *Animal Farm* and *Nineteen*

Eighty-Four, appears in a rudimentary and limited way—in the form of Mrs. Creevy's harsh authoritarianism and Dorothy's descent into a condition of radically diminished consciousness for the purpose of regaining a past at once timeless and free of sexual tensions. Not until *Animal Farm* is the pathetic futility of the individual's Utopian dream of personal regeneration broadened into a collective tragedy; and the gap existing in *A Clergyman's Daughter* between the central character's psychosexual malaise and an irredeemable civilization is not bridged until *Nineteen Eighty-Four*, where we find the sexual discontents of the protagonist linked to the totalitarian imperatives of a State bent on eradicating the autonomous individual and transforming society into a mindlessly submissive primal horde.

Notes

1. *A Clergyman's Daughter* (New York: Harcourt, Brace and Co., 1960), p. 245. Page references will be placed within parentheses in the text whenever this can be done without confusing the reader.

2. *The Road to Wigan Pier* (New York: Harcourt, Brace and Co., 1958), p. 17.

3. "Notes on the Way" (1940), in *The Collected Essays, Journalism and Letters of George Orwell*, eds. Sonia Orwell and Ian Angus (New York: Harcourt, Brace and Co., 1968), II, 15. Unless otherwise indicated, references to Orwell's non-fictional writings are from the four-volume *Collected Essays*.

4. "Notes on the Way," II, 15–16. All italics are in the original.

5. "As I Please" (1943), III, 57; "Will Freedom Die with Capitalism?" *The Left News*, No. 58 (1941), p. 1683.

6. Introduction to *British Pamphleteers: From the Sixteenth Century to the French Revolution*, eds. George Orwell and Reginald Reynolds (London: Allen Wingate, 1948), pp. 9–10.

7. "Looking Back on the Spanish War" (1943), II, 259–260; "Inside the Whale" (1940), I, 515; "Occupation's Effect on French Outlook," *Observer* (London), 4 March 1945, p. 5.

8. "Wells, Hitler and the World State" (1941), II, 143,

9. "Notes on the Way," II, 16.

10. "Catastrophic Gradualism" (1945), IV, 17–18.

11. *Burmese Days* (New York: Harcourt, Brace and Co., 1962), p. 42.

12. John Atkins, *George Orwell: A Literary and Biographical Study* (New York: Frederick Ungar, 1954), p. 267; Laurence Brander, *George Orwell* (London: Longmans, Green and Co., 1954), pp. 93–95; Jenni Calder, *Chronicles of Conscience: A Study of George Orwell and Arthur Koestler* (University of Pittsburgh Press, 1968), pp. 87–89; Christopher Hollis, *A Study of George Orwell: The Man and His Works* (Chicago: Henry Regnery Company, 1956), p. 68; Frank W. Wadsworth, "Orwell as a Novelist: The Early Work," *UR* 22 (1955), 98.

13. Indicative of Orwell's emphasis on the subjective significance of Dorothy's experiences is the fact that nowhere in the novel are we given any reliable information as to whether or not the young woman has, at some time either during or after the evening of her visit to Warburton's home, yielded to his entreaties and run off with him, as Mrs. Semprill claims. All we can be sure of is that Dorothy suffers an attack of amnesia after hurrying away from Warburton's and later turns up in London. Orwell's refusal to fill in this gap suggests that the

surrealistic implications of the events of the narrative are more important than the events themselves. As one reviewer put it: "For all its realism of scene, . . . *A Clergyman's Daughter* is not in a fundamental sense a 'realistic' novel. The story of the clergyman's daughter . . . is . . . credible, but the writing that makes it so is of exactly the variety that can sometimes give fantasy concreteness." (C.C., review of *A Clergyman's Daughter*, *Saturday Review of Literature*, 15 August 1936, p. 21.)

In Dubious Battle: George Orwell and the Victory of the Money-God

Nicholas Guild*

When Gordon Comstock, the moth-eaten hero of George Orwell's *Keep the Aspidistra Flying*, finally capitulates to the conditions of real life by giving up his war on money, marrying his pregnant mistress, and going back to work for the New Albion Publicity Company, he is obviously doing something of which his creator approves, and yet critics of the novel frequently cite this ending as its greatest fault. John Wain, claiming that "Orwell originally intended the story to be a sardonic, bitter little parable about what happens to the soul of a society that plants itself in money and still expects to flower," maintains that "in the closing pages everything collapses, tripped up by one of the author's basic confusions. . . . what ought to be a fine, gloomy satiric ending turns unexpectedly into a renascence,"[1] and Sir Richard Rees states that "In the end he [Gordon] is a disastrously defeated rebel."[2]

Both of these statements imply that the novel would have been more consistent and that Gordon's conduct would have been more admirable if he had never been blackjacked by Rosemary's pregnancy into re-entering middle-class life, if he had been allowed to continue his downward slide into the subworld of poverty. This, in turn, assumes that Gordon was right to declare war on money in the first place, that the moral victory he believed himself to have won by embracing the shabby life of a bookshop assistant was somehow real. Except incidentally, however, is *Keep the Aspidistra Flying* a satire, or even a criticism, of what Gordon calls the "money-world"? The conventional wisdom seems to be that it is. According to the back jacket of my edition, Lionel Trilling regarded it as "a *summa* of all the criticisms of a commercial civilization that have ever been made," but such a conclusion seems questionable. If Orwell's purpose was to examine a commercial society, he certainly chose an odd perspective. Except in a purely negative way, Gordon is not a creature of the money-world; rather he is a refugee from it. Although he is continually

*Reprinted with permission from *Modern Fiction Studies* 21 (1975):49–56. © Purdue Research Foundation.

meditating on the horrors concealed behind Corner Table's ratlike smile and the general beastliness of twentieth-century culture, his major preoccupation is not with the evils involved in the possession of money or the desire to possess it but with the evils of being without it. Gordon's rantings against "a civilization of stockbrokers and their lip-sticked wives, of golf, whiskey, ouija-boards and Aberdeen terriers called Jock"[3] ring curiously false, and it is impossible to doubt that he would willingly have traded economic places with his rich parlor-socialist friend Ravelston. Gordon is most convincing when he bewails the bloodiness of life on two quid a week.

To argue that in the course of writing *Keep the Aspidistra Flying* Orwell changed his conception of its meaning, a necessary assumption if we are to believe that the novel begins as an attack on "commercial civilization" and ends as a hymn of praise to middle-class values, is to disregard what he tells us of the roots of Gordon's rebellion. The war on money is born of Gordon's revulsion against the genteel poverty of his spiritless relatives and of his own sense of inferiority:

> Gordon thought it all out, in the naive selfish manner of a boy. There are two ways to live, he decided. You can be rich, or you can deliberately refuse to be rich. You can possess money, or you can despise money; the one fatal thing is to worship money and fail to get it. He took it for granted that he himself would never be able to make money. It hardly even occurred to him that he might have talents which could be turned to account. That was what his schoolmasters had done for him; they had rubbed into him that he was a seditious little nuisance and not likely to "succeed" in life. He accepted this. Very well, then, he would refuse the whole business of "succeeding"; he would make it his especial purpose *not* to "succeed." Better to reign in hell than serve in heaven; better to serve in hell than serve in heaven, for that matter. Already, at sixteen, he knew which side he was on. He was *against* the money-god and all his swinish priesthood. He had declared war on money; but secretly, of course. (pp. 44–45)

Ten or twelve years ago I saw one of Jules Feiffer's little cartoon stories about a small boy who in the first frame laments, "Eleven years old, and I can't play baseball." In the course of the story, however, he decides that there's "something bad, something unhealthy" about "the way they [the other little boys who can play baseball] *gather* together, the way they *choose* up sides," and by the end he is able to console himself with the reflection that "it's a good thing they wouldn't let me play; otherwise I might never have noticed." This little boy provides an exact analogy to Gordon Comstock, who, because he is convinced that if he makes any attempt to succeed he will only perpetuate the flattened-out, lifeless pattern of the other members of his depressing family, develops a philosophy of dynamic failure. He will make a virtue of necessity. He will not simply slide passively into the inevitable; he will thumb his nose at the success which under any circumstances he believes he can never have and will rush willingly into the arms of poverty.

But Orwell makes it quite clear that this resolve is formed in complete ignorance of the real nature of poverty: "Vaguely he looked forward to some kind of moneyless, anchorite existence. He had a feeling that if you genuinely despise money you can keep going somehow, like the birds of the air. He forgot that the birds of the air don't pay room rent. The poet starving in a garret — but starving, somehow, not uncomfortably — that was his vision of himself" (p. 49).

Along with British imperialism, poverty is one of the major themes of Orwell's early writings, and just as his chief concern with imperialism is the spiritual imprisonment endured by the imperialist, so among the principal horrors of poverty is the crushing burden of isolation it imposes on the poor. The lack of money poisons the relations between men and between men and women, a point driven home again and again by Orwell in his essays and the autobiographical *Down and Out in Paris and London* and by Gordon Comstock in *Keep the Aspidistra Flying*. According to Gordon, most of the inconveniences of living on two quid a week are social: you can't go down to the Crichton for a quick one with Flaxman because you don't have any money; Paul Doring doesn't bother to tell you that he's changed the date of his literary tea-party because you're poor and, therefore, can be safely ignored; you can only pay your best friend short and infrequent visits because the difference in your incomes makes real equality nearly impossible; and your girl friend won't sleep with you because you can't afford to marry her if she becomes pregnant and because even privacy costs money in a cold climate. Sometimes even the money you do have doesn't do you any good; witness Gordon's Joey:

> Because how can you buy anything with a threepenny-bit? It isn't a coin, it's the answer to a riddle. You look such a fool when you take it out of your pocket, unless it's in among a whole handful of other coins. "How much?" you say. "Three-pence," the shop-girl says. And then you feel all round your pocket and fish out that absurd little thing, all by itself, sticking on the end of your finger like a tiddlywink. The shop-girl sniffs. She spots immediately that it's your last threepence in the world. You see her glance quickly at it — she's wondering whether there's a piece of Christmas pudding still sticking to it. And you stalk out with your nose in the air, and can't ever go to that shop again. (p. 4)

With reference to another passage, but one also involving the infamous Joey, David L. Kubal claims that "Orwell satirizes Gordon's vanity and obsession with money,"[4] and certainly there is something a trifle neurotic about Gordon's preoccupation with his own poverty, but it is an error to assume that Orwell is merely poking fun at his harried, moth-eaten little hero. If Gordon is neurotic, his neurosis is endemic to his condition.

Describing elsewhere his own experience in Paris of having to make ends meet on six francs (approximately one shilling) a day, Orwell comments that "it was too difficult to leave much thought for anything else,"[5] and, although his income is five or six times what Orwell's was, the same holds true for Gordon. Gordon's fixation on his money troubles tends to make us despise him as a self-pitying little weakling until it is understood within the context of Orwell's other writings on the subject of poverty, and then we discover that Gordon is merely reflecting what Orwell himself had found to be the case. All through the beginning of Chapter 6, for instance, Gordon laments the fact that the lack of money makes him repulsive to women, a fancy we are reluctant to credit at first but which Orwell confirms in *Down and Out in Paris and London*: "For the first time I noticed, too, how the attitude of women varies with a man's clothes. When a badly dressed man passes them they shudder away from him with a quite frank movement of disgust, as though he were a dead cat" (p. 129).

Another of Gordon's recurring complaints is that the lack of money has destroyed his capacity to write: "Of all types of human being, only the artist takes it upon him to say that he 'cannot' work. But it is quite true; there *are* times when one cannot work. Money again, always money! Lack of money means discomfort, means squalid worries, means shortage of tobacco, means ever-present consciousness of failure—above all it means loneliness. How can you be anything but lonely on two quid a week? And in loneliness no decent book was ever written. It was quite certain that *London Pleasures* would never be the poem he had conceived—it was quite certain, indeed, that it would never even be finished" (p. 31). A year after the publication of *Keep the Aspidistra Flying*, Orwell returned to the relationship between money and artistic achievement: "You can't settle to anything, you can't command the spirit of *hope* in which anything has got to be created, with that dull evil cloud of unemployment hanging over you."[6]

Gordon even reflects many of Orwell's less justifiable pet prejudices. For instance, Gordon believes that the literary establishment, of which the *Primrose Quarterly* serves as a symbol, is a closed corporation whose response to a grubby little interloper such as himself must inevitably be, "We don't want your bloody poems. We only take poems from chaps we were at Cambridge with. You proletarians keep your distance" (p. 77). Indefensible as this may be, it seems to have been Orwell's real opinion. According to George Woodcock, "at the best of times, Orwell was inclined to a kind of mild paranoia in his relationships with the literary world, which he regarded as a racket run by 'nancy poets' and mutual-back-scratchers from Cambridge."[7]

Granted that Gordon is not a tramp or an unemployed coal miner and that his hardships are correspondingly diluted versions of what Orwell experienced and observed in his various contacts with poverty, but they are none the less real; we are not justified in writing off Gordon's analysis of life on two quid a week as simply the whining of a gutless failure because the isolation and spiritual paralysis of which he complains are real. They are the inevitable products of a meager income.

So this is the final wisdom to which Gordon's rebellion has led him. Poverty is revealed as a kind of spiritual death, a squalid, nasty business that isolates a man from normal human contacts and annihilates his ability to create. If the novel has one major organizing idea, it is not the evils of middle-class values or "The deadening effect of serving the money-god";[8] throughout, Gordon suffers precisely because he has rejected middle-class values and precisely because he has refused to serve the money-god. As is the case in most of Orwell's early work, the central theme of *Keep the Aspidistra Flying* is poverty. Contrary to our expectations, the parody of I Corinthians 13 that serves as the book's motto, far from being merely a clever little piece of incidental irony, is a literal truth which it is the purpose of the novel to demonstrate.

Gordon is, of course, perfectly well aware of all this and has been from that first moment of sticky boredom on page one. His education, as it were, has already been completed by the beginning of the novel; there is no particular development, no change, in his character. Rather like Marlow's Faust in the last act, he has really attained his salvation, even as he damns himself. The various chapters simply examine different facets of the essentially static situation into which Gordon's self-imposed poverty has thrust him; he is the same person throughout, but apparently helpless, unable to free himself. All that is needed is something, some catalyst, that will release him to follow his destiny in marriage and the freedom of service to the aspidistra, and this catalyst is provided by Rosemary's pregnancy. Nonetheless, Gordon's salvation is assured from the first chapter.

The reason it is such a foregone conclusion is that Gordon has grasped the essential fact that in wishing London would be blown to hell by squadron after squadron of bombing planes and in hating Corner Table's mindless grin, he is "merely objectifying his own inner misery" (p. 84). As he explains to Ravelston, the degeneracy of Western Culture is really a side-issue with him:

> If the whole of England was starving except myself and the people I care about, I wouldn't give a damn. . . . All this talk we make—we're only objectifying our own feelings. It's all dictated by what we've got in our pockets. I go up and down London saying it's a city of the dead, and our civilisation's dying, and I wish war would break out, and God knows what; and all it means is that my wages are two quid a week and I wish they were five. (p. 90)

It really isn't much of a jump from recognizing this to giving up the war on money and rejoining the human race under the shade of the aspidistra.

And Gordon really wants to abandon his rebellion. For instance, he recognizes in marriage "a trap set for you by the money-god," and yet he really wants to fall into that trap:

> Nevertheless he perceived that in a way it is necessary to marry. If marriage is bad, the alternative is worse. For a moment he wished that he were married; he pined for the difficulty of it, the reality, the pain. And marriage must be indissoluble, for better for worse, for richer for poorer, till death do you part. The old Christian ideal — marriage tempered by adultery. Commit adultery if you must, but at any rate have the decency to *call* it adultery. None of that American soulmate slop. Have your fun and then sneak home, juice of the forbidden fruit dripping from your whiskers, and take the consequences. Cut-glass whiskey decanters broken over your head, nagging, burnt meals, children crying, clash and thunder of embattled mothers-in-law. Better that, perhaps, than horrible freedom? You'd know, at least, that it was real life that you were living. (p. 104)

These are obviously the thoughts of a man who in some sense has already made up his mind. Given Gordon's perception of the alternatives with which he is faced, it can be nothing but pure funk that keeps him from abandoning the struggle and going back to work for the New Albion.

Speaking of Saint Francis, Kenneth Clark, remarks that "his belief that in order to free the spirit we must shed all our earthly goods is the belief that all great religious teachers have had in common — eastern and western, without exception."[9] Divested of its religious significance, this is precisely the kind of freedom through renunciation that Gordon wishes to achieve, but it is a freedom with which only a saint could be happy, and Gordon is not a saint.

Nor is there any indication in the novel that Gordon is in any sense diminished by not being a saint. In his essay on Gandhi, Orwell remarks that "The essence of being human is that one does not seek perfection, that one *is* sometimes willing to commit sins for the sake of loyalty, that one does not push asceticism to the point where it makes friendly intercourse impossible, and that one is prepared in the end to be defeated and broken up by life, which is the inevitable price of fastening one's love upon other human individuals. No doubt alcohol, tobacco, and so forth are things that a saint must avoid, but sainthood is also a thing that human beings must avoid."[10]

For most of us it would be as easy to live any kind of meaningful life outside the money-world as it would be to live outside the atmosphere of the earth. We have to have our incomes and our families, our dreams of material success and our fear of losing our jobs, because for most of us these things in large measure define what it is to be alive. This is what Gordon's rebellion has taught him, and this is the reason that, for most of *Keep the Aspidistra Flying*, his poverty so utterly poisons his life.

Thus Gordon's reintroduction into middle-class life is inevitable; he could not go on picking at the festering sores of his economic malnutrition forever. Rosemary's pregnancy was, in Aristotelian terms, the efficient cause of his apostasy, but the final cause was his own realizaiton of what is actually entailed in refusing to live within the shadow of the aspidistra.

Once the novel is understood within these terms, the problem of its ending disappears. Gordon's choice was never between the New Albion Publicity Company and an heroic struggle to escape the deadening influences of a capitalisitc society, but between the New Albion Publicity Company and spiritual death. In the end, he commits a sin for the sake of loyalty, loyalty to Rosemary and their unborn child, and in committing that sin he recaptures his humanity. Living in the money-world involves a measure of corruption, but at least it is living; the only other alternative involves cutting oneself off from the things that let us know we are alive. In the end, Gordon makes the inevitable, the only right decision. The price of purity is simply too high.

Notes

1. John Wain, "Here Lies Lower Binfield: On George Orwell," *Encounter*, 97 (October 1961), 76.

2. Sir Richard Rees, George Orwell: *Fugitive from the Camp of Victory* (Carbondale: Southern Illinois University Press, 1962), p. 36.

3. George Orwell, *Keep the Aspidistra Flying* (New York: Harbrace Paperbound Library, N.d.), p. 129.

4. David L. Kubal, "George Orwell and the Aspidistra," *The University Review*, 37 (October 1970), 62.

5. George Orwell, *Down and Out in Paris and London* (New York: Harbrace Paperbound Library, N.d.), p. 16.

6. George Orwell, *The Road to Wigan Pier* (New York: Berkeley Medallion, N.d.), p. 78.

7. George Woodcock, *The Crystal Spirit: A Study of George Orwell* (Boston: Little, Brown & Co., 1966), p. 14.

8. Keith Alldritt, *The Making of George Orwell: An Essay in Literary History* (London: St. Martin's Press, 1969), p. 33.

9. Kenneth Clark, *Civilisation, a Personal View* (New York: Harper & Row, 1969), p. 78.

10. George Orwell, "Reflections on Gandhi," *The Collected Essays, Journalism and Letters of George Orwell* (New York: Harcourt, Brace and World, 1968), IV, 457.

The Times of Their Lives:
George Orwell's *Coming Up*
for Air

Joseph Browne*

A major slogan of *1984* explains, "Who controls the past, controls the future." In that novel's context this was meant in the most politically oppressive and psychologically destructive sense; in the more positive context of George Orwell's *Coming Up for Air* it denotes what T. S. Eliot has called the "historical sense," which is a sense of the timeless and the temporal and of the timeless and the temporal together; it is also what "makes a writer most acutely conscious of his place in time, of his own contemporaneity."[1]

George Orwell, more than most writers, was "acutely conscious of his place in time," especially in late 1938 and early 1939 when he was writing *Coming Up for Air* and doubly preoccupied with the changes that had been wrought by World War I and the potential changes threatened by an imminent World War II. Given his unusual blend of socialism and conservatism, however, Orwell was ambivalent about the past and tradition. He insisted on change and reform while longing for the stability and values of his childhood and the recently concluded Victorian era. As V. S. Pritchett correctly observed in 1946, "His traditions are those of the Right, and he cannot forgive the world for driving him to the Left."[2] In 1936 Orwell had moved from London to the more primitive but preferred living conditions of the village of Wallington in Hertfordshire, where he lived until 1940 except for the seven months spent in Morocco writing *Coming Up for Air* and recovering from tuberculosis. In an autobiographical note written in April 1940, Orwell, reflecting on his rural and urban years, listed a series of likes and dislikes; the former were all from the past or were unrelated to time (e.g., gardening, tobacco, beer, candlelight, and coal fires); the latter were all related to his present day: "motor cars, the radio, tinned food, central heating. . . ."[3] Thus, for Orwell, time, be it the past, present, or future, one's awareness or ignorance of it, one's recollection or repression of it, and one's particular involvement or noninvolvement with it, was a vital issue, as illustrated by the various characters he carefully selected to portray in *Coming Up for Air*.

In "Recapturing the Past in Fiction," Mary Lee Settle argues that "The present in which the writer writes, no matter how far in the past the subject may be, is reflected in the selection of that subject. The years when I was writing informed the past I chose."[4] In *The Lion and the Unicorn* (1941) Orwell had emphasized a similar thesis: "And above all, it is *your* civilization, it is *you*. However much you hate it or laugh at it, you will

*From *the CEA Critic* 47, no. 4 (Summer 1985):51–60. Reprinted by permission of the author.

never be happy away from it for any length of time. The suet pudding and the red pillar-boxes have entered into your soul. Good or evil, it is yours, you belong to it, and this side the grave, you will never get away from the marks that it has given you."[5] Just how marked Orwell was by his civilization, especially by the 1920s and 1930s, is evident throughout this essay, most markedly in the "England Your England" section where he denounced certain aspects of his England:

> However much one may hate to admit it, it is almost certain that between 1931 and 1940 the National Government represented the will of the mass of the people. It tolerated slums, unemployment and a cowardly foreign policy. Yes, but so did public opinion. It was a stagnant period, and its natural leaders were mediocrities. (31)

> The mishandling of England's domestic problems during the nineteen-twenties had been bad enough, but British foreign policy between 1931 and 1939 is one of the wonders of the world. Why? What had happened? What was it that at every decisive moment made every British statesman do the wrong thing with so unerring an instinct? (37)

> England is the most class-ridden country under the sun. It is a land of snobbery and privilege, ruled largely by the old and silly. (33)

These attitudes are especially evident in *Coming Up for Air*, which was set in 1938 on the eve of World War II with more than half of its narrative actually consisting of the protagonist's Proustian remembrances of things past, specifically the twenty years prior to World War I. Russell Baker's comments in his autobiography, *Growing Up*, about the atomic conclusion to World War II are equally applicable to World War I and to someone like Orwell, who was born in 1903 and was old enough to have witnessed and acknowledged the two different worlds of pre- and post-World War I England. For Baker, as well as for Orwell, "Doors were closing forever on our past, but we could not hear them slam. Soon the world we had known and the values we had lived by in that world would become so obsolete that we would seem to Americans of the new age as quaint as travelers from an antique land."[6] Just such a traveler is George Bowling, the fat, frustrated and forty-five year old narrator/protagonist of *Coming Up for Air*. By giving Bowling a birthday in 1893, a decade earlier than his own, Orwell entrenched him more firmly in the Victorian world and in the twentieth-century, pre-World War I ethos than he himself had been. This increases the disruption and disorientation effected by World War I as well as the fear and fatalism Bowling experiences because of the impending World War II; it also accentuates "the marks" that his civilization had given him.

George Bowling has no delusions about himself, the past, the present, or the future. When Edmund Fuller reviewed the first American edition of *Coming Up for Air* in 1950, his judgment of Bowling was somewhat extreme except for his acceptance of him as a completely credible person. "He is a British Babbitt, a confessed bounder, a little repellent, a little pathetic, thoroughly human."[7] Actually, Bowling is a blend of George Orwell, H. G. Wells's Mr. Polly, T.S. Eliot's J. Alfred Prufrock, and James Joyce's Leopold Bloom; yet, in spite of this array of progenitors, Bowling, to Orwell's credit, is a distinct individual. Although he acknowledges being "a little broad in the beam, with a tendency to be barrel-shaped," Bowling adamantly insists that "mentally, I'm not altogether fat . . . there's a thin man inside. . . ."[8] The "thin man" inside George Bowling is demonstrably George Orwell, who had admitted to his "own character constantly intruding on that of the narrator"[9] when he was writing the novel, an intrusion facilitated by the novel's first-person narration. Many of Bowling's comments and concerns echo or approximate Orwell's, particularly as expressed in *The Road to Wigan Pier* and *Homage to Catalonia*, written just before *Coming Up for Air*, and *Inside the Whale* and *The Lion and the Unicorn*, written immediately after it. Except for its ending, H. G. Wells's *The History of Mr. Polly* remarkably parallels *Coming Up for Air* in theme, structure, and protagonist. The Wells novel is referred to in *Coming Up for Air* (141), and Orwell has attested to his "great admiration for Wells" and to *Coming Up for Air* being "Wells watered down."[10] Bowling's Prufrock and Bloom features resulted from Orwell's esteem for those fictional characters as completely believable human beings. He had praised "The Love Song of J. Alfred Prufrock" for "carrying on the human heritage," and summarized that poem as "The hesitations of a middle-aged highbrow with a bald spot."[11] He believed that *Ulysses* summed up better than any book he knew, "the fearful despair that is almost normal in modern times,"[12] and considered Bloom as someone "you could imagine yourself talking to" and as "a rather exceptionally sensitive specimen of the man in the street."[13] In his essay, "Inside the Whale," Orwell explained that "the truly remarkable thing about *Ulysses*" was the "commonplaceness of its material." He believed that Joyce's "real achievement" was "to get the familiar on to paper:" "Here is a whole world of stuff which you have lived with since childhood; stuff which you supposed to be of its nature incommunicable, and somebody has managed to communicate it. The effect is to break down, at any rate momentarily, the solitude in which the human being lives."[14] It is just this sense of shared humanity which Orwell creates through George Bowling's narrative and the thorough communicability of the novel that are the "remarkable thing" and "real achievement" of *Coming Up for Air*.

When Orwell began *Coming Up for Air*, he wrote to a friend that Bowling was a "typical middle-aged bloke with about £5 a week and a house in the suburbs, and he's also rather thoughtful and fairly well educated, even slightly bookish. . . ."[15] A direct, but more refined, descendant of George Flaxman, the crass and corpulent traveling salesman of *Keep the Aspidistra Flying*, George Bowling tells us in his concise, candid self-appraisal, "I'm vulgar, I'm insensitive, and I fit in with my environment" (23). There are, however, parts of his environment that, as he would say, he "can hardly stick the sight of" (8), namely, his wife Hilda, who is "one of those people who get their main kick in life out of foreseeing disasters" (7–8), and his two children, or as he occasionally likes to call them, "Unnatural little bastards!" (101). But it is not just the wife, the kids, the miserable little row house in the suburbs that is "a prison with the cells all in a row" (12), or his job as an insurance salesman which he knows is a swindle, that drives George into his mid-life crisis and his "brooding on the future and the past" (180); it is his new false teeth and a frankfurter! When the last of his real teeth goes, George knows that "the time when you can kid yourself that you're a Hollywood sheik is definitely at an end" (5). When he decides to test his temporary teeth with a frankfurter in a fast-food shop, he learns that more than his sheikdom has ended.

> The frankfurter had a rubber skin, of course, and my temporary teeth weren't much of a fit. I had to do a kind of sawing movement before I could get my teeth through the skin. And then suddenly—pop! The thing burst in my mouth like a rotten pear. A sort of horrible soft stuff was oozing all over my tongue. But the taste! For a moment I couldn't believe it.
>
> It gave me the feeling that I'd bitten into the modern world and discovered what it was really made of. That's the way we're going nowadays. Everything slick and streamlined, everything made out of something else. Celluloid, rubber, chromium-steel everywhere, arc-lamps blazing all night, glass roofs over your head, radios all playing the same tune, no vegetation left, everything cemented over, mock-turtles grazing under the neutral fruit-trees. But when you come down to brass tacks and get your teeth into something solid, a sausage for instance, that's what you get. Rotten fish in a rubber skin. Bombs of filth bursting inside your mouth. (27–28)

This growing disgust with the present together with a variety of other repugnant sensory stimuli drives George back into his past, to the time before World War I when "it was always summer" (120) and to much more positive and pleasant sensory experiences:

> I can feel the grass round me as tall as myself, and the heat coming out of the earth. And the dust in the lane, and the warm greeny light coming through the hazel boughs. (44)

> The white dusty road . . . the smell of night-stocks, the green pools under the willows, the splash of Burford Weir—that's what I see when I close my eyes and think of "before the war." (120)

Similar sensory passages abound in the novel, and George, hyperconscious of both the past and present stimuli and their effects, observes,

The past is a curious thing. It's with you all the time. I suppose an hour never passes without your thinking of things that happened ten to twenty years ago, and yet most of the time it's got no reality, it's just a set of facts that you've learned, like a lot of stuff in a history book. Then some chance sight or sound or smell, especially smell, sets you going, and the past doesn't merely come back to you, you're actually in the past. It was like that at this moment. (131)

Although Orwell had apparently never read Proust, this passage, as well as many others in *Coming Up for Air*, replicates a persistent Proustian theme and technique, especially as articulated in the "Overture" of *Swann's Way*: "the smell and taste of things remain poised a long time, like souls, ready to remind us, waiting and hoping for their moment, amid the ruins of all the rest; and bear unfalteringly, in the tiny and almost impalpable drop of their essence, the vast structure of recollection." [16] This "vast structure of recollection" or sensory process by which we often reenter the past, and then try to rediscover what is real and essential, and to reencounter the "fundamental self" is the basis of Henri Bergson's *Time and Free Will: An Essay on the Immediate Data of Consciousness* in which he discusses the two selves that exist concurrently in time. The first self, or what Bergson calls the "shadow of the self," exists as a numerical multiplicity of duration of conscious states in which "Consciousness . . . substitutes the symbol for the reality, or perceives the reality only through the symbol. As the self thus refracted, and thereby broken to pieces, is much better adapted to the requirements of social life in general and language in particular, consciousness prefers it, and gradually loses sight of the fundamental self." The second self, or the "fundamental self," exists as a qualitative multiplicity or duration which is "ever changing and inexpressible because language cannot get hold of it without arresting its mobility or fit it into its common-place forms without making it into public property."[17] George Bowling acknowledges these two selves when he distinguishes between the past as "a set of facts" and actually being in the past. Midway through the novel he echoes Bergson:

I know that in a sense one never forgets anything. You remember that piece of orange-peel you saw in the gutter thirteen years ago, and that coloured poster of Torquay that you got a glimpse of in a railway waiting-room. But I'm speaking of a different kind of memory. In a sense I remembered the old life in Lower Binfield. I remembered my fishing rod and the smell of sainfoin and mother behind the brown teapot and Jackie the bullfinch and the horse-trough in the market place. (145)

Half of *Coming Up for Air* consists of George's recollection of the past, actually of two pasts (again, the pre- and post-World War I periods) and although it always seemed summertime in the first past, he is not oblivious to the negatives and unpleasantries; they just seemed to have multiplied out of all reasonable proportion after World War I because life's sense of permanence and natural progression was irreparably shattered:

> The houses had no bathrooms, you broke the ice in your basin on winter mornings, the back street stank like the devil in hot weather, and the churchyard was bang in the middle of the town, so that you never went a day without remembering how you'd got to end. And yet what was it that people had in those days? A feeling of security, even when they weren't secure. More exactly, it was a feeling of continuity. (125)

> They thought it was eternity. You couldn't blame them. That was what it felt like. (127)

Whatever minimal and unverbalized cognizance he may have of Bergson's "qualitative multiplicity" and "fundamental self" relates directly to the first past, which ended abruptly in 1914. Bergson's "creative evolution" or the "continuous progress of the past which gnaws into the future and which swells as it advances," simply discontinued, and Bowling was left with a very fragmented sense of self and a "feeling of disbelief in everything" (144). Orwell concluded *The Lion and the Unicorn* by stating his conviction that "Nothing ever stands still. We must add to our heritage or lose it, we must grow greater or grow less, we must go forward or go backward" (126–27). Bowling has no choice. Reluctant to go forward, he goes backward to find the fundamental self, to renew a creative evolution, and then to progress into the future.

Although it is a much more intensely symbolic novel than *Coming Up for Air*, Margaret Atwood's *Surfacing* parallels Orwell's work considerably beyond their synonymous titles. Atwood's narrator-protagonist, a commercial artist in New York, returns to her parents' remote Canadian homestead and to the forest primeval with sufficient fervor to make Rousseau's "noble savage" appear an ignoble urbanite by comparison. Like Bowling, she realizes that she had a good childhood; yet she is disconnected from it; she seeks to reenter it, only to discover that "nothing is the same" and that she does not "know the way any more." Having gone back, however, and relearned the way, she can now reenter her own time and place with a sense of direction and continuity. In her critical study, *Survival: A Thematic Guide to Canadian Literature*, Atwood spoke even more explicitly to the issue of the past in the present: "Part of where you are is where you've been. If you aren't too sure where you are, or if you're sure but don't like it, there's a tendency, both in psychotherapy and in literature to retrace your history to see how you got there."[18] Atwood's comments read like a summary of the other half of *Coming Up for Air* which consists of George's self-prescribed psychotherapeutic journey back to his hometown "to try and recover the past" (270). Naturally and predictably he fails, and his five days in Lower Binfield succeed only in confirming Thomas Wolfe's famous admonition. At the novel's end George asks himself, "Why had I bothered about the future and the past, seeing that the future and the past don't matter?" (277–78). Although these sentiments indicate George's basic concern for the here and now, they also reveal a resignation and despair that were natural for him and his contemporaries. Having survived the war to end all wars, they were suddenly confronted with another war—the very thought of which had coerced George into his past only to find that what World War I had really ended was a way of life that would appear forever separate and distinct from, rather than a part of, the present. George Bowling is, however, as he is fond of telling us, a survivor, and he knows that the "future and the past" do matter, and that without them there would be no present from which he could have formed that perspective in the first place. But if George time-travels from the present to the future to the past and back to the present, then other characters in the novel exist, solely and minimally at best, in a variety of time warps.

Hilda Bowling has been married to George for fifteen years, and in terms of that marriage, he regularly asks, "Why the hell did I do it?" (155). His best answer is that she came from a world that so intrigued and perplexed him that he had no "grasp of what she was really like" (156) until after the marriage. According to George, Hilda originated in a poverty stricken, Anglo-Indian, middle-class from which she would do anything, even marry him, to escape. In 1923, when they were married, he was trying to establish himself in the present while she tried to escape into the future and her family had already escaped into the past. When George first visits her home he observes that her mother "was so colourless that she was just like one of the faded photos on the wall," and that her father "was almost invisible" (157). As for the home itself, he explains, "It's almost impossible, when you get inside these people's houses, to remember that out in the street it's England and the twentieth century. As soon as you set foot inside the front door you're in India in the 'eighties' " (157).

Thus, on the one hand we have Hilda's parents incapable of life except as atrophied beings in an artificial past, vestigial appendixes from British imperialism, and on the other hand is Hilda, traumatized by her unnatural upbringing in a financially and spiritually impoverished world which left "a fixed idea not only that one always is hard-up but it's one's duty to be miserable about it" (160). She cannot enjoy the present because of the past, and she wants the future to come, but knows it will be joyless and threatening, as evidenced by her lugubrious refrain, "Next week we'll be in the poorhouse" (160). Incapable of maintaining what William James called a "sense of futurity" because her past has been so warped by her parents' obsession with their past, Hilda semi-exists as this novel's most wretched being on the periphery of life, unable to cope with the past, present, or future. In *Beyond the Tragic Vision*, Morse Peckham states that "before we can think historically, we must think humanly, psychologically, socially."[19] Hilda, however, cannot think historically—that is, with a sense of individual and social growth—because her own history has rendered her a psychological misfit and social outcast. Growing up in the ersatz Anglo-Indian world of her parents, she has become permanently repulsed by the past, frightened by the present, and terrified of the future. George, however, has had an enjoyable past, but it was terminated so abruptly that he is perplexed by the present and almost as terrified of the future as Hilda because he has experienced what one war did to his life, and he knows that another is menacingly near.

Where Hilda's parents have remained in the immediate past, and Hilda cannot relate positively to any time frame, George's friend "Old Porteous," a retired public school master, lives so exclusively in a world of Greek and Latin antiquity that he has become oblivious to the present and the future. "Old Porteous" would certainly be among those "intellectuals" whom Orwell excoriates in *The Lion and the Unicorn* whose "marked characteristic is the emotional shallowness of people who live in a world of ideas and have little contact with physical reality" (47). Of the many defects Orwell perceived in the "English Intelligentsia," he was especially embittered by "their severance from the common culture of the country" (48). Nevertheless, it soothes George Bowling occasionally to visit Porteous's world because it is not "the same world as trams and gas-bills and insurance companies" (183). It is 1938 A.D., not B.C., however, and George realizes that Porteous's ignorance of Hitler and Stalin and his blindness to change have made him a dead man because he is incapable of change; he just "says the same things and thinks the same thoughts over and over again. There are a lot of people like that. Dead minds, stopped inside" (188). It was obviously people like Hilda's parents and Porteous whom Orwell had in mind when he wrote the conclusion to *Homage to Catalonia*, which was published just months before he began work on *Coming Up for Air*, "all sleeping the deep, deep sleep of England, from which I sometimes fear that we shall never wake till we are jerked out of it by the roar of bombs."[20]

When George returns to Lower Binfield, his hometown, and to the cemetery where his parents are buried, he meets the vicar whom he has not seen in twenty-five years, since the time when he (George) was twenty-five and the vicar was George's current age, forty-five. Suddenly, in a very Joycean epiphany, the past, present, and future become distinct yet inseparable entities; they achieve a oneness, an organic unity, and he realizes exactly what "the passage of time" (277) really means and that to progress spiritually and emotionally it is necessary to go back, even if, like Proust at the conclusion of *Swann's Way*, we also realize that "remembrance of a particular form is but regret for a particular moment."[21] Bowling, of course, truly regrets, and has resigned himself to, the inevitable passing of countless particular moments, but he has more than just regret and resignation; he has the pleasure of knowing these moments have happened to him and that they will always remain as irreducible parts of his life and his times.

Appropriately, it is now little more than forty-five years since Orwell wrote *Coming Up for Air*; it is also 1985, when there is another palpable threat of world war together with countless technologies and technological devices to minimize, dehumanize, or destroy us unless, like George Orwell and George Bowling, we return to and understand the past in order to live properly in the present and plan prudently and protectively for the future. Near the end of *The Lion and the Unicorn* Orwell explained that "to preserve is always to extend" (124), and only through preservation and extension can we accommodate the times of our lives in a continuous creative evolution from the past into the present and on to the future.

Notes

1. T. S. Eliot, *Selected Prose of T. S. Eliot*, ed. Frank Kermode (New York: Farrar, Straus & Giroux, 1975), 38.

2. V. S. Pritchett, "The Rebel," *New Statesman and Nation* 31 (16 February 1946): 124.

3. George Orwell, "Autobiographical Note" in *The Collected Essays, Journalism and Letters of George Orwell*, ed. Sonia Orwell and Ian Angus (New York: Harcourt, Brace & World, 1968), 2:23–24; hereafter cited as *CEJL*.

4. Mary Lee Settle, "Recapturing the Past in Fiction," *New York Times Book Review*, (12 February 1984). 1, 36–37.

5. George Orwell, *The Lion and the Unicorn* (London: Secker & Warburg, 1941) 12; hereafter cited in the text.

6. Russell Baker, *Growing Up* (New York: New American Library, 1983), 228.

7. Edmund Fuller, "Posthumous Orwell Reissues," *Saturday Review of Literature* 33 (18 February 1950): 18–19.

8. George Orwell, *Coming Up for Air* (New York: Harcourt Brace Jovanovich, 1969), 23. Hereafter cited in the text.

9. *CEJL*, 4:422.

10. *CEJL*, 4:422.

11. *CEJL*, 1:525.

12. *CEJL*, 1:121.

13. *CEJL*, 1:127.

14. *CEJL*, 1:495.

15. *CEJL*, 1:358.

16. Marcel Proust, *Swann's Way*, trans. C. K. Scott Moncrieff (New York: Random House, 1956), 65.

17. Henri Bergson, *Time and Free Will: An Essay on the Immediate Data of Consciousness*, trans. F. L. Pogson (New York: Harper Brothers, 1960), 128–29.

18. Margaret Atwood, *Survival: A Thematic Guide to Canadian Literature* (Toronto: Anansi, 1971), 112.

19. Morse Peckham, *Beyond the Tragic Vision* (New York: George Braziller, 1962), 31.

20. George Orwell, *Homage to Catalonia* (New York: Harcourt Brace Jovanovich, 1980), 232.

21. Proust, *Swan's Way*, 611.

Nonfiction

Down and Out in Paris and London: The Conflict of Art and Politics
David L. Kubal*

The dominant, critical attitude of the last twenty years or more has made it difficult to evaluate the relationship between political thought and literature. Because of the influence of the "New Criticism," which holds at bottom that ideas as such do not belong in literature, works with an obvious political purpose are generally viewed suspiciously. Lionel Trilling has defined this attitude as part of the liberal imagination which sees an opposition between experience and ideas and asserts that literature must involve only the former. These critics miss, according to Trilling, the fact that ideas are not abstractions but have their sources in the emotions. To deny the validity of ideas as material for the novel or the poem, therefore, is to divide the artist from both reality and a means of structuring his work.

The question of the effects of politics on art is, of course, a central one in a consideration of George Orwell. He believed that it was impossible for a writer of his generation to avoid a social commitment. Because of the historical situation, the collapse of capitalism and the advent of Fascism the writer had a responsibility to deal with politics. It was, after all, the principal reality of his time. As he said, "When you are on a sinking ship your thoughts will be about sinking ships" (*England Your England*, p. 17). Further, he did not view ideas, political or otherwise as alien to literature. On the contrary, he asserts in "Charles Dickens" that "every writer, especially every novelist, *has* a 'message,' whether he admits it or not, and the minutest details of his work are influenced by it. All art is propaganda. . . . On the other hand, not all propaganda is art" (*Critical Essays*, p. 45). In this sense everything he wrote was propaganda. Even before he gave his allegiance to socialism his works reveal a socio-political purpose. Previous to 1936, it is true, he does not advocate any particular ideology; nevertheless, *Down and Out in Paris and London, Burmese Days, The Clergyman's Daughter*, and *Keep the Aspidistra Flying* are products of alarm and disgust *vis à vis* social conditions. They are meant as protests; their

*Reprinted from *Midwest Quarterly* 12 (1970); 199–209, by permission of the author and *Midwest Quarterly*.

purpose is to elicit something besides an esthetic response. Obviously, a critical approach which reacts in abhorrence to any kind of "message" or is repulsed by ideas not carefully disguised as metaphor would dismiss Orwell as a polemist. The question of when the doctrinal aspect of a work impinges upon, mitigates or destroys its artistic value has not, consequently, received adequate attention.

Orwell himself never completely worked out a satisfactory answer to the problem of judging political literature. He does suggest a standard in the essay, "Why I Write," where he points out that "What I have most wanted to do throughout the past ten years is to make political writing into an art" (*England Your England*, p. 13). To achieve this end, the writer must, he insists, find some way to reconcile his life and interests with his political responsibility. To exemplify the difficulty of this task, he refers to *Homage to Catalonia*, still his finest book, in which he tried "very hard . . . to tell the whole truth without violating my literary instincts." It is flawed, however, as he agrees, by his inclusion of a long chapter defending the Trotskyists and indicting the newspapers for their distortion of the truth. In explanation he says, "I could not have done otherwise. I happened to know, what very few people in England had been allowed to know, that innocent men were being falsely accused. If I had not been angry about that I should never have written the book."

Regardless of his excuse, what remains is *Homage to Catalonia's* lack of coherence. It is not, importantly, that Orwell treated diametrically opposed matters: his defense of the P.O.U.M. and exposé of the journalists' lies are directly related to his central aim. He fails by presenting these facts as a commentator rather than as a participant, which is the controlling point of view in the book. In other words, the sense of immediacy and involvement which forcefully convinces us of his purpose are dissipated when he breaks the narrative line and proceeds to editorialize. Although he does not understand it, the flaw ultimately stems from a distrust of his art. He obviously felt such an urgency and public responsibility to reveal the truth in this particular case that he believed personal dramatization would obscure the facts. This commitment results, on the contrary, in heavy-handed propaganda.

Although Orwell never arrived at any final clarity concerning the problem, he at least implies here one means of deciding whether a work of political intent is art or propaganda. He thought that only when the writer presents his ideas as part of human experience, shows them as having a basis in sentiment and emotion, would polemic be raised to the level of art. When character is employed merely as a vehicle for argument or situation as illustration for point of view, the end is propaganda. Ideas, in fact, become most effective when they are concretized and given an emotional dimension. This is not the same as insisting that they must appear in literature only as metaphor, myth or symbol; they can be presented explicitly as they are, for example, in Lionel Trilling's novel, *The Middle of the Journey*. This is what Orwell suggests when he says:

> My starting point [in writing] is always a feeling of partisanship, a sense of injustice. When I sit down to write a book, I do not say to myself, "I am going to produce a work of art." I write it because there is some lie that I want to expose, some fact to which I want to draw attention, and my initial concern is to get a hearing. But I could not do the work of writing a book, or even a long magazine article, if it were not also an aesthetic experience. Anyone who cares to examine my work will see that even when it is downright propaganda it contains much that a full-time politician would consider irrelevant. I am not able, and I do not want, completely to abandon the world-view that I acquired in childhood. So long as I remain alive and well I shall continue to feel strongly about prose style, to love the surface of the earth, and to take a pleasure in solid objects and scraps of useless information. It is no use trying to suppress that side of myself.

But it was also his ideas, his political commitment, he thought, which enabled him to produce works of artistic worth. For as he says in concluding "Why I Write," "looking back through my work, I see that it is invariably where I lacked a *political* purpose that I wrote lifeless books and was betrayed into purple passages, sentences without meaning, decorative adjectives and humbug generally."

As early as 1933 in his first book, *Down and Out in Paris and London*, Orwell attempted to reconcile his artistic and political aims. In fact he presented it as a novel, although he had, quite obviously, another intention in mind. His main purpose is moral and, in the largest meaning of the word, political: he wants to reveal the condition of a certain segment of society and to suggest those responsible. The book, however, is not free from invention. In *The Road to Wigan Pier* he admitted that a few of the incidents were created and the whole rearranged. But only in the loosest sense might we take it as a novel. He does not attempt to develop character very greatly or plot; it is episodic, with the narrator — an undisguised Orwell — providing the principal unity. To judge *Down and Out* as a novel, then, would not only be unfair but also would tend to obscure the book's real value. If one needed a definition, one might call it a dramatic autobiography, a "form" which he employs again in *Wigan Pier* and *Homage to Catalonia*, where he tries to elevate personal experience to general relevance.

Down and Out is seminal in other ways as well. As in almost all of Orwell's works, the main character begins in naïvete and proceeds to knowledge, another manner of stating the theme of search. Its effectiveness stems from the fact that he portrays this movement in his protagonist. Thus, for the most part he brings the reader himself to a sense of discovery. The narrator's initiation into the underworld, nevertheless, is never total.

He remains the middle-class Englishman to the end; complete identity with poverty is impossible because there is always the alternative of a tutoring position in England and a friend in the background ready with a loan. Throughout the journey the narrator, one feels, is in a constant state of amazement. Continuously surprised, his curiosity never abates. Whatever he undergoes, moreover, two or three days without eating, working as a *plongeur* or tramping from spike to spike, he always remains somewhat detached from the experience itself. At the end of the adventure Orwell admits, "At present I do not feel that I have seen more than the fringe of poverty"; at least, though, as he says, "That is a beginning" (*Down and Out*, p. 213).

Orwell's simplicity is seen particularly in regard to the manners, morals and living conditions of the poor. For example, in a brief incident which takes place in a London coffee-shop, he indirectly satirizes his own ignorance:

> "Could I have some tea and bread and butter?" I said to the girl.
> She stared. "No butter, only marg," she said, surprised. (p. 132)

In negotiating for a permanent job in Paris, he discovers that his class sense of honor is an outmoded commodity in the jungle. Out of work and hungry, he loses a prospect because he is unwilling to lie about how long he will stay. Boris, the Russian immigrant who had found him the opportunity, berates him:

> "Idiot! Species of idiot! What's the good of my finding you a job when you go and chuck it up the next moment? How could you be such a fool as to mention the other restaurant? You'd only to promise you would work for a month."
> "It seemed more honest to say I might have to leave," I objected.
> "Honest! Honest! Who ever heard of a *plongeur* being honest? *Mon ami*" — suddenly he seized my lapel and spoke very earnestly — "*mon ami*, you have worked here all day. You see what hotel work is like. Do you think a *plongeur* can afford a sense of honour?" (pp. 59–50)

Orwell, on the other hand, also learns about those who exploit the *plongeurs* and the tramps. The pawnshop owners, the hotel managers, even the hostel operators all use and de-humanize the outcasts.

His pilgrimage, thus, becomes a moral encounter in modern society, an initiation into the knowledge of good and evil; from this he comes to a sense of deterioration. In fact, despite the exhilarating effect which Bozo's and Boris' defiance and will to survive have on Orwell, the dominant and unifying theme of the book is one of decay. For example, our first vision of Paris is of a "very narrow street — a ravine of tall, leprous houses, lurching towards one another in queer attitudes, as though they had all been frozen in act of collapse" (p. 5). In London, too, everything appears in the state of decomposition. Entering a "dosshouse" for the first time, he says a "boy led me up a rickety unlighted staircase to a bedroom. It had a sweetish reek of paregoric and foul linen; the windows seemed to be tight shut, and the air was almost suffocating at first" (p. 130).

Indeed, the principal value of *Down and Out* is the author's creation of the experience of physical corruption. His presentation of the city reminds the reader of Dickens' *Our Mutual Friend*, George Moore's *Esther Waters*, George Gissing's *New Grub Street*, and, particularly, Conrad's *The Secret Agent*. It is inhuman, monstrous and destructive. His use of vivid detail is not merely descriptive but it also functions to sustain the reader's indignation and to suggest society's spiritual condition. The portrayal has its sources in Orwell's own moral horror which was transmuted before composition into a desire to inform and convince. His primary purpose consists in communicating a message, and his avid belief in the truth of what he has seen is behind the immediacy of his vision. *Down and Out*, in fact, illustrates to a great extent how the propaganda motive can inform and strengthen the esthetic effect.

His characterization also appears to be substantially influenced by Dickens. Paddy Jaques, Orwell's mate on the tramp, is the only one of the three major characters who might be called typical or average. Boris and Bozo, however, are eccentrics. The former has been an officer and a son of a rich man before the revolution. A comic figure, he combines the manner of an aristocrat with the appearance of a beggar. Even though he is something of a stock character, the gentleman down on his luck (a figure, by the way, which again emerges briefly in a London dosshouse and the manner in which the author obviously sees himself), Boris is individuated by his humor and cunning. He also assumes the role of the narrator's first mentor, teaching him the mores of the underground society and a way of survival. Paddy and Bozo complete his education in England, the first showing him how to endure physically, and the second, intellectually and artistically.

A sidewalk screever, Bozo exists as an image of the independent artist. Like Boris, he has come down in the world. After an injury to his foot, he could not get a regular job and so has taken to drawing political cartoons on the pavements. He impresses Orwell with his facility with French and his reading — Zola, Shakespeare, and Swift — as well as his idea of personal and artistic integrity. For example, Bozo satirizes various politicians and parties. And as he says, "I'm what they call a serious screever. I don't draw in blackboard chalk like these others. I use proper colours the same as what painters use; bloody expensive they are, especially the reds" (p. 161). Later as Orwell is watching him draw, he is amazed by his knowledge of his art: "From the way he [Bozo] spoke he might have been an art critic in a picture gallery. I was astonished. I confessed that I did not know which Aldebaran was — indeed, I had never noticed that the stars [in the drawing] were of different colours" (p. 164).

But of more importance to Orwell is Bozo's attitude toward poverty. At one point the author says to him:

> "It seems to me that when you take a man's money away he's fit for
> nothing from that moment."
> "No, not necessarily. If you set yourself to it, you can live the same
> life, rich or poor. You can still keep on with your books and your ideas.
> You just got to say to yourself, 'I'm a free man in here'—and he tapped
> his forehead—and you're all right." p. 165)

Bozo demonstrated to him the way a man and an artist might live without
the middle-class and their money ethic—which the latter detested and
feared. During his time in Paris and London, he was obviously looking for
an alternative mode of living. Realizing the moral and intellectual
corruption which conformity to middle-class society produced, but in
doubt about the effects of poverty, Orwell saw Bozo's and Boris' way of life
as an illustration of a means of maintaining integrity beyond the limits of
society. Furthermore, he understood that their attitude was not simply a
negation or a glorification of failure. For, as he observes about the
sidewalk screever, "he had neither fear, nor regret, nor shame, nor self
pity. He had faced his position, and made a philosophy for himself"
(p. 165).

The characters in *Down and Out*, therefore, are largely counter-
pointed to the setting. Paris and London are presented as corrosive and
debilitating cities, while the people—especially the ones Orwell focuses
on—who inhabit them manage to retain their humanity and identity. In
this way the author achieves his dual purpose, an exposé of society's
condition and the assertion that the lower classes possess the interior
strength to survive. This juxtaposition is a part of all his work, even
Nineteen Eighty-Four. The quality of the characterization also indicates
that propaganda was not Orwell's sole motive; for his creations are often
seen as more than victims and never presented with the sentimentality
which mitigates, let us say, Dickens' portrait of the workingman, Stephen
Blackpool, in *Hard Times*. Besides, the narrator is quite capable of
criticizing the outcasts for their lack of gratitude and their vindictiveness.

Finally, however, if his characters are vivid because of his careful use
of detail and dialogue, they are closer in caricatures than personalities. In
other words, they exist almost entirely on the surface and their gestures
and speech do not indicate any depth of feeling or thought. His failure in
characterization is, of course, a limitation of his naturalistic method and
also substantiates his disclaimer of any thorough knowledge of poverty.

Down and Out also reveals Orwell's distrust of art. The book falls
roughly into two parts, the first dealing with his experiences in Paris, and
the second, London. At the end of each section Orwell steps out of the role
of narrator-character and comments upon and interprets the action. And
so he ends the first part by saying:

> To sum up. A *plongeur* is a slave, and a wasted slave, doing stupid and
> largely unnecessary work. He is kept at work, ultimately, because of a
> vague feeling that he would be dangerous if he had leisure. And

educated people, who should be on his side, acquiesce in the process, because they know nothing about him and consequently are afraid of him. I say this of the *plongeur* because it is his case I have been considering; it would apply equally to numberless other types of workers. These are only my ideas about the basic facts of a *plongeur's* life, made without reference to immediate economic questions, and no doubt largely platitudes. I sent them as a sample of the thoughts that are put into one's head by working in a hotel. (p. 121)

Not only does he fall occasionally into this rather obvious political moralizing, but he also adds an inappropriate discussion of underworld slang and language in chapter xxii, certainly an interesting observation and one he wanted very much to make. But he included it without regard for the narrative integrity. Later in his career he admitted in a letter to Julian Symons that "One difficulty I have never solved is that one has masses of experience which one passionately wanted to write about . . . and no way of using them up except by disguising them as a novel." Even though *Down and Out* is not strictly speaking a novel, we see in this incident an example of Orwell failing to exercise his critical judgment by introducing an experience which has no precise relevance to what he is doing.

The author's political moralizing is a flaw because it is for the most part redundant. The dramatic episodes, which take up the vast bulk of the book, have already carried his point and, in fact, have done it much more convincingly. Instead of a unified reworking of a personal experience designed to delineate the agony of poverty and heroism of the poor, we are left with something of an inductive syllogism. The confusion results from Orwell's inability to solve the problem of form. As in *Homage to Catalonia* he initially realizes the greater effectiveness of character and situation, but once into the work decides a "prose gloss" is necessary. The fact that this same problem occurs not only in *Down and Out* but in several other works, including his last, *Nineteen Eighty-Four*, suggests that he had an innate suspicion of the imagination; that is, he saw it as partially inadequate when one had to cope with ideas. In political thought he preferred common sense, the straightforward, the concrete; in his art as well, especially in those works with a pointed political purpose, he appears impatient with the dramatic. On the one hand, he did not wish to write mere polemics, on the other, he felt the urgency and need for facts in view of the social situation. When these contradictory impulses were unresolved, the results were often a lack of structural and narrative coherence and over-simplified propaganda.

Despite these exceptions, Orwell demonstrates in his first book an ability to convey the ugliness and depression of poverty. If his characterization lacks depth and the structure is unsteady, his description is extraordinarily persuasive. His powers of observation and use of detail to portray the substratum of the modern city make *Down and Out* more than simply a tract. Throughout the book there is an underlying moral horror, the presence of a highly sensitive conscience reacting to a diseased society. No one of Orwell's generation was able to create the experience of the city better than he.

Bibliographical Note

George Orwell, "Writers and Leviathan," *England Your England* (London, 1953).

―――, *Critical Essays* (London, 1946).

―――, *Down and Out in Paris and London* (London, 1949).

Julian Symons, "Orwell: A Reminiscence," *London Magazine*, III (September, 1963), 33–49.

Foreword [to *The Road to Wigan Pier*]

Victor Gollancz*

This foreword is addressed to members of the Left Book Club (to whom *The Road to Wigan Pier* is being sent as the March Choice), and to them alone: members of the general public are asked to ignore it. But for technical considerations, it would have been deleted from the ordinary edition.

I have also to make it clear that, while the three selectors of the Left Book Club Choices — Strachey, Laski and myself — were all agreed that a Foreword was desirable, I alone am responsible for what is written here — though I think that Laski and Strachey would agree with me.

Why did we think that a Foreword was desirable? Because we find that many members — a surprisingly large number — have the idea that in some sort of way a Left Book Club Choice, first, represents the views of the three selectors, and, secondly, incorporates the Left Book Club "policy." A moment's thought should show that the first suggestion could be true only in the worst kind of Fascist State, and that the second is a contradiction in terms: but we get letters so frequently — most interesting and vital letters — which say: "Surely you and Laski and Strachey cannot believe what So-and-So says on page so-and-so of Such-and-Such a book," that there can be no doubt at all that the misconception exists.

The plain facts are, of course, (a) that the three selectors, although they have that broad general agreement without which successful committee work is impossible, differ as to shade and *nuance* of opinion in a hundred ways; (b) that even if they were in perfect agreement on every point, nothing could be worse than a stream of books which expressed this

*Reprinted with permission from *The Road to Wigan Pier* (London: Gollancz, 1937), ix–xxii.

same point of view over and over again; and (c) that their only criterion for a Choice is whether or not the reading and discussion of it will be helpful for the general struggle against Fascism and war. And that brings me on to this question of Left Book Club "policy." The Left Book Club has no "policy": or rather it has no policy other than that of equipping people to fight against war and Fascism. As I have said elsewhere, it would not even be true to say that the People's Front is the "policy" of the Left Book Club, though all three selectors are enthusiastically in favour of it. What we rather feel is that by giving a wide distribution to books which represent many shades of Left opinion (and perhaps, most of all, by providing facilities for the discussion of those books in the 300 local centres and circles that have sprung up all over the country) we are creating the mass basis without which a genuine People's Front is impossible. In other words, the People's Front is not the "policy" of the Left Book Club, but the very existence of the Left Book Club tends towards a People's Front.

But we feel that a Foreword to *The Road to Wigan Pier* is desirable, not merely in view of the misconception to which I have referred, but also because we believe that the value of the book, for some members, can be greatly increased if just a hint is given of certain vital considerations that arise from a reading of it. The value can be *increased*: as to the positive value itself, no one of us has the smallest doubt. For myself, it is a long time since I have read so *living* a book, or one so full of a burning indignation against poverty and oppression.

The plan of the book is this. In Part I Mr. Orwell gives a first-hand account of the life of the working class population of Wigan and elsewhere. It is a terrible record of evil conditions, foul housing, wretched pay, hopeless unemployment and the villainies of the Means Test: it is also a tribute to courage and patience—patience far too great. We cannot imagine anything more likely to rouse the "unconverted" from their apathy than a reading of this part of the book; and we are announcing in the current number of *The Left News* a scheme by means of which we hope members may make use of the book for this end. These chapters really *are* the kind of thing that makes converts.

In the second part, Mr. Orwell starts with an autobiographical study, which he thinks necessary in order to explain the class feelings and prejudices of a member of "the lower upper-middle class," as he describes himself: and he then goes on to declare his adherence to Socialism. But before doing so he comes forward as a devil's advocate, and explains, with a great deal of sympathy, why, in his opinion, so many of the best people detest Socialism; and he finds the reason to lie in the "personal inferiority" of so many Socialists and in their mistaken methods of propaganda. His conclusion is that present methods should be thrown overboard, and that we should try to enrol everyone in the fight for Socialism and against

Fascism and war (which he rightly sees to be disasters in the face of which little else is of much importance) by making the elemental appeal of "liberty" and "justice." What he envisages is a great league of "oppressed" against "oppressors"; in this battle members of all classes may fight side by side — the private schoolmaster and the jobless Cambridge graduate with the clerk and the unemployed miner; and then, when they have so fought, "we of the sinking middle class . . . may sink without further struggles into the working class where we belong, and probably when we get there it will not be so dreadful as we feared, for, after all, we have nothing to lose but our aitches."

Now the whole of this second part is highly provocative, not merely in its general argument, but also in detail after detail. I had, in point of fact, marked well over a hundred minor passages about which I thought I should like to argue with Mr. Orwell in this Foreword; but I find now that if I did so the space that I have set aside would be quickly used up, and I should wear out my readers' patience. It is necessary, therefore, that I should limit myself to some of the broader aspects.

In the first place, no reader must forget that Mr. Orwell is throughout writing precisely as a member of the "lower upper-middle class" or, let us say without qualification, as a member of the middle class. It may seem stupid to insist on this point, as nothing could be clearer than Mr. Orwell's own insistence on it: but I can well imagine a reader coming across a remark every now and again which infuriates him even to the extent of making him forget this most important fact: *that such a remark can be made by Mr. Orwell is* (if the reader follows me) *part of Mr. Orwell's own case.* I have in mind in particular a lengthy passage in which Mr. Orwell embroiders the theme that, in the opinion of the middle class in general, the working class smells! I believe myself that Mr. Orwell is exaggerating violently: I do not myself think that more than a very small proportion of them have this quaint idea (I admit that I may be a bad judge of the question, for I am a Jew, and passed the years of my early boyhood in a fairly close Jewish community; and, among Jews of this type, class distinctions do not exist — Mr. Orwell says that they do not exist among any sort of Oriental). But clearly *some* of them think like this — Mr. Orwell quotes a very odd passage from one of Mr. Somerset Maugham's books — and the whole of this chapter throws a most interesting light on the reality of class distinctions. I know, in fact, of no other book in which a member of the middle class exposes with such complete frankness the shameful way in which he was brought up to think of large numbers of his fellow men. This section will be, I think, of the greater value to middle class and working class members of the Left Book Club alike: to the former because, if they are honest, they will search their own minds; to the latter, because it will make them understand what they are "up against" — if they do not understand it already. In any case, the moral is that the class division of

Society, economic in origin, must be superseded by the classless society (I fear Mr. Orwell will regard this as a wretched and insincere cliché) in which alone the shame and indignity so vividly described by Mr. Orwell — I mean of the middle class, not of the lower class — will be impossible.

Mr. Orwell now proceeds to act as devil's advocate for the case against Socialism.

He looks at Socialists as a whole and finds them (with a few exceptions) a stupid, offensive and insincere lot. For my own part I find no similarity whatsoever between the picture as Mr. Orwell paints it and the picture as I see it. There is an extraordinary passage in which Mr. Orwell seems to suggest that almost every Socialist is a "crank"; and it is illuminating to discover from this passage just what Mr. Orwell means by the word. It appears to mean anyone holding opinions not held by the majority — for instance, any feminist, pacifist, vegetarian or advocate of birth control. This last is really startling. In the first part of the book Mr. Orwell paints a most vivid picture of wretched rooms swarming with children, and clearly becoming more and more unfit for human habitation the larger the family grows: but he apparently considers anyone who wishes to enlighten people as to how they can have a normal sexual life without increasing this misery as a crank! The fact, of course, is that there is no more "commonsensical" work than that which is being done at the present time by the birth control clinics up and down the country — and common sense, as I understand it, is the antithesis of crankiness. I have chosen this particular example, because the answer to Mr. Orwell is to be found in his own first part: but the answers to Mr. Orwell's sneers at pacifism and feminism are as obvious. Even about vegetarianism (I apologize to vegetarians for the "even") Mr. Orwell is astray. The majority of vegetarians are vegetarians not because "they want to add a few miserable years to their wretched lives" (I cannot find the exact passage at the moment, but that is roughly what Mr. Orwell says), but because they find something disgusting in the consumption of dead flesh. I am not saying that I agree with them: but anyone who has seen a man — or woman — eating a raw steak (*saignant*, as the French say so much more frankly) will feel a sneaking sympathy.

The fact is that in passages like that to which I have referred, and in numerous other places in this part of the book, Mr. Orwell is still a victim of that early atmosphere, in his home and public school, which he himself has so eloquently exposed. His conscience, his sense of decency, his understanding of realities tell him to declare himself a Socialist: but fighting against this compulsion there is in him all the time a compulsion far less conscious but almost — though fortunately not quite — as strong: the compulsion to conform to the mental habits of his class. That is why Mr. Orwell, looking at a Socialist, smells out (to use a word which we have already met in another connection) a certain crankiness in him; and he finds, as examples of this crankiness, a hatred of war (pacifism), a desire to see woman no longer oppressed by men (feminism), and a refusal to withhold the knowledge which will add a little happiness to certain human lives (birth control).

This conflict of two compulsions is to be found again and again throughout the book. For instance, Mr. Orwell calls himself a "half intellectual"; but the truth is that he is at one and the same time an extreme intellectual and a violent anti-intellectual. Similarly he is a frightful snob — still (he must forgive me for saying this), and a genuine hater of every form of snobbery. For those who can read, the exhibition of this conflict is neither the least interesting nor the least valuable part of the book: for it shows the desperate struggle through which a man must go before, in our present society, his mind can really become free — if indeed that is ever possible.

I have said enough, I think, to show, by means of one example, the way in which I should venture to criticise the whole of this section of the book. But there is another topic here which cannot be passed over without a word or two. Among the grave faults which Mr. Orwell finds in Socialist propaganda is the glorification of industrialism, and in particular of the triumphs of industrialisation in the Soviet Union (the words "Magnito-gorsk" and "Dnieper" make Mr. Orwell see red — or rather the reverse). I have a fairly wide acquaintance among Socialists of every colour, and I feel sure that the whole of this section is based on a misunderstanding. To leave Russia out of account for the moment, no Socialist of my acquaint-ance *glorifies* industrialism. What the Socialist who has advanced beyond the most elementary stage says (and I really mean what he *says*, not what he *ought to say*) is that capitalist industrialism is a certain stage which we have reached in the business of providing for our needs, comforts and luxuries: that though it may be amusing to speculate on whether or not a pre-industrialist civilisation might be a more attractive one in which to live, it is a matter of plain common sense that, whatever individuals may wish, industrialism will go on: that (if Mr. Orwell will forgive the jargon) such "contradictions" have developed in the machine of capitalist industri-alism that the thing is visibly breaking down: that such break-down means poverty, unemployment and war: and that the only solution is the supersession of anarchic capitalist industrialism by planned Socialist industrialism. In other words, it is not industrialism that the Socialist advocates (a man does not advocate the sun or the moon), but Socialist industrialism as opposed to capitalist industrialism.

Mr. Orwell, of course, understands this quite elementary fact per-fectly well: but his understanding conflicts with his love of beauty, and the result is that, instead of pointing out that industrialism can be the parent of beauty, if at all, then only under planned Socialist industrialism, he turns to rend the mythical figure of the Socialist who thinks that gaspipe chairs are more beautiful than Chippendale chairs. (Incidentally, gaspipe chairs *are* more beautiful than the worst Chippendale chairs, though not nearly as beautiful as the best.)

As to the particular question of the Soviet Union, the insistence of Socialists on the achievements of Soviet industrialisation arises from the fact that the most frequent argument which Socialists have to face is precisely this: "I agree with you that Socialism would be wholly admirable if it would work—but it wouldn't." Somewhere or other Mr. Orwell speaks of intelligent and unintelligent Socialists, and brushes aside people who say "it wouldn't work" as belonging to the latter category. My own experience is that this is still the major *sincere* objection to Socialism on the part of decent people, and the major *insincere* objection on the part of indecent people who in fact are thinking of their dividends. It is true that the objection was more frequently heard in 1919 than in 1927, in 1927 than at the end of the first Five Year Plan, and at the end of the first Five Year Plan than to-day—the reason being precisely that quite so direct a *non possumus* hardly carries conviction, when the achievements of the Soviet Union are there for everyone to see. But people will go on hypnotising themselves and others with a formula, even when that formula is patently outworn: so that it is still necessary, and will be necessary for a long time yet, to show that modern methods of production *do* work under Socialism and *no longer work* under capitalism.

But Mr. Orwell's attack on Socialists who are for ever singing pæans of praise to Soviet industrialisation is also connected with his general dislike of Russia—he even commits the curious indiscretion of referring to Russian commissars as "half-gramophones, half-gangsters." Here again the particular nature of Mr. Orwell's unresolved conflict is not difficult to understand; nor is it difficult to understand why Mr. Orwell states that almost all people of real sensitiveness, and in particular almost all writers and artists and the like, are hostile to Socialism—whereas the truth is that in several countries, for instance in France, a great number, and probably the majority, of writers and artists are Socialists or even Communists.

All this is not to say that (while this section gives, in my view, a distorted picture of what Socialists are like and what they say) *Socialists themselves* will not find there much that is of value to them, and many shrewd pieces of, at any rate, half-truth. In particular I think that Mr. Orwell's accusation of arrogance and dogmatism is to a large extent justified: in fact as I think back on what I have already written here I am not sure that a good deal of it is not itself arrogant and dogmatic. His accusation of narrowness and of sectarianism is not so well grounded to-day as it would have been a few years ago: but here also there is still plenty of room for improvement. The whole section indeed is, when all has been said against it, a challenge to us Socialists to put our house and our characters in order.

Having criticised us in this way (for though Mr. Orwell insists that he is speaking merely as devil's advocate and saying what other people say, quite often and quite obviously he is really speaking *in propria persona* — or perhaps I had better say "in his own person," otherwise Mr. Orwell will class me with "the snobs who write in Latinised English" or words to that effect) Mr. Orwell joins us generously and whole-heartedly, but begs us to drop our present methods of propaganda, to base our appeal on freedom and liberty, and to see ourselves as a league of the oppressed against the oppressors. Nothing could be more admirable as a first approach; and I agree that we shall never mobilise that vast mass of fundamentally decent opinion which undoubtedly exists (as, for instance, the Peace Ballot showed) and which we *must* mobilise if we are to defeat Fascism, unless we make our first appeal to its generous impulses. It is from a desire for liberty and justice that we must draw our militant strength; and the society which we are trying to establish is one in which that liberty and that justice will be incarnate. But between the beginning in that first impulse to fight, and the end when, the fight won, our children or our children's children will live in the achievement, there is a great deal of hard work and hard thinking to be done — less noble and more humdrum than the appeal to generosities, but no less important if a real victory is to be won, and if this very appeal is not to be used to serve ends quite opposite to those at which we aim.

It is indeed significant that so far as I can remember (he must forgive me if I am mistaken) Mr. Orwell does not once define what he *means* by Socialism; nor does he explain *how* the oppressors oppress, nor even what he understands by the words "liberty" and "justice." I hope he will not think I am quibbling: he will not, I think, if he remembers that the word "Nazi" is an abbreviation of the words "National Socialist"; that in its first phase Fascism draws its chief strength from an attack on "oppression" — "oppression" by capitalists, multiple stores, Jews and foreigners; that no word is commoner in German speeches to-day than "Justice"; and that if you "listen in" any night to Berlin or Munich, the chances are that you will hear the "liberty" of totalitarian Germany — "Germans have become free by becoming a united people" — compared with the misery of Stalin's slaves.

What is indeed essential, once that first appeal has been made to "liberty" and "justice," is a careful and patient study of just *how* the thing works: of *why* capitalism inevitably means oppression and injustice and the horrible class society which Mr. Orwell so brilliantly depicts: of *the means* of transition to a Socialist society in which there will be neither oppressor nor oppressed. In other words, *emotional* Socialism must become scientific Socialism — even if some of us have to concern ourselves with what Mr. Orwell, in his extremely intellectualist anti-intellectualism, calls "the sacred sisters" Thesis, Antithesis and Synthesis.

What I feel, in sum, is that this book, more perhaps than any that the

Left Book Club has issued, clarifies — for me at least — the whole meaning and purpose of the Club. On the one hand we have to go out and rouse the apathetic by showing them the utter vileness which Mr. Orwell lays bare in the first part of the book, and by appealing to the decency which is in them; on the other hand we have so to equip ourselves by thought and study that we run no danger, having once mobilised all this good will, of seeing it dispersed for lack of trained leaders — lance corporals as well as generals — or even of seeing it used as the shock troops of our enemies.

George Orwell and *The Road to Wigan Pier*
Richard Hoggart*

The Road to Wigan Pier has been disliked by almost all commentators on Orwell. Tom Hopkinson calls it his worst book and Laurence Brander "his most disappointing performance." Disappointment began when the typescript reached the desk of its publisher, Victor Gollancz, who had commissioned the essay. It duly appeared in 1937 but with a preface in which Mr. Gollancz, though doing his best to be fair and to appreciate fully what he had been offered, showed his disagreement on every page.

He had good reason to be surprised, for this must be one of the oddest responses to a commission which even the Left Book Club inspired. The club was intended to mobilize and nourish socialist thought. With his co-editors John Strachey and Harold Laski, Mr. Gollancz issued each month to club members, under the imprint of his own publishing house but in distinctive limp orange covers, a book designed to help these ends. He had asked George Orwell to write a "condition of England" book, a documentary on the state of the unemployed in the North, a book of descriptive social analysis. What he got was a book in two equal halves, neither of them what he had asked for. Part one seems to be roughly on the contracted subject but approaches it most idiosyncratically. Part two is partly cultural autobiography, partly opinionation about socialism by a man who had then a patchy idea of the nature of socialism.

The truth was that socialism was at that time fairly new to Orwell, and *Wigan Pier* was his first directly political book. Nor was he much known, so that the club editors were to some extent chancing their collective arm. Orwell had published his first book. *Down and Out in Paris and London* (social observation but not directly political writing), four years before. He had followed it at yearly intervals with three novels,

*Reprinted from *The Road to Wigan Pier* (London: Heinemann, 1965), by permission of the author.

all interesting but the first probably the best (*Burmese Days, A Clergy-man's Daughter, Keep the Aspidistra Flying*). When the Gollancz commission came he was living in Essex, keeping a village store and writing. He threw up the shop to go North for this book. But there was no great financial loss, if any: the shop produced only £1 a week and up to the age of 37 Orwell, so he used to say, never earned more than £3 a week from his writings. He did not go back to the Essex shop. After handing over the typescript of *Wigan Pier* he set out for Spain to enlist on the Government side (but characteristically chose to serve with the militia of a minority group on the extreme left). The relentless enquiry which had led him from filthy work in Paris kitchens to London dosshouses and the Brookers's tripe-shop-cum-boarding house finally brought him to the front near Huesca where, luckily for him, he got a bullet in the neck and so eventually came home.

It was not a pilgrimage for which anything in Orwell's background gave a prior hint. He was born Eric Blair (the 'Orwell' came from a river near which he once lived in Suffolk) into the upper classes. With his characteristic effort at precision in matters of class Orwell called himself in this book a member of "the lower upper middle classes." His point was that his father was a public servant, not a landowner nor a big business-man; so, though he had the rank, status and tastes of a gentleman, his salary was modest. He was, in fact, a minor official in the Indian Customs service and George was born in Bengal, in 1903. He was, as was usual, sent to a preparatory school in England, a school which he described with great bitterness in the essay "Such, such were the joys." From there he won a scholarship to Eton which he also wrote about, though with less bitterness. When the time came to leave Eton Orwell was unsure of his plans and in particular unsure about whether or not he should try to go to Cambridge. A tutor, with what reasons we do not certainly know, suggested that he should take a job abroad. Orwell joined the Indian Imperial police and served for five years (1922–1927) in Burma. In some respects the central character of *Burmese Days*, Flory, is Orwell himself.

It is plain, from *Wigan Pier* as well as from many of Orwell's other writings, that he was reacting intensely against his social and educational background, was much of the time trying to cast off his class. But he always respected certain characteristic virtues of his class, such as fair-mindedness and responsibility. And it is worth remarking at this early point that in some deep-seated ways Orwell was himself characteristic of his class and (though he was an acute analyst) didn't always realise how much this was so himself. To begin with, he had a kind of fastidiousness (which is not the same as gentility) which never deserted him and which much of the time he was fighting. But it was there. It was reinforced by his phenomenally sharp sense of smell: he could *smell* his way through complex experiences. Thus, he tells us in this book that at first he found the English working-classes physically repulsive, much more repellent than Orientals. Look, too, at a tiny but characteristic moment in this book. He constantly drove himself into extreme and unpleasant situations and could describe them with exactness. One of the best passages in *Wigan Pier* is the description of the nature of work down the mine. It is terribly hard and grimy work, and Orwell wanted his readers to know this. In the course of his description he says that he suddenly put his hand on "a dreadful slimy thing among the coal dust." Orwell uses that word "dreadful" frequently and usually means something really inspiring horror. So one wonders what it will prove to be this time. It is in fact a quid of chewed tobacco spat out of a miner's mouth. Not a particularly pleasant thing to put your hand on; but, for a man who had deliberately subjected himself to the trials and squalors which Orwell had, hardly a "dreadful" thing, one would have thought. So the phrase unintentionally acts as a sudden shifter of perspective: used in that way, it comes straight out of the vocabulary of the class which Orwell's journeys were a way of escaping from. Inevitably, in describing this little incident in full (but one could hardly make the point otherwise) I have given it too much weight. It is a small pointer but an accurate one to a quality that Orwell never lost and which was partly (but not wholly; he was also *by nature* fastidious) socially-acquired.

At other times (and this quality can be seen in part 2 of *Wigan Pier* and most notably in the essay "England Your England") Orwell revealed a particular kind of toughness in manner, a sort of anti-intellectual pugnacity which reminds you of a no-nonsense upper-class colonel. This from a man who could a few chapters before talk so warmly and gently about working-class interiors. The two characteristics do not blend: they remain throughout Orwell's short life (he died in 1950) a contradictory mixture.

More important, to this tracing of Orwell's deep-seated connections with his class, he was one of the latest in a long and characteristic English line: those dissidents which a system that is in so many ways designed to reproduce its own kind has always managed to produce richly. In this aspect of his character Orwell joins hands, among men of this century, with Lawrence of Arabia. They went in different directions, geographically and intellectually: but in their tempers they had much in common.

All these tensions finally brought Orwell out of the Indian Imperial Police and sent him on the first phase of his journey to the lower depths. He had to go, of that there is no doubt. But why? There are easy answers and hard answers to this question, and all probably have some truth in them. But to establish anything like a satisfactory *order* of reasons would require a much fuller study of Orwell — not only of his works but of his life — than we have had so far (or than we are likely to have if his wishes are respected, since he asked that there should be no biography).

In trying to touch bottom, Orwell most obviously was reacting against imperialism and his own guilt as a former agent of imperialism. He came to regard it as evil. Not just because one side was a tyrant to the other: not all the British rulers were tyrannical, and Orwell was as likely to dislike a Buddhist priest as a British colonial policeman. He believed that imperialism was evil because it distorted the moral character of both the oppressor and the oppressed.

So when he came back to an England in the grip of a slump, with millions unemployed and therefore many more millions *directly* affected by unemployment he felt that he knew what he had to do. He had to associate himself with the oppressed half of England rather than with his own kind by birth and training. He had to feel for himself the pressures the poor felt and suffer them; he had to get to know the victims of injustice, had to "become one of them." He had to try to root out the class-sense within himself. He did not have a romantic idea of what that last duty meant; he knew it always means trying to root out a part of yourself.

But that explanation, though it contains some of the truth, is not the whole. The whole truth is more varied. To touch bottom for Orwell was a very complicated release indeed, a shedding of guilt but also a positive test to which he was impelled. Phrases like the following occur throughout his work and are typical of an important characteristic of the Orwellian stance: "it had to be done," "there was nothing else for it," "it is a kind of duty." They are brave phrases and have a grandeur; they are also the phrases of a very vulnerable man and an obsessively *driven* man, a man with at times a burning sacrificial egoism. As so often with writers, Orwell's use of language, the words and images he instinctively chose, show this more quickly and surely than his actual statements. Describing his first trip to the rock-bottom poor, the fear and then the relief when a down-and-out lumbered straight at him — and then embraced him and offered him a cup of tea, he says: "I had a cup of tea. It was a kind of baptism." It is the image which stands out.

By nature Orwell was a lonely man. He wanted to belong to a coherent society, he longed for a sense of communion. But he could never quite believe in the eventual good effect of any man-made groups. "No one who feels deeply about literature, or even prefers good English to bad, can accept the discipline of a political party," he said in his introduction to the first volume of *British Pamphleteers* which he edited with Reginald Reynolds. He could just as characteristically have said, "No one who feels deeply about *life* . . . can accept . . ." In an interesting chapter of *Culture and Society* Raymond Williams discusses Orwell's representative importance as a modern intellectual, representative of "the disassociation between the individual and society which is our deepest crisis." The argument is interesting and subtle and should be read. But this condition may well be, as Mr. Williams recognises, as much a matter of individual temperament as of the climate of the age; Orwell's attitude was at least as much personal as representative.

It may be that, more deeply than he knew (and this is ironic since he so much distrusted intellectuals who did not belong). Orwell was temperamentally a lonely, isolated intellectual. He was always seeking out the lepers of life, yet he shrank instinctively from physical contact. Critics of Orwell who are committed to a creed will of course carry their interpretation of Orwell's "metaphysical loneliness" further. In his full-length study of Orwell Mr. Christopher Hollis, who is a Roman Catholic, sees him as a deeply religious man who, for reasons both temperamental and cultural, could not accept any religion; sees him as a believer without a religion, a man full of convictions, full not only of a moral sense but of metaphysical assumptions (hence — without them in the background — his convictions, to Mr. Hollis, would be meaningless).

Certainly the passion behind much of Orwell's feeling was inspired by a very un-material sense of man; and at key moments his language often moved into the metaphors of religion. This can be seen in the baptism image just quoted. Just before Gordon Comstock and Rosemary, in *Keep the Aspidistra Flying*, decide to marry rather than get rid of their unborn child by abortion, Orwell says, of Gordon: "He knew it was a dreadful thing they were contemplating — a blasphemy, if the word had any meaning." In its image and in its doubling back upon itself at the end that sentence nicely catches the "religious" feeling of Orwell and the dry metaphysical unexpectancy. He was an intensely moral man. He knew in his bones, to quote a phrase he accurately described as evidence of the natural religion of many working-class people, that "we are here for a purpose." But he could settle in no church and with no formal religion.

Though he found membership of organised groups difficult Orwell had an exceptionally strong feeling that we are members one of another, that we belong to each other, that all men are brothers. No one ever needed to remind Orwell that he should not send to find for whom the bell tolls; he knew. That was partly why he went to Spain and the other places. During the war, it is said, he and his first wife deliberately went short on their rations (Orwell thought this hastened his wife's death) so that there would be more for other people. The remarkable fact here is not that they went short; others did that. But most went short so as to help someone *known* to be in need, someone identified — an old lady down the road or a local hospital. The Orwells went short so that there would be "more for others," and this is both a saintly and an intensely familial act. It conceives the whole nation as one family. It doesn't calculate or assume that if you let yourself go short some official will make away with what you have saved, or someone else down the road will waste it anyway, so why bother. Orwell had a rooted sense of Britain as a family, as a continuing community (he was, to use one of his own distinctions, a patriot but not a nationalist). "England is a family with the wrong members in control," he said in an epigram which neatly catches his attitude: it assumes that we are a family, and it grumbles about the way the family is being run. This doubleness is itself very much a family attitude, a basic acceptance and a readiness to criticise in a way we would not be happy to accept from outsiders.

These impulses seem to have been moving the man who set out North to fulfil Victor Gollancz's commission. No wonder the result was a surprise. The North of England was stranger to Orwell than Burma. Not only had he spent many years out of England; he was by class and domicile apart from the heavy industrial areas of the North. They hit him hard, and the harder because he saw them at the worst time, at the bottom of the slump. He set out to recreate as vividly and concretely as he could the shock of this world of slag heaps and rotting basements, of shabby men with grey clothes and grey faces and women looking like grandmothers but holding small babies — *their* babies, all of them with the air of bundles of old clothes roughly tied up: the world of the Means Test and of graduates nearly penniless and canvassing for newspaper sales. This is the Thirties alright, for many in the working-classes a long drawn-out waste and misery which only the preparations for the war of 1939 ended. Whatever the qualifications we make to Orwell's account we would falsify our own history if we tried to qualify it out of existence. These things happened not long ago in this country (as they are happening in many other countries now); and it matters greatly — matters, as Orwell would have been the first to admit, far more than simply the need to get *his* record right — that we should take their emotional measure.

The qualifications are many and critics have not spared them. Orwell, as John Beavan points out, picked out the most depressed of the working-classes. The respectable working-class figure hardly at all in his pages. He chose the miners and, more, the unemployed miners. He chose also people on Public Assistance, the unemployable and the shabbily itinerant, the kind of people who land up at the Brookers'.

All these qualifications are true. So is the charge that Orwell sometimes sentimentalises working-class life. His famous description of a working-class interior *is* slightly idealised and "poetic." His account of the working-class attitude to education is oversimplified, and given a touch of the noble savage.

Before we look more closely at these charges we could add some others which are not so evident. Orwell's picture of working-class life, even of that good side typified in a working-class interior, is too static, is set like a picture caught at a certain moment. So it becomes in part a nostalgic looking back (and for Orwell himself probably also suggested an un-anxious calm, free of status-striving, which was a balm to him). In general his portrayal of the working-classes in *Wigan Pier* has not sufficient perkiness and resilience, is a bit dispirited. One can see why, given the kinds of people he chose to describe. Still, he did offer it as a picture of "the working-class." Later, in his full length work, *Nineteen Eighty-Four* (in all but this a terrifyingly hopeless novel) Orwell was to say "if there is hope it lies in the proles." But from the "proles" of *Wigan Pier* we would not get much hope of resistance and rebirth. There is just a hint now and again of a related quality, the ability to soldier on, to stick together and bear it, that basic stoicism which Orwell himself possessed and which may have been one of the reasons why he found the disposition of working-class people so immediately attractive.

When all has been said Orwell's picture, though not the whole truth, was truer than almost all the other documentary material which came out of the documentary 'thirties. It was true to the *spirit* of its place and time and (with the reservations noted) its people. It was true to the spirit of the misery: "and this is where it all led — to labyrinthine slums and dark back kitchens with sickly, ageing people creeping round and round them like black beetles. It is a kind of duty to see and smell such places now and again, especially smell them, lest you should forget that they exist; though perhaps it is better not to stay there too long."

Orwell's picture was true too to the spirit of some of the good qualities in this environment. He was not foolish when he said that he felt inferior to a coal-miner though he has been called so; within the terms defined in that first part of *Wigan Pier* he was talking humane good sense then. He may have sometimes sentimentalised working-class interiors. But fundamentally he is not wrong to praise working-class interiors. It demanded, especially then, a special sort of insight and hold on truth to be able to speak about the "sane and comely" home life those interiors represented. And it is not at all foolish — as some have called it — it is sensible and humane, to say that the memory of working-class interiors "reminds me that our age has not been altogether a bad one to live in."

It is important to be sure of our own motives here. Some writers on Orwell, sympathetic though they are to much of his work, have tried to shuffle off this side because it makes them uncomfortable. But he knew what he was about. It is no accident that again and again in this book he directly addressed himself to people of his own class. The "old ladies living in retirement at Brighton" are representative figures for a great many more, for politicians and businessmen and writers and rentiers and university lecturers. It was to these above all that Orwell was speaking. He was trying to correct that conveniently distant vision of other people's problems, that face-saving view of slum life and slum dwellers, which the training of his class offered him: he was insisting that people *do* hate living in slums (remember the sight of a young woman poking at a blocked waste pipe which printed itself on his memory as the train carried him South again), that even if some have become so dispirited as not to seem to mind, or have adapted themselves, it is still rotten — rotten for them and rotten for what it does to the souls of those of us who are willing to let other people live like that. These attitudes die hard and they are not dead yet.

In the beginning of its second half *Wigan Pier* is autobiographical about the sense of class. Inevitably, Orwell has been accused of exaggerating, of carrying on wars already long dead. He did exaggerate now and again; this was rough polemical writing. But it is important to say, and say firmly, that Orwell's sense of the importance and the pervasiveness of class in Britain was sound, sounder than that of most of those who criticise him for it. He feels the smallness of small snobbery accurately. He grasps the rooted nature of class feeling and the immense effort needed to grow out of it. He knew (as many people today still do not recognise) that it cannot be got rid of with a smile, or by calling a garage mechanic "Charlie." To believe that it can is one of the continuing self-deceptions of the British. Orwell was right to stress the subtle pervasive force of class, the way in which it cuts across and sometimes surmounts economic facts.

The professedly socialist parts of the book which follow are not so easily defended. The comic-grotesque gallery of cranks whom Orwell attacked — pacifists, feminists, fruit-juice drinkers, Quakers, birth-control fanatics, vegetarians, nature-cure quacks, nudists and "nancy poets" — these were to him the left-wing intelligentsia, the literary intellectuals and the middle-class socialists. Towards them all he was intemperately violent.

Of course, there is some truth in what he says. A man with Orwell's insight could not fail to score some shrewd hits. But at bottom his attack was probably inspired as much as anything by his puritanical mistrust of self-indulgence, physical or mental. His great antagonism to the left-wing intelligentsia was founded in his feeling that they were intellectually and imaginatively self-indulgent. He sombrely hated what seemed to him moral shallowness. He thought them prim and out of touch with decent ordinary life. He thought they wanted to have things both ways, to get socialism on the cheap whilst remaining undisturbed in their own fundamental attitudes and habits. He thought they wanted to remain dominative or at least distantly paternal in their attitude towards the workers rather than to recognise the need for a radical change of outlook. In his view, they thought they could remain vaguely international in their socialism without facing the full implication of their beliefs (which Orwell had proved in action he *was* ready to face). They thought they could be true socialists and yet keep their prosperity, though that was founded on the subjection of millions of coloured people; "we all live by robbing the Asiatic coolies." For Orwell, responsibility, responsibility in action, existed all the time, was heavy and had to be obeyed.

All this is useful. But Orwell did not leave it there. He was grossly unfair to his victims. At one moment he was asserting that working-class habits are better than middle-class and seemed to be mocking the middle-classes and urging them to drop their middle-class habits. At another moment he was warning them not to dare to try. At yet another time he was telling them that they cannot drop their middle-class habits anyway because they are too ingrained. At still another time he said that he could not drop middle-class habits himself. It is a confused, harsh and one-sided attack and omits altogether the history of good and self-forgetful action which many middle-class socialists have shown. On the other hand, Orwell idealised some working-class socialists and omitted to criticise—it would have been easy to do so—the limitations of, for example, some professional trade unionist politicians.

More than all this, his attack purported to be an attack on the main body of socialists. As such it is fantastically inadequate in scope. The left-wing intelligentsia are only a small part of the labour movement (though a valuable part). Outside them there is a complicated range of other people and groups: unions, co-operatives, local branches, chapels, friendly societies and the like. All these and many other groups and individual make up the texture of British socialism.

Something similar could be said about Orwell's attack on machine society which also runs through this part of the book. He had a continuing fierce suspicion of the emergence of a beehive state, a rage which later lay behind his two most famous books—*Animal Farm*, where it was controlled as an apparently light-hearted allegory, and *Nineteen Eighty-Four* in which it erupted into terror (but by then Orwell was a sick and indeed dying man). His tirades in *Wigan Pier*, though sometimes pointed, have nothing like the edge and force of D. H. Lawrence's. One may often agree with him because one has long accepted the particular point (without being clear what next can be done about it), but Orwell did not often illuminate the issues. Here, as in some other places, one has to be on guard not to be carried away by him. He had such an *honest* voice, as we all say; he so often said, outright, things we have all wanted to say and have been inhibited from saying, that we are in danger of being swept away. We have sometimes to distinguish between sentimentality and hysteria on the one hand and a just rage and pity on the other.

Wigan Pier, more than any other book of Orwell's, shows a host of contradictions in his thinking—between an absolutist and a tolerantly gentle man; between a resilient man, out to get things done by communal political action, and a dark despairer; between one who urged the need for revolutionary changes in our thinking and a man with a deep-seated sense that things would always go on much as they always had ("every revolutionary opinion draws part of its strength from a secret conviction that nothing can be changed," he says in this book, and elsewhere: "on balance life is suffering, and only the very young or the very foolish imagine otherwise"); between a pessimist and an optimist who believed in the eventual triumph of ordinary good sense. These things came together in his interest in working-class people. His pity for their condition made him want to bring about change for them; his basic, stoical acceptance and unexpectancy made him—with one part of himself—not really believe in the efficacy of change and made him also admire, with a peculiarly close natural feeling, the *stillness* of working-class interiors. It is probably useful to follow a reading of *Wigan Pier* with *Homage to Catalonia*, in which Orwell describes his experiences in the Spanish Civil

War. This is much more variously spirited book and much surer of itself. By then some of the things so far unproved for Orwell at the time of *Wigan Pier*, especially about his capacity to live up to his own convictions, had been proved.

There is a danger at this point of making *Wigan Pier* sound too faulty, too unfinished to be worth much attention. This would be a serious mistake. It has some impressive parts and is, as a whole, unforgettable. When we are trying to explain this we usually say that it is because of Orwell's exceptional honesty. What does "honesty" mean here? And is honesty in itself enough to make a memorable writer, whatever it may imply for a man as a man? I think that honesty here means a certain way of seeing and the possession of the power of showing what it is you have seen. It means a certain manner and *quality* of perception, and a style which isolates it. It means an eye for telling gesture and incident — for instance, the ability to notice that the mine's offices had a rubber stamp which said simply "death stoppages"; realizing that, you know unforgettably how much the risk of death is accepted in mining. It means the sense of detail and verisimilitude which allowed Orwell to create atmosphere in much the same way as Defoe and Cobbett. We do not easily forget the exact description of the "fillers" work at the coal-face, or the budget of a family on P.A.C., or the "scrambling for the coal" on the slag-heaps, or Mr. Brooker's dirty thumb finding its way into everything.

We mean also by Orwell's "honesty" his training himself to get rid as far as possible of the expected, the social-class, response. You can almost feel him disciplining himself to the point at which, when he looks up and says "what different universes different people inhabit," such an obvious remark seems to have the fresh validity of a self-forged truth. He tests on himself, bites between his teeth, the kind of socially conventional coinage which most of us merely accept; he tests it by talking flat out about the smell of working-class people or about assumed differences in status and the misery they cause.

All this seems a down-to-earth common sense though it is in fact so uncommon as to be a form of high intelligence. The total effect, which is why we use the word "honesty" so often, is as though we saw the thing, the scene, the incident as though for the first time.[1] To be able to write like this was partly due to natural gifts, partly deliberate professional practice (Orwell always meant to be a writer); and partly it is the product of a moral tension. It is informed by an urgent, nonconforming and humane personality.

To embody this outlook Orwell forged his peculiar style. It is, at first glance, clear and neutral, one of the least literary or involuted or aesthetic (one of Orwell's bad words) styles. 'Good prose is like a windowpane' he said, and set about stripping his down. Like Yeats, Orwell thought there was "more enterprise in walking naked." His style was a function of his search for truth. He thought of it as a weapon, a political weapon (which is not the same as a *party* political weapon); "I have been forced into becoming a pamphleteer," he said in "Why I Write." He was in no doubt about the importance of language in this respect, as we may easily see from his essay on "Politics and the English Language" and even more from his invention of Newspeak in *Nineteen Eighty-Four*. But his sense of the relations between language, thought and imagination was sometimes superficial.

The style Orwell forged was direct, active, cogent and epigrammatic. It rarely qualifies; it has not many "perhapses" or "somewhats" or "rathers" or "probables" or "sort of" or "on the whole." It uses short and ungenteel words wherever possible and says "bum" instead of "behind" or "belly" instead of "stomach." It is directed at a "you" outside, who has to be convinced; when Orwell is impassioned the "you's" succeed one another like an indictment. It is demonstrative—"Here is this frightful business of . . ." and "One of those ready-made steak puddings. . . ." It gives the reader a feeling of relief because it refuses to pussyfoot. It says, "This swindle . . ." and you feel firm ground under your feet. It has a distinctive kick and energy. One critic, Richard Rees, calls it "debonair." This is not the word that would come first to mind, but when you think about it you realise that it is true and helpful, since it reduces the risk of talking about Orwell's style as though it were only that of a plain honest George.

When Orwell was moved his style lifted to match his feeling and the reader himself feels as though he is confronting experience rawly and nakedly. Look, for instance, at the opening page of *Wigan Pier*. There is the short direct placing paragraph referring to the mill-girls' clogs and factory whistles and then we are straight into the description of the Brookers' lodging house. Notice especially how the epithets and images all work to build up a particularly loathsome impression. They are thrown at the reader, like blows with a wet dish cloth. The opening of E. M. Forster's *A Passage to India* makes an interesting comparison, not so as to award comparative marks but to see how far Orwell had gone in removing the "civilized" modulations, the literary and "read" air from his style so as to arrive at an immediate and demotic voice:

> Except for the Marabar Caves—and they are twenty miles off—the city of Chandrapore presents nothing extraordinary. Edged rather than washed by the river Ganges, it trails for a couple of miles along the bank, scarcely distinguishable from the rubbish it deposits so freely. There are no bathing-steps on the river front, as the Ganges happens not to be holy here; indeed there is no river front, and the bazaars shut out the wide and shifting panorama of the stream.

At its best this voice of Orwell's is charitable, morally earnest and convincing. At its worst, it can deceive us by the misuse of just those qualities which elsewhere make its strength. The apparently clear run of the prose can, like that of Matthew Arnold's at times, be deceptive. Orwell can commit, and commits in the second part of *Wigan Pier*, most of the faults he attacks in others. He can write loosely and in cliché. Very soon after the opening of the second part of this book he is writing about the "dreary wastes of Kensington," of their inhabitants as "vaguely embittered' and of their "favourite haunts." He overuses certain words for quick effects, words such as "frightful," "dreadful," "awful" and "evil-smelling." He sometimes overcharges his metaphors and this is usually a sign of emotional looseness. After talking about the evils of imperialism with a man from the Educational Service he had met on the train, he says in this book: "In the haggard morning light when the train crawled into Mandalay we parted as guiltily as any adulterous couple." Some of his larger generalisations only slip by us at a quick reading because he has built up a reputation with us as an honest broker: on a closer reading we find that the invoice has been incorrectly made out. He uses limiting labels as a form of Instant Insult; there are plenty of examples of this in *Wigan Pier*.

So it is easy to see why some people are suspicious of Orwell, why those of us who are drawn to him need to be on our guard so as not to be seduced by his manner in itself. I use that curious choice of words deliberately because Orwell was one of those writers who gives the reader a particularly strong sense of himself as a man. His personality is inextricably intertwined with his writing; his life and art were mutually complimentary political acts, in the larger than usual sense I defined above. As Lionel Trilling says, he belongs to that group of writers who *are* what they write.

He always drove himself hard and no doubt hastened his death, at the age of 47, by forcing himself to finish *Nineteen Eighty-Four* whilst living on the damp and remote island of Jura. For all the apparent straightness of his manner he was, as we have seen, a peculiarly complex and ambiguous man. No doubt all of us are complex and ambiguous, but Orwell differed both in the strength of his ambiguity and in the fact that he expressed it in his life and in his writing at the same time (and with less than the usual artistic indirection). He was tolerant, generous, brave, charitable and compassionate; he was also irritable, fierce, bitter, and indignant (but not "righteously indignant" in the self-righteous sense). He was at one and the same sceptical and sentimental, conservative and radical, unideological or abstract and intensely moralistic (this is a specially English combination), insular and internationally-minded, austere and full of fellow feeling.

Orwell has often been called "the conscience of his generation." Alexander Trocchi, whilst agreeing in general, added that the 'conscience' of a generation is not the "consciousness" of a generation but a less penetrating, because too immediately committed, entity, one too much tied to political action here and now. Similarly, Tom Hopkinson argues that Orwell suffered because he was "without historical perspective" and adds that this gave him the peculiar intensity of his attention to matters of the present day. One can agree so far here—whilst reflecting that Orwell himself might have said that some kinds of "historical perspective" can make us lose all sense of urgency and intensity in working for reform, so that we more easily accept the inevitability of misery.

But there is truth in both these criticisms and they do help to define Orwell's limits. To call Orwell the "conscience" of his generation is just and fair praise. In his actions and his writing he is representative. In spite of his frequent wrong-headedness we recognise in him a passionate concern. All of us may not be able to accept all his moral solutions; but we are bound to respect his moral *stance*. For exiles of Orwell's kind a moral stance rather than a moral programme is probably the only way in which they can speak to a fellow feeling in other men.

It is therefore a temper of heart and mind that we must respond to in Orwell. In trying to define that temper briefly we find ourselves using (and he would have been unlikely to object) old-fashioned phrases. We say, for example, that he stood for *common decency*; and though that phrase is difficult to define and often woolly, with Orwell it defined a hope which he tried to embody in action, it indicated his active commitment to the notion of brotherhood and kindly dealing.

It is easy, too easy, to say that the conditions described in the first part of *Wigan Pier* have almost wholly gone today, and so to feel more comfortable in not taking the book more seriously. One might speculate on what Orwell's own reactions would be if he were to come back to Britain 30 years after *Wigan Pier* was written and 15 years after his own death. He would certainly have been one of the warmest to welcome all the clear improvements—beginning with the lines of miners' cars which now stand at the pitheads (but on which we too often congratulate ourselves). He would no doubt have enjoyed himself in mordantly attacking those who so much resent the new prosperity that they accuse the working-classes, now that they have T.V. sets and washing-machines, of becoming materialistic. He would certainly have pointed out that for all our increased prosperity plenty of people—many more than most of us wish to recognise—are still living in miserable conditions on little money.[2] He would have seen, what many of us do not wish to see, that there are still two Britains divided at the Trent, that the Saturday afternoon shopping crowds in Bradford and Leicester still *look* different. He would no doubt have pointed out that when he reported in the middle Thirties Wigan had over 2,000 houses standing which had been condemned; and that in the Sixties, it has been estimated, it would cost 45 million pounds to complete the slum clearance of Oldham alone.

It would have been particularly instructive to hear him comment on whether the increasing attempt now being made to unify the working-classes and the middle-classes as bland consumers seemed near that kind of union between the classes which he urges in the last pages of this book. At that point he would probably have gone, more directly than he was always tempted to do in his writing in the Thirties, into what is at bottom his overriding theme — not so much the physical conditions of people but the quality of life offered to them. And on this George Orwell, today, would have been a fascinating and, I think, a disturbing voice.

Notes

1. Two particularly effective short pieces in this kind are "A Hanging" and "Killing an Elephant."

2. As may be seen from the works of, for example, Professors Titmuss and Townsend.

Life against Odds: *Homage to Catalonia*
George Woodcock*

If I were asked to pick the best of Orwell's books, I would immediately name *Animal Farm*. If I were asked which I liked most, I would select *Homage to Catalonia*. And this would not be merely because the book records a passage in history which has a peculiar emotional resonance for so many of us who were young thirty years ago. Many books do that, but from rereading most of them one gets little pleasure. The great virtue of *Homage to Catalonia* is not merely that it brings the period back to life in one's mind, but that it does so with such exceptional radiance. The best thing that might be said about the book was actually said by Matthew Arnold about the novels of Tolstoi:

> But the truth is that we are not to take *Anna Karenina* as a work of art; we are to take it as a piece of life. A piece of life it is. The author has not invented and combined it, he has seen it; it has all happened before his inward eye, and it was in this wise that it happened. . . The author saw it all happening so — saw it, and therefore relates it; and what his novel in this way loses in art it gains in reality.

Homage to Catalonia was a feat quite different from any other of Orwell's works. He left Spain in July 1937, and wrote the book so quickly that in April 1938 it was already off the press; this he appears to have done without any records to aid him, since, as he tells us, his diaries were confiscated by the Communist police when they raided his hotel room in Barcelona. The reason for his success was obviously that the experiences in Spain had been so intense that he was able to live through them again in the light of the inner eye, and to transfer them to the page in such a way that to the reader also the scenes appear with the greatest luminosity. To

*Reprinted from *The Crystal Spirit: A Study of George Orwell* (New York: Schocken, 1984), 163–74, by permission of the author.

reread *Homage to Catalonia* is an experience quite unlike rereading most other books, for so vivid and direct has the first impression been that afterwards it is like recollecting part of one's own life.

This, indeed, is the book in which Orwell comes nearest to his ideal of writing "good prose" that is "like a windowpane." He tells us how, when he was working on it, he tried "very hard . . . to tell the whole truth without violating my literary instincts." And if *Homage to Catalonia* seems singularly effortless in comparison with, say, *Down and Out in Paris and London*, it has much more formal grace and cohesion than *The Road to Wigan Pier*, which appears to have been written in just about the same length of time. It is true that the narrative is broken by chapters of political discussion defending the POUM party against accusations of plotting with Franco, and putting forward an astute analysis of the role of the Communists in the Spanish Civil War. At the time of publication it looked as though these passages of very topical political argument would spoil the book for later readers, and a decade after writing it Orwell seemed to agree with a critic who said to him, "Why did you put in all that stuff? You've turned what might have been a good book into journalism." He defended himself with the remark that he could not have done otherwise, because his anger at the thought of innocent men being falsely accused was one of his main motives for writing this particular book.

In fact, both Orwell and his critic were wrong. There are some rare writers, realistic by nature rather than by intellectual conviction, who can introduce argument or exposition into narrative writing without producing the usual shattering break of tone; one of them — to renew the comparison — was Tolstoi. There are also journalists who can write so truly for their own time that they raise journalism into literature and give it a permanent validity; one of these was Swift. Tolstoi and Swift were men of Orwell's own stamp, which possibly explains why he wrote long essays relentlessly analyzing their faults. He, like them, was a moralist, and it was the moral passion that carried his best works to the level of high literary art. Even his concern for purity of style and language was a moral concern, springing out of his conviction that the real aim of literature was to tell the truth, in his case the political truth. Nowhere is this shown more brilliantly than in *Homage to Catalonia*, where a political passion — the quest for human equality — led him into the most meaningful and possibly — in spite of everything — the happiest experience of his life.

Orwell went to Spain with letters of introduction from the British Independent Labor Party. He had written rather scathingly of the members of that organization in *The Road to Wigan Pier*, and he himself — despite the fact that he was already a declared Socialist — belonged to no party; the connection was possibly due to the fact that at this time the *Adelphi*, to which he still contributed regularly, was following the ILP world revolutionary line. His original intention was to visit the front as a war correspondent, but one can reasonably assume that he went there with some hope of joining in. Like so many others, he was caught up in the peculiar crusading atmosphere of the time even before he reached the Spanish border. In one of his columns in the *Tribune*, dated September 15, 1944, he looked back on his journey to Spain and recollected how he quarreled with a taxi driver in Paris and then took the night train towards the Pyrenees. The passage is an almost essential key to *Homage to Catalonia*:

> The train, a slow one, was packed with Czechs, Germans, French-men, all bound on the same mission. Up and down the train you could hear one phrase repeated over and over again, in the accents of all the languages of Europe — *là-bas* (down there). My third-class carriage was full of very young, fair-haired, underfed Germans in suits of incredible shoddiness — the first *ersatz* cloth I had seen — who rushed out at every stopping place to buy cheap wine and later fell asleep in a sort of pyramid on the floor of the carriage. About halfway down France the ordinary passengers dropped off. There might still be a few nondescript journalists like myself, but the train was practically a troop train, and the countryside knew it. In the morning, as we crawled across southern France, every peasant working in the fields turned round, stood sol-emnly upright, and gave the anti-Fascist salute. They were like a guard of honor, greeting the train mile after mile.

To anyone who thinks of French peasants in normal times, the guard of honor seems like a sheer flight of fantasy. But the year 1936, the year of the Popular Front, of the great sit-in strikes in Paris, of the Spanish Civil War, did not belong to the normal times of European history. Last winter, when I had given a lecture on Orwell and his contemporaries on a dreary Canadian campus, a young student came up and began to question me about the Thirties. Just before he went, a look of something very close to envy came over his face. "It was a time when one believed," he said. And 1936 particularly was a year when many people were filled with a secular faith that would not have seemed possible even at the end of 1935, and which was to be no longer possible after the middle of 1937. Remembering that season when the millennium did not seem an impossible dream, I can imagine that the peasants of the Languedoc did in fact salute the trains going down to the Spanish border. But I also think that Orwell himself was in the exalted and adventurous state of mind that gives an epic significance even to small actions.

Certainly he responded with intense feeling to his first sight of Barcelona, which in December 1936, when he arrived, still had the appearance of a citadel of resurgent anarchism. Going straight from England, he found the aspect of the city "something startling and overwhelming." Everything impressed him: the buildings draped with Socialist and Anarchist flags, the revolutionary posters, the gutted churches, the abolition of tipping and servile forms of speech, the loudspeakers playing revolutionary songs far into the night.

> And it was the aspect of the crowds that was the queerest thing of all. In outward appearance it was a town in which the wealthy classes had practically ceased to exist. Except for a small number of women and foreigners there were no "well-dressed" people at all. Practically everyone wore rough working-class clothes, or blue overalls or some variant of the militia uniform. All this was queer and moving. There was much in it that I did not understand, in some ways I did not even like it, but I recognized it immediately as a state of affairs worth fighting for. Also I believed that things were as they appeared.

In this atmosphere, to join the militia "seemed the only conceivable thing to do," and Orwell, since his references were from the ILP, joined one of the units sponsored by POUM, the dissident Marxist party which, though he did not know it at the time, was the object of a particularly malignant hatred on the part of the Stalinists, rapidly gaining control in Republican Spain because Russia alone was sending appreciable supplies of arms to the Republican side. Orwell, still politically rather green, was actually sympathetic to the Communists because they seemed to have the most efficient plans for carrying on the war, and at one time he even contemplated joining the International Brigade. Not until he had been in Spain for five months did he get a glimpse, which stayed in his mind for the rest of his life, of the face behind the Communist mask.

Altogether Orwell served about four months on the Aragon and Teruel fronts. Owing to the stalement which had been reached by this time in Aragon, he was engaged in comparatively little actual fighting, but he was nearly killed in May 1937 when a bullet went through his throat, miraculously missing the carotid artery, and gave his voice its characteristically monotonous tone by permanently damaging his vocal cords. On this occasion he imagined for a few moments that he was dying; the thoughts that flashed through his mind provide an excellent answer to those who have claimed that an urge to suicide drove him to the deadly Hebrides. His first thought, he notes, was "conventionally enough" for his wife, now in Barcelona: "My second was a violent resentment at having to leave this world which, when all is said and done, suits me so well. I had time to feel this very vividly. The stupid mischance infuriated me. The meaninglessness of it!"

From what I know of Orwell, he never felt differently to the day of his death, and I am sure that in the last moment of life, with whatever consciousness remained to him, he resented leaving it.

At the same time, though he admits to having been often afraid, he never avoided the situations which were dangerous to life, and his observations have that vibrant clarity with which one perceives one's surroundings in the moments of peril when time slows down and everything takes on a preternatural sharpness of outline. He describes conditions at the front, the daily boredom, the occasional excitement of patrols and attacks, the filth and the cold, and does it better than most men who have written on war, but what he remembers with most warmth is the unique sense of comradeship and equality which he experienced in those early months of fighting on the government side. For this reason he saw his time at the front as "a kind of interregnum in my life," different from anything that had gone before and probably from anything that would happen afterwards.

> I had dropped more or less by chance into the only community of any size in Western Europe where political consciousness and disbelief in capitalism were more normal than their opposites. Up here in Aragon one was among tens of thousands of people, mainly though not entirely of working-class origin, all living at the same level and mingling on terms of equality. In theory it was perfect equality, and even in practice it was not far from it. There is a sense in which it would be true to say that one was experiencing a foretaste of socialism.

What Orwell had found was a little society in which, once and once only in his life, he could feel completely removed from a situation where there were ruled and rulers; a society which was not—like that of the derelicts—below the class line, but in which he could mingle, without any sense of caste, with men of every origin. And this was worth so much to him that in memory it canceled out all the boredom, the physical discomfort and the danger. He found it "so different from the rest of my life that already it has taken on the magic quality which, as a rule, belongs only to memories that are years old."

As Orwell saw afterwards, this was a situation which had happened almost by accident, and which probably owed a great deal to the fact that it had arisen "among Spaniards, who, with their innate decency and their ever-present anarchist tinge, would make even the opening stages of socialism tolerable if they had the chance." It would not continue once the "enormous game" of world power politics moved into the Iberian Peninsula. Later events disappointed Orwell, but they did not disillusion him with what he had seen in the beginning. In June 1937, after he had recognized the aims of the Communists and had seen the beginning of reaction in Catalonia, he could still write to Cyril Connolly, from the sanatorium where he was convalescing from his throat wound, "I have seen wonderful things, and at last really believe in socialism, which I never did before." Even at the end of *Homage to Catalonia*, after he had told the terrible story of the mass frame-up of the POUM by the Communists, and had prophesied that whichever side won Spain was doomed to live under some roughly Fascist kind of government, he was still able to remark: "Curiously enough the whole experience has left me with not less but more belief in the decency of human beings."

Later on, I shall return to the influence of Spain on Orwell's socialist ideas. Meanwhile, *Homage to Catalonia* is not concerned only with the existence, among all the filth and discomfort of a civil war, of a miniature and temporary working model of the libertarian society. If Orwell's experiences brought him for the first time and last time the kind of acceptance into a casteless comradeship of workingmen which he had always desired, afterwards they turned him into that modern symbol of human alienation, the man on the run, and introduced him to the kind of political caste system—the rule of the party elite—which in his later novels took the place of the socially organized caste system he had known in England and, on a more intensified scale, in Burma.

When the Spanish Civil War first broke out it seemed as though the class system had been given a geographical shape, so that the old ruling class was safely behind the Fascist lines, and the workers and their friends on the Republican side could proceed to create a society in which caste differences would no longer exist. Something like a social revolution did actually occur in Catalonia, when the industrial workers took over the factories and the peasants seized the large estates. But history has not yet produced any revolution that failed to create a new class system. In Spain a number of forces soon combined against the revolutionary society which Orwell had observed when he reached Barcelona in December 1936. Equality and freedom have a difficult time in any war, and in Spain the advocates of military efficiency were soon arguing for the reintroduction of a discipline based on a hierarchical officer class. Then, because of their peculiar relation to Russia, the only source of arms for the Republican side, the Communists moved towards a position of power; in order to ensure success they assumed an antirevolutionary line which appealed to the remnants of the propertied classes. The result was a triple reconstruction of the caste system, militarily with the formation of an officer corps, politically with the consolidation of the Communist Party and its private police organization into a ruling elite, and socially in the re-emergence of the middle class and of blatant economic inequalities, as Orwell found when he returned to Barcelona in April 1937, after several months on the Aragon front. It was no longer the revolutionary Mecca in which he had arrived a mere four months before:

> The change in the aspect of the crowds was startling. The militia uniform and the blue overalls had almost disappeared; everyone seemed to be wearing the smart summer suits in which Spanish tailors specialize. Fat prosperous men, elegant women and sleek cars were everywhere.

But more sinister things were happening in the political field. It is in the nature of any totalitarian party to eliminate its own heretics first, and so the Communist Party set out to make an example of the heterodox Marxists of the POUM by the double process of vilification and physical extermination. As we have seen, Orwell was by accident involved in this persecuted group. *Homage to Catalonia* takes on darker tones as he describes the internecine war in Barcelona, and particularly the period when he stood guard on the roof of a cinema above the barricaded streets in May 1937, during the fighting between the Communists and the police on one side and the Anarchists and the POUM on the other. After he had been sent to the Teruel front and had come back wounded at the end of May, he found the threat of political terror brooding over the city:

> It is not easy to convey the nightmare atmosphere of that time —
> the peculiar uneasiness produced by rumors that were always changing,
> by censored newspapers and the constant presence of armed men. . . .
> There were times when I caught my ears listening for the first shots. It
> was as though some huge evil intelligence were brooding over the town.

And then the storm broke, POUM was suppressed, its members and supporters were hunted down, and Orwell suddenly realized what Continental novelists like Koestler and Silone were writing about when he was forced, like one of their characters, to live for a short time the life of a hunted man, a secretive, double life: "It was an extraordinary, insane existence. . . . By night we were criminals, but by day we were prosperous English visitors — that was our pose, anyway."

Orwell was more fortunate than most of his POUM comrades. Not merely did he evade arrest and manage eventually to cross the frontier, but he was even able to penetrate as a visitor into one of the noisome prisons in which some of his friends were being held. The lessons about totalitarian police methods which he learned during those days on the run, and the lessons about totalitarian distortions of history which he afterwards absorbed when he came to study the Communist accounts of what happened in Catalonia during those early months of May and June 1937, stayed in his mind and helped to shape both *Animal Farm* and *Nineteen Eighty-Four*. From this point onward the organized political elite began to take the place of a socially defined upper class in the vision of a caste world which shaped his works of fiction.

Yet the final effect of *Homage to Catalonia* is, strangely enough, not somber. The shadows of the latter days cannot overcome the radiance of clear colors that glow in the impressionistic prose, vigorous as Spanish revolutionary posters, which portrays the most dramatic moments. There are many such moments, but for Orwell the most vivid memory of all was that of the Italian militiaman who spontaneously shook his hand at the Lenin Barracks in Barcelona on the day before he joined the militia. He began his book with it and returned to it six years later in his essay "Looking Back on the Spanish Civil War."

> When I remember — oh, how vividly! — his shabby uniform and
> fierce, pathetic, innocent face, the complex side issues of war seem to
> fade away and I see clearly that there was at any rate no doubt as to who

was in the right. In spite of power politics and journalistic lying, the central issue of the war was the attempt of people like this to win the decent life which they knew to be their birthright.

Homage to Catalonia is in its way an elegy on men like this once seen and never forgotten Italian, but it is not a lament for their ideals. In "Looking Back on the Spanish Civil War" Orwell quotes a poem he wrote about that strange meeting. The last two verses, clumsy yet astonishingly tender, might be taken as a lyrical summary of all that he learned from the Spanish Civil War:

> Your name and your deeds were forgotten
> Before your bones were dry,
> And the lie that slew you is buried
> Under a deeper lie:
>
> But the thing that I saw in your face
> No power can disinherit;
> No bomb that ever burst
> Shatters the crystal spirit

There is a certain archaic grandeur about the setting of Orwell's experiences in *Homage to Catalonia*, and even about the actors. For, by the accident of history, he has entered a small, simplified society dominated by a few broad ethical concepts which gain value because of the material primitiveness of existence. These badly armed militiamen, guarding their mountaintops with very little but their ideals, seem a great deal nearer to the men who fought at Thermopylae and Marathon than to the great mechanized armies of modern times. It was doubtless this sense of living in a world snatched out of history that made Orwell recollect it immediately afterwards as something which had "the magic quality" of "memories that are years old."

Like the Anarchists beside whom he fought, and with whom he had more in common than he would usually admit, Orwell tended to see the present as a time of particular moral degeneracy. He looked forward with somewhat less confidence than they did to a better world in the future, but he shared their feeling that in past times, golden or at least silver ages, human existence had been more meaningful and more natural than it was becoming in the mid-twentieth century. But, while the Anarchists have always tended to set a distant focus on the Middle Ages or even on the tribal periods of human development, Orwell looked to a time into which his own memory reached – the last decades before the First World War broke apart the fabric of an ordered life which England had developed during the nineteenth century.

Homage to Catalonia ends on a vibrantly lyrical note, but its last words are not of Spain; they are of England, and they express all of Orwell's love for the country he had known in his childhood, and all his fears for its future. He describes crossing the Channel after his flight from Barcelona, and the impression — shared by almost everyone on returning from the Continent — of the extraordinary sleekness of the southern English landscape.

The Essays [of George Orwell]   J. R. Hammond*

Orwell's career as an essayist began with the publication of "A Farthing Newspaper" in 1928 and ended with "Reflections on Gandhi" almost exactly twenty years later. He began as an unknown writer on the brink of poverty and ended as a literary figure known and respected throughout the English-speaking world and beyond. These twenty years saw the depression, massive unemployment, the rise of Hitler and Mussolini, the Spanish Civil War, the Second World War, post-war reconstruction and the dawn of the nuclear age. His themes embraced not only these momentous issues but hop-picking, boys' comics, seaside postcards, English cooking, precise directions for making a cup of tea, murders, and the mating habits of the toad. He wrote extensively on political, social and literary topics and was also a prolific book reviewer. In all he wrote some 100 essays, 70 book reviews and 72 contributions to "As I Please" in *Tribune*. In the process his style matured from the diffident (but still recognisably Orwellian) tone of the early essays to the polished, self-assured, incisive manner which has made his name a hallmark for all that is finest in modern English letters.

During his lifetime he published four volumes of essays: *Inside the Whale* (1940), *The Lion and the Unicorn* (1941), *Critical Essays* (1946) and *The English People* (1947). There are also four posthumously published collections: *Shooting an Elephant* (1950), *England Your England* (1953), *Such, Such Were the Joys* (1953) and *The Collected Essays, Journalism and Letters* (1968). These will now be discussed in turn.

Inside the Whale and Other Essays consists of three extended essays written during 1939–40: "Charles Dickens," "Boys' Weeklies" and "Inside the Whale," each of which reflects Orwell's fascination with the literary and intellectual background of his times. "Charles Dickens," the longest of his essays, should be studied carefully by any reader interested in either Dickens or Orwell for it is a perceptive exercise in literary criticism in its own right and tells us much about Orwell's characteristic preoccupations. In an autobiographical note written in 1940[1] he described Dickens as one of the novelists "I care most about and never grow tired of," and in

*Reprinted with permission from *A George Orwell Companion* (New York: St. Martin's Press, 1982), 187–227.

discussing Dickens's work he sought at the same time to express his indebtedness to a writer who was an important formative influence on his own approach to literature.

The essay is significant for the insights it provides into Orwell's concerns and attitudes for in analysing Dickens's novels he reveals *inter alia* his own radicalism, his interest in the surfaces of life, his curiosity, his interest in social forces and his deep-rooted class consciousness. It is a sustained attempt to define Dickens's moral and philosophical attitudes and to identify the assumptions underlying the novels. In attempting this broad theme he transcends the boundaries of the conventional literary essay and embraces sociological and historical discussion. What interests Orwell throughout is Dickens's world-view:

> I have been discussing Dickens simply in terms of his "message," and almost ignoring his literary qualities. But every writer, especially every novelist, *has* a "message," whether he admits it or not, and the minutest details of his work are influenced by it. All art is propaganda. Neither Dickens himself nor the majority of Victorian novelists would have thought of denying this.

Central to the essay is Orwell's discussion of two philosophical positions: the revolutionary, who argues that there can be no lasting improvement in human affairs until *the system*, i.e., the basic structure of society, has been radically changed; and the moralist, who asserts that human nature must itself change before social improvements can be achieved. He demonstrates the intellectual weakness of the moralistic position as exemplified by Dickens whilst at the same time acknowledges his profound admiration for the warm humanitarian vision which animates the novels. Dickens's works continue to be read and enjoyed, he concludes, because they are inspired by a fundamental human decency and not by a political belief. Orwell is quick to perceive that Dickens was untypical of the novelists of his period in combining a radical critique of society with a nostalgic longing to return to the simplicity and picturesqueness of an earlier period. The combination of these two attitudes in one and the same person was also characteristic of Orwell himself. (It can surely be no accident that Orwell and Gissing, both of whom wrote fine essays on Dickens, shared a nostalgia for the past. Gissing was also a writer whose work Orwell greatly admired.)[2] This is one illustration of the manner in which the essay continually illuminates his own attitudes and beliefs. At one point he remarks:

> His radicalism is of the vaguest kind, and yet one always knows that it is there. That is the difference between being a moralist and a politician. He has no constructive suggestions, not even a clear grasp of the nature of the society he is attacking, only an emotional perception that something is wrong.

When writing this he must have been aware that much the same criticism could be made of his own novels, particularly *Keep the Aspidistra Flying*, and that he was by no means innocent himself of some of the charges he levels against Dickens, e.g., his failure to understand manual workers.

At the root of his discussion is an examination of how far a novel can convey a political idea and remain a work of art. "The thing that drove Dickens forward into a form of art for which he was not really suited, and at the same time caused us to remember him, was simply the fact that he was a moralist, the consciousness of 'having something to say.' " The phrase "a form of art for which he was not really suited" is interesting and once again has a direct relevance to himself. It is as if Orwell is aware that the novel of character in the English tradition was a medium outside his legitimate range and that in commenting upon Dickens's aims and motivations he is at the same time analysing his own purposes as a creative writer. In this sense the essay is, as it were, a mirror: implicit within it is a comparison of his own artistic intentions with those of Dickens and an illuminating commentary upon the rationale of twentieth-century literature.

Despite the highly questionable nature of some of Orwell's critical judgements—e.g., "Heep, of course, is playing a villainous part, but even villains have sexual lives; it is the thought of the 'pure' Agnes in bed with a man who drops his aitches that really revolts Dickens"—and the attribution to Dickens of traits of which he was guilty himself—e.g., "When he writes about Coketown he manages to evoke, in just a few paragraphs, the atmosphere of a Lancashire town as a slightly disgusted southern visitor would see it"—the essay as a whole is a masterly appraisal of Dickens's strengths and weaknesses. Orwell is acutely perceptive about Dickens's limitations as a novelist yet at the same time is generous in his praise for the enduring elements in his work: his memorable characters, his love of detail, his descriptive powers and, above all, the sheer vitality of his invention.

"Charles Dickens" is an entirely characteristic essay which bears upon it the stamp of Orwell's idiosyncratic approach. There is the tendency to make sweeping generalisations unsupported by evidence, e.g., "All art is propaganda," "His [Tolstoy's] characters are struggling to make their souls, whereas Dickens's are already finished and perfect"; the fascination with sociological and polemical discussion; the preoccupation with issues of class and background; the continual presence of the stimulating phrase, e.g., "Any writer who is not utterly lifeless moves upon a kind of parabola, and the downward curve is implied in the upper one." What attracted him to Dickens was that the Victorian novelist represented for him the qualities of a liberal humanitarian which he so much admired: decency, honesty, generosity, compassion. Because he admired Dickens so much the essay is more balanced than his essays on Swift, Tolstoy, Kipling or Wells and is for that reason one of his finest pieces of literary criticism. It tells us much about Orwell that in 1939 when the war clouds were ominously gathering he chose to forget his immediate concerns and write a long, discursive, humane essay on a long-dead English novelist. He concluded his survey with an attempt to visualise Dickens's face:

> It is the face of a man who is always fighting against something, but who fights in the open and is not frightened, the face of a man who is *generously angry* — in other words, of a nineteenth-century liberal, a free intelligence, a type hated with equal hatred by all the smelly little orthodoxies which are now contending for our souls.

"Boys' Weeklies" belongs to a category of sociological discussion which came increasingly to fascinate Orwell and which subsequent writers, most notably Richard Hoggart in *The Uses of Literacy*, have made their own. It is an examination of boys' weekly papers from a sociological and literary standpoint, concentrating in particular on the stories featuring Billy Bunter and Greyfriars School. The significant aspect of the essay is not the analysis itself — much of which is highly critical and provoked a lengthy riposte from Frank Richards, the author of the Billy Bunter stories — but the fact that he felt that weekly comics were an interesting and appropriate subject for serious analysis:

> You never walk far through any poor quarter in any big town without coming upon a small newsagent's shop. . . . Probably the contents of these shops is the best available indication of what the mass of the English people really feels and thinks. Certainly nothing half so revealing exists in documentary form.

This is the prelude to a detailed examination of *Magnet* and *Gem*. Throughout the discussion the question which fascinates Orwell is: what are the assumptions and values underlying the Greyfriars stories? The stories are analyzed from the point of view of their language, their relation to real life at a public school, the literary influences upon them and the social and political attitudes implicit within them. Such an exercise had not been attempted before and here Orwell was breaking new ground. He was astute enough to see that the values implicit in the stories would be imbibed by those who read them and therefore devotes considerable attention to defining the mental outlook suggested by Greyfriars. It is an outlook, he suggests, utterly remote from the contemporary world. The mental atmosphere deduced from *Gem* and *Magnet* is that of the year 1910, a world in which "nothing ever changes, and foreigners are funny." This safe, secure, solid world in which Billy Bunter and his friends have their adventures (never growing any older) bears no relationship to life in a real public shool and is totally removed from the problems of the real world. It is a make-believe world in which behaviour is determined by schoolboy ethics of right and wrong and where the predominant appeal is one of snobbishness.

Despite some rather wild generalisations (e.g., "*All* fiction from the novels in the mushroom libraries downwards is censored in the interests of the ruling class") "Boys' Weeklies" remains an impressive piece of writing which pointed the direction in which much of his finest journalism was to follow. In arguing that one's boyhood reading was important and left an indelible impression on the mind he was drawing attention to a neglected field of sociological study and it is entirely characteristic of Orwell that he concentrates his discussion on *Gem* and *Magnet* "because they are more interesting psychologically than the others" and because they had survived almost unchanged into the 1930s.

The intellectual curiosity which is such a distinctive feature of his work can be discerned in "Boys' Weeklies," as in "The Art of Donald McGill" and much of his journalism of the period. Always the questions which fascinate him are: What do boys read between the ages of ten and fifteen? At what age do they cease reading comics? Is readership of public school stories confined to one particular social class? Do children from poor backgrounds read boys' weeklies? Are comics also read by adults? This curiosity ranges from the minutiae of everyday living to fundamental questions of attitude and belief. There can also be discerned indications of that curious ambivalence which is present at many points in his novels and essays. He is, for example, highly critical of the Billy Bunter stories because they are set in an unchanging world of *c.* 1910 where "The King is on his throne and the pound is worth a pound" and "Everything is safe, solid and unquestionable" — yet this is precisely the world looked back upon with such nostalgia in *Coming Up For Air.* Again, he notes with apparent disapproval the fact that in the school stories sex as a topic is completely taboo and yet concludes his discussion with the comment that "on its level the moral code of the English boys' papers is a decent one."

"Boys' Weeklies" is then the work of a highly original and yet ambivalent mind, a man who was both fascinated and repelled by the subculture of weekly comics and attracted above all by the question of their influence on the adolescent. He appears to have been conscious of its inconsistencies for when he learned that Frank Richards had been invited to reply he wrote "I look forward to this with some uneasiness, as I've no doubt made many mistakes. . . ."[3] Re-reading the essay today one is impressed afresh with Orwell's skill in assembling and ordering his material, his insight into the imaginative world of the schoolboy and his gift for presenting a discussion in which issues are examined from both a literary and a sociological standpoint. One can only applaud his courage and honesty in approaching such a large subject with his characteristic verve.

His passionate interest in and concern for literature, including the debate on "commitment" which so exercised the writers of his generation, found renewed expression in "Inside the Whale," a lengthy essay on which he worked during the autumn of 1939. The title owes its origin to his contention that there were two schools of thought in twentieth-century literature. On the one hand were those who, like Henry Miller, were "inside the whale," i.e., indifferent to the world political crisis and sealed off from political affairs inside a womb-like cushioned space. Their attitude could be summarised as "Give yourself over to the world-process, stop fighting against it or pretending that you control it; simply accept it, endure it, record it." Contrasted to this were those—including, by definition, Orwell himself—who were or strived to be "outside the whale," that is, actively involved in world affairs and committed both in writing and in personal activities to helping to change the direction of human advancement.

Much of the essay takes the form of a discursive commentary on the novels of Henry Miller, a writer who was considered at that time *outré* and therefore unfashionable to praise. His comments on Miller, particularly on *Tropic of Cancer*, are penetrating and intelligent. The quality in Miller's writing which Orwell finds most attractive is its sense of optimism and happiness, even when describing sordid or unpleasant events. He contrasts this atmosphere with the pessimism which was so characteristic of the novels and poetry of the inter-war years, concluding that "On the whole the literary history of the 'thirties seems to justify the opinion that a writer does well to keep out of politics."

In an angry passage he discusses the sheltered life led by the fashionable writers of the 1930s and contrasts this implicitly with his own experience:[4] "It is the same pattern all the time; public school, university, a few trips abroad, then London. Hunger, hardship, solitude, exile, war, prison, persecution, manual labour—hardly even words." The point Orwell is making here is that the inexperience of life which was a feature of middle-class education meant that (for example) the excesses of the Stalin regime were condoned by many well-meaning intellectuals simply because they were incapable of grasping the reality of totalitarian government. There is a wider sense however in which the passage is peculiarly apposite to an examination of Orwell as a literary figure: that is that his unusual combination of experiences since leaving Eton—poverty in London and Paris, teaching in private schools, the bookshop, observing the life of the unemployed, Spain—had inevitably given him a difference of perspective compared with that of his contemporaries. This can be seen, for example, in his awareness of the passivity of ordinary people:

> For the ordinary man is also passive. Within a narrow circle (home life, and perhaps the trade union or local politics) he feels himself master of his fate, but against major events he is as helpless as against the elements. So far from endeavouring to influence the future, he simply lies down and lets things happen to him.

It was perceptive of Orwell to see that this passivity had exercised a profound influence on the literature of the present century: that the most memorable books about the 1914–18 war had been written "not by propagandists but by *victims*." This acknowledgement that the social and political forces which had shaped the twentieth-century crisis were beyond the comprehension of ordinary people and that all one could do in the circumstances was "to endure" was, he felt close to the attitude of Miller and in the sharpest contrast to the omniscience which was then fashionable in political writing.

His difference of perspective can also be seen in his assertion that every book, every work of art, has an implicit message: "And no book is ever truly neutral. Some or other tendency is always discernible, in verse as much as in prose, even if it does no more than determine the form and the choice of imagery." The discussion of Henry Miller leads on to an examination of the works of Housman, Lawrence and Joyce, but at each stage of the analysis his concern is with the writer's point of view, the underlying *attitude* which determines his themes and presentation of material. The writers of the inter-war years were characterised, he felt, by a pessimism of outlook, a "tragic sense of life" which led them to seek escape from the concerns of the moment in remote lands or psychological problems having little or no bearing on the significant events of the period—the Russian Revolution, the rise of Nazism and Fascism, the Spanish Civil War. His own attitude, as he expressed it some years later in "Why I Write" was that "When I sit down to write a book, I do not say to myself, 'I am going to produce a work of art.' I write it because there is some lie that I want to expose, some fact to which I want to draw attention, and my initial concern is to get a hearing." Implicitly, then, throughout "Inside the Whale" Orwell is defining his own approach to literature by comparison with that of the novelists and poets of his generation. As the essay proceeds the reader becomes increasingly aware that Orwell is distancing himself from such writers as Auden and Connolly and allying himself with Miller, not because he is in agreement with Miller's attitudes but because he respects and understands the indifference to world affairs which lay behind such works as *Tropic of Cancer*. Orwell had met Miller whilst *en route* for Spain in 1936 and had become convinced that his indifference was fundamentally honest, borne of a profound belief that the individual was powerless to change the course of world events. It was this honesty, this absence of pose, which deeply appealed to the Englishman.

Above all his distinctive voice can be seen in his awareness that totalitarianism and intolerance were about to engulf Europe:

> What is quite obviously happening, war or no war, is the break-up of *laissez-faire* capitalism and of the liberal-Christian culture. . . . Almost certainly we are moving into an age of totalitarian dictatorships—an age in which freedom of thought will be at first a deadly sin and later on a meaningless abstraction. The autonomous individual is going to be stamped out of existence.

This presage of some of the major themes of *Nineteen Eighty-Four* is remarkable in a work written on the eve of the Second World War (war had been declared whilst the essay was in draft). As early as 1939 he had recognised that freedom of thought would become "a meaningless abstraction," that the individual would be "stamped out of existence," that liberalism as an idea and a political reality would perish over much of the earth. His experiences in Spain had convinced him that totalitarianism was now the most insidious menace facing mankind and that the implications of this fact upon literature and art would be far-reaching. "Good novels," he observed, "are written by people who are *not frightened.*" There could be no literature of enduring value until the present conflict and its implicit threat to the free mind had passed. Until then the only option open to the creative writer was to endure, to record, to accept what happened to him without deluding himself that by his actions he could affect the shape of history.

Seen in the conspectus of his work as a whole *Inside the Whale* is a seminal book which concerns itself with many of Orwell's most fundamental preoccupations. To his friend Geoffrey Gorer he confided: "I find this kind of semi-sociological literary criticism very interesting & I'd like to do a lot of other writers but unfortunately there's no money in it. All Gollancz would give me in advance on the book was £20!"[5] Despite the limited appeal of the book it was favourably reviewed and earned for him a wide reputation as a critic. All three essays bear upon them the unmistakeable stamp of Orwell the iconoclast and man of ideas. The tendency to make sweeping judgements (e.g., "Considered as a poem 'Grantchester' is something worse than worthless")is as inseparable a part of his personality as his enthusiasm for Dickens and his striking use of metaphor. What lifts these essays above the level of journalism is their ability to stimulate thought, to suggest novel ways of approach, to probe beneath the surface of each argument to reveal the hitherto unsuspected considerations beneath. Orwell's approach throughout is individual and unconventional. The essay on Dickens is much more sociological and historical than the conventional literary analysis; that on "Boys' Weeklies" begins as a review of weekly comics but soon extends into a discussion of language and social mores; the title essay, whilst ostensibly a discussion of Henry Miller and his approach to literature, is in reality a profoundly serious statement of his own intellectual position. At each stage of the discussion he raises social, cultural, literary or aesthetic arguments which reveal the wide range of his reading and compel the reader to re-examine the issues in question from unusual points of view. Here, then, in his first volume of collected essays, can be discerned those qualities which were to earn for him a world-wide reputation as a man of letters: clarity of language, vividness of analogy, penetrating analysis of problems and diversity of argument. Above all there is an ability to see through pretension and hypocrisy, a gift for weighing up an issue with fairness and sifting the essentials of a problem from the dross. It is indeed prose "like a window pane."

During the autumn of 1940 Orwell was at work on a lengthy polemical essay "The Lion and the Unicorn: Socialism and the English Genius," which was published as a booklet in February 1941. This was the first volume in a series of booklets, the "Searchlight Books," which were intended to discuss a range of wartime problems and offer possible solutions to them. The series was edited by Orwell and T. R. Fyvel and, although the original conception was not fully realised — of the projected seventeen titles ten only were published during 1941–3 — it was an imaginative scheme which contributed significantly to the wider discussion of some fundamental contemporary issues.

"The Lion and the Unicorn" is a remarkable piece of writing in which Orwell ranges widely over the English character and attempts to define the prospects for radical social reform within its context. Part One, "England Your England," is a brilliantly written summary of English national characteristics which was later reprinted separately and has become well known in its own right. The title is taken from W. E. Henley's poem "For England's Sake":

> What have I done for you,
> England, my England?
> What is there I would not do,
> England, my own?

He begins with a careful definition of what it is that constitutes Englishness: a survey of those qualities and traits which distinguish England from other nations. He concludes that these may be summarised as dislike of abstract thought; privateness; gentleness; hatred of militarism; liking for anachronisms; respect for legality; patriotism; emotional unity. In these pages his own affection for England and English culture (including its weaknesses) is clearly evident and in a striking paragraph he conveys in a memorable series of images a microcosm of national life.

> The clatter of clogs in the Lancashire mill towns, the to-and-fro of the lorries on the Great North Road, the queues outside the Labour Exchanges, the rattle of pin-tables in the Soho pubs, the old maids biking to Holy Communion through the mists of the autumn morning — all these are not only fragments, but *characteristic* fragments, of the English scene. . . . Yes, there *is* something distinctive and recognisable in English civilisation. It is a culture as individual as that of Spain. It is somehow bound up with solid breakfasts and gloomy Sundays, smoky towns and winding roads, green fields and red pillar-boxes. It has a flavour of its own.

Orwell is impressed above all with the sense that, in spite of its diversity and class-consciousness, England was still emotionally one nation; he is struck by "the tendency of nearly all its inhabitants to feel alike and act together in moments of supreme crisis." Whilst acknowledging this sense of identity he discerns two significant trends in twentieth-century social history: the decline of ability in the English ruling class and the enlargement of the middle class through the rise of a new stratum of technicians and artisans. As evidence of the decay of ability in those in positions of power he cites the foreign policy pursued by British governments in the 1930s: the refusal to perceive the reality of Nazism and Fascism and the ambivalent attitude of Britain towards the traumatic events in Spain. This decline in integrity and intellectual grasp had been accompanied by the blurring of the old "class" divisions. A new, indeterminate social class of technicians, engineers and publicists was emerging and this would exercise a profound influence on the future.[6] The post-war world, he felt, would be vastly different from that of 1940, but "England will still be England, an everlasting animal stretching into the future and the past, and, like all living things, having the power to change out of recognition and yet remain the same."

In Part Two, "Shopkeepers at War," Orwell states the case *against* private capitalism and *for* a socialist society. His indictment of capitalism — "that is, an economic system in which land, factories, mines and transport are owned privately and operated solely for profit" — is essentially that it did not work and was wholly inappropriate in wartime conditions. It is characteristic of Orwell that he is not content simply to pose "a socialist society" as an alternative to this but proceeds to define more precisely his own understanding of the phrase. Socialism for him, he insists, is not only the common ownership of the means of production but also "approximate equality of incomes . . . political democracy, and abolition of all hereditary privilege, especially in education." His conception of socialism at this time is therefore considerably more far-reaching than that advanced in *The Road to Wigan Pier*. Indeed, having urged (in another memorable phrase) that "England is a family with the wrong members in control" he extends the argument to embrace an open advocacy of revolution:

> It is only by revolution that the native genius of the English people can be set free. Revolution does not mean red flags and street fighting, it means a fundamental shift of power. . . . What is wanted is a conscious open revolt by ordinary people against inefficiency, class privilege and the rule of the old.

He perceives that the war effort will inevitably involve immense sacrifices for the British people but is convinced that these sacrifices will be borne, willingly and cheerfully, provided that they know what they are fighting for and are presented with realistic hopes of a better life after the war.

Orwell's most earnest aspiration is that post-war England will be a more egalitarian and just society, a society in which gross inequalities of income and opportunity will have been eradicated. His essential thesis is that the war and revolution are inseparable—there was no prospect of establishing a socialist society without first defeating Hitler; conversely, Hitler could not be defeated without fundamental social and economic changes.

The discussion is continued in the third and final section, "The English Revolution." Here he argues the case for a popular socialist movement: the use of the word *movement* is deliberate, for he is advocating a current of thought, not simply a political party—a movement "that actually has the mass of the people behind it."

What is urgently needed, he argues, is a clear definition of war aims. These should include, in his view, the "nationalisation of land, mines, railways, banks and major industries"; the limitation of incomes; reform of the educational system; immediate Dominion status for India; and the declaration of a formal alliance with countries overrun by the Fascist powers. A popular movement motivated by a statement of aims approximating to such a programme could achieve a fundamental shift in the direction of domestic and foreign policies. He recognises however that a government inspired by such policies "will transform the nation from top to bottom, but it will still bear all over it the unmistakeable marks of our own civilisation," the peculiar, illogical civilisation which is quintessentially England.

"The Lion and the Unicorn" was well received and made a brief but significant impact upon the English intelligentsia. In a warm review in the *New Statesman* V. S. Pritchett compared Orwell with "the two outstanding figures of our tradition of pamphleteering, Cobbett and Defoe," and praised his lucidity and outspokenness. It was one of a number of radical booklets published in the early war years including Wells's *The Commonsense of War and Peace* and Sir Richard Acland's *Unser Kampf* and, whilst much of the discussion has inevitably become obsolete with the passage of time, it remains an interesting and valiant attempt to stimulate thought on some crucial issues of the day. He seems to have seriously underestimated the strength of national unity as a factor overriding all other considerations. As George Woodcock expressed it: "Few even among the Socialists agreed with him on the wisdom of attempting a total social transformation in the mid-career of a world war, and the majority of the people were interested mainly in staying alive and staying uninvaded."[7] On the other hand it could be argued that the Labour victory of 1945 confirmed much of Orwell's analysis and his prescience in realising that social change would take a distinctively English form. In defining English characteristics and then advocating revolutionary changes *within their context* he was unquestionably breaking new ground and rehearsing themes and issues which continued to fascinate him during the remainder of his life. But perhaps its deepest significance lies in the evidence it affords of his profound emotional attachment towards England:

> And above all, it is *your* civilisation, it is *you*. However much you hate it or laugh at it, you will never be happy away from it for any length of time. The suet puddings and the red pillar-boxes have entered into your soul. Good or evil, it is yours, you belong to it, and this side the grave you will never get away from the marks that it has given you.

Reading this passage one can only speculate afresh regarding his feelings on returning from Burma in August 1927 and from Paris at the end of 1929. Undoubtedly his ability to see England from the outside "warts and all" and to write with loving detachment of its strengths and foibles, was one of his most distinctive achievements. Writing as one who had been brought up in a comparatively sheltered English middle-class environment and had twice, of his own volition, removed himself from it, he expressed in "The Lion and the Unicorn" his deep affection for his country and his understanding of its special attributes. It is plainly the work of a writer who cared passionately for his native land and believed with fervent intensity in the resilience and adaptability of its people.

Critical Essays (published in the United States under the title *Dickens, Dali and Others*) contains, in addition to "Charles Dickens" and "Boys' Weeklies," eight essays written during the years 1941–5. All are exercises in literary or sociological analysis. "The Art of Donald McGill" is a survey of comic seaside postcards, a subject in which Orwell had a lifelong interest; "Benefit of Clergy" is a review of Salvador Dali's autobiography; and "Raffles and Miss Blandish" is a review of James Hadley Chase's *No Orchids for Miss Blandish* and a commentary on its underlying assumptions. The remaining five are assessments of writers who had each, in their various ways, influenced his own literary development: Wells, Kipling, Yeats, Koestler and Wodehouse. Of this material the most significant from the point of view of Orwell's distinctive approach to life and literature are "Wells, Hitler and the World State" and "Raffles and Miss Blandish."

The writings of H. G. Wells exercises a profound influence on Orwell as man and writer. As a schoolboy he had eagerly read *The Country of the Blind* and *A Modern Utopia* and frequently acknowledged his indebtedness to Wells as a literary and intellectual force. "Wells, Hitler and the World State'" is a curious mixture of criticism and praise. It is ostensibly a review of Wells's *Guide to the New World*, a collection of newspaper articles published in 1941, but soon widens into an assessment of Wells and of his place in modern literature. He is generous in his praise:

> But is it not a sort of parricide for a person of my age (thirty-eight) to find fault with H. G. Wells? Thinking people who were born about the beginning of this century are in some sense Wells's own creation. . . . I

doubt whether anyone who was writing books between 1900 and 1920, at any rate in the English language, influenced the young so much. The minds of all of us, and therefore the physical world, would be perceptibly different if Wells had never existed.

Orwell's central criticism is that Wells's nineteenth-century, English, middle-class background — remarkably similar to that of Dickens — meant that he was incapable of understanding the irrationality of such men as Hitler. Wells's advocacy of a Declaration of Human Rights and a federal world control of the air was academic until Hitler and his armed forces had been eliminated. This fundamental question, Orwell urged, had never been faced by Wells who continued to believe that man would behave in a rational manner. Although Orwell overstates his case somewhat — his indictment overlooks Wells's pessimistic writings such as *The Croquet Player* and *Mr. Blettsworthy on Rampole Island* — unquestionably there is some substance in his criticism. There is a tendency in Wells's novels to underestimate the immense power of evil in human affairs and Orwell is one of the very few critics to have drawn attention to this fact.

The essay is, however, rather more than a conventional exercise in literary criticism. Apart from its shrewd assessment of Wells's strengths and weaknesses as a creative writer it contains a moving account of his significance to those of Orwell's generation. It is not difficult to imagine, in the light of this, the impact of *The Country of the Blind* on the young Eric Blair when he and Cyril Connolly read it at St. Cyprian's in 1914 and the liberating effect it must have had on his intelligence (as late as 1941[8] he listed one of the stories in this collection, "A Slip Under the Microscope," as one of his favourite short stories). "Traditionalism, stupidity, snobbishness, patriotism, superstition and love of war seemed to be all on the same side," he observes: "there was need of someone who could state the opposite point of view." Of deeper significance is his recognition that such forces as nationalism and militarism had proved to be far more powerful influences in the twentieth century than movements for world unity and were, moreover, not affected by reasoned argument. This acknowledgement of the growing power of irrational forces such as hatred, bigotry and intolerance is of fundamental importance to his intellectual development and was to play a decisive role in the conception of *Animal Farm* and *Nineteen Eighty-Four*. "Creatures out of the Dark Ages have come marching into the present, and if they are ghosts they are at any rate ghosts which need a strong magic to lay them." It is these same "creatures out of the Dark Ages" — hatred, cruelty and violence — which found expression in the Two Minutes Hate and the torture chambers of the Ministry of Love.

"Raffles and Miss Blandish" owed its origin to Orwell's deep admiration for the novels of E. W. Hornung, an enthusiasm which had remained unchanged since his boyhood. Jacintha Buddicom, in her memoir *Eric and Us*, records: "Eric was a great admirer of Hornung, Conan Doyle's brother-in-law. He thought it rather nice for Holmes and Raffles to be in

the same family." Throughout the essay he makes it plain that the appeal
of the Raffles novels for him is the gentlemanly code of conduct on which
they depend:

> Hornung was a very conscientious and on his level a very able writer.
> Anyone who cares for sheer efficiency must admire his work. However,
> the truly dramatic thing about Raffles, the thing that makes him a sort
> of byword even to this day . . . is the fact that he is *a gentleman*. Raffles
> is presented to us — and this is rubbed home in countless scraps of
> dialogue and casual remarks — not as an honest man who has gone
> astray, but as a public-school man who has gone astray.

Orwell then devotes several pages to an examination of Raffles's code
of behaviour and a comparison of this with *No Orchids for Miss Blandish*.
For him the difference between the two is a moral one. "Raffles and
Bunny, after all, are gentlemen, and such standards as they do have are
not to be violated." To Raffles friendship is sacred; he is chivalrous towards
women; he will never abuse hospitality; he is deeply patriotic. Orwell also
draws attention to the absence of sadism and violence in Hornung's stories:
the novels, though convincing, are notable for their genteelism. There is
little bloodshed and few corpses. He concludes that the Raffles novels were
written at a time "when people had standards," when not to play the game
was simply not done, when there was a clearly understood and accepted
dividing line between good and evil.

This gentlemanly tone is then contrasted with that of *No Orchids*.
Orwell finds the sordidness and brutality of the latter utterly repugnant.
In the completest contrast to Hornung's work, Chase's novel apparently
accepts no standards:

> . . . it takes for granted the most complete corruption and self-seeking
> as the norm of human behaviour . . . such things as affection, friend-
> ship, good nature or even ordinary politeness simply do not enter. Nor,
> to any great extent, does normal sexuality. Ultimately only one motive is
> at work throughout the whole story: the pursuit of power.

The discussion is then widened to embrace a comparison of *No Orchids*
with the crime novels of Edgar Wallace and William Faulkner. Orwell
shrewdly detects that despite superficial similarities the mental atmosphere of Chase's novel is fundamentally different. What he finds so
reprehensible about *No Orchids* and stories of its type is that for him they
symbolised a new departure in escapist fiction: a departure from the
essentially civilised, gentlemanly world of Sherlock Holmes and Raffles to
a world of violence, cruelty, sadism and amorality. The distinction was a
crucial one, having repercussions throughout literature. On the one hand
was a society governed by an ethical code, in which crime was invariably
punished and in which there was a sharp distinction between legality and
illegality. On the other hand was a society in which there were no
standards, in which might was always right and the prime motivation was

an insatiable quest for power. It was the dichotomy between a world governed by *values* and one dominated by unprincipled brutality.

Orwell concludes his analysis with a discussion of the relationship between *No Orchids* and Fascism. In a striking passage which clearly anticipates the sadism of *Nineteen Eighty-Four* he summarises the attitudes which he felt were implicit in such fiction:

> It is a daydream appropriate to a totalitarian age. In his imagined world of gangsters Chase is presenting, as it were, a distilled version of the modern political scene, in which such things as mass bombing of civilians, the use of hostages, torture to obtain confessions, secret prisons, execution without trial, floggings with rubber truncheons, drownings in cess-pools, systematic falsification of records and statistics, treachery, bribery and quislingism are normal and morally neutral, even admirable when they are done in a large and bold way.

This list of features of modern warfare, almost all of which he had witnessed at first hand in Spain, was for him the world of *No Orchids* writ large. The frightening aspect for Orwell was that such books ministered to a power-instinct, to an unspoken lust for dominance regardless of social consequences. It was, he felt, no accident that *No Orchids* reached its greatest popularity at the time of the Battle of Britain and the blitz. Between the heroes of popular fiction in 1900 and 1940 there was an unbridgeable gulf. It was a gulf which he profoundly deplored. Whilst acknowledging that the reading of his boyhood was not free of snobbishness it represented an essentially moral culture whose passing would have the most insidious consequences for civilisation.

"Raffles and Miss Blandish" merits an important place in the canon since it encapsulates within its short compass a number of his most characteristic themes. Throughout there is an emphasis on morality: on a code of ethics or standards upon which civilised conduct should be based. Orwell was a profoundly *moral* writer. His concern for ethical standards in writing and in behaviour is implicit in his work as novelist, essayist and critic over a period of twenty years. Lionel Trilling described him epigrammatically as "a virtuous man."[9] The essay, however, is more than a plea for morality in literature. It goes beyond this to point out the relationship between the values inherent in one's reading and the attitudes of the reader: "People worship power in the form in which they are able to understand it." A generation which had imbibed novels of this calibre would be unlikely to question policies based upon duplicity and torture. Above all the essay provides powerful evidence of Orwell's deepening pessimism in the face of totalitarianism and warfare. In both this and "Looking Back on the Spanish War" (written in the previous year) can be discerned the apprehension of a sensitive man, a man alarmed at the rise of Nazism, Fascism and Communism and powerless to do more than voice his protest at the insidious advance of falsehood and the denial of objective realities.

The English People, published in August 1947, was written considerably earlier. It was commissioned by Collins in 1943 for their "Britain in Pictures" series and written in the Spring of 1944 following the completion of Animal Farm (in common with Animal Farm it was subject to a long delay in publication due to the wartime paper shortage). Superficially The English People covers much the same ground as The Lion and the Unicorn — a discussion of the English national character and an assessment of the probable future of the English people — and the apparent similarity between the two essays has meant that the later work has received comparatively scant attention from literary critics. It is in fact a much more balanced and carefully written essay than The Lion and the Unicorn and reveals interesting modifications of some of his views.

The opening section, "England at First Glance," is an attempt to define English characteristics as they would appear to a foreign observer:

> It is worth trying for a moment to put oneself in the position of a foreign observer, new to England, but unprejudiced, and able because of his work to keep in touch with ordinary, useful, unspectacular people. . . . Almost certainly he would find the salient characteristics of the English common people to be artistic insensibility, gentleness, respect for legality, suspicion of foreigners, sentimentality about animals, hypocrisy, exaggerated class distinctions, and an obsession with sport.

The discussion which is so brilliantly foreshadowed in this paragraph has a twofold significance. First, it should be acknowledged that in attempting to identify and examine the distinctive qualities of the English people he was exploring ground which had not been penetrated in this way before. It is not until Geoffrey Gorer's pioneering study Exploring English Character (1955) that we find a similar sociological approach to the problem of delineating English culture. Orwell, with his intellectual curiosity, his ability to see his native country from outside, his freedom from xenophobia and freshness of outlook was uniquely qualified to attempt such an assessment. The capacity to look dispassionately at one's own country, to assess its strengths and weaknesses and identify its peculiarities must be exceedingly rare. In The English People he demonstrated once again his gift for presenting sociological discussion in a readable and popular form. Continually one is aware of his fascination with the rich diversity of national and regional life, his ability to grasp the essentials of a complex reality, his unrivalled forte for the memorable phrase and the penetrating simile. Always he is curious to learn why things are as they are. Why, for example, had England "produced poets and scientists rather than philosophers, theologians, or pure theorists of any description"? Why did a manual worker wear a cloth cap whereas a non-manual worker wore one only for golf or shooting? What is the English attitude towards temperance and sexual morality? Orwell's curiosity ranges over the whole field of life, work and recreation and embraces the smallest details of daily living. The result is an essay which combines sociological commentary with an invigorating and highly individual freshness of approach.

Second, his distinctive voice is discernible at each stage of the analysis. In his essay on Dickens he had described a phrase of Dickens's as being "as individual as a fingerprint." The same comment could well be applied to Orwell himself. In the passage quoted above, for example, there occurs the phrase "and able because of his work to keep in touch with ordinary, useful, unspectacular people": a characteristic touch from the author of *The Road to Wigan Pier*. (Notice also the use of the phrase "Almost certainly": a very common Orwellian device). Throughout the discussion he is at pains to point out that "the real England is not the England of the guide-books," that the visitor has to probe beneath outward appearances to find the reality of English life and that not all English traits are praiseworthy. It is his unusual ability to draw attention to the less attractive features of the national persona as well as the more commendable, and to discuss both with equal dispassionateness, which makes Orwell such a fascinating guide. He dwells on the "gentle-mannered, undemonstrative, law-abiding English of today," but also enlarges on our apparent indifference to ugliness, our conservative eating habits, our irrationality and class jealousy. Again and again the reader is struck by his honesty: by his commendable power of impartial discussion and his gift for summarising complex nuances in simple, lucid, polished prose. As an example of this one has only to turn to the final sentence of the introductory section: "And he [the imaginary observer] might end by deciding that a profound, almost unconscious patriotism and an inability to think logically are the abiding features of the English character, traceable in English literature from Shakespeare onwards." It would be difficult to better this sentence as a summation of the national character expressed in language of the utmost economy and precision. Rarely can the quintessence of Englishness have been expressed with such felicity.

Orwell follows this introduction with three sections concerned respectively with moral outlook, politics and class structure. In these he displays to the full his intense curiosity regarding beliefs and attitudes and an extraordinary faculty for identifying the essentials of a problem. Topics such as religious belief, attitudes to violence, puritanism, freedom of thought and political consciousness are discussed with frankness and a complete absence of rancour. At each stage of his analysis he presents both sides of the question and is careful to warn the reader against too facile an interpretation of the evidence. In his discussion of "The English Class System" for example, after describing the broad social classes into which the population may be classified he adds cautiously: "This roughly fits the facts, but one can draw no useful inference from it unless one takes account of the subdivisions within the various classes and realises how deeply the whole English outlook is coloured by romanticism and sheer snobbishness." His fascination with the minutiae of class gradations is again abundantly evident and after noting the survival of the outward forms of feudalism—a hereditary aristocracy, the monarchy, the House of Lords—he discusses the increasing fluidity of class differences and foresees that "the tendency of the working class and the middle class is evidently to merge." Throughout these pages one is impressed anew with Orwell's unobtrusive skill as an essayist. Behind the deceptive simplicity of his style there is evident a compassionate intelligence borne of wide reading and shrewd observation. It is, however, not a conventional intelligence but one with a highly idiosyncratic (and decidedly un-Etonian) approach: that of a man who is intensely absorbed by matters of belief and emotion and is concerned above all else to present a balanced appraisal of his subject whilst not losing sight of the essentially quixotic nature of the English character. Even such an apparently simple statement as "They have the virtues and the vices of an old-fashioned people" contains within it a wealth of truth and yet is expressed with the conciseness of an aphorism. *The English People*, in fact, bears all the hallmarks of a work which has been most carefully thought out and revised.

There follows an engrossing section on "The English Language" in which he displays all that fascination with linguistics which came to the fore in "Politics and the English Language" (1946) and the Appendix on "The Principles of Newspeak" in *Nineteen Eighty-Four*. His discussion of English vocabulary and grammar is marked by a quiet erudition and an acute awareness of the subtleties of language. In a passage which strikingly anticipates some of the finest writing of his last years he observes:

> To write or even to speak English is not a science but an art. There are no reliable rules: there is only the general principle that concrete words are better than abstract ones, and that the shortest way of saying anything is always the best. . . . Whoever writes English is involved in a struggle that never lets up even for a sentence.

A new line of argument is opened up by his observation that " 'Educated' English has grown anaemic because for long past it has not been reinvigorated from below" and his perceptive comment that those who are in daily contact with physical reality—factory workers, miners, engineers, soldiers—are those likeliest to use simple concrete language. The vitality of English as a written and spoken tongue depended upon its continual reinvigoration through metaphors and words based firmly on everyday realities. He concludes with the vivid statement: "Language ought to be the joint creation of poets and manual workers, and in modern England it is difficult for these two classes to meet."

In a final section, "The Future of the English People," Orwell looks ahead to the probable shape of English society in the post-war decades.

Urging the need for "a rising birthrate, more social equality, less centralisation and more respect for the intellect" he anticipates some of the recommendations of the Beveridge Plan of 1944, *Full Employment in a Free Society*, which laid the foundations of the Welfare State. His practical proposals are an odd mixture of authoritarianism and social welfare. He advocates penal taxation so that childlessness becomes "as unbearable an economic burden as a big family is now" but at the same time argues the case for less inequality of wealth and greater democracy in education. There is also a cogent advocacy of decentralisation including more autonomy for Scotland and Wales, generous endowment of provincial universities, the subsidising of provincial newspapers and wider teaching of local history and topography. This co-existence within Orwell of dictatorial and libertarian attitudes is an interesting example of that ambivalence which makes him so rewarding a writer to study in depth. He is capable within the same essay of a generalisation such as "the centralised ownership of the press means in practice that unpopular opinions can only be printed in books or in newspapers with small circulations" and the most profound assessments of national traits.

At the end of his life Orwell prepared a statement for his literary executors indicating which of his works he preferred not to see reprinted. This list included both *The Lion and the Unicorn* and *The English People*.[10] His inclusion of them would seem to indicate his awareness of their limitations and his sense that with the passage of time some of his comments would inevitably "date." Of the two *English People* seems the most likely to survive, if only because of its publication in the "Britain in Pictures" series: a series now much sought after by collectors. To read it in its original form, alongside illustrations by Ardizzone, Lowry and Henry Lamb, is to realise afresh Orwell's unusual achievement and to acknowledge that in such essays he was attempting to define his own attitudes towards the land he loved so much. In doing so he placed on record a wealth of penetrating comment and appraised the English psyche with a fresh, humanitarian vision.

Shooting an Elephant, the collection on which he was working sporadically during the last year of his life, includes much of Orwell's very finest work. There are a number of essays which could only have come from his pen—"Books versus Cigarettes," a careful examination of the cost of reading compared with that of smoking and entertainment; "Good Bad Books" and "Decline of the English Murder," two characteristic pieces which testify to his fascination with popular culture; and "Some Thoughts on the Common Toad" and "A Good Word for the Vicar of Bray," two delightful essays which reveal his abiding affection for the English countryside and a simple joy in the passing of the seasons. The collection contains four essays which seem destined to earn for him a permanent niche in English letters: "A Hanging," "Shooting an Elephant," "How the

Poor Die" and "Politics and the English Language." These will repay careful study by all who seek to understand Orwell and his distinctive contribution to the intellectual climate of our times.

It is significant that "A Hanging" is the only example of his apprenticeship years as a writer — i.e., the only work originally published under the name Eric Blair — which Orwell considered worthy of preservation. It was published in the *Adelphi* in August 1931 and is markedly different in style from the rather pretentious book reviews he was contributing to the magazine at that time (the only other enduring piece of work from this period is his essay "The Spike," published in April of the same year, which he later reshaped to form part of *Down and Out in Paris and London*). Immediately the reader commences "A Hanging" he is arrested by the direct, individual, assured tone of the opening paragraph:

> It was in Burma, a sodden morning of the rains. A sickly light, like yellow tinfoil, was slanting over the high walls into the jail yard. We were waiting outside the condemned cells, a row of sheds fronted with double bars, like small animal cages. Each cell measured about ten feet by ten and was quite bare within except for a plank bed and a pot for drinking water. In some of them, brown silent men were squatting at the inner bars, with their blankets draped round them. These were the condemned men, due to be hanged within the next week or two.

Already can be discerned here a number of those literary touches which were to become a hallmark of the mature Orwell. There is the vivid phrase: "a sodden morning of the rains"; "the condemned cells . . . like small animal cages." There is the striking imagery: "A sickly light, like yellow tinfoil. . . ." Observe also the characteristic preoccupation with detail: "Each cell measured about ten feet by ten." At the outset of his narrative he is concerned to set the scene for the reader with the utmost precision.

The incident described in "A Hanging" — the execution of a nameless Indian and the realisation on the part of the narrator of the intrinsic wrongness of capital punishment — forms the framework for one of his most memorable and haunting essays. One is impressed, firstly, with its starkness. We are given no details of the prisoner's identity, nor of his offence, nor of his innocence or guilt. The narrator himself remains anonymous throughout: he is simply "I," one of the officials who observe the hanging and drink together when it is over. The episode itself is told without preamble; it is simply related, as if it was a chapter from a volume of recollections of Burma. This very starkness adds immeasurably to its power: clearly the incident had made a deep impression on Orwell and each detail of it was etched permanently on his memory. Although "A Hanging" is much closer in time to his Burmese experiences than the novel *Burmese Days* it must be borne in mind that even here he is looking back on an occurrence dating from five years previously. It seems clear therefore that the entire episode was one on which he had brooded long and deeply. The only way in which he could exorcise it from his mind was to commit it to paper and in doing so transfix indelibly each terrible detail of the execution and its impact on his consciousness.

From the moment that the hanging is set in motion — "Eight o'clock struck and a bugle call, desolately thin in the wet air, floated from the distant barracks" — the story moves inexorably to its conclusion. The walk to the gallows, the pursuit of an escaped dog, the hangman and the gallows, the final prayer of the doomed man, the hanging, the relief of the onlookers: all are described in prose of astringent lucidity. The climax of the essay occurs not at the conclusion but at the instant of Orwell's realisation of the inhumanity of judicial death:

> And once, in spite of the men who gripped him by each shoulder, he stepped slightly aside to avoid a puddle on the path. It is curious, but till that moment I had never realised what it means to destroy a healthy, conscious man. When I saw the prisoner step aside to avoid the puddle I saw the mystery, the unspeakable wrongness, of cutting a life short when it is in full tide.

Thus, an apparently trivial incident while on the way to the gallows acts as a catalyst, leading the narrator to meditate on the meaning of premature death. The prisoner, who at the beginning of the essay has been described in unsympathetic terms — he is a "puny wisp" of a man with a comic moustache "absurdly too big for his body" — becomes after the moment of realisation a fellow human being, united with the narrator in a common humanity: "He and we were a party of men walking together, seeing, hearing, feeling, understanding the same world; and in two minutes, with a sudden snap, one of us would be gone — one mind less, one world less." This shift from alienation to a recognition of kindred, from condescension to complete emotional identity, forms a powerful element within the structure of the essay and provides it with a convincing *raison d'être*. This ability to identify himself with the underdog, to achieve a sense of affinity with downtrodden or despised individuals, was to prove one of his greatest strengths as a novelist and critic.

Superficially "A Hanging" and "Shooting an Elephant" have much in common. Both describe incidents Orwell had witnessed in Burma, both are overtly critical of imperialism in practice, and both describe an apparently minor occurrence which serves as a watershed in the life of the narrator. The essays are however very different in spirit and intent. "A Hanging" is the work of a tiro, and for all its brevity is unquestionably the result of a long process of polishing and revision. It is not, moreover, a conscious political document: Blair in 1931 was still feeling his way towards his mature political position and was still years away from the social awareness of *The Road to Wigan Pier*. "Shooting an Elephant," by contrast, was written in 1936 when Orwell was an established writer with a clearly defined viewpoint: already by this time he had come to the view that everything he wrote was written "directly or indirectly, *against* totalitarianism and *for* democratic Socialism, as I understand it." It has therefore a much more deliberate didactic intention than the earlier piece. This is not to deny in any way its literary qualities, which are undeniable — the essay has been described as "one of the masterpieces of the genre in this century"[11] — but to suggest that it needs to be approached with some caution. It should be treated as a literary recreation, as an artefact consciously shaped to point a moral, rather than as a piece of reportage.

The editor of the magazine *New Writing* wrote to Orwell in May 1936 inviting him to submit a contribution. He replied with a diffidence that was all too typical:

> I am writing a book at present & the only other thing I have in mind is a sketch (it would be about 2,000–3,000 words), describing the shooting of an elephant. It all came back to me very vividly the other day & I would like to write it, but it may be that it is quite out of your line.[12]

It seems incredible that one of the most celebrated essays of modern times was first mooted with such apparent casualness. Fortunately the editor replied that he would indeed be pleased to publish "the sketch" and Orwell set to work.

In contrast to the consciously literary, dispassionate manner of "A Hanging," the tone of "Shooting an Elephant" is one of acute emotional involvement. The incident described took place at Moulmein in Lower Burma, where he was for a time, sub-divisional police officer. Here, he declares, he was "hated by large numbers of people — the only time in my life that I have been important enough for this to happen to me." Before turning to the central episode of the essay the atmosphere of hatred is carefully described: the bitterness of anti-European feeling, the humiliations and insults to which Europeans were subject, the loathing Orwell felt for his job. As a uniformed agent of the occupying power he was an obvious target for petty indignities which he found "perplexing and upsetting." At the same time he was oppressed by feelings of guilt at the blatant injustices of the imperial regime; the floggings, executions and imprisonments convinced him of the evil of imperialism and of his own role within it. "But," he adds, "I could get nothing into perspective. I was young and ill-educated and I had had to think out my problems in the utter silence that is imposed on every Englishman in the East." (The use of the phrase "ill-educated" in this context is curious and significant. Orwell must have been aware that having spent five years at Eton he had had the benefit of an education only available to a privileged minority. He may well have felt, however, that a public school education ill-fitted him for the harsh realities of service in remote outposts of empire.)

The crux of the story is then described. A tame elephant has escaped from its keeper and has run amok, causing much damage and killing livestock. As a police officer Orwell is requested to deal with the situation. On arriving at the locality in question he finds that the elephant has now calmed down and is browsing contentedly in a field. Since the animal now appears to be harmless he realises that, although he is armed with a rifle, it would be wrong to shoot it: the elephant has now recovered from its attack of madness and appears to be as harmless as a cow. However, a large crowd of Burmese has gathered round, confidently expecting the beast to be shot. At this moment he senses that, whether he wishes to or not, he will have to do what the crowd expects of him; failure to do so would result in intolerable humiliation.

> And suddenly I realised that I should have to shoot the elephant after all. The people expected it of me and I had got to do it; I could feel their two thousand wills pressing me forward, irresistibly. And it was at this moment, as I stood there with the rifle in my hands, that I first grasped the hollowness, the futility of the white man's dominion in the East. Here was I, the white man with his gun, standing in front of the unarmed native crowd — seemingly the leading actor of the piece; but in reality I was only an absurd puppet pushed to and fro by the will of those yellow faces behind. I perceived in this moment that when the white man turns tyrant it is his own freedom that he destroys.

The story thus becomes a powerful parable of the emptiness of imperial domination. Much against his will, for he feels that it would be murder to do so, he proceeds to shoot the elephant. The animal takes a long time to die even though he has aimed at the brain and heart. Its tortured gasping in its death agonies become intolerable and at last he can stand it no longer. He leaves the scene, abandoning the elephant to the natives who will strip the body for the meat and tusks.

Both "A Hanging" and "Shooting an Elephant" might well have found a place within the structure of *Burmese Days*, but some instinct persuaded Orwell to present them as separate essays rather than as incidents in a novel. Both gain significantly from this treatment. The two incidents stand out, sharp and clear, divorced from all extraneous matter. There remains indelibly impressed on the mind a series of unusually vivid impressions: the prisoner stepping aside to avoid the puddle; the impassioned praying of the doomed man; the terrible finality of the gallows; the excited, expectant crowd swarming around the policeman and the elephant; the lingering, painful, unbearable death of the stricken beast. The skill with which both incidents become the focal point of a parable is impressive in its dexterity. "I perceived in this moment that when the white man turns tyrant it is his own freedom that he destroys. . . . He wears a mask, and his face grows to fit it." The power of his invective is more telling than any number of polemical tracts.

In March 1929 Orwell was for two weeks a patient in the Hôpital Cochin in Paris, desperately ill with pneumonia. This was an old-fashioned hospital maintained for the teaching of medical students and was at that time "a stronghold of French medical obscurantism."[13] His experiences during those two weeks were such that they were etched unforgettably on his memory and when he came to write about them in 1946 he could recollect in terrible detail each stage of his ordeal. No one has excelled him in the art of grim understatement:

> After the questioning came the bath—a compulsory routine for all newcomers, apparently, just as in prison or the work-house. My clothes were taken away from me, and after I had sat shivering for some minutes in five inches of warm water I was given a linen nightshirt and a short blue flannel dressing-gown—no slippers, they had none big enough for me, they said—and led out into the open air. . . . Someone stumbled in front of me with a lantern. The gravel path was frosty under-foot, and the wind whipped the nightshirt round my bare calves.

This scene forms the prelude to a series of nightmarish vignettes in which the antique practices of the hospital are described with Dickensian intensity. It is as if the reader is being conducted on a journey backwards through time. The cupping (the application of heated glasses to the body to draw out blood), the forcible subjection to a mustard poultice, the cramped ward with its rows of beds containing emaciated patients, the foul odours, the sense that each patient was a *specimen* and not a human being: all are described in a terse, emotionless prose reminiscent of *Down and Out in Paris and London*. Horror is piled relentlessly upon horror— patients dying like animals, corpses left exposed to view, the unspeakable atmosphere of death and decay—until the cumulative effect becomes almost unbearable. Long after "How the Poor Die" has been read these impressions remain ingrained on the memory; the essay has the stark, inhuman quality of a short story by Edgar Allan Poe.

The significance of the essay lies precisely in this element of verisimilitude. "How the Poor Die" is a moving and unforgettable document because it does not claim to be other than a factual account of an experience undergone by Orwell himself. There is no element of artificiality (as in the Etonian posing as a London tramp, or in the hop-picking scenes in *A Clergyman's Daughter*) but instead an attempt to describe as honestly as possible all that he saw and underwent. The essay gains immeasurably from this absence of pose. He was not pretending to be ill, nor pretending to be poor. He was admitted to the hospital as a pauper and was treated accordingly, suffering cruelty and indifference on the same terms as the other patients. As a result he is able to identify himself totally with the poor; he was one of them. It would not be too much to claim that his experience of hospitalisation was the turning point in the development of his unique literary style. However harrowing the experience at the time, the submerging of himself in identical conditions with others in like circumstances and the opportunity thus afforded of observing poverty *from the inside* proved to be a decisive step in the forging of his personality.

"Politics and the English Language," written for *Horizon* in April 1946, has justifiably become one of Orwell's most renowned essays. It was written when he was at the height of his powers and at a time when, with *Animal Farm* completed and *Nineteen Eighty-Four* at the planning stage, he was increasingly preoccupied with language and its repercussions on literature and politics. He is at pains to make clear at the outset that his concern stems not from linguistic theory or pedantic purism but from an essentially *moral* concern for the establishment of truth:

> Modern English, especially written English, is full of bad habits which spread by imitation and which can be avoided if one is willing to take the necessary trouble. If one gets rid of these habits one can think more clearly, and to think clearly is a necessary first step towards political regeneration: so that the fight against bad English is not frivolous and is not the exclusive concern of professional writers.

He proceeds to examine five extracts from recently published books and pamphlets and analyses these for their faults; these faults are discussed at length under the headings "dying metaphors," "operators or verbal false limbs," "pretentious diction," and "meaningless words." Throughout the discussion his concern is with the clarity and honesty of language, with "language as an instrument for expressing and not for concealing or preventing thought." He stresses that the careless use of language has an insidious effect since it corrupts thought by the introduction of meaningless phrases, clichés and platitudes which muffle clear statement. This concern with the capacity of language to express clear thought was Orwell's obsession: it had been his King Charles's Head since *Homage to Catalonia* (indeed its roots can be traced much earlier, in Gordon Comstock's preoccupation with language and his distaste for advertising slogans). What angered him was that in the twentieth century "political speech and writing are largely the defence of the indefensible." Imperialism, purges, nuclear weapons and political imprisonments could only be defined by phrases and sentences which were essentially bromides: statements designed to conceal rather than reveal the truth. In his view politicians had been responsible for much of the decay in the English language since political communication had to consist largely of euphemism, vagueness and subjective statement.

The process, Orwell concludes, is not irreversible. Through the application of a number of simple rules—the avoidance of hackneyed metaphors and similes, the avoidance of long words where short ones will suffice, the removal of unnecessary words, the shunning of passive words and foreign phrases—English could become once again a language of meaning and precision. This, he recognizes, will "demand a deep change of attitude in anyone who has grown used to writing in the style now fashionable." It would demand an end to lazy habits of thought, a refusal to use worn-out phrases and a conscious determination to achieve the utmost clarity of statement.

This was to be his major preoccupation during the remainder of his life: a passionate concern for the use of English as an accurate and explicit instrument for the communication of ideas. It underlies all his work from the war years onwards and was to find its final and most moving expression in *Nineteen Eighty-Four*.

Such, Such Were the Joys and *England Your England* are the American and English editions respectively of a second fine collection of posthumously published essays. The English edition differs from the former in that the long autobiographical essay "Such, Such Were the Joys" is omitted: for legal reasons it was considered inadvisable to publish this in Britain at the time. The essay had its origins in an exchange of correspondence between Orwell and his old friend Cyril Connolly in 1938.

Writing to Connolly apropos the latter's *Enemies of Promise* Orwell commented: "I wonder how you can write about St. Cyprian's. It's all like an awful nightmare to me, & sometimes I think I can still taste the porridge (out of those pewter bowls, do you remember?)"[14] The phrase "awful nightmare" is revealing and indicates the deep impact which his preparatory school experiences made upon him. Following the publication of *Enemies of Promise* Connolly invited him to write his reminiscences of St. Cyprian's for publication in the magazine *Horizon*. These reminiscences, which took the form of a novella-length essay, were not published until 1953 and did not appear in book form in Britain until 1968 with the publication of the *Collected Essays*. Orwell forwarded the manuscript to his publisher F. J. Warburg in May 1947 with a covering note: "I am sending you separately a long autobiographical sketch. . . . I haven't actually sent it to Connolly or *Horizon*, because apart from being too long for a periodical I think it is really too libelous to print, and I am not disposed to change it, except perhaps the names."[15]

The title is taken from "The Echoing Green" one of Blake's *Songs of Innocence* with which he had been familiar since childhood:

> Such, such were the joys
> When we all, girls and boys,
> In our youth time were seen,
> On the Echoing Green.

The selection of this line for the title of his most painful and deeply-felt essay can only be ironical: far from being an evocation of childhood happiness it is a bitterly wrought indictment of childhood sufferings, a scathing account of mental and emotional repression in the years before 1914. In common with *Down and Out in Paris and London* and "Shooting an Elephant" the essay needs to be approached with some caution as a fragment of autobiography. In deliberately casting the sketch in the form of an indictment, omitting all the happier aspects of his memories (apart from one beautifully written passage eulogising the joys of summer) he has created a powerful but highly selective document, a polemic which is so carefully fashioned and intensely conceived that it achieves the status of a work of art.

The essay is divided into six sections, each concerned with a different aspect of his childhood world: the effect is to view his memories from a number of different perspectives. The sections are concerned respectively with the violent punishment meted out to him for bed-wetting; the emphasis upon hereditary wealth and competitive examinations; the squalor and neglect which was a feature of some private schools; the prevailing sexual codes; the social and moral values inculcated by the school; and a comparison of his own schooling with that of the contemporary child. At the outset Orwell is careful to warn the reader of the distorting effects of memory (assuming that the essay was written in 1940 he was attempting to recall events that had occurred twenty-eight years previously):

> In general, one's memories of any period must necessarily weaken as one moves away from it. . . . At twenty I could have written the history of my school days with an accuracy which would be quite impossible now. But it can also happen that one's memories grow sharper after a long lapse of time, because one is looking at the past with fresh eyes. . . .

With candour and bitterness he describes the harsh regime of St. Cyprian's: the canings, the bullyings, the snobbishness, the petty humiliations, the discomfort, the acute unspoken misery which only childhood can know. What it can mean to a sensitive child to be removed from home at the age of eight and thrust into the uncongenial environment of a boarding school is vividly conveyed. At that age, Orwell asserts, he was in a state of sexual and worldly innocence; his years at St. Cyprian's were a painful introduction into a world of sexual repression, learning by rote, a code of "get on or get out" and the hierarchy of wealth. His feeling that he was innately inferior and doomed to failure was reinforced by the prevailing code that strength and power mattered above all else: "There were the strong, who deserved to win and always did win, and there were the weak, who deserved to lose and always did lose, everlastingly." The emphasis on games, on the passing of examinations as an end in itself, on the social cachet of wealth, on the virtue of winning: all these were anathema to him. He did not question the prevailing values, however, since as a child he was too young and inexperienced to put other values in their place; he accepted his inferiority. (At one point he comments drily: "The conviction that it was *not possible* for me to be a success went deep enough to influence my actions till far into adult life." How far is this an accurate statement of his outlook as a young man and how far is it a rationalisation?) The technique employed is akin to that of "How the Poor

Die" — the relentless accumulation of detail upon detail to achieve an effect of unforgettable squalidness. The overwhelming impression is one of a boy who was a misfit: unbearably unhappy, realising to his chagrin that he had been accepted at reduced fees, unable to accommodate himself to a world in which physical prowess was the touchstone of achievement, a boy immersed in a lonely, introspective world of his own. The traumas of childhood, he adds, can be immense. The adults and bullies who seem to a child terrifying and all-powerful would seem from his mature perspective quite harmless: but to the child they assume monstrous, nightmarish proportions: "Whoever writes about his childhood," he concludes, "must beware of exaggeration and self-pity. I do not claim that I was a martyr or that St. Cyprian's was a sort of Dotheboys Hall. But I should be falsifying my own memories if I did not record that they are largely memories of disgust."

The question which has fascinated critics and biographers since Orwell's death is how far "Such, Such Were the Joys" can be accepted as a literal statement of fact: how reliable is it as a recreation of his boyhood? The question is by no means easy to answer (and is not made any easier by his deceptively simple, direct style) but may most fruitfully be approached by separating its two aspects — the qualities of the essay as a literary composition and its reliability as a factual record of his schooling. From a purely literary standpoint "Such, Such Were the Joys" must be accepted as one of Orwell's finest creations. Lucid, intelligent and fluent, it is a most carefully assembled piece of work and bears all the hallmarks of a closely revised text which has been long mulled over. The power of the writing is such that certain details remain in the mind long after the essay has been laid aside: the caning from the headmaster, the long walks on the Sussex downs, the earnest homily on the Temple of the Body, the tearful interrogations from the headmaster's wife. It is in this direction that the enduring value of the essay lies — as a memorable *interpretation* of schooling, a deliberately selective account of boyhood unhappiness written from the vantage point of adulthood. Its value as autobiography is more problematic. Memory is notoriously unreliable and before accepting the essay at its face value one has to place it in context alongside contemporary evidence: letters written at the time and the testimony of his friends and fellow pupils.[16] The evidence seen as a totality is not by any means a picture of unrelieved misery, although his account is confirmed in many of its particulars. The conclusion must be that he has carefully selected his material in order to present a case; the formulation of a dispassionate account of his school days was not his intention, since this would have involved the inclusion of episodes which did not minister to his overall design. In the last analysis it is therefore as a *literary* exercise that it must be judged and in these terms it has to be acknowledged as a wholly coherent and moving composition.

It is significant that Orwell concludes the essay with the reflection:

"Now, however, the place is out of my system for good. Its magic works no longer. . . ." In forcing himself to dwell on painful childhood memories and to ponder episodes long consigned to neglected corners of the mind he succeeded in exorcising from his imagination a part of his life he had looked back upon with repugnance. In doing so he fashioned one of his most absorbing and personal essays.

"Such, Such Were the Joys" is one more instance of Orwell's technique of using his personal reminiscences as a basis for the presentation of radical ideas. "All art," he wrote elsewhere, "is propaganda." One may disagree with this statement while acknowledging that in the fusion of the two media he achieved a purposive and dynamic literary form.

The Collected Essays, Journalism and Letters published in four volumes in 1968 contains all the essays in the collections discussed above together with much of his journalism, his wartime diary, and a generous selection of his letters. It amounts in all to some 500 items and represents an impressive achievement for a man who was for much of his life in poor health and died at the age of 46. Of all this material — which embraces the whole range of his life, work and thought from 1920 to 1949 — the most enduring pieces (apart from those discussed in the previous pages) are his memorable essay "Why I Write" and the numerous contributions he wrote for *Tribune* under the title "As I Please." Taken together these indicate the wide range of his interests, the depth of his concern for human betterment and the seriousness with which he approached his work. Above all they reveal the unshakeable moral stance which lay at the root of his art.

Between December 1943 and February 1945 Orwell contributed to *Tribune* a regular weekly column under the title "As I Please" and continued this at irregular intervals thereafter until April 1947. In all he contributed 72 "As I Please" columns covering some 230 separate topics ranging from cosmetics to transport and from air raids to Christianity. The scope of the column embraced comments on the war effort, literary discussion, commentary on religious and philosophical ideas, discussion of current affairs, gardening, prominent people, and in fact any topic which took his fancy. Its catholicity must have been for him a large part of its appeal for it permitted him to comment on a diversity of issues without obliging him to confine his attention to politics or literature. The result is a fascinating exercise in a now unfashionable genre: the causerie. Tolerant, humane, stimulating and idiosyncratic, "As I Please" was and is a major contribution to the art of the pot-pourri. The contributions illustrate the diversity of his reading and interests, his willingness to espouse unpopular causes and his gift for stimulating his readers with apposite and thought-provoking commentary:

> That seems to be a fixed rule in London: whenever you do by some chance have a decent vista, block it up with the ugliest statue you can find.

The fact is that we live in a time when causes for rejoicing are not numerous. But I like praising things, when there is anything to praise, and I would like here to write a few lines . . . in praise of the Woolworth's Rose.

With no power to put my decrees into operation, but with as much authority as most of the exile "governments" now sheltering in various parts of the world, I pronounce sentence of death on the following words and expressions: Achilles' heel, jackboot, hydra-headed, ride roughshod over, stab in the back, petty-bourgeois, stinking corpse, liquidate, iron heel, blood-stained oppressor, cynical betrayal, lackey, flunkey, mad dog, jackal, hyena, blood-bath.

With great enjoyment I have just been rereading *Trilby*, George du Maurier's justly popular novel, one of the finest specimens of that "good bad" literature which the English-speaking peoples seem to have lost the secret of producing.

Two days ago, after a careful search in Hyde Park, I came on a hawthorn bush that was definitely in bud, and some birds, though not actually singing, were making noises like an orchestra tuning up. Spring is coming after all, and recent rumours that this was the beginning of another Ice Age were unfounded.[17]

The column gained him a wider readership than any of his books with the exception of *Animal Farm* and stimulated a lively correspondence. His readers were alternately amused, irritated, exasperated and enlightened by his wide-ranging comments; many were annoyed by his quirkiness, his refusal to respect the wartime convention that the Soviet Union was not to be criticised, and his frequent forays into apparently minor topics. Many more found the column essential reading and turned to his page before studying the remainder of the paper. In its unusual combination of earnestness and good humour, its liberality of subject matter, its evidence of diverse reading and an acute eye for neglected byways of knowledge "As I Please" is a fascinating reflection of Orwell's personality and indicates many aspects of his complex make-up. George Gissing, in the preface to his *Private Papers of Henry Ryecroft*, wrote: "But in this written gossip he revealed himself more intimately than in our conversation of the days gone by. . . . Here he spoke to me without restraint, and, when I had read it all through, I knew the man better than before." The same might be said of "As I Please." Freed from the conventions of the novel and the documentary, he was able to exploit to the full his formidable talents as ranconteur, iconoclast and man of letters. Viewed in their entirety these short pieces are among the finest contributions to the English essay written in this century.

"Why I Write," written in 1946 and since frequently anthologised, is one of the very few essays in which Orwell discusses his own approach to literature. The editors of the *Collected Essays* have wisely placed it at the beginning of the collection since it is in a real sense a summary of his intellectual position and of the motives which led him to embark on a literary life.

After describing his early efforts to write poetry and short stories he makes the perceptive comment:

> . . . I do not think one can assess a writer's motives without knowing something of his early development. His subject-matter will be determined by the age he lives in—at least this is true in tumultuous, revolutionary ages like our own—but before he ever begins to write he will have acquired an emotional attitude from which he will never completely escape.

This emotional attitude, he acknowledged, was of crucial importance in the development of any writer and particularly so in his own case: "if he escapes from his early influences altogether, he will have killed his impulse to write."

The most interesting section of the essay to the student of his work is that in which Orwell examines his own motives as a writer. By temperament, he admits, he is a person in which egotism, aesthetic enthusiasm and historical impulse would normally outweigh political purpose. "In a peaceful age I might have written ornate or merely descriptive books, and might have remained almost unaware of my political loyalties. As it is I have been forced into becoming a sort of pamphleteer." The word *forced* in this connection tells us much concerning his attitudes; clearly he felt impelled by a powerful urge which he could not resist or ignore. The Spanish Civil War was the turning point, the catalyst which changed him from a littérateur uncertain of his motives and ideals to a politically committed writer with conscious aims and a vision of his ideal society. But the artistic purpose which shaped his work remained unchanged:

> What I have most wanted to do throughout the past ten years is to make political writing into an art. My starting point is always a feeling of partisanship, a sense of injustice. . . . But I could not do the work of writing a book, or even a long magazine article, if it were not also an aesthetic experience.

Again, Orwell deliberately uses the phrase "I could not"; not "I would not wish to" or "I would find it difficult to," but *I could not*. It was simply not possible for him to write a book, however politically motivated, which was not also an artistic whole demanding the utmost attention to language. "And yet it is also true," he concludes, "that one can write nothing readable unless one constantly struggles to efface one's own personality. Good prose is like a window pane." For twenty years he had striven to make a permanent impression on English literature, to become a novelist and essayist in the manner of Swift. In doing so he had fashioned a distinctive prose style—simple, direct, and apparently effortless—recognised as Orwellian and sharpened to maturity in the writings of his final decade. What this had cost him in terms of health and happiness and sheer hard work can only be guessed at. Towards the end of the essay occurs the revealing passage: "Writing a book is a horrible, exhausting struggle, like a long bout of some painful illness. One would never undertake such a thing if one were not driven on by some demon. . . ." Rarely can a writer have laid bare his innermost feelings with such honesty or expressed so tellingly the travail of literary effort.

For all these reasons "Why I Write" occupies an important place in his work and forms a fitting conclusion to a discussion of Orwell as essayist. It was entirely characteristic of him that this essay, so finely and thoughtfully written, was prepared not for syndication in the major magazines but for *Gangrel*, a journal with a tiny circulation and which could have offered at best only a nominal payment. He was always willing to devote much of his energies on causes or publications in which he deeply believed.

As an essayist Orwell's achievement was very considerable. In volume, range and intellectual depth his essays are unrivalled in this century and reveal the extraordinary diversity of his reading and interests. Their subject matter is unusually catholic when one reflects that he was an essentially English writer from a solid Anglo-Indian background: the range of topics at his disposal is in itself a reminder that he was no ordinary writer. In these shorter pieces—so painstakingly written and so eloquent of the man—he combined the two great traditions of English letters. On the one hand there is the solid *belles-lettres* tradition of Hazlitt and Stevenson: the memorable, polished essay on life and literature and the passing scene. To this category belong such fine pieces as "Some Thoughts on the Common Toad," "A Good Word for the Vicar of Bray," "Mark Twain" and "Tobias Smollett." These reflect his deep affection for the countryside, his pleasure in the simple joys of the open air and the world of literature. On the other hand there is the radical, questioning tradition of Defoe and Swift; to this category belong such characteristic essays as "Looking Back on the Spanish War," "The Prevention of Literature" and "Writers and Leviathan." In these he deployed to the full his passionate concern for human welfare, his concern for justice and the utmost freedom of thought and expression. There is a sense in which he not only made a significant contribution to those two strands but added a third mainstream of his own: that of the searching, incisive essay dealing with neglected aspects of daily living. Examples of this genre are "A Nice Cup of Tea," "Books vs. Cigarettes," "Decline of the English Murder" and "In Defence of English Cooking." Here he displayed his fascination with the minutest details of everyday life and his gift for illuminating these with penetrating comment. No detail of living was too small to escape his notice; and to each topic, whether it was the cost of reading or the weightiest matters of international politics, he brought to bear the same critical intelligence.

When one considers the range of his essays, their consistent readability and overall literary qualities, one turns to Orwell with renewed respect. With the passage of time much of his political and wartime journalism will inevitably diminish in interest yet one has the firm impression that the bulk of his essays will continue to be read and enjoyed. In such pieces as "A Hanging," "Shooting an Elephant," "Charles Dickens" and "How the Poor Die" he made a lasting contribution to English literature and moreover enlarged the horizons of the English essay in a significant and dynamic way.

Notes

1. *The Collected Essays, Journalism and Letters of George Orwell*, edited by Sonia Orwell and Ian Angus (London: Secker & Warburg, 1970), 2, 7.

2. Cf. Orwell's essay "George Gissing," *CEJL* 4, 119.

3. *CEJL* 1, 165.

4. Cf. Gissing's comments in *The Private Papers of Henry Ryecroft*, Autumn, XXI: "Many biographical sketches have I read . . . but never one in which there was a hint of stern struggle, of the pinched stomach and frozen fingers. I surmise that the path of 'literature' is being made too easy."

5. *CEJL* 1, 165.

6. Cf. H. G. Wells, *Anticipations* (1900), Chapter 3: "Developing Social Elements," for an interesting forecast of the emergence of this new class.

7. George Woodcock, *The Crystal Spirit* (London: Cape, 1967), 205.

8. *New Statesman*, 25 January 1941.

9. "George Orwell and the Politics of Truth," included in Raymond Williams (ed.), *George Orwell*.

10. See Bernard Crick, *George Orwell: A Life* (Boston: Little, Brown, 1980), 402.

11. Stansky and Abrahams, *The Unknown Orwell* (London: Constable, 1972), 166.

12. *CEJL* 1, 79.

13. Woodcock, 96.

14. *CEJL* 1, 135.

15. *CEJL* 4, 85.

16. Cf. Buddicom, Jacintha, *Eric and Us*, Chapter 5, "Were Such the Joys?"

17. These quotations are taken from "As I Please" articles reprinted in *CEJL* as follows: 3, 12; 3, 16; 3, 27; 4, 65; 4, 81.

Bibliography

Trends in Orwell Criticism: 1968–1984

Paul Schlueter*

As a glance at each annual MLA International Bibliography for the past fifteen years will attest, there has not exactly been a flood of essays and books on Orwell, though the total has been respectable. Indeed, at times it seems as if one discernible trend is that recent commentators on Orwell appear not to have read much of the excellent work on Orwell done earlier than 1968, all of which is carefully and astutely annotated in Jeffrey and Valerie Meyers, *George Orwell: An Annotated Bibliography of Criticism* (New York: Garland Publishing Co., 1977).

Any summary of Orwell's criticism could of course be arranged as I have done, in various major categories, such as (A) Orwell's life, (B) General studies, and (C) Orwell's writings, with each of these — and especially the last — easily subdivided. Using such a simple breakdown with the array of pre-1968 criticism on Orwell, we can easily see that earlier book-length commentaries on Orwell's life were dominated by those who had known Orwell, like those of Richard Rees (1951), Cyril Connolly (1948), and T. R. Fyvel (1950 and 1959). Other early biographical studies still worth consulting include essay-length memoirs by Avril Dunn, Orwell's sister (1961), and John McNair (1962), Paul Potts (1957), Anthony Powell (1967), and Julian Symons (1963), some of his friends. (Later writings by Fyvel, Reese, and Symonds are described further in this checklist; all others are fully described in the Meyers bibliography.)

Some of the major critical works from before 1968 include important books by Richard Rees (1962), Richard Voorhees (1954), and George Woodcock (1966), as well as various introductory studies such as those by John Atkins (1954), Laurence Brander (1954), B. T. Oxley (1967), and Edward Thomas (1965). Some of the essays and portions of books from earlier years still worth consulting include those by E. M. Forster (1951), T. R. Fyvel (1956), Christopher Hollis (1956), as well as the many excellent pieces by Irving Howe (including two from 1956 and one from 1969), Frederick Karl (1962), Q. D. Leavis (1940), Ellen Leyburh (1956), Stephen Lutman (1967), John Mander (1960), John Morris (1950), Conor

---

*Expanded and reprinted with permission from *College Literature* 11 (1984).

Cruise O'Brien (1965 and 1968), Henry Popkin (1954), V. S. Pritchett (1950), Ricardo Quintana (1961), Philip Rahv (1949), Philip Rieff (1954), Isaac Rosenfeld (1950 and 1956), Richard Rovere (1956), Bertrand Russell (1950), Julian Symons (1949), Lionel Trilling (1952), John Wain (1954, 1957, and 1961), Brian Way (1960), Richard Voorhees (1955 and 1961), Anthony West (1958), Angus Wilson (1954), Edmund Wilson (1946), and George Woodcock (1946 and 1950). These may well be accounted the best of the general criticism on Orwell prior to 1968.

As with more recent work on Orwell, studies of *1984* dominated earlier criticism. Worth mentioning in this regard are portions of books or essays by Isaac Deutscher (1960), Langdon Elsbree (1959), A. E. Dyson (1965), Mark Hillegas (1967), Irving Howe (1950), Martin Kessler (1957), Jennifer McDowell (1962), Ralph Ranald (1967), Mark Schorer (1949), Jerome Thale (1962), Lionel Trilling (1949), and Richard Voorhees (1956). The only still-valuable earlier criticism of *Animal Farm* are pieces by Alvin Kernan (1962) and Arthur Schlesinger, Jr. (1946). Stephen Spender's 1950 essay on *Homage to Catalonia* is among the very few essays still worth consulting on that work, and Malcolm Muggeridge's 1950 and 1962 essays on *Burmese Days* are perhaps still the best on that novel. A number of engaging pieces were done on *The Road to Wigan Pier*, including those by Victor Gollancz (1937), Richard Hoggart (1965), Dwight MacDonald (1959), C. C. Martindale (1939), Philip Toynbee (1959), Fredric Warburg (1960), and Richard Wollheim (1960). Frank Wadsworth's three 1956 essays on Orwell's early, middle, and late periods are still provocative also.

The reason for starting this retrospective summary of recent work on Orwell with 1968 is easily explained: the fall of 1968 saw the publication of the invaluable *Collected Essays, Journalism, and Letters of George Orwell*, which enabled us to see exactly how complex and varied a writer Orwell was compared to what we had concluded on the basis of the major novels alone. Now, with two additional volumes scheduled for publication in the near future, a six-volume set of such material will make the picture of Orwell even more varied, his works even more ripe for analysis.

At the risk of over-simplifying what has been done on Orwell over the past fifteen years, it seems to me, as I said previously, that a summary of trends on Orwell criticism could best be approached by using three major groupings:

A: Orwell's Life

B: General Studies

C: Orwell's Writings

Each of these, of course, could be sub-divided, but for practical purposes only the latter two major headings will be broken down into discrete — and presumably valid — subheads. Particularly important items are preceded by asterisks. Only works in English are cited; some items appear under more than one heading.

A: ORWELL'S LIFE

The life of George Orwell, which seems always to have intrigued critics, now appears to have become a biographical subject worth endless variations on the same theme. It was long believed (as Bernard Crick mentions in the preface to his biography) that Orwell's will forbade the publication of any "authorized" biography, but whether this is now considered to have been an authentic prohibition, one fostered by Orwell's widow, or merely another apocryphal tale, it did effectively eliminate any substantial biographical work from appearing until the first half of the two-volume work by Stansky and Abrahams (see below), *The Unknown Orwell* (1972) and *Orwell: The Transformation* (1980). Stansky and Abrahams thoroughly investigated Orwell's origins and acquaintances, in the process interviewing many of Orwell's survivors and friends. But these are strange volumes of biography: the authors seem to feel, especially in the earlier volume, in which Orwell's first thirty years are presented, that some kind of schizophrenia exists, with Eric Blair the ordinary bloke who had a variety of experiences and Orwell somehow a kind of alter ego who wrote about these incidents. True, the authors do bring in vast quantities of useful details, but not much of a picture of Orwell the complex, real person results, and as a result the overall portrait is one of a too-extreme demarcation between Blair and Orwell, between the man and the writer, between the petit-bourgeois school-teacher and the deeply committed, compassionate prophet.

A far more balanced, persuasive, and definitive biography is Bernard Crick's *George Orwell: A Life* (1980), a work approved by Orwell's widow and one far surpassing those by Stansky and Abrahams in its incisive honesty, its judicious use of all the encyclopedic detail, and its candid appraisal of Orwell's actual relations with the left. Crick is less concerned with literary analysis than most other biographers have been, but he surpasses these others in his more complete picture of Orwell as a decent, intelligent man, as a moralist, as a writer with a sardonic perspective on the absurdities of his day, and as one of the least categorizable writers of the modern world. Crick is only marginally better than Stansky and Abrahams in presenting the live, warm persona who became known as Orwell, but he does a far better job in suggesting Orwell's passionate political sensitivity and imagination.

Since Crick's book there has appeared another, much slighter work, a memoir by T. R. Fyvel (1982), which Crick himself has called "the best short, general introduction to Orwell's life and work for the general reader." Fyvel's is a more limited work, to be sure. It focuses, on the negative side, on the same kind of Freudian split in Orwell that one would have thought had been relinquished to critical oblivion; and, on the positive, discusses Orwell's belated awareness of the Jewish predicament in Europe and the threat of Nazism. And, like George Woodcock, whose writings on Orwell remain valuable, Fyvel had the advantage of knowing Orwell. Unlike almost all the biographical efforts thus far, Fyvel's presents a warm, even nostalgic portrait of Orwell the man.

Fyvel had written extensively on Orwell back in the 1950s — on both his life and on his relations with the "Jewish question." In addition to having had the advantage of personal friendship with Orwell, he had few of the personal causes to defend that other early writers on Orwell seemed to have. Fyvel's review of Christopher Hollis' lopsidedly Christian *A Study of George Orwell* (1956), for example, rejected Hollis' connection that Orwell was really a right-wing apologist, a stance, ironically, that has recently been given far more exposure than it warrants (see below, B. 4).

There is still work to be done on details of the life, to be sure; but even now, after all the pages written about Orwell the man and Orwell the writer, little genuine sense of how the one related to the other has been provided. More than many recent writers, Orwell is an enigma, a puzzle offering tantalizing appeal to the biographer but little fresh substance after all the mysteries are explained away; and although this means that there will really be no end to the biographical speculations that are likely to be offered, little more of the essence of Orwell is likely to be gleaned than we have thus far in the works described in this section. After all, how many variations can researchers come up with about Orwell's essential "decency" that all biographers have mentioned since John Atkins' still-useful 1954 book? Still, if one were to select any single book as the most nearly indispensable biography of Orwell thus far written, the clear and obvious choice must be Crick's.

Charpier, Jacques. "George Orwell, a 'Tory Anarchist.' " *UNESCO Courier,* January 1984, pp. 4–7.
*Coppard, Audrey and Bernard Crick, eds. *Orwell Remembered.* London: Ariel, 1984; New York: Facts on File, 1984.
*Crick, Bernard. *George Orwell: A Life.* London: Secker and Warburg. 1980; as *George Orwell.* New York; Alfred A. Knopf, 1981.
*Fyvel, T[osco] R. *George Orwell: A Personal Memoir.* London: Weidenfeld and Nicolson; New York: Macmillan, 1982.
————. "The Years at *Tribune.*" *The World of George Orwell.* Ed. Miriam Gross, pp. 112–115.
Greer, Herb. "Orwell in Perspective." *Commentary,* March 1983, pp. 50–54.
Jones, Landon Y. "George Orwell." *People,* January 9, 1984, pp. 38, 41–42, 45.
Meyer, Michael. "Memories of George Orwell." *The World of George Orwell.* Ed. Miriam Gross, pp. 128–133.
Meyers, Jeffrey. "Orwell's Painful Childhood." *Ariel,* 3 (1972), 54–61.
*Muggeridge, Malcolm. "A Knight of the Woeful Countenance." *The World of George Orwell.* Ed. Miriam Gross, pp. 166–175.

O'Flinn, Paul. "Orwell and *Tribune*." *Literature and History*, 6 (1980), 201–218, 173.

Shelden, Michael. "Orwell and His Publishers: New Letters." *TLS*, January 6, 1984, pp. 15–17.

Stafford, Tim. "The Life and Hard Times of George Orwell." *Christianity Today*, January 13, 1984, pp. 26, 70–71.

*Stansky, Peter, and William Abrahams. *The Unknown Orwell*. New York: Alfred A. Knopf, 1972.

*_____. *Orwell: The Transformation*. New York: Alfred A. Knopf, 1980.

Thompson, John. *Orwell's London*. London: Fourth Estate, 1984.

*Wadhams, Stephen, ed. *Remembering Orwell*. London: Penguin, 1984. Introduction by George Woodcock.

B: GENERAL STUDIES

The overwhelming bulk of commentary on Orwell unfortunately falls within this vague catch-all category, primarily because so little of it takes any particular stance, critical or otherwise, but instead offers variations on established facts and interpretations. It is unfair, of course, to suggest that works that are introductory or general in nature have nothing to offer even the sophisticated reader, for the mere art of rearranging or reinterpreting the familiar can lead to unusual or new insights. Hence the breakdown offered within this section suggests some of the more promising areas of investigation by scholars.

B. 1: Collections of Essays

Of these six collections, Meyers' is the most useful, since it includes over a hundred reviews and evaluations from throughout Orwell's entire career. Williams' is lopsidedly political, though some good, more objective pieces (such as those by Lionel Trilling and John Wain) are included. Also valuable is the special issue of *Modern Fiction Studies*, since it includes, in addition to a checklist of criticism, valuable new essays by Richard Voorhees, Meyers, and others. The Gross collection is mixed; only reminiscences by Malcolm Muggeridge and William Empson have much real merit.

Gross, Miriam, ed. *The World of George Orwell*. London: Weidenfeld and Nicolson, 1971; New York: Simon and Schuster, 1972. Contains eighteen essays.

*Meyers, Jeffrey, ed. *George Orwell: The Critical Heritage*. London: Routledge and Kegan Paul, 1975.

Modern Fiction Studies, 21, 1 (1975).

Norris, Christopher, ed. *Inside the Myth: Orwell: Views from the Left*. London: Lawrence & Wishart, 1984.

Williams, Raymond, ed. *George Orwell: A Collection of Critical Essays*. Englewood Cliffs, N.J.: Prentice-Hall, 1974.
*College Literature, 11, 1 (1984).

B. 2: Essays and Books

Alldritt, Keith. *The Making of George Orwell: An Essay in Literary History*. London: E. Arnold, 1969; New York: St. Martin's, 1970.
Alver, Leonard. "The Relevance of George Orwell," *English Literature and Language*, 8 (1971), 65–79.
*Ash, Timothy Garton. "A Waiter's Year." *Times Literary Supplement*, February 8, 1985, pp. 147–148.
Auden, W. H. "George Orwell." *Spectator*, 226 (January 16, 1971), 86–87.
Browning, Gordon. "Toward a Set of Standards for Anti-Utopian Fiction." *Cithara*, 10, 1 (1970), 18–32.
*Donoghue, Denis. "Plain English." *London Review of Books*, 6, 24 (December 20, 1984–January 24, 1985), 7–8.
Edelheit, Steven. *Dark Prophecies: Essays on Orwell and Technology*. New York: Revisionist Press, 1977.
Elkins, Charles L. "George Orwell, 1903–1950." *Science Fiction Writers: Critical Studies of the Major Authors from the Early Nineteenth Century to the Present Day*. Ed. Everett F. Bleiler. New York: Scribner, 1982, pp. 233–241.
George, Alan, ed. *Unwelcome Guerrilla: George Orwell and The New Statesman*. London: New Statesman, 1984. Introduction by Bernard Crick.
Gillie, Christopher. *Movements in Modern English Literature, 1900–1940*. Cambridge: Cambridge Univ. Press, 1975.
Glusman, John A. "The Style Was the Man." *Literary Review*, 25 (1982), 431–447.
Hodge, Bob, and Roger Fowler. "Orwellian Linguistics." *Language and Control*. Ed. Roger Fowler et al. London: Routledge and Kegan Paul, 1979, pp. 6–25.
*Howe, Irving. "George Orwell: 'As the Bones Know.' " *Harper's Magazine*, 238 (January 1969), 97–103; reprinted in *Decline of the New*. New York: Harcourt, Brace and World, 1970, pp. 269–279.
Hunter, Jefferson. "Orwell's Prose: Discovery, Communion, Separation." *Sewanee Review*, 87 (1979), 436–454.
Hunter, Lynette. *George Orwell: The Search for a Voice*. Milton Keynes, England: Open University Press, 1984.
*Justman, Stewart. "Orwell's Plain Style." *University of Toronto Quarterly*, 53 (1984), 195–203.
Katz, Wendy R. "Imperialism and Patriotism: Orwell's Dilemma in 1940." *Modernist Studies: Literature and Culture 1920–1940*, 3 (1979), 99–105.

Knapp, John V. "Orwell's Fiction: Funny But Not Vulgar." *Modern Fiction Studies*, 27 (1981), 294–301.

*Kubal, David L. *Outside the Whale: George Orwell's Art and Politics*. Notre Dame, Ind.: University of Notre Dame Press, 1972.

Lang, Berel. "The Politics and Art of Decency: Orwell's Medium." *South Atlantic Quarterly*, 75 (1976), 424–433.

*Lee, Robert A. *Orwell's Fiction*. Notre Dame, Ind.: Univ. of Notre Dame Press, 1969.

Lewis, Peter. *George Orwell: The Road to 1984*. New York and London: Harcourt Brace Jovanovich, 1981.

Leys, Simon. "Orwell: The Horror of Politics." *Quadrant*, 28, 12 (December 1983), 9–21.

*Lief, Ruth Ann. *Homage to Oceania: The Prophetic Vision of George Orwell*. Columbus: Ohio State Univ. Press, 1969.

McNally, Cleo. "On Not Teaching Orwell." *College English*, 38 (1977), 553–566.

Meyer, Alfred G. "The Political Theory of Pessimism: George Orwell and Herbert Marcuse." *The Future of Nineteen Eighty-Four*. Ed. Ejner J. Jensen. Ann Arbor: University of Michigan Press, 1984, pp. 121–135.

*Meyers, Jeffrey. *A Reader's Guide to George Orwell*. London: Thames and Hudson, 1975; Totowa, N.J.; Littlefield, Adams & Co., 1977.

———. "George Orwell, the Honorary Proletarian." *Philological Quarterly*, 47 (1969), 526–549.

New, Melvyn. "Ad nauseum: A Satiric Device in Huxley, Orwell, and Waugh." *Satire Newsletter*, 8 (1970), 24–28.

O'Flinn, J. P. "Orwell on Literature and Society." *College English*, 31 (1970), 603–612.

Paley, Alan. *George Orwell: Writer and Critic of Modern Society*. Charlottesville: Univ. of Virginia Press, 1974.

Philmus, Robert M. "In Search of Orwell." *Science Fiction Studies*, 6 (1979), 327–332.

Spender, Stephen. *Love-Hate Relations: English and American Sensibilities*. London: Hamish Hamilton; New York: Random House, 1974, pp. 254–261.

Steiner, George. "True to Life." *New Yorker*, 45 (March 29, 1969), 139–151.

Symons, Julian. "A Passion for Justice." *Folio* (1970), 86–91.

Taylor, Richard K. S., ed. *George Orwell*. Bradford, England: Univ. of Leeds, Dept. of Adult Education, 1981.

Thody, Philip. "The Curiosity of George Orwell." *Univ. of Leeds Review*, 12 (1969), 69–80.

Wain, John. *A House for the Truth*, London: Macmillan, 1972; New York: Viking Press, 1973, pp. 43–66.

———. "Orwell and the Intelligentsia." *Encounter*, 21 (December 1968), 72–80.

_____. "In the Thirties." *The World of George Orwell.* Ed. Miriam Gross, pp. 76–90.

Warncke, Wayne. "George Orwell's Critical Approach to Literature." *Southern Humanities Review*, 2 (1968), 484–98.

Williams, Raymond. *Orwell.* London: Fontana Books; New York: Viking Press, 1971.

Woodcock, George. "Orwell's Changing Repute." *Queen's Quarterly*, 88 (1981), 250–255.

_____. "Orwell, Blair, and the Critics." *Sewanee Review*, 83 (1975), 524–536.

Workman, Gilliam. "Orwell Criticism." *Ariel*, 3 (1972), 62–73.

Zehr, David M. "George Orwell: the Novelist Displaced." *Bucknell Review*, 27 (1982). 17–31.

*_____. "George Orwell." *Dictionary of Literary Biography*, Vol. 15. Ed. Bernard Oldsey, 407–422.

_____. "Orwell and the Proles: Revolutionary or Middle-Class Voyeur?" *Centennial Review*, 27 (1983), 30–40.

B. 3: Orwell and Other Writers

Comparing Orwell to other writers is of course not new, as the repeated comparisons with Aldous Huxley and Yevgeny Zamyatin in earlier years — and now — attest. In addition to those writers specifically tied in with *1984* — such as Anthony Burgess and H. G. Wells — there has also been a wave of clever, sometimes persuasive, sometimes unconvincing, studies. Comparing Orwell to Fyodor Dostoevsky (in *Notes from the Underground*), as Roman S. Struc did, is a valid inter-relationship; and so are the parallels with Arthur Koestler that several critics have come up with, though comparisons of Orwell with Charles Dickens, Jonathan Swift, T. S. Eliot, and Jack London might say more about the critic than the subjects of the criticism. Still other, less obvious comparisons, such as the essay in which Orwell is related to the Marxist critic Christopher St. John Sprigg, who wrote under the name Christopher Caudwell, are suggestive but still in need of more than mere assertion.

Armytage, W. H. G. "Orwell and Zamyatin." *Yesterday's Tomorrows: An Historical Survey of Future Societies.* London: Routledge and Kegan Paul, 1968, pp. 160–164.

Beadle, Gordon. "George Orwell and Charles Dickens: Moral Critics of Society." *Journal of Historical Studies*, 2 (1969–70), 245–55.

Beauchamp, Gorman. "Of Man's Last Disobedience: Zamyatin's We and Orwell's *1984*." *Comparative Literature Studies*, 10 (1973), 285–301.

Brantley, Daniel. "Charisma in Literature: An Examination of Fictional Charismatic Leadership." *West Georgia College Review*, 14 (May 1982), 16–25. On Dostoevsky.

Brown, Edward J. "Zamyatin's *We* and *Nineteen Eighty-Four*." *On Nineteen Eighty-Four*. Ed. Peter Stansky. New York: W. H. Freeman, 1983, pp. 159–169.

*Calder, Jenni. *Chronicles of Conscience: A Study of George Orwell and Arthur Koestler*. Pittsburgh: Univ. of Pittsburgh Press; London: Secker and Warburg, 1968.

Connors, James. "Zamyatin's *We* and the Genesis of *1984*." *Modern Fiction Studies*, 21 (1975), 107–124.

Espey, David B. "George Orwell vs. Christopher Caudwell." *Illinois Quarterly*, 36, 4 (1974), 46–60.

Fyvel, T. Y. "Arthur Koestler and George Orwell." *Astride the Two Cultures: Arthur Koestler at 70*. Ed. Harold Harris. London: Hutchinson, 1975; New York: Random House, 1976.

Gloversmith, Frank. "Changing Times: Orwell and Auden." *Class, Culture, and Social Change: A New View of the 1930's*. Ed. Frank Gloversmith. Brighton, Sussex: Harvester, 1980.

Mudrick, Marvin. "Herzen and Orwell: Political Animals." *On Culture and Literature*. New York: Horizon Press, 1970, pp. 15–28.

*Ross, Michael L. " 'Carrying on the Human Heritage': From *Lady Chatterley's Lover* to *Nineteen Eighty-Four*." *D. H. Lawrence Review*, 17 (1984), 5–28.

Scruggs, Charles. "George Orwell and Jonathan Swift: A Literary Relationship." *South Atlantic Quarterly*, 76 (1977), 177–189.

Sperber, Murray A. "The Author as Culture Hero: H. G. Wells and George Orwell." *Mosaic*, 14, 4 (Fall 1981), 15–29.

Stewart, Ralph. "Orwell's Waste Land." *International Fiction Review*, 8 (1981), 150–152.

*Struc, Roman. "George Orwell's *1984* and Dostoevsky's 'Underground Man.' " *Proceedings: Pacific Northwest Conference on Foreign Languages*. Ed. Walter C. Kraft. Corvallis, Ore.: Oregon State Univ., 1973, pp. 217–220.

Tambling, Victor R. S. "Following in the Footsteps of Jack London: George Orwell, Writer and Critic." *Jack London Newsletter*, 11 (1978), 63–70.

Warncke, Wayne. "George Orwell's Dickens." *South Atlantic Quarterly*, 69 (1970), 373–381.

———. "George Orwell on T. S. Eliot." *Western Humanities Review*, 26 (1972), 265–270.

B. 4: Orwell and Politics

Since one could justifiably claim that all that Orwell wrote dealt with politics, such a subhead may seem unnecessary. Yet some particularly valuable studies have appeared that take a larger view of politics than, say, purely left-wing or right-wing perspectives. The political right-wing has been especially busy in discovering and claiming Orwell for its own, just as some years back the political left decried Orwell's "betrayal" of its cause. Since this issue is dealt with at length in the following titles and in numerous other places, only a few of the many works on the subject can be cited. It should be stated, though, that right-wing claims for Orwell seem a particularly ludicrous example of special pleading; see, for particularly extreme examples, the essays by Kirk and Podhoretz. Extreme examples from the left can be found in the items by Raskin.

Eagleton, Terry. "George Orwell and the Lower Middle-Class Novel." *Exiles and Emigrés: Studies in Modern Literature*. London: Chatto and Windus; New York: Schocken Books, 1970, pp. 71–107.

Hartley, Roger. "Orwell: Political Criticism and Fictional Vision." *Practices of Literature and Politics*. Ed. Francis Barker et al. Colchester: University of Essex, 1979, pp. 232–244.

Hobbs, Albert H. "Welfarism and Orwell's Reversal." *Intercollegiate Review*, 6 (1970), 105–112.

Ingle, Stephen J. "The Politics of George Orwell: A Reappraisal." *Queen's Quarterly*, 80 (1973), 22–33.

Jain, Jasbur. "Orwell and Imperialism." *Banasthali Patrika*, 16 (1971), 1–7.

_____. "Orwell: The Myth of a Classless Society." *Quest*, 72 (1971), 95–100.

_____. "The Vision of Orwell." *Rajasthan Univ. Studies in English*, 5 (1971), 68–86.

Kirk, Russell. "George Orwell's Despair." *Intercollegiate Review*, 5 (1968), 21–25.

Nisbet, Robert. "*1984* and the Conservative Imagination." *1984 Revisited: Totalitarianism in Our Century*. Ed. Irving Howe. New York: Harper & Row, 1983, pp. 180–206.

Podhoretz, Norman. "If Orwell Were Alive Today." *Harper's Magazine*, 266 (January 1983), 30–37; see also "An Exchange on Orwell" by Podhoretz and Christopher Hitchens, *Harper's Magazine*, 266 (February 1983), 56–58.

Raskin, Jonah. "George Orwell and the Big Cannibal Critics." *Monthly Review*, 35, 1 (May 1983), 40–45.

_____. *The Mythology of Imperialism*, New York: Random House, 1971, pp. 46–52.

Rees, Richard. "George Orwell." *The Politics of Twentieth-Century Novelists*. Ed. George A. Panichas. New York: Hawthorne Books, 1971, pp. 85–99.

Rossi, John. "Why the Left Hates Orwell." *Intercollegiate Review*, 17 (1982), 97–105.

Rowse, A. L. "The Contradictions of George Orwell." *Contemporary Review*, 241 (1982), 186–194.

Smith, Malcolm. "George Orwell, War, and Politics in the 1930's." *Literature and History*, 6 (1980), 219–234.

*Swingewood, Alan. "George Orwell, Socialism and the Novel." *The Sociology of Literature*. Ed. Diana T. Laurenson and Alan Swingewood, London: MacGibbon and Kee, 1971; New York: Schocken Books, 1972, pp. 249–75.

Watson, George. "Orwell and the Spectrum of European Politics." *Journal of English Studies*, 1 (1971), 191–97.

Winegarten, Renée. *Writers and Revolution*, London and New York: New Viewpoints, 1974, pp. 294–313.

*Zwerdling, Alex. *Orwell and the Left*. New Haven, Conn.: Yale Univ. Press, 1974.

B. 5: Religious Approaches to Orwell

Given the apocalyptic nature of Orwell's best-known novels, it is not surprising that religious as well as political perceptions and interpretations of Orwell are common. In addition to the many superficial treatments of Orwell's work found in well-meaning warnings about the "last days" of the earth, there have been a few such studies worth a glance by virtue of their scholarly solidity, balanced perspective, or overall moderation of tone. Geoffrey Ashe was one of the first to make such an emphasis; his various essays from the 1950's are still readable, though somewhat dated, as, to a greater extent, are those by Neville Braybrooke and Christopher Hollis from the same decade.

Beadle, Gordon. "George Orwell and the Death of God." *Colorado Quarterly*, 23 (1974), 51–63.

Faulkner, Peter. "Orwell and Christianity." *New Humanist*, 89 (1973), 270–273.

Homberger, Eric. "A Social Theology: On Orwell." *Encounter*, 43 (July 1974), 70–73.

Kantzer, Kenneth S. "Orwell's Fatal Error." *Christianity Today*, January 13, 1984, pp. 10, 12.

Rossi, John. "Orwell and Catholicism." *Commonweal*, 103 (June 18, 1976), 404–406.

Sandison, Alan. *The Last Man in Europe: An Essay on George Orwell*. London: Macmillan: New York: Barnes and Noble, 1974.

Small, Christopher. *The Road to Miniluv: George Orwell, the State, and God*. London: Gollancz, 1974; Pittsburgh: Univ. of Pittsburgh Press, 1976.

B. 6: Psychological Approaches to Orwell

As with the preceding sub-sections of this essay, psychological studies of Orwell have been common, though not always so labeled. For it seems as if most studies of Orwell try to a greater or lesser extent to figure out the identity of the "true" George Orwell, perhaps as this relates to the "real" Eric Blair, possibly in terms more easily resolved objectively. In any event, such studies are interesting, if sometimes amusing, simply because from among the masses of jargon and retrospective analysis an occasional valid insight can be found.

Carter, Thomas. "Group Psychology Phenomena of a Political System as Satirized in *Animal Farm:* An Application of the Theories of W. R. Bion." *Human Relations,* 27 (1974), 525–546.

Fiderer, Gerald. "Masochism as Literary Strategy: Orwell's Psychological Novels." *Literature and Psychology,* 20 (1970), 3–21.

*Kubal, David. "Freud, Orwell, and the Bourgeois Interior." *Yale Review,* 67 (1978), 389–403.

Nair, K. Narayanan. "Orwell's Guilt Complex and the Submersion-Reversion Pattern in His Writings." *Literary Studies: Homage to Dr. A. A. Aiyer.* Ed. K. P. K. Menon et al. Trivandrum, India: A. S. Aiyer Memorial Committee, 1973.

Smith, Marcus. "The Wall of Blackness: A Psychological Approach to Orwell." *Modern Fiction Studies,* 14 (1968–69), 423–433.

*Smyer, Richard I. *Primal Dream and Primal Crime: Orwell's Development as a Psychological Novelist.* Columbia: Univ. of Missouri Press, 1979.

C: ORWELL'S WRITINGS

This section is arranged chronologically; it will be evident at once that the early novels have been analyzed far less frequently — and intensely — in the past fifteen years than the later ones, and that there appears to be a certain amount of repetitiveness in, say, the studies of *Burmese Days* or *The Road to Wigan Pier.* For the most part, these earlier works have been given more biographical than formal analysis, which suggests at the very least an area offering relatively untapped possibilities for scholarship.

C. 1: The Early Writings in General

Crompton, Donald. "False Maps of the World: George Orwell's Autobiographical Writings and Early Writings." *Critical Quarterly,* 16 (1974), 149–169.

Eagleton, Terry. "George Orwell and the Lower Middle-Class Novel." *Exiles and Emigrés.* London: Chatto and Windus; New York: Schocken Books, 1970, pp. 71–107.

*Kubal, David. "George Orwell: The Early Novelist." *Arizona Quarterly,* 27 (1971), 59–73.

Pawling, Chris. "George Orwell and the Documentary in the Thirties." *Literature and History*, 4 (1976), 81–93.

C. 2: *Down and Out in Paris and London* (1933)

*Kubal, David. *"Down and Out in Paris and London:* The Conflict of Art and Politics." *Midwest Quarterly*, 12 (1970), 199–209.

Mayne, Richard. "A Note on Orwell's Paris." *The World of George Orwell.* Ed. Miriam Gross, pp. 40–45.

Ramsey, Roger. " 'Down and Out': Orwell's First Novel." *Arizona Quarterly*, 32 (1976), 154-170.

Ross, William T. " 'My Theme Is Poverty': Orwell's *Down and Out in Paris and London.*" *Modernist Studies: Literature and Culture 1920-1940*, 1, 2, (1974), 31–39.

Smyer, Richard. "Loss of Innocence in George Orwell's *Down and Out in Paris and London.*" *South Dakota Review*, 8 (1970–71), 75–83.

C. 3: *Burmese Days* (1934)

*Beadon, Roger. "With Orwell in Burma." *Listener*, 81 (May 29, 1969), 755.

Greenberger, Allen. *The British Image of India: A Study in the Literature of Imperialism 1880-1960.* London and New York: Oxford Univ. Press, 1969; pp. 85–92, 174–176, and *passim.*

Gross, John. "Imperial Attitudes." *The World of George Orwell.* Ed. Miriam Gross, pp. 32–38.

*Htin Aung, Maung. "George Orwell and Burma." *Asian Affairs*, 57 (1970), 19–28; reprinted in *The World of George Orwell.* Ed. Miriam Gross, pp. 20–30.

_____. "Orwell of the Burma Police." *Asian Affairs*, 60 (1973), 181–186.

Islam, Shamsul. "George Orwell and the Raj." *World Literature Written in English*, 21 (1982), 341–347.

Jain, Jasbir. "Orwell and Imperialism." *Banasthali Patrika*, 14 (1971), 1–7.

Knapp, John. "Dance to a Creepy Minuet: Orwell's *Burmese Days*, Precursor of *Animal Farm.*" *Modern Fiction Studies*, 21 (1975), 11–29.

*Lee, Robert. "Symbol and Structure in *Burmese Days*: A Revaluation." *Texas Studies in Literature and Language*, 11 (1969), 819–835.

Lewis, Robin. "Orwell's *Burmese Days* and Forster's *A Passage to India*: Two Novels of Human Relations in the British Empire." *Massachusetts Studies in English*, 4 (1974), 1–36.

*Meyers, Jeffrey. "The Ethics of Responsibility: Orwell's *Burmese Days.*" *University Review*, 35 (1968), 83–87.

_____. "Orwell in Burma." *American Notes and Queries*, 11 (1972), 52–54.

Nakaji, Hiromichi. "Nats in the Novels of Burma by Orwell and Takey-ama." Kyoritsu Women's Junior College, Tokyo. *Collected Essays by the Members of the Faculty in Commemoration of the 20th Anniversary*, No. 17. Tokyo: Kyoritsu Women's Junior College, 1973, pp. 115–126.

Odle, Francis. "Orwell in Burma." *Twentieth Century*, 179 (1972), 38–39.

C. 4: *A Clergyman's Daughter* (1935)

Smyer, Richard. "Orwell's *A Clergyman's Daughter*: The Flight from History." *Modern Fiction Studies*, 21 (1975), 31–47.

C. 5: *Keep the Aspidistra Flying* (1936)

Byrne, Katherine. "George Orwell and the American Character." *Commonweal*, 100 (April 12, 1974), 135–137.

Guild, Nicholas. "In Dubious Battle: George Orwell and the Victory of the Money-God." *Modern Fiction Studies*, 21 (1974), 49–56.

*Kubal, David. "George Orwell and the Aspidistra." *University Review*, 37 (1970), 61–67.

Schoenl, William. "Abstract Phraseology, Orwell, and Abortion." *Intellect*, 103 (November 1974), 125–127.

C. 6: *The Road to Wigan Pier* (1937)

*Beadle, Gordon B. "George Orwell's Literary Studies of Poverty in England." *Twentieth-Century Literature*, 24 (1978), 188–201.

Dodd, Philip. "The Views of Travellers: Travel Writing in the 1930's." *Prose Studies*, 5 (1982), 127–138.

Hamilton, Ian. "Along the Road to Wigan Pier." *The World of George Orwell*. Ed. Miriam Gross, pp. 54–61.

*Hoggart, Richard. "George Orwell and *The Road to Wigan Pier*." *Critical Quarterly*, 7 (1965), 72–85.

Parrinder, Patrick. "Updating Orwell: Burgess's Future Fictions." *Encounter*, 56, 1 (January 1981), 45–53.

Smith, Stan. "Scars and Emblems: 1936 and the Crisis of the Subject." *Practices of Literature and Politics*. Ed. Francis Barker et al. Colchester: University of Essex, 1979, pp. 344–379.

Spender, Stephen. *Love-Hate Relations: English and American Sensibilities*. London: Hamish Hamilton; New York: Random House, 1974, pp. 255–259.

Stevenson, John. "Myth and Reality: Britain in the 1930's." *Crisis and Controversy: Essays in Honour of A. J. P. Taylor*. Ed. Alan Sked and Chris Cook. London: Macmillan; New York: St. Martin's Press, 1976, pp. 90–109.

C. 7: *Homage to Catalonia* (1939)

Bal, Sant Singh. "The Spanish Civil War and Orwell's Ethics of Commitment." *Commonwealth Quarterly*, 3, 11 (1979), 68–84.

*Beadle, Gordon B. "George Orwell and the Spanish Civil War." *Duquesne Review*, 16 (1971), 3–16.

*Benson, Frederick. *Writers in Arms: The Literary History of the Spanish Civil War.* New York: New York Univ. Press 1967; London: Univ. of London Press, 1968, pp. 117–123, 286–289, and *passim*.

Carr, Raymond. "Orwell and the Spanish Civil War." *The World of George Orwell.* Ed. Miriam Gross, pp. 64–73.

*Hoskins, Katharine. *Today the Struggle: Literature and Politics During the Spanish Civil War.* Austin: Univ. of Texas Press, 1969, pp. 90–92, 101–104, and *passim*.

Jamal, Zahir. "Orwell in Spain." *Renaissance and Modern Studies*, 20 (1976), 54–64.

*Cowley, Malcolm. " 'No Homage to Catalonia' ": A Memory of the Spanish Civil War." *Southern Review*, 18 (1981), 131–140.

*Lutman, Stephen. "Orwell's Patriotism." *Journal of Contemporary History*, 2 (1967), 149–158.

Matthews, Herbert. *A World in Revolution.* New York: Scribner, 1971, pp. 11, 43–45, and *passim*.

*Meyers, Jeffrey. " 'An Affirming Flame': Orwell's *Homage to Catalonia*." *Arizona Quarterly*, 27 (1971), 5–22.

Sperber, Murray A. " 'Marx: G. O.'s Dog': A Study of Politics and Literature in George Orwell's *Homage to Catalonia*." *Dalhousie Review*, 52 (1972), 226–36.

*Weintraub, Stanley. "Homage to Utopia." *The Last Great Cause: The Intellectuals and the Spanish Civil War.* New York: Weybright and Talley; London: W. H. Allen, 1968, pp. 88–119.

Wykes, David. "Orwell in the Trenches." *Virginia Quarterly Review*, 59 (1983), 415–435.

C. 8: *Coming Up for Air* (1939)

*Fink, Howard. "*Coming Up for Air:* Orwell's Ambiguous Satire on the Wellsian Utopia." *Studies in the Literary Imagination*, 6, 2, (1973), 51–60.

*_____. "The Shadow of Men Like Gods: Orwell's *Coming Up for Air* as Parody." *H. G. Wells and Modern Science Fiction.* Ed. Darko Suvin and R. M. Philmus. Lewisburg, Pa.: Bucknell Univ. Press, 1977, pp. 144–158.

Hunter, Jefferson. "Orwell, Wells and *Coming Up for Air*." *Modern Philology*, 78 (1980), 38–47.

*Meyers, Jeffrey. "Orwell's Apocalypse: *Coming Up for Air.*" *Modern Fiction Studies*, 21, 1 (1975), 69–80.

Poznar, Walter. "Orwell's George Bowling: How to Be." *Wascana Review*, 14 (1979), 80–90.

Van Dellen, Robert J. "George Orwell's *Coming Up for Air*: The Politics of Powerlessness." *Modern Fiction Studies*, 21, 1 (1975), 57–68.

C. 9: *Animal Farm* (1945)

Carter, Thomas. "Group Psychology Phenomena of a Political System as Satirized in *Animal Farm*: An Application of the Theories of W. R. Bion." *Human Relations*, 27 (1974), 525–546.

Cooper, Nancy M. "*Animal Farm*: An Explication for Teachers of Orwell's Novel." *California English Journal*, 4 (1968), 59–69.

Davis, Robert M. "Politics in the Pig-Pen." *Journal of Popular Culture*, 2 (1968), 314–20.

*Eliot, T. S. "T. S. Eliot and *Animal Farm*: Reasons for Rejection." *Times* (London), January 6, 1969, p. 9.

Hoggart, Richard. "Walking the Tight Rope: *Animal Farm.*" *Speaking to Each Other*, v. 2. New York: Oxford Univ. Press; London: Chatto and Windus, 1970, pp. 108–110.

Kressel, Marilyn. "Pigs on Two Feet: George Orwell Through the Prism of Watergate." *Intellect*, 103 (1974), 192–195.

Lee, Robert A. "The Uses of Form: A Reading of *Animal Farm.*" *Studies in Short Fiction*, 6 (1969), 557–73.

*Meyers, Jeffrey. "Orwell's Bestiary: The Political Allegory of *Animal Farm.*" *Studies in the Twentieth Century*, 8 (1971), 65–84.

Smyer, Richard I. "*Animal Farm*: The Burden of Consciousness." *English Language Notes*, 9 (1971), 55–59.

*Warburg, Fredric. "*Animal Farm* and *1984.*" *All Authors Are Equal.* London: Hutchinson, 1973; New York: St. Martin's Press, 1974, pp. 8–15, 35–58, 92–120, 205–206.

C. 10: *1984* (1949)

Abrahams, William. "*Nineteen Eighty-Four*: The Book." *On Nineteen Eighty-Four.* Ed. Peter Stansky. New York: W. H. Freeman, 1983, pp. 2–8.

*Adelson, Joseph. "The Self and Memory in *Nineteen Eighty-Four.*" *The Future of Nineteen Eighty-Four.* Ed. Ejner J. Jensen. Ann Arbor: University of Michigan Press, 1984, pp. 111–119.

Allen, Francis A. "*Nineteen Eighty-Four* and the Eclipse of Private Worlds." *Michigan Quarterly Review*, 22 (1983), 517–540.

Avishai, Bernard. "Orwell and the English Language." *1984 Revisited.*

Ed. Irving Howe. New York: Harper and Row, 1983, pp. 57–71.

Babcock, Barbara Allen. "Lawspeak and Doublethink." *On Nineteen Eighty-Four.* Ed. Peter Stansky, pp. 86–91.

*Bailey, Richard W. "George Orwell and the English Language." *The Future of Nineteen Eighty-Four.* Ed. Ejner J. Jensen, pp. 23–46.

Barnsley, John R. " 'The Last Man in Europe': A Comment on George Orwell's *1984." Contemporary Review,* 239 (1981), 30–34.

Barr, Alan. "The Paradise Behind *1984." English Miscellany,* 19 (1968), 197–203.

Baruch, Elaine Hoffman. " 'The Golden Country': Sex and Love in *1984." 1984 Revisited.* Ed. Irving Howe, pp. 47–56.

Baskett, Sam. "*1984* and the Term Report." *College English,* 18 (November 1956), 99–101.

Beauchamp, Gorman. "From Bingo to Big Brother: Orwell on Power and Sadism." *The Future of Nineteen Eighty-Four.* Ed. Ejner J. Jensen, pp. 65–85.

———. "Future Words: Language and the Dystopian Novel." *Style,* 8 (1974), 462–76.

*———. "Of Man's Last Disobedience: Zamyatin's *We* and Orwell's *1984." Comparative Literature Studies,* 10 (1973), 285–301.

Bloombecker, Jay. "Friend and Foe: Computers in *1984." PC Magazine,* 3, 1 (January 24, 1984), 172–173, 176–177.

*Bolton, W. F. *The Language of 1984: Orwell's English and Ours.* Knoxville: Univ. of Tennessee Press, 1984.

Brown, Edward James. *Brave New World, 1984, and We: An Essay on Anti-Utopia: Zamiatin and English Literature.* Ann Arbor, Mi.: Ardis, 1976.

———. "Zamiatin's *We* and *Nineteen Eighty-Four." On Nineteen Eighty-Four.* Ed. Peter Stansky, pp. 159–169.

Browning, Gordon. "Toward a Set of Standards for Evaluating Anti-Utopian Fiction." *Cithara,* 10 (1970), 18–32.

Carpenter, Luther P. "*1984* on Staten Island." *1984 Revisited.* Ed. Irving Howe, pp. 72–85.

Clayton, Raymond B. "The Biomedical Revolution and Totalitarian Control." *On Nineteen Eighty-Four.* Ed. Peter Stansky, pp. 76–84.

Comfort, Alex. "1939 and 1984: George Orwell and the Vision of Judgment." *On Nineteen Eighty-Four.* Ed. Peter Stansky, pp. 15–22.

Connors, James. " 'Do It to Julia': Thoughts on Orwell's *1984." Modern Fiction Studies,* 16 (1970), 463–73.

———. "Zamyatin's *We* and the Genesis of *1984." Modern Fiction Studies,* 21, 1 (1975), 107–24.

Craig, Gordon A. "Triangularity and International Violence." *On Nineteen Eighty-Four.* Ed. Peter Stansky, pp. 24–32.

Crick, Bernard. "*Nineteen Eighty-Four*: Satire or Prophecy?" *Dutch Quarterly Review,* 13 (1983), 90–102.

*Currie, Robert. "The 'Big Truth' in *Nineteen Eighty-Four*." *Essays in Criticism*, 34 (1984), 56–69.

*Doctorow, E. L. "On the Brink of 1984." *Playboy*, February 1983, pp. 78–80, 156–158, 160, 162.

Drell, Sidney D. "Newspeak and Nukespeak." On *Nineteen Eighty-Four*. Ed. Peter Stansky, pp. 34–42.

*Ehrlich, Paul R. and Anne H. Ehrlich. "1984: Population and Environment." *On Nineteen Eighty-Four*. Ed. Peter Stansky, pp. 49–55.

*Esslin, Martin. "Television and Telescreen." *On Nineteen Eighty-Four*. Ed. Peter Stansky, pp. 126–138.

*Feder, Lillian. "Selfhood, Language and Reality: George Orwell's *Nineteen Eighty-Four*." *Georgia Review*, 37 (1983), 392–409.

Ferguson, Alfred R. "Newspeak, the First Edition: Tyranny and the Decay of Language." *Michigan Quarterly Review*, 14 (1975), 445–53.

Fink, Howard. "Newspeak: The Epitome of Parody Techniques in *Nineteen Eighty-Four*." *Critical Survey*, 5 (1971), 155–63.

Gottlieb, Annie, ed. "Is *1984* Really Here?" *McCall's*, January 1984, pp. 20, 96, 98–101, 119. Contains statements by Walter Mondale, Gloria Steinem, John Glenn, Norman Lear, John Naisbitt, Phyllis Schlafly, Carl Bernstein, and Arthur Schlesinger, Jr.

Howe, Irving, ed. *1984 Revisited: Totalitarianism in Our Century*. New York: Harper & Row, 1983.

*Hynes, Samuel, ed. *1984: A Collection of Critical Essays*. Englewood Cliffs, N.J.: Prentice-Hall, 1971.

Jensen, Ejner J. "*1984*." *Horizon*, January–February 1984, p. 15.

John, George. "Towards a Stylistic Analysis of Orwell's *1984*." *Rice Univ. Studies in English*, 11 (1978), 57–65.

*Lowenthal, Richard. "Beyond Totalitarianism?" *1984 Revisited*. Ed. Irving Howe, pp. 209–267.

McBee, Susanna. "U.S. Still a Far Cry from World of *1984*." *U.S. News and World Report*, December 26, 1983–January 2, 1984, pp. 90–91, 93.

McGinn, Robert E. "The Politics of Technology and the Technology of Politics." *On Nineteen Eighty-Four*. Ed. Peter Stansky, pp. 67–75.

*McNamara, James, and Dennis J. O'Keefe. "Waiting for 1984: On Orwell and Evil." *Encounter*, 59, 6 (December 1982), 43–48.

Mellor, Anne K. " 'You're Only a Rebel from the Waist Downwards': Orwell's View of Women." *On Nineteen Eighty-Four*. Ed. Peter Stansky, pp. 115–125.

*Meyers, Jeffrey. "The Evolution of *1984*." *English Miscellany*, 23 (1972), 247–61.

*Miller, Mark Crispin. "The Fate of *1984*." *1984 Revisited*. Ed. Irving Howe, pp. 19–46.

Mueller, William. *Celebration of Life: Studies in Modern Fiction*. New York: Sheed and Ward, 1972, pp. 169–187.

New, Melvyn. "Orwell and Antisemitism: Toward *1984.*" *Modern Fiction Studies*, 21, 1 (1975), 81–106.

Nisbet, Robert. "*1984* and the Conservative Imagination." *1984 Revisited.* Ed. Irving Howe, pp. 180–206.

*Patai, Daphne. "Gamesmanship and Androcentricism in Orwell's 1984." *PMLA*, 97 (1982), 856–870.

*Philmus, Robert M. "The Language of Utopia." *Studies in the Literary Imagination*, 6, 2 (1973), 61–78.

Ranald, Ralph. "George Orwell and the Mad World: The Anti-Universe of *1984.*" *South Atlantic Quarterly*, 64 (1967), 544–553.

Rankin, David. "Orwell's Intention in *1984.*" *English Language Notes*, 12 (1975), 188–92.

Roazen, Paul. "Orwell, Freud, and *1984.*" *Virginia Quarterly Review*, 54 (1978), 675–695.

*Robinson, Paul. "For Love of Big Brother: The Sexual Politics of *Nineteen Eighty-Four.*" *On Nineteen Eighty-Four*. Ed. Peter Stansky, pp. 148–158.

*Ross, Michael L. " 'Carrying on the Human Heritage': From *Lady Chatterley's Lover* to *Nineteen Eighty-Four.*" *D. H. Lawrence Review*, 17 (1984), 5–28.

Rule, James B. "*1984* — The Ingredients of Totalitarianism." *1984 Revisited.* Ed. Irving Howe, pp. 166-179.

Samuels, Dorothy J. "Computer Scan: No Place to Hide." *PC Magazine*, 3, 1 (January 24, 1984), 164–167.

Sheldon, Leslie E. "Newspeak and Nadsat: The Disintegration of Language in *1984* and *A Clockwork Orange.*" *Studies in Contemporary Satire*, 6 (1979), 7–13.

Siegel, Paul N. "The Cold War: *1984* Twenty-five Years After." *Confrontation*, 8 (1974), 148–56.

Smith, Marcus. "The Wall of Blackness: A Psychological Approach to *1984.*" *Modern Fiction Studies*, 14 (1968), 423–33.

Smyer, Richard I. "*1984*: The Search for the Golden Country." *Arizona Quarterly*, 27 (1971), 41–52.

*Sperber, Murray. " 'Gazing into the Glass Paperweight': The Structure and Psychology of Orwell's *1984.*" *Modern Fiction Studies*, 26 (1980), 213–226.

Stafford, Tim. "*1984*: Can Orwell's Nightmare Still Become Reality?" *Christianity Today*, January 13, 1984, pp. 22–26.

*Stansky, Peter, ed. *On Nineteen Eighty-Four*. New York: W. H. Freeman, 1983.

*Steiner, George. "Killing Time." *New Yorker*, December 12, 1983, pp. 168, 171–178, 181–182, 184, 186, 188.

*Steinhoff, William. *George Orwell and the Origins of 1984*. Ann Arbor: Univ. of Michigan Press; London: Weidenfeld and Nicolson, 1975. British edition entitled *The Road to 1984.*

*_____. "Utopia Reconsidered: Comments on *1984.*" *No Place Else: Explorations in Utopian and Dystopian Fiction.* Ed. Eric S. Rabkin, Martin H. Greenberg, and Joseph D. Olander. Carbondale: Southern Illinois Univ. Press, 1983, pp. 147–161.

Strasser, Johanno, "*1984*: Decade of the Experts?" trans. John E. Woods. *1984 Revisited.* Ed. Irving Howe, pp. 149–165.

Struc, Roman S. "George Orwell's *Nineteen Eighty-Four* and Dostoevsky's 'Underground Man'." *Proceedings: Pacific Northwest Conference on Foreign Languages.* Ed. Walter C. Kraft. Corvallis, Ore.: Oregon State Univ., 1973. 217–20.

Trafford, Abigail. "Orwell's *1984* — Coming True?" *U.S. News and World Report*, December 26, 1983–January 2, 1984, pp. 86–87.

Traugott, Elizabeth Closs. "Newspeak: Could It Really Work?" *On Nineteen Eighty-Four.* Ed. Peter Stansky, pp. 92–102.

Vose, G. Michael. "1984 and Beyond." *Byte*, January 1984, pp. 100–101.

*Walzer, Michael. "On 'Failed Totalitarianism.'" *1984 Revisited.* Ed. Irving Howe, pp. 102–121.

Warburg, Fredric. "*Animal Farm* and *1984.*" *All Authors Are Equal.* London: Hutchinson, 1973; New York: St. Martin's Press, 1973, pp. 8–15, 35–38, 92–120, 205–206.

*Watt, Ian. "Winston Smith: The Last Humanist." *On Nineteen Eighty-Four.* Ed. Peter Stansky, pp. 103–114.

Wellborn, Stanley N. "Big Brother's Tools Are Ready, but. . . ." *U.S. News and World Report*, December 26, 1983–January 2, 1984, pp. 88–89.

Westlake, J. H. J. "Aldous Huxley's *Brave New World* and George Orwell's *Nineteen Eighty-Four*: A Comparative Study." *Neueren Sprachen*, 21 (1972), 94–102.

Wiessler, David A. "Language Takes a Turn for 'Plusungood.'" *U.S. News and World Report*, December 26, 1983–January 2, 1984, p. 95.

Wilding, Michael. "Orwell's *1984*: Rewriting the Future." *Sydney Studies in English*, 2 (1976–1977), 38–63.

*Wilt, Judith. "Behind the Door of *1984*: 'The Worst Thing in the World.'" *Modernism Reconsidered.* Ed. Robert Kiely and John Hildebidle. Cambridge: Harvard Univ. Press, 1983, pp. 247–262.

*Zimbardo, Philip G. "Mind Control: Political Fiction and Psychological Reality." *On Nineteen Eighty-Four.* Ed. Peter Stansky, pp. 197–215.

*Zwerdling, Alex. "Orwell and the Techniques of Didactic Fantasy." *Twentieth Century Interpretations of "1984."* Ed. Samuel Hynes. Englewood Cliffs, N.J.: Prentice-Hall, 1971, pp. 88–101.

C. 11: Miscellaneous Writings

Coombes, John. "A New Dissection of Orwell's Elephant." *Practices of Literature and Politics.* Ed. Francis Barker et al. Colchester: Univ. of Essex, 1979, pp. 245–257. "A Hanging."

*Freedman, Carl. "Writing, Ideology, and Politics: Orwell's 'Politics and the English Language' and English Composition." *College English*, 43 (1981), 327–340.

Klitzke, Robert. "Why Is the Collected Orwell Not the Complete Orwell?" *International Fiction Review*, 10 (1983), 125–129. On *The Collected Essays, Journalism and Letters*.

Oram, Richard W. "George Orwell's 'A Hanging' and Thackeray." *American Notes & Queries*, 21 (1983), 108–109.

Orwell, George. *Orwell: The Lost Writings*. Edited, with an introduction by W. J. West. New York: Arbor House, 1985.

*Parrinder, Patrick. "George Orwell and the Detective Story." *Journal of Popular Culture*, 6 (1973), 692–696; reprinted in *Dimensions of Detective Fiction*. Ed. Larry N. Landrum et al. Bowling Green, Oh.: Bowling Green Univ. Popular Press, 1976, pp. 64–67.

Rank, Hugh. "Mr. Orwell, Mr. Schlesinger, and the Language." *College Composition and Communication*, 28 (1977), 159–165.

Shapiro, Marjorie. "George Orwell's Criticism." *Connecticut Review*, 6, 2 (1973), 70–75.

Smith, Susan Harris. "No Orchids for George Orwell." *Armchair Detective*, 9 (1976), 114–115.

INDEX